GEORGE WASHINGTON
BICENTENNIAL EDITION

# THE WRITINGS OF
# GEORGE WASHINGTON

From the Houdon Bust, modeled from life at Mount Vernon in 1785.   Here reproduced by permission of the Mount Vernon Ladies' Association of the Union

# THE WRITINGS OF

# George
# Washington

from the

## Original Manuscript Sources
### 1745–1799

Prepared under the direction of the UNITED STATES
GEORGE WASHINGTON BICENTENNIAL COMMISSION
and published by authority of CONGRESS

JOHN C. FITZPATRICK, *Editor*

## Volume 5
### May, 1776 – August, 1776

United States
Government Printing Office
Washington

PRINTED

APRIL, 1932

# UNITED STATES GEORGE WASHINGTON BICENTENNIAL COMMISSION

## President of the United States
### Chairman

*Vice President of the United States*
*Speaker of the House of Representatives*

| United States Senate | House of Representatives |
|---|---|
| SIMEON D. FESS, *Vice Chairman*<br>Ohio | WILLIS C. HAWLEY<br>Oregon |
| ARTHUR CAPPER<br>Kansas | JOHN Q. TILSON<br>Connecticut |
| CARTER GLASS<br>Virginia | JOSEPH W. BYRNS<br>Tennessee |
| MILLARD E. TYDINGS<br>Maryland | R. WALTON MOORE<br>Virginia |

### Presidential Commissioners

| | |
|---|---|
| MRS. ANTHONY WAYNE COOK<br>Pennsylvania | C. BASCOM SLEMP<br>Virginia |
| MRS. JOHN DICKINSON SHERMAN<br>Colorado | WALLACE MCCAMANT<br>Oregon |
| HENRY FORD<br>Michigan | ALBERT BUSHNELL HART<br>Massachusetts |
| GEORGE EASTMAN*<br>New York | BERNARD M. BARUCH<br>New York |

### Executive Committee

THE SENATE AND HOUSE
COMMISSIONERS
C. BASCOM SLEMP
MRS. ANTHONY WAYNE COOK
BERNARD M. BARUCH

### Historian

PROF. ALBERT BUSHNELL HART

### Associate Directors

REPRESENTATIVE SOL BLOOM
———— ————

### Executive Secretary
WILLIAM TYLER PAGE

———

*Deceased.

# ADVISORY COMMITTEE
## ON THE WRITINGS

# TABLE OF CONTENTS
## 1776

[vii]

# LIST OF ILLUSTRATIONS

# TABLE OF SYMBOLS

The following symbols have been used to denote the place of deposit of Washington letters not found in draft or letter-book form in the *Washington Papers* in the Library of Congress:

| | |
|---|---|
| Indicating that the letter is in Washington's own handwriting | * |
| Chicago Historical Society | [CH.H.S.] |
| Clements Library, University of Michigan | [C.L.] |
| Connecticut Historical Society | [C.H.S.] |
| Connecticut State Library | [C.S.L.] |
| Harvard College Library | [HV.L.] |
| Haverford College | [HD.C.] |
| Historical Society of Pennsylvania | [H.S.P.] |
| Huntington Library | [H.L.] |
| Maine Historical Society | [M.H.S.] |
| Maryland Historical Society | [MD.H.S.] |
| Massachusetts Historical Society | [MS.H.S.] |
| J. P. Morgan Library | [M.L.] |
| New Hampshire Historical Society | [N.H.H.S.] |
| New York Historical Society | [N.Y.H.S.] |
| New York Public Library | [N.Y.P.L.] |
| New York State Library | [N.Y.S.L.] |
| Rhode Island Historical Society | [R.I.H.S.] |
| Rhode Island Society of the Cincinnati | [R.I.S.C.] |
| Society of the Cincinnati | [S.C.] |
| University of Chicago Library | [U.C.L.] |
| University of Pennsylvania Library | [U.P.] |
| Virginia Historical Society | [V.H.S.] |
| Virginia State Library | [V.S.L.] |

# THE WRITINGS OF
# GEORGE WASHINGTON

# THE WRITINGS OF
# GEORGE WASHINGTON

———◆———

## GENERAL ORDERS

Head Quarters, New York, May 1, 1776.
Parole Shelbourne. Countersign Townsend.
The Majors of brigade are to see that every Regiment in their respective Brigades, take their proper Share of all duties that the service requires.

### AFTER ORDERS

Col. McDougall's, and Col Ritzema's Regiments to be mustered on Saturday Morning, at Ten O'Clock, upon the Common, near the Laboratory, where the Commissary General of Musters will attend.

## To MAJOR GENERAL CHARLES LEE

New York, May [1], 1776.
My Dear Lee, Your favour of the 5th ult. from Williamsburgh, the first I have received from you since you left this city, came to my hands by the last post. I thank you for your kind congratulations on our possession of Boston. I thank you for your good wishes in our future operations, and hope that every diabolical attempt to deprive mankind of their inherent rights and privileges, whether made in the East, West, North, or South, will be attended with disappointment and disgrace, and that the authors in the end will be brought to such punishment, as an injured people have a right to inflict.

General Howe's retreat from Boston was precipitate, beyond anything I could have conceived. The destruction of the stores at Dunbar's camp after Braddock's defeat was but a faint image of what was seen at Boston; artillery carts cut to pieces in one place; gun carriages in another; shells broke here; shot buried there, and everything carrying with it the face of disorder and confusion, as also of distress.

Immediately upon their embarkation, I detached a brigade of five regiments to this city, and upon their sailing, removed with the whole army hither except four regiments at Boston, and one at Beverly, &c. for the protection of those places, the stores and barracks there, and for erecting works for defending the harbour of the first. Immediately upon my arrival here I detached four regiments by order of Congress to Canada (to wit, Poor's, Patterson's Greaton's, and Bond's) under the command of Brigadier Thompson, and since that, by the same authority, and in consequence of some unfavourable accounts from that quarter, General Sullivan and six other regiments, namely Stark's, Read's, Wain's, Irvine's, Wind's, and Dayton's, have moved off for that department; the four last regiments are of Pennsylvania, and New Jersey. The first brigade arrived at Albany the twenty-fourth ultimo, and were moving on, when accounts came from thence the twenty-seventh. The other brigades must all be at Albany before this, as some of the regiments failed ten days ago, and the last four, and the winds were favourable. This has left us very weak at this place, whilst I have my fears that the reinforcement will scarce get to Canada in time, for want of teams to transport the troops, &c. to Fort George, and vessels to convey them on afterwards.

We have done a great deal of work at this place. In a fortnight more, I think the city will be in a very respectable posture of defence. Governor's-Island has a large and strong work erected, and a regiment encamped there. The point below, called Red-Hook, has a small, but exceeding strong barbet battery; and several new works are constructed, and many of them almost executed at other places.

General Ward, upon the evacuation of Boston, and finding there was a probability of his removing from the smoke of his own chimney, applied to me, and wrote to Congress for leave to resign. A few days afterwards, some of the officers, as he says, getting *uneasy* at the prospect of his leaving them, he applied for his letter of resignation, which had been committed to my care; but, behold! it had been carefully forwarded to Congress, and, as I have since learnt, judged so reasonable (*want of health* being the plea) that it was instantly complied with. Brigadier Fry, previous to this, also conceiving that there was nothing entertaining or profitable to an old man, to be marching and counter-marching, desired, immediately on the evacuation of Boston (which happened on the 17th of March) that he might *resign his commission on the 11th of April:* the choice of the day became a matter of great speculation, and remained profoundly mysterious till he exhibited his account, when there appeared neither more or less in it, than the completion of three calendar months; the pay of which he received without any kind of compunction, although he had never done one tour of duty, or, I believe, had ever been out of his house from the time he entered till he quitted Cambridge.

So much for two Generals: I have next to inform you, that the Pay-master-general, Colonel Warren, not finding it convenient to attend the army, from the various employments and avocations in which he was engaged, also resigned his commission, and is succeeded by our old aid, Palfrey.

When I was speaking of the distressed situation of the king's troops, and the Tories, at their evacuation of Boston, I might have gone on, and added, that their misfortunes did not end here. It seems, upon their arrival at Halifax, many of the former were obliged to encamp, although the ground was covered deep with snow; and the latter, to pay six dollars a week for forty upper rooms, and stow in them, men, women, and children, as thick, comparatively, as the hair upon their heads. This induced many of these gentry to return, and throw themselves upon the mercy and clemency of their countrymen, who were for sending them immediately back, as the properest and severest punishment they could inflict, but death being preferred to this, they now wait, in confinement, any other that may be thought due to such parricides.

All the ships of war have left this place, and gone down to the Hook, except the Asia, which lays five miles below the Narrows, and about twelve or fourteen from hence. I could have added more, but my paper will not admit of it. With compliment, therefore, to the gentlemen of my acquaintance with you, and with the most fervent wishes for your health and success, I remain, etc.[1]

## To GOVERNOR JONATHAN TRUMBULL

New York, May 2, 1776.

Sir: I received your favor of the 22d Ulto. and am sorry to Inform you, that it is not in my power at this time to refund to your Colony the Powder lent the Continent; our Magazine here being very low and the pressing demands from Canada obliging me immediately to forward Sixty Barrels thither. Should any Inconveniency result to the Colony from not having it, It will give me much unneasiness; you may rest assured, that as soon as I possibly can, I will make a return of it.

The Commissary General has not presented the Account yet; when he does, it shall be immediately paid. I am etc.

[1] From *Memoirs of the Late Charles Lee, Esq.*

## To COLONEL JAMES CLINTON

New York, May 2, 1776.

Sir: Having received Information that there is a Number of Arms at one Wiltseys at the Fishkills, among the Officers Baggage which came from St. Johns, I request and authorize you to make Inquiry about them and to secure all you can find. I am, etc.[2]

## GENERAL ORDERS

Head Quarters, New York, May 2, 1776.

Parole Granby.   Countersign Wilkes.

The first, second, and fourth Brigades, to encamp to morrow in the forenoon; each Regiment to be drawn up on their Regimental Parade, at eight O'Clock in the morning, and directly march to the Ground, mark'd out for their Encampment, when they are immediately to pitch their tents—The Qr. Mr. General will provide Camp-Equipage, Wood, and Straw, necessary for the Encampment.

The Brigadiers General, or Officers commanding, will attend to the Encampment of their respective Brigades and see that one Regiment does not encroach upon another, but encamps exactly upon the Ground assigned.

The Chief Engineer Lieut. Col. Putnam, to send every evening the Details for the working Parties wanted for the next day, to Major Genl. Putnam, who will provide Boats, and give the necessary Orders for marching them to the places where they are to work, and will also direct, the entrenching Tools to be properly distributed.

Corporal John Weaver, of Capt. Williams[3] Independent Company of Rifflemen, tried at a late General Court Martial,

---

[2] The "Letter Book" copy by George Lewis mistakenly attributes this to George Clinton.

[3] Capt. Otho Holland(?) Williams, of the Maryland riflemen.

whereof Col. Baldwin was President, for "getting drunk, when on duty." The Court find the Prisoner guilty of the Charge, and do sentence him to be reduced to the Ranks, and whipped Thirty Lashes on his bare back.

Jno. McGarra of Capt. Stephenson's[4] Independent Company of Riffle-men, tried at the above General Court Martial, for "mutinous behaviour," is found guilty by the Court, and sentenced to be whipped Fifteen Lashes on his bare back.

Samuel Londers and Abner Fuller, of Capt. Bissell's[5] Company, in Col Huntington's Regiment, tried at the above General Court Martial for "Desertion"—The Court finding the Prisoners guilty of the Charge, do sentence each of them to receive Thirty Lashes, on his bare back. The General approves of the foregoing Sentences, and orders the execution of them to morrow Morning at Guard mounting.

The General Court Martial, whereof Col: Baldwin is President, is dissolved.

### GENERAL ORDERS

Head Quarters, New York, May 3, 1776.
Parole Albany.    Countersign Quebec.

A General Court Martial of the Line, consisting of one Colonel, one Lieut. Colonel, one Major, and ten Captains, to sit to morrow morning at Ten O'Clock, to try all such Prisoners as shall be brought before them—All Evidences, and Persons concerned, to attend the court.

Frederick Roach, a Matross in the Regiment of Artillery, tried at a late General Court Martial, whereof Col. Baldwin was President for "Insulting and striking Capt. Hull[6] and for insulting some Inhabitants on Long-Island"—The Court

---

[4] Capt. Hugh Stephenson, of the Virginia riflemen.
[5] Capt. Ebenezer Fitch Bissell, of the Seventeenth Continental Infantry.
[6] Capt. William Hull, of the Nineteenth Continental Infantry.

finding the Prisoner guilty of the charge, do sentence him to be whipped Thirty nine Lashes, on his bare back.

Edward McCartney of Capt. Hardenburgh's[7] Company, in Col Ritzema's Regiment, tried at the above General Court Martial, for "Desertion"—is found guilty by the Court, and by them sentenced to receive thirty-nine Lashes, on his bare back.

John Maxfield of Capt. Tylers[8] Company, in Colonel Huntington's Regiment, tried by the above General Court Martial for "Desertion"—The Court finding the Prisoner guilty of the Charge, do sentence him to be whipped Thirty-nine Lashes on his naked back for said offence.

Charles Bowen of Capt. Potter's[9] Company, in Col. Dayton's Regiment, tried by the above General Court Martial for "Desertion" is found guilty by the Court and sentenced to be whipp'd Thirty Lashes on his bare back.

The General approves of each of the foregoing sentences, and orders them to be put in Execution to morrow morning at guard mounting.

## To MAJOR GENERAL PHILIP SCHUYLER

New York, May 3, 1776.

Dear Sir: I received your Favour of the 27th. Ulto., Yesterday Evening with its several Inclosures, and in Part Answer thereto, refer you to mine of the 29th., which probably will have come to Hand ere now; but least any accident has prevented it, I will again inform you, that in Obedience to an Order of Congress, I have detached six more Regiments under General Sullivan, in Addition to those with General Thompson, to reinforce our Army in Canada: all of which, except a

[7] Capt. Cornelius Hardenburgh, of the Third New York Regiment.
[8] Capt. Abraham Tyler, of the Seventeenth Continental Infantry.
[9] Capt. Samuel Potter, of the Third New Jersey Regiment.

few Companies, are embarked, and as the Situation of our Affairs in that Quarter is not so promising as we could wish, and an early Arrival of them may be of the most infinite Advantage to us; I shall repeat my Request, and in full Confidence, trust, that you will do every Thing in your Power to hasten their March. I have sent forward with them 60 Barrels of Powder, which is all can be spared from hence at this Time, which I hope will arrive safe.

The Commissary, I have been importunate with: He tells me eight Hundred Barrels of Pork are gone to Albany, and that he every Day expects a further Quantity from Connecticut, which he will order to you, as soon as it comes, without stopping here.

You will also receive three Boxes of Money, said to contain 300,000 Dollrs. which from my Letter from Congress accompanying it, are for Canada. Your's probably will be more particular; but I should think, my dear Sir, if the whole will not be more than sufficient to pay the Troops, and the Claims there, tho' some of it might be intended for you, that it will be adviseable to send it forward. You will have it in your Power to get a further Supply before long, to satisfy your Engagements. Those in Canada either with our Men or others, should not remain unpaid at this critical and interesting Period. You however, will be better able to judge what should be done in this Instance, than I possibly can. With Respect to your military Chest when replenished, I see no Impropriety in your giving Warrants as usual. It seems to be necessary and of Consequence must have my Approbation.

The Quarter Master has forwarded a Parcel of intrenching Tools, and other Necessaries with about 500 Tents, the latter to be equally and properly distributed amongst this last Detachment. No more can be had at this Time.

You will also receive the Chain which General Lee order'd and which I think should be sent to and fix'd at the Place it is designed for, with all possible Expedition. It may be of great Service and Benefit.

In Respect of Sailors to cruize and pass in the Lakes; on the 24th. Ulto., I gave a Warrant to a Captain Jacobus Wynkoop for 276⅔ Dollars for a Month's advance Pay for himself, Officers and Men, who are engaged in that Service; Of this, I there advised you, of their different Pay that you might take an Account of it, and know what they are to receive in future.

I am exceedingly sorry you should have been so indisposed: I had hoped you would get perfectly restored so as not only to have seen the End of this Campaign; but your great Labour and unwearied Assiduity in the Cause of your Country, crowned with Success, and the Blessings of Freedom; you have my most fervent Wishes for it.

I have just received an Arrangement of the Companies allotted by the Committee of Safety to Colonels Wynkoop and Clinton, for their Regiments, a Copy of which you have inclosed, by which you will see they are differently arranged from what you expected or I knew. I have, therefore, countermanded an Order, which was issued to Colo. Wynkoop before, and directed him (the Companies at Albany being in his Regiment) to repair immediately to you, for such Directions and Orders respecting his Regiment, as you may judge necessary to give. This you will employ at the Posts you mentioned, and for the Communication. I can spare no more from hence, the ten Regiments already detached, having weakened us here too much. The four Companies of Colo. Clinton's Regiment at the Highland Fortifications, I intend shall remain there, for carrying on and garrisoning those Works, and which will be joined by another. Those on Long Island will be kept there. I am etc.

## To COLONEL CORNELIUS D. WYNKOOP[10]

New York, May 3, 1776.

Sir: Since the Adjutant General's Letter to you of the first Inst., I have received from the Committee of Safety a Note of the Companies belonging to each Regiment and the Places where they are stationed: by which I find four of the Companies belonging to Colonel Clinton's Regiment are at Fort Montgomery and Fort Constitution, which will answer the Purposes intended when the Order was sent to you to repair thither; which Order I now think proper to countermand, as I have received by Express from General Schuyler a Letter wherein he mentions the Necessity of having a Regiment stationed on the Communication betwixt Albany and Canada. You will, therefore, Sir, on Receipt hereof—repair to Albany, and obey such Orders as you may receive from General Schuyler respecting your Regiment. I am, etc.

## To LIEUTENANT COLONEL
## HENRY BEEKMAN LIVINGSTON[11]

Head Quarters, New York, May 4, 1776.

Sir: You will on Receipt hereof give Orders to the Officers of the Battalion, of which you are Lieut. Colonel, to join their respective Companies; which if you do not find compleat let an Officer from each go on the recruiting Service, and if in Want of Arms, you must apply to the Committee of Safety, to procure them for you if possible.

There are four Companies belonging to your Regiment now stationed at Fort Montgomery and Fort Constitution.

---

[10] Of the Fourth New York Regiment.
[11] Of the Third New York Regiment.

You will repair thither and if no superior Officer is there, you must take the Command, and look to the Works now carrying on there, which you must exert yourself in seeing finished as soon as possible. The three Companies of your Regiment stationed on Long Island are to remain there; The other Company you will order to join you at the Forts, with all convenient Speed. I am, Sir, etc.

### GENERAL ORDERS

Head Quarters, New York, May 4, 1776.
Parole Montreal.   Countersign St. Johns.

The weather proving wet and cold, the Regiments that did not encamp Yesterday, are to remain in the present quarters, until Monday Morning; when they are to march, and encamp upon the Ground assigned them.

The undernam'd Officers are appointed by the General, to oversee the works laid out by the Engineer: Capt. Chapman[12] of Col Prescot's Regiment; Lieut. Cole[13] of Col Wyllys's Regiment, Lieut. Fish[14] of Col. Larnard's Regt.; and Lieut. Goodall[15] of Col Reed's Regiment.

The Colonels, or commanding Officers of regiments, are to be particular in obliging their Quarter Masters, constantly to attend to the cleaning the Streets of their encampment, and especially to the digging, and fixing the Necessaries, in the place appointed for that purpose; which are every morning to be lightly covered with fresh Earth, and at stated times filled up, and new ones dug; To the end that all obnoxious, and unwholesome Smells, be prevented from infecting the camp,

---

[12] Capt. James(?) Chapman, of the Tenth Continental Infantry.
[13] Lieut. Marcus Cole, of the Twenty-second Continental Infantry.
[14] Lieut. Thomas Fish, of the Third Continental Infantry.
[15] Lieut. Nathan Goodale, of the Thirteenth Connecticut Infantry.

the Quarter Masters are also carefully to see all Filth and Carrion, in, or near their encampments, immediately buried.

The Honorable the Continental Congress, have been pleased to appoint William Palfrey Esqr., to be Pay Master General of the Army of the United Colonies; he is to be respected, and obeyed as such.

Col Parsons's, and Col Huntington's Regiments, to be muster'd in the Front of their encampment, upon Tuesday Morning next—They are to prepare their Rolls accordingly. The Muster Master General will attend at eight o'Clock.

William Winslow, Soldier in Capt: Johnson's[16] Company, in Col McDougall's Regiment, tried at a late General Court Martial, whereof Col Baldwin was President, for "Desertion," is acquitted by the Court—The General orders the prisoner to be released from his confinement, and wishes he could add his approbation, of the proceedings of the court martial.

## GENERAL ORDERS

Head Quarters, New York, May 5, 1776.
Parole Franklin.   Countersign Chace.

The commanding Officers of Regiments, to send a Return to the Quarter Master General, of the Armourers, and Smiths in their respective Corps, when such as are necessary for the service of the Army will be draughted.

Col Wyllys's, and Col Arnold's Regiments, are to be muster'd in the front of their encampment, upon Wednesday Morning next at eight o'clock, when the Commissary General of the Musters will attend.

The Officers commanding the Guards, in and near the encampment, are to be particularly attentive to prevent any waste,

---

[16] Capt. John Johnson, of the First New York Regiment.

or depradation, being committed upon the Fields, Fences, Trees, or Buildings about the camp. Turf is not to be permitted to be cut, unless by the express orders of the Chief Engineer, and any non-commissioned Officer, or Soldier, who is detected cutting any of the Trees, or Shrubs, or destroying any of the Fences, near the camp, will be confined, and tried for disobedience of orders. The Quarter Master General will supply a certain Quantity of boards for flooring, for the tents of every Regiment, which are upon no account to be converted to any other use.

The Officers, and Soldiers, order'd upon Command under Lieut. Col Tupper,[17] of which a Roll is this day deliver'd to the several Brigade Majors, are to be continued upon that Command until further Orders, and the Regiments they are severally draughted from, are to have an allowance in the Roll of duty accordingly.

## To THE PRESIDENT OF CONGRESS

New York, May 5, 1776.

Sir: I am honored with your favor of the 20th. ulto., and observe what Congress have done respecting the settlement of the Pay Masters Accounts. This seems expedient as he is out of Office, and I am certain will be attended with but little if any difficulty, nothing more being necessary thereto, than to compare the Warrants with his debets, and the receipts he has given with his Credits.[18] I wish every other Settlement as easy, and that a Committee was appointed to examine and audit the Accounts on which the Warrants are founded, particularly

---

[17] Lieut. Col. Benjamin Tupper, of the Twenty-first Continental Infantry.

[18] The former Paymaster General of the Continental Army, James Warren, had resigned and had been directed to hand in his vouchers and papers to the Superintendents of the Treasury, which was a standing committee of Congress, appointed Feb. 17, 1776.

those of the Quarter Master and Commissary General;—they are long and high in amount, consisting of a variety of charges, and of course more intricate, and will require time and an extraordinary degree of attention, to adjust and liquidate in a proper manner. Upon this Subject I did myself the Honor to write you a considerable time ago.[19]

Having had several complaints from the officers in the Eastern Regiments, who have been and are engaged in recruiting, about the expence attending it, and for which they have never been allowed any thing, tho' the officers in these Governments have, as I am informed, I shall be glad to know whether the allowance of 10/, granted to the officers for every man Inlisted by the resolve of Congress in is general and indiscriminate, or confined to the Middle Districts: If general, must I have retrospect to the time of the Resolve, and pay for the intermediate services or only for future Inlistments.[20]

In a Letter I wrote Congress the 25th of December, I inclosed one I had received from Jacob Bailey Esquire, about opening a Road from Newbury to Canada; I received another on the 15th. Ulto. and from his Account and the intelligence of others, I have no doubt of the practicability of the measure, and am well informed that the distance will be considerably shortened; In so much, that our Troops going to Canada from any part of the New England Governments, Eastward of Connecticut River, or returning from thence Home, will perform their March in five or Six days less than by going or returning any way now used.

Add to this, that the road may be carried to Missisque River, as is said, from whence the Water Carriage to St. Johns is good,

---

[19] On May 10 Congress directed that the resolves of April 1, governing the settlement of accounts, be sent to Washington.

[20] On May 10 Congress resolved that the resolution of January 17 was general in its operation, and included, therefore, the troops of the Eastern Department; allowance was to be made for all the troops enlisted since that date.

except forty odd Miles, or so far to the Northward, as to keep clear of the Lake altogether and which will afford an easy pass to and from Canada at all Seasons. The benefits resulting from this Rout, will be so great and Important, that I have advanced Col: Bailey Two hundred and fifty pounds to begin with and directed him to execute his plan: no doubt it will require a more considerable advance to accomplish it, but the whole will be soon sunk.

The expence saved, by shortning six days pay and provisions for the Men returning to the Eastern Governments, at the expiration of this Campaign, will be almost, if not more than, equal to the Charge of Opening it: If not, as in all probability there will be often a necessity for detachments of our Troops from those Governments, to go and return, It will soon be repaid.[21]

By a Letter from General Schuyler of the 27th. Ulto. I find General Thompson and his Brigade had arrived at Albany. General Sullivan with the last, except three or four Companies of Colonel Wayne's Regiment, not yet come, is embarked and gone, and probably will be soon there. I am apprehensive from General Schuyler's Account, they will not proceed from thence with the expedition wished, owing to a difficulty in getting Teams and provender for the Cattle necessary to carry their Baggage, and a scarcity of Batteaux for transporting so great a Number; tho' he is using the utmost Industry and deligence to procure them. Should they be retarded for any considerable time, It will be exceedingly unfortunate, as we are much weakened here by their going, and our Army in Canada not strengthened. I have sent with the last Brigade sixty Barrels of Powder and other Stores and Intrenching Tools, a supply being wanted; also the Chain for a Boom

---

[21] On May 10 Congress in its resolves approved, and directed Washington to prosecute the plan.

at the Narrows of Richlieu, and the three Boxes of Money brought me by Mr. Hanson, and have wrote General Schuyler to have the Boom fixed, as soon as possible. The Commissary too has forwarded about Eight Hundred Barrels of Pork, and is in expectation of a further Quantity from Connecticut, which will go on without stopping here.

As the magazines from whence the Northern and Eastern Armies will occasionally receive supplies of Powder, will probably be kept here, and our Stock is low and inconsiderable, being much reduced by the Sixty Barrels sent to Canada, I shall be glad to have a Quantity immediately forwarded. Our Stores should be great, for if the Enemy make an Attack upon the Town, or attempt to go up the North River, the expenditure will be considerable. Money too is much wanted, the Regiments that are paid, have only received to the first of April, except those of Pennsylvania and Jersey gone to Canada, they are paid up to the last of April. By a Letter from General Ward, I find his Chest is just exhausted, the Money left with him for the Payment of the five Regiments at Boston and Beverly, being almost expended, by large Drafts in favor of the Commissary and Quarter Master, and in fitting out the Armed Vessels. I would here ask a question, towit, Whether as Mr. Warren's Commission is superseded by Mr. Palfrey's appointment, It will not be necessary to fix upon some person to pay the Troops at those places, or are the payments to go thro' his hands? he does not incline to do anything in the Affair without the direction of Congress.

I have inclosed you a return of the last Brigade detached and also of the forces remaining here, and as it is a matter of much importance to know the whole of our strength from time to time and to see it at one view, for regulating our Movements with propriety, I wish it were a direction from Congress to the Commanding Officers in the different Districts to make Monthly returns to the Commander in Chief of the Continental Army, of the State of their Troops in their department, and also of the Military Stores: such direction will probably make them more attentive than they otherwise would be. I could not get a return of the Army in Canada, all last year.[22]

I beg leave to lay before Congress, a Copy of the proceedings of a Court Martial upon Lieutenant Grover[23] of the 2d. Regiment, and of his defence, which I should not have troubled them with, had I not conceived the Courts Sentence upon the facts stated in the proceedings, of a singular nature; the small fine imposed, by no means adequate to the enormity of his offence and to be a dangerous and pernicious tendency: for these reasons, I thought it my duty to lay the proceedings before them, in order to their forming such a Judgment upon the Facts, as they shall conceive right and just, and advancive of the Public Good. At the same time I would mention, that I think it of material consequence that Congress should make a resolve, taking away the supposed right of succession in the Military line from one Rank to another, which is claimed by many upon the happening of vacancies, and upon which principle this Offence seems to have originated in a great measure, and this extraordinary Judgment to be founded; declaring that no succession or promotion can take place in case of vacancies, without a Continental Commission giving and Authorizing it. It is of much importance to check and entirely suppress this Opinion and claim, become too prevalent already, and which have an obvious tendency to Introduce Mutiny and disorder: Or if they conceive the Claim good, and that it should take

---

[22] On May 10 Congress passed a resolution to this effect.

[23] Lieut. Thomas Grover. He was tried for disobedience of orders and using insulting language to his superior officer. The proceedings of his court-martial and his defense, dated Apr. 29, 1776, are in the *Washington Papers*.

place, that they will declare it so, that the point may be known and settled in future.[24] I have the Honor &ca.[25]

## *To THE PRESIDENT OF CONGRESS

New York, May 5, 1776.

Sir: I have so often, and so fully communicated my want of Arms to Congress, that I should not have given them the trouble of receiving another Letter upon this Subject, at this time, but for the particular application of Colo. Wain of Pensylvania, who has pointed out a method by which he thinks they may be obtain'd.

In the hands of the Committee of Safety at Philadelphia, there are, according to Colo. Wain's Acct. not less than two or three thousand stand of Arms for Provincial use; from hence, he thinks a number might be borrowed by Congress; provided they are replaced with Continental Arms, as they are brought into the Magazine in that City. At a crisis so important as this, such a loan might be attended with most signal advantages while the defenceless state of the Regiments, if no relief can be had, may be productive of fatal Consequences.

To give Congress some Idea of our Situation with respect to Arms, (and justice to my own Character requires that it should be known to them, altho' the world at large will form their opinion of our strength from numbers, without attending to circumstances) it may not be amiss to Inclose a Copy of a Return which I received a few days ago from the Troops in the Highlands,[26] and add, that by a Report from Colo. Retzema's Regiment of the 29th ulto., there appeared to be only 97

---

[24] On May 10 it was resolved "That this Congress has hitherto exercised, and ought to retain the power of promoting the officers in the continental service according to their merit; and that no promotion or succession shall take place upon any vacancy, without the authority of a continental Commission."

[25] In the writing of Robert Hanson Harrison.

[26] The return from Isaac Nicoll, colonel of New York Militia, presented a state of the garrisons at Fort Montgomery on April 23, and at Fort Constitution on April 29. This return, dated Apr. 29, 1776, is in the *Washington Papers*.

Firelocks and Seven Bayonets belonging thereto, and that all
the Regiments from the Eastward are deficient from Twenty
to Fifty of the former.

Four of those Companies at the Fortifications in the Highlands belonging to Colo. Clintons Regiment but in what condition the residue are, on acc't. of Arms, and how Col. Wynkoop's
Men are provided I cannot undertake to say, but am told most
miserably; as Col. Dayton's (of New Jersey) and Col. Wain's
of Pennsylvania also are. This Sir, is a true tho' melancholy
description of our Situation; the propriety therefore of keeping Arms in Store when Men in actual pay are wanting of
them and who it is to be presumed will, as they ought, bear the
heat and burthen of the day, is submitted with all due deference
to the superior judgment of others.

I cannot, by all the enquiries I have been able to make, learn,
what number of arms have been taken from the Tories, where
they lay, or how they are to be got at.

The Committee of Safety for this Colony have assured me
that no exertions of theirs shall be wanting to procure Arms;
but our sufferings in the meanwhile may prove fatal, as Men
without are in a manner useless.

I have therefore thought of Imploying an Agent, whose sole
business it shall be, to ride through the middle and interior
parts of these Governments for the purpose of buying up such
Arms as the Inhabitants may Incline to sell, and are fit for use.[27]

The designs of the Enemy are too much behind the Curtain, for me to form any accurate opinion of their Plan of
Operations for the Summers Campaign; we are left to wander
therefore in the field of conjecture, and as no place, all its
consequences considered, seemed of more Importance in the
execution of their grand Plan, than possessing themselves of

---

[27] The resolve of May 14, 1776, authorized Washington to employ such an agent,
but ignored the reported stores in Philadelphia. The Secret Committee was ordered to
send to camp the muskets that were at Newport, R. I.

Hudsons River; I thought it advisable to remove, with the Continental Army to this City, as soon as the Kings Troops evacuated Boston, but if the Congress from their knowledge, information, or believe, think it best for the general good of the Service, that I should go to the Northward, or elsewhere, they are convinced I hope, that they have nothing more to do, than signify their Commands. With great respect, I have the Honor etc.

### To THE NEW YORK COMMITTEE OF SAFETY

New York, May 6, 1776.

Gentlemen: I beg leave to refer to your examination Joseph Blanchard and Peter Puillon, who were yesterday apprehended, the former on suspicion of carrying on a correspondence with persons on board the King's ships, the latter of having supplied them with some provision, in violation of, and contrary to, the regulations which have been adopted for preventing such practices. There are witnesses against both, which are ordered to wait on you; and also some papers found in possession of Mr. Blanchard, which, though previous to your resolves in point of date, indicate an intimacy between him and Colonel Fanning, the Secretary, to whom, I am told, he has written since their publication, and his knowledge of them. I am, etc.

P. S. Captain Gibbs[28] will deliver the papers.[29]

### GENERAL ORDERS

Head Quarters, New York, May 6, 1776.
Parole Virginia.    Countersign Lee.

The Colonels, and commanding Officers of Regiments are again reminded, of the propriety of immediately providing

---

[28] Capt. Caleb Gibbs was commandant of the Commander in Chief's Guard.
[29] The text is from Force's *American Archives*.

their men with cloathing, and necessaries; that they may be ready to march, or embark, upon the shortest notice; The General wishes to impress this strongly, upon the minds of the Colonels; because no Excuse will be taken to delay their departure, the moment that it becomes necessary. It is recommended to those Corps which are not already supplied with Uniforms, to provide hunting Shirts for their men.

Colonel Hands, and Col. Littles Regiments, to be mustered upon Thursday morning at Long Island: The Colonels to acquaint Commissary General Moylan with the places where, and the hour when, it is most convenient for the mustering, and to provide their Rolls accordingly.

## GENERAL ORDERS

Head Quarters, New York, May 7, 1776.

Parole Devonshire.   Countersign Cavendish.

Every Regiment encamped in the Line, and every Regiment in the Brigade, upon Long-Island, exclusive of their Quarter, and Rear Guards, are to mount a picquet every evening at Retreat beating, at Sun-sett; consisting of one Captain, two Subalterns, three Serjeants, one Drum, one Fife, and fifty Rank and File; They are to lay upon their Arms and be ready to turn out at a minute's notice. One Colonel, one Lieut. Colonel, and one Major, to mount every evening at sun set, as Field Officers of the picquet: Immediately upon any Alarm, or Order from the Brigadier General of the day, the picquets are to form in the front of their respective encampments, and there wait the Orders of the Field Officers commanding the picquet—The Field Officer commanding the picquet, is instantly to obey the Orders of the Brigadier General of the day.

A Brigadier General to mount every morning, at Ten o'Clock, who will receive all reports, visit all the out guards in the day time, and report all extraordinaries to the Commander in Chief.

A Brigade Major of the day, is constantly to attend Head Quarters, to receive all extraordinary Orders, and to distribute them immediately to the brigades.

The Colonel, Lieut. Colonel, and Major of the same picquet; the former to go the Grand Rounds and the two latter the visiting Rounds of the camp.

Brigadier General Greene, will order the same picquet to be mounted by the Regiments, in his Brigade, as are mounted by those in the Grand Camp; he will also direct, one Field Officer to mount daily, to command them—Genl. Greene will report all extraordinaries to the Commander in Chief.

Col Prescot, or Officer commanding upon Nutten, or Governors Island, and the officer commanding at Red-hook to report all extraordinaries to the Commander in Chief; Upon any appearance of an enemy, the commanding Officer at Red-hook will also dispatch a messenger to Genl. Greene.

The Officer commanding the Riffle-men upon Long-Island, will constantly report all extraordinaries to Brigadier Genl. Greene, and the Officer commanding upon Staten-Island, will do the same to the Commander in Chief.

## To THE PRESIDENT OF CONGRESS

New York, May 7, 1776.

Sir: At a Quarter after seven this Evening I received by Express a Letter from Thomas Cushing Esquire Chairman of a Committee of the Honorable General Court, covering one from the Committee of Salem Copies of which I do myself the Honor to transmit to Congress that they may Judge of the Intelligence contained therein and direct such measures to be

taken upon the occasion as they may think proper and necessary. I would observe, that supposing Captain Lee's Account
to be true in part, there must be a mistake, either as to the
Number of Troops, or the Ships. If there are no more Ships
than what are mentioned, It is certain there cannot be so many
Troops; of this however Congress can Judge as well as myself,
and I submit it to them, whether upon the whole circumstances and the Incertainty of their destination, If they were
met with at all, they choose that any forces shall be detached
from hence, as they will see from the returns transmitted Yesterday, the number of Men here, is but small and inconsiderable and what is much to be regretted, no small part of those
without Arms. perhaps by dividing and subdividing our force
too much, we shall have no one post sufficiently guarded. I shall
wait their direction and whatever their order is will comply
with it as soon as possible. I have &ca.

P. S: I had by the Express, a Letter from General Ward, containing an Account similar to that from the Salem committee,
and by way of Captain Lee. Should the Commissioners arrive,
How are they to be received and treated? I wish the direction
of Congress upon the Subject, by return of the Bearer.[30]

### To COLONEL ALEXANDER McDOUGALL

New York, May 7, 1776.

Sir: I received your Favour upon the Subject of Rations, and
agreeable to your Request have inclosed a List of Rations allowed
the Officers of the Regiments before Boston. Those in Service the
1st of July, have been allowed from that Time; Others appointed
to Office since, from the Dates of their Commissions.

Having never given any Direction about the Officers alluded
to, or any others, except those that were immediately under

---

[30] In the writing of Robert Hanson Harrison.

my Command, I would observe that I do not mean to do it in this Instance, as they were acting in a distinct and different District. I am, etc.

### GENERAL ORDERS

Head Quarters, New York, May 8, 1776.

Parole Manchester.   Countersign York.

John Fowler, Soldier in Capt. Winship's[31] Company, in Col Nixon's Regiment, tried at a late General Court Martial, whereof Col Huntington was President, for "Deserting from his guard and being three days absent from his Regiment without leave," is found guilty by the court, and sentenced to receive Twenty Lashes, upon the bare back, for the said offence.

Timothy Dawney, Soldier in Capt. Curtiss[32] Company, in Col Learnards Regiment, tried by the same General Count Martial, for "attempting to stab Joseph Laffin, assaulting John Phipps, and for snapping a loaded musket at Luther Proute"; The Court finding the Prisoner guilty of the charge, order him to be whipp'd Thirty-nine Lashes upon the bare back, and order him to be drum'd out of the army.

John Reling, of Capt. Hamilton's[33] Company, in the New-York Artillery, tried by the same General Court Martial for "Desertion," is found guilty of breaking from his confinement, and sentenced to be confin'd for Six days, upon bread and water.

The General approves the sentence of all the above mentioned Trials, and commands them to be put in execution at such time and place, as the commanding Officers of the several Corps, shall direct.

---

[31] Capt. Ebenezer Winship, of the Fourth Continental Infantry.
[32] Capt. Samuel Curtiss, of the Third Continental Infantry.
[33] Capt. Alexander Hamilton.

The commanding Officers of Regiments and Corps are to be answerable that such of their Officers, and Soldiers, as are seized with the Infection of the small-pox, are instantly removed to the Island assign'd for the reception of all those, who have that distemper, and the Surgeons of regiments, are carefully to report when any person is supposed to be infected, that he may be removed without delay.

## To MAJOR GENERAL ARTEMAS WARD

New York, May 9, 1776.

Sir: Your Letters of the 27th. and 28th. Ulto. came in Course to Hand; I am glad that you have given your Attention to the Works, which I doubt not by this Time are compleat. It will give me Pleasure to hear they are: For should these Accounts of Hessians and Hanoverian Troops coming over prove true, it is possible the Enemy may make some Attempts to regain a Footing in your Province.

I have represented to Congress the Want you was in for Cash, to which I have not yet received an Answer: When I do, you shall be informed thereof.

The Account you give of the Vessels at Beverley, being unfit for Service, surprizes me prodigiously; I was taught to believe very differently of the Ship Jenny, by Commodore Manley, and Captain Bartlett, who you mention to have given you their Opinion of them. The Brigantine from Antigua was also thought very fit to arm.

Doctor Brown's[34] Accounts are more immediately in the Director General's of the Hospital Department. When he arrives here, I shall give them to him for his Inspection.

---

[34] Probably Dr. William Brown, of Alexandria, Va., and, later, director general of the hospital, Middle Department.

Mr. Singletorry's Account is easily settled, as he has the Commissary's Receipt for the Arms. If the Account of the Loss of the Arms was more particular, it would be more regular and satisfactory.

A Letter is just come to my Hands from Winthrop Sargent[35] Esqr. Agent for the Navy at Gloucester; He says, there are some Women and Children whom he is obliged to maintain at the Continl. Expense; also a Number of Men taken in some of the last Prizes. You will please to examine into their Situation; If Prisoners of War they should be sent into some Inland Place and confined; If Tories, the General Court are the proper Persons to take Cognizance of them.

I see by the public Prints, that the Prizes at Beverley are to be sold the 20th Inst.: As by the Obstructions put on Commerce in General, there may appear but few Purchasers for the Vessels: of Course, they may be sold vastly under their Value, I think you had best have some Persons in whom you can confide, present at the Sale, with Power to purchase the large Ship, and the Brig from Antigua, if he finds them going very much under their Value.[36] It is not above two or three Years since the Ship cost £3000 Sterlg. She is to be sure something worse for the Wear, and I believe is not remarkably well found at present, as she has been pillaged for the Use of our armed Vessels, which must make a considerable Abatement of her Value. The Brigantine is, I suppose, in the same Predicament; but a good Judge will easily know their Value.

Wm. Watson Esqr. of Plymouth, advises that the Prizes *Norfolk* and *happy Return,* are condemn'd; and desires I would appoint a Day for Sale of them, and their Cargoes: This you will please to do, letting them be advertised in the Papers, at least a Fortnight before the Sale. I am, etc.

---

[35] Winthrop Sargent, then agent for Continental armed vessels.
[36] To be fitted out as additional Continental armed vessels.

## To THE COMMITTEE
## OF THE MASSACHUSETTS LEGISLATURE[37]

New York, May 9, 1776.

Sir: I received your favor of the 3d Inst. on Tuesday Evening, covering that of the Committee of Salem to your Honble. Court; and judging the Intelligence interesting and Important, I immediately forwarded Copies of both to Congress by the Express for them to give such Orders and direction respecting it, as they might think proper and requisite. I am not yet favored with their Answer; as soon as it comes, I will send it you by the Express, and whatever measures they direct me to pursue, I will attempt to put in execution with all Possible dispatch. The Account having come thro' different hands, I hope it is exaggerated; It appears inconsistent and impossible in part; certainly there is a mistake, either as to the Number of Troops or the Ships, there must be more of the latter or fewer of the former; 60 Vessels could not bring 12,000 Men, unless they are much larger than usual, besides provisions and Stores: nor should such a fleet and Armament be coming, do I think it altogether probable, that an account of their destination and Views, could be so distinctly and accurately given to the Master, who informed Captn. Lee; I should rather suppose, that they would wish to take us by surprize. For these reasons, and as their destination may be elsewhere, and as the Army here is greatly Weakened and reduced by Ten of the Strongest Regiments being ordered to Quebec; I could not think myself authorized to detach any reinforcement from hence, without the direction of Congress; least by dividing the Army into small parties, we should have no place secure and guarded; Assuring you at the same time, I shall be always ready and happy to give you every Assistance in my power against our common

---

[37] Thomas Cushing was chairman of this committee.

Enemies, when it can be done consistently with the public good. I am &ca.

## To GEORGE MASON

New York, May 10, 1776.

Dear Sir: The uncertainty of my return, and the justice of surrendering to Mr. Custis, the Bonds which I have taken for the Monies raised from his Estate and lent out upon Interest. As also his Moiety of his deceased Sister's Fortune (consisting of altogether of Bonds &c.) obliges me to have recourse to a friend to see this matter done, and a proper Memorandum of the transaction made. I could think of no person in whose friendship, care and Abilities I could so much confide, to do Mr. Custis and me this favour as yourself; and, therefore, take the liberty of Soliciting your Aid.

In Order that you may be enabled to do this with ease and propriety, I have wrote to the Clerk of the Secretary's Office, for attested Copies of my last settled Accounts with the General Court in behalf of Mr. Custis and the Estate of his deceased Sister; with which and the Bonds, I have desired him and Mr. Washington to wait upon you for the purpose above mentioned.

The Amount of the Balance due, upon my last settled Accounts, to Mr. Custis, I would also have assigned him out of my Moiety of his Sister's Bonds; and, if there is no weight in what I have said, in my Letter to Mr. Lund Washington, concerning the rise of exchange, and which, to avoid repetition, as I am a good deal hurried, I have desired him to shew you, I desire it may meet with no Notice, as I want nothing but what is consistent with the strictest justice, honour, and even generosity; although I have never charged him or his Sister, from the day of my connexion with them to this Hour, one Farthing, for all the trouble I have had in managing their Estates, nor for any expense they have been to me, notwithstanding some hundreds of pounds would not reimburse the Monies I have actually paid in attending the public Meetings in Williamsburg to collect their debts, and transact these several matters appertaining to the respective Estates.

A variety of occurrences, and my anxiety and hurry to put this place, as speedily as possible, into a posture of defence, will not, at this time, admit me to add more than that I am, etc.

## To LUND WASHINGTON

New York, May 10, 1776.

Dear Lund: As I am not able to form any Idea of the time of my return, and as it is very reasonable and just that Mr. Custis should be possessed of his Estate, although it is not in my power (circumstanced as I am at present) to Liquidate the Accounts and make a final settlement with him, I have wrote to the Clerk of the Secretary's Office for Authentic Copies of the last Accounts which I exhibited against him and the Estate of his deceased Sister. With these (for I have directed them to be sent to you) and the bundle of Bonds which you will find among my Papers, I would have Mr. Custis and you repair to Colonel Mason, and get him, as a common friend to us both, as a Gentleman well acquainted with business and very capable of drawing up a proper Memorandum of the transaction, to deliver him his own Bonds, which, if my memory fails me not, and no changes have happened, are in one parcel and indorsed; and at the same time deliver him as many Bonds out of the other parcel, endorsed Miss Custis's Bonds, as will pay him his Moiety of her Fortune, and the Balance which will appear due to him from me, at my last settlement with General Court.

How the Acct. will then stand between us, I cannot, with precision, say, but believe the Balance will be rather in my favour than his.

In my last settlement of the Estate of Miss Custis (which you will have sent to you, I expect, by Mr. Everard) every Bond, Mortgage, &c. were fully accounted for and will be the best Ground to found the dividend (between Mr. Custis and myself) upon, lest any of the Bonds or Mortgages should be misplaced, or in the Office.

Mr. Mercer's Bonds I have promised to take into my part, and as there are Wheat and other Accounts opened between that Estate and me, I should be glad to have them allotted accordingly. In like manner, I promised to take Mr. Robert Adams's debt upon myself and believe the last Mortgage from him was taken in my own Name. As to the others, I do not care how they are divided, nor was I anxious about these, further than that it served to comply with their desires, founded (I believe) on an Opinion, that I should not press them for the Money.

The Bank stock must, I presume, be equally divided between us. Long before I left Virginia, I directed it to be sold, writing to Messieurs Cary and Co., who had always received the dividends, to negotiate the matter: In consequence they sent me a power of Attorney, and a great deal of formal stuff for Mrs. Washington and myself to execute before the Governor. This we did, literally as required, and transmitted, since which the Directors of the Bank have prescribed another Mode, and I have had forwarded to me another set of Papers to be executed also before the Governor, which has never been in my power to do, as they arrived but a little while before I set out for the Congress last Spring. Thus the matter stands, as far as I know, with respect to the Money in the Funds.[38]

---

[38] This bank-stock matter was not finally settled until after the Revolutionary War.

There is another matter, which I think justice to myself requires a mention of, and that is with respect to the Sterling Balance which it will appear I was owing Mr. Custis upon last settlement. It was then, and ever since has been, my intention to assign him as many Bonds, carrying Interest, as would discharge this Ballance, but my attendance upon Congress in the Fall 1774, and Spring 1775, put it out of my power to attend the General Courts at this Sessions; consequently no Order could be taken, or account rendered, of this matter; and now, by the rise of exchange, if I was to turn Current Money Bonds into Sterling, I should be a considerable sufferer, when I had not, nor could have, any interest in delaying of it; and that it was so delayed, was owing to the Reasons abovementioned, it being a practice to let out his Money upon Interest, as soon as it came to my Hands.

The many matters, which hang heavy upon my hands at present, do not allow me time to add, but oblige me to request, as I have not wrote fully to Colonel Mason on this subject, that you will shew him, and, if necessary, let him have this Letter. I am etc.

## GENERAL ORDERS

Head Quarters, New York, May 10, 1776.
Parole Nassau.   Countersign Williams.

The Colonel of Artillery, constantly to employ the whole of the officers, and men off guard, in placing the Guns upon their proper platforms, providing a sufficient quantity of filled Cartridges, and fix'd Ammunition for each Gun; seeing the Shot, Rammers, Spunges and Ladles with all the necessary *Atraile,* brought to the Batteries where they are to be used, and continually keeping as many men, as can work, filling cannon, and musket cartridges, and doing all the various duty required in the Laboratory. The heaviest Mortars to be placed in the Batteries to the sea-line, and a proper quantity of Fuses to be drove, and Shells fill'd, for each mortar—The light Mortars to be placed in the Forts, near the encampments.

Joseph Child of the New York Train of Artillery tried at a late General Court Martial whereof Col. Huntington was President for "defrauding Christopher Stetson of a dollar, also for drinking Damnation to all Whigs, and Sons of Liberty, and for profane cursing and swearing."—The Court finding the prisoner guilty of profane cursing and swearing and speaking contemptuously of the American Army, do sentence him to be drum'd out of the army.

Zodiac Piper of Capt. Ledyard's[39] Company and Thos. Watkins of Capt. Lyon's[40] Company, both in Col. McDougal's Regiment, tried by the same General Court Martial, for "being concern'd in a riot on Saturday night"—The Court find the Prisoner, Piper, guilty of being from his quarters at an unseasonable hour, and being concern'd, in raising a disturbance in the streets, and do sentence him to be confined six days, upon bread and water, for said offence: The Court are of opinion, that the Prisoner, Watkins, is guilty of being out of his quarters at unseasonable hours, and of profane cursing and swearing, and do sentence him to be confin'd six days; upon bread and water—and be fined one sixth of a dollar for profane swearing, as by the 3rd Article is prescribed.

The General approves of the foregoing Sentences, and orders them to take place to morrow morning at Guard mounting.

## To THE PRESIDENT OF CONGRESS

New York, May 11, 1776.

Sir: I am now to acknowledge the receipt of your favors of the 4th and 7th Instant, with their several Inclosures, and am exceedingly glad that before the Resolution of Congress

---

[39] Capt. Benjamin Ledyard, of the First New York Regiment.
[40] Capt. David Lyon, of the First New York Regiment.

respecting Lieut. Col. Ogden came to hand, I had ordered him to join his regiment and had quelled a disagreeable Spirit of mutiny and desertion which had taken place and seemed to be rising to a great degree in consequence of it: In order to effect It, I had the Regiment paraded, and ordered two more at the same time under Arms convinced them of their error and Ill conduct and obtained a promise for their good behaviour in future. To such as had absconded I gave pardons on their assurances to return to their duty again.

In my Letter of the 5th Instant, which I had the honor of addressing you, I mentioned to Congress the refractory and mutinous conduct of Lieut. Grover of the 2d Regiment, and laid before them a Copy of the proceedings of a Court Martial upon him, and of his defence, with a view that such measures should be adopted as they shou'd think adequate to his crime. I would now beg leave to inform them, that since then he has appeared sensible of his mis-conduct, and having made a written acknowledgement of his Offence and begged pardon for it, as by the inclosed Copy will appear, I thought it best to release him from his confinement, and have ordered him to join his Regiment, which I hope will meet their approbation and render any determination as to him unnecessary; Observing at the same time, that I have endeavoured and I flatter myself not ineffectually, to support their authority and a due subordination in the Army, I have found it of importance and expedient to yield many points, in fact, without seeming to have done it, and this to avoid bringing on a too frequent discussion of matters, which in a political view ought to be kept a little behind the Curtain, and not be made too much the subjects of disquisition. Time only can eradicate and overcome customs and prejudices of long standing; they must be got the better of, by slow and gradual advances.

I would here take occasion to suggest to Congress, (not wishing or meaning of myself to assume the smallest degree of power in any instance) the propriety and necessity of having their Sentiments respecting the filling up of Vacancies and issuing Commissions to Officers, especially to those under the rank of Field Officers. Had I literally complied to the directions given upon this Subject, when I first engaged in the Service, and which I conceived to be superceded by a subsequent resolve for forming the Army upon the present establishment, I must have employed one clerk for no other business, than Issuing Warrants of Appointment and giving information to Congress for their confirmation or refusal. It being evident from the nature of things, that there will be frequent changes and vacancies in Office, from death and a variety of other causes, I now submit it to them and pray their direction, whether I am to pursue that mode and all the Ceremonies attending it, or to be at liberty to fill up and grant Commissions at once to such as may be fit and proper persons to succeed.

When I came from Cambridge, I left instructions with Col. Knox of the Artillery Regiment, for the regulation of his Conduct and among other things, directed him immediately to send forward to this place, Lieut: Col: Burbeck, who notwithstanding he received orders for that purpose, has refused to come, considering himself as he says in his Answer to Colonel Knox's Letter (Copies of which I have enclosed) bound in point of Generosity to stay in the Service of the province, tho' I am told by Colonel Knox, that some of the Members of the General Court hearing of the matter, informed him, that they did not consider him engaged to them, and that he had no just pretext for his refusal. I thought it right to lay this matter before Congress and submit it to them, whether Colo. Burbeck, who will or will not serve the Continent, or go, to this or that place as it may suit him and square with his pretended notions of generosity, should be longer continued in Office.[41]

Before I have done, with the utmost deference and respect, I would beg leave to remind Congress of my former Letters and Applications, respecting the appointment of proper persons to superintend and take directions of such Prisoners, as have already fallen and will fall into our hands, in the course of the War; being fully convinced, if there were persons appointed for and who wou'd take the whole Management of them under their care, that the Continent would save a considerable sum of money by it, and the Prisoners be better treated and provided with real necessaries, than what they now are, and shall take the liberty to add, that it appears to me a matter of much importance and worthy of consideration, that particular and proper places of security should be fixed on and established in the interior parts of the different Governments for their reception. Such Establishments are agreeable to the Practice and usage of the English and other Nations and are founded on principles of necessity and public utility. The advantages which will arise from them, are obvious and many; I shall only mention two or three: they will tend much to prevent escapes, which are difficult to effect, when the Public is once advertized, that the Prisoners are restrained to a few stated and well known places and not permitted to go from thence, and the more Ingenious among them, from discriminating and spreading their artful and pernicious Intrigues and Opinions throughout the Country, which would Influence the Weaker and wavering part of Mankind and meet with too favorable a hearing. Further it will be less in their power to join and assist our Enemies in cases of Invasion, and will give us an Opportunity always to know

---

[41] Lieut. Col. William Burdeck. On May 25 Congress resolved that he be dismissed from the Continental service.

from the returns of those appointed to superintend them, what number we have in possession, the force sufficient to check and suppress their Hostile views in Times of emergency, and the expenses necessary for their maintenance and support. Many other reasons might be adduced to prove the necessity and expediency of the measure, I shall only subjoin one more and then have done on the Subject, which is, that many of the Towns where prisoners have been already sent, not having conveniencie for, or the means of keeping them, complain they are burthensome, and have become careless, inattentive, and altogether indifferent, whether they escape or not, and those of them that are restricted to a close confinement, the limits of Jail, neglected and not treated with the care and regard, which Congress wish.

I have not received further Intelligence of the German Troops since my Letter of the 7 Inst. covering Mr. Cushing's dispatches; but least the account of their coming should be true, may it not be advisable and good policy, to raise some Companies of our Germans to send among them, when they arrive, for exciting a spirit of disaffection and desertion? If a few trusty, sensible fellows could get with them, I should think they would have great weight and influence with the common Soldiery, who certainly have no enmity towards us, having received no Injury, nor cause of Quarrell from us.

The measure having occurred and appearing to me expedient, I thought it prudent to mention it for the consideration of Congress.

Having received a Letter from General Ward, advising that Congress have accepted of his resignation and praying to be relieved; and it being necessary that a General Officer should be sent to take the command of the Troops at Boston, especially if the Army should arrive which is talked of, and which some consider as a probable event, I must beg leave to recommend to Congress the appointment of some Brigadier Generals, not having more here (nor so many at this Time) than are essential to the Government and conducting the Forces and Works carrying on. Generals Sullivan and Thompson being ordered to Canada, I cannot spare one more General Officer from hence, without injuring the service greatly. and leaving the Army here without a sufficient number.[42]

Having frequent applications from the Committee of Safety and others about an Exchange of Prisoners being frequently made and not having Authority to pursue any other mode, than that marked out by a resolve of Congress some considerable time ago, I hope they will pardon me when I wish them to take into consideration such parts of my Letter of the 22d Ulto. as relate to this Subject and for their determination upon it. I shall then have it in my power to give explicit and satisfactory Answers to those who shall apply. I have the Honor &ca.[43]

## GENERAL ORDERS

Head Quarters, New York, May 11, 1776.
Parole The Congress.   Countersign Hampden.

All Officers, non-commissioned Officers and Soldiers, belonging to the Regiments at present encamped, are on no pretence (sickness excepted) to lay out of their respective encampments.

---

[42] On May 14, in compliance with the above request, Congress resolved that General Washington should order a major general to take command in the Eastern Department and also send a brigadier general to that department. On May 16 Horatio Gates was appointed a major general and Thomas Mifflin a brigadier general. John Adams, in a letter to Hancock (May 16), records: "I have written to Genl. Washington to request him, if agreable, that those gentlemen may take the command in Boston."

[43] In the writing of Robert Hanson Harrison, who also copied this letter into the "Letter Book" record and made many variations and changes therein, which do not, however, alter the meaning. The text here used is from the letter signed and sent, which is a much stronger composition than the "Letter Book" copy. Maj. Gen. Horatio Gates's memorandum on England's method of treating prisoners was inclosed by Washington and is filed with this letter in the *Papers of the Continental Congress*.

Col Wyllys's Regiment, to march to morrow morning, at eight o'clock, and encamp on the ground, marked out for them in their brigade.

The Regiment and Company of Artillery, to be quarter'd in the Barracks of the upper and lower Batteries, and in the Barracks near the Laboratory—As soon as the Guns are placed in the Batteries to which they are appointed, the Colonel of Artillery, will detach the proper number of officers and men, to manage them—These are to encamp with the Brigades they are posted with.

The Colonel of Artillery, to order all the cannon and musquet Cartridges, to be filled in a room appointed for that purpose, in the upper battery, near the bowling Green Cannon and Musquet Powder, sufficient for the above purpose to be lodged in the Magazine prepar'd to receive it, in the upper battery.

All the Boat Builders, Carpenters and Painters, in the several Regiments and Corps, to be sent to Major General Putnam's quarters, to morrow morning at Six o'Clock, to receive his orders.

His Excellency has been pleased to appoint, Hugh Hughes Esqr., Assistant Quarter Master General—he is to be obeyed as such.

Serjt. John Smith, of Capt. Adams's[44] Company, in Col Irvine's Regt. tried at a late General Court Martial, whereof Col Huntington was president, for "forging an order on the Commissary General, in the Name of Col Irvine, with an Intent of defrauding the Continent, in drawing Twenty two shillings and six pence, for rations which were not due"—The Court finding the prisoner guilty of the charge, do sentence him to be reduced to the ranks, and to be mulcted two months pay.

The General approves the above sentence, and orders Col. Irvine to see it put in execution.

---

[44] Capt. Robert Adams, of the Sixth Pennsylvania Regiment.

## GENERAL ORDERS

Head Quarters, New York, May 12, 1776.

Parole Madrid.   Countersign Paris.

The Carpenters, Boat Builders, and Painters, who were selected for the public service this morning, by Major Genl. Putnam, are to parade to morrow morning at Sunrise, in the Street opposite to Genl. Putnam's, where they will receive his orders.

Corpl. John Crossly of Capt. Ledyards Company, in Col. McDougall's Regiment, tried at a late General Court Martial, whereof Col Huntington was president, for "Desertion." The Court find the prisoner guilty of the charge, and do sentence him to be reduced to a private, and mulcted one month's pay— The General approves the above sentence, and orders it to take place immediately.

## GENERAL ORDERS

Head Quarters, New York, May 13, 1776.

Parole Holland.   Countersign Martinico.

Major Genl. Putnam, with the Brigadiers General, Spencer, and Lord Stirling, to examine, and make report of the proper places to be fixed upon for the particular alarm posts of each regiment.

Col Webb's, and Col. Nixon's regiments to be muster'd, wednesday morning at eight o'Clock, upon their regimental parades, in the front of their encampment.

## To GOVERNOR NICHOLAS COOKE

New York, May 13, 1776.

Sir: I received your favor of the 6th Inst., for which and Its several Inclosures, I return you my thanks.

Agreeable to my promise, on the 30th Ulto. I wrote Congress respecting the state of your Colony, importuning their Attention to it, and that proper measures should be adopted for its relief and defence. A copy of the Letter you have inclosed for your perusal and further satisfaction.

It gives me much pleasure, to hear there is so much unanimity among you, and that the Inhabitants of Newport have come to the laudable and necessary Resolution you mentioned; If united, your exertions most probably will have the desired effect; and tho' they should not be so fully answered, as men of over sanguine dispositions hope and expect; yet they will be productive of great benefits and advantages to the Colony and at the same time promote the public good. I am &c.

## To ISAAC SEARS

New York, May 13, 1776.

Sir: I received your favor of the 2d Inst. and am fully of opinion with you, that the Resolves of Congress, should be strictly adhered to; As the regulation of the Price of Tea, or any other Article, is quite foreign to my department, I shall leave such Matters to the Provincial Congress before whom I will this day lay your Letter, and I doubt not they will take such steps as will put a stop to the evil you are apprehensive of. I am &c.

## To THE NEW YORK LEGISLATURE

New York, May 13, 1776.

Sir: As applications are frequently made by officers of Militia, that came for the defence of this city, for their pay, I enclose you a resolve of Congress on that subject, which passed the 26th. of April. You have also, herewith, a letter I received from Mr. Sears, of New Haven, the subject of which is of consequence, but very foreign to my department. I doubt not but your honourable Convention will take the matter under consideration, and put a stop to the evil Mr. Sears is apprehensive of. I have the honor to be, etc.[45]

### To MAJOR GENERAL ARTEMAS WARD

New York, May 13, 1776.

Sir: Your Favour of the 4th. Inst. with Return of the Division of the Army under your Command is come to Hand.

The Account you give of your Progress in fortifying the Town and Harbour of Boston is very agreeable. When the Works are compleated, I think you will have but little to apprehend from the Enemy, should they incline to pay you another Visit.

Inclosed is a Petition from Colonel Varnum, which I beg you will attend to: If the Facts are as set forth therein, he must be redressed; for if such Practices as he complains of are given the least Countenance to, it will have the Worst of Consequences, by encouraging Soldiers to shift from one Regiment to another, and throw the whole Army into Confusion.

I have had no Advice from Congress relative to your Resignation.[46] I shall write them this Day to know whom they may think proper to appoint to the Command in your State. When I receive their Answer, you shall be informed thereof.

Inclosed is a Copy of a Resolve of Congress respecting the Cannon in the Colony of Massachusetts Bay.[47] I am, Sir, etc.

### To COLONEL DAVID WATERBURY

New York, May 13, 1776.

Sir: Governor Trumbull has been pleased to mention you to me as a proper Person to succeed to the Command of the Regiment, lately General Arnold's.

---

[45] The text is from Force's *American Archives.*
[46] Ward's resignation had been accepted by Congress on April 23.
[47] The resolve of May 7, 1776, permitting the cannon in Boston that had not been removed by General Washington to remain there for the protection of the town.

If you incline to engage in the Service again, I should be obliged to you for signifying as much; in Order that I may lay the Matter before Congress for their Approbation. I am, etc.

## GENERAL ORDERS

Head Quarters, New York, May 14, 1776.

Parole St. Eustatia.    Countersign Amboy.

Christian Mazure of Capt. Wylley's[48] Company, in Col. McDougalls Regiment, tried at a late General Court Martial, whereof Col Huntington was president, for "Desertion,": The Court find the prisoner guilty of the charge and do sentence him to receive Twenty Lashes on his bare back.

John McFarling of Capt. Sharpe's[49] Company, in Col Daytons Regiment, tried by the above General Court Martial for "Desertion," is acquitted by the court.

John Cooper of Capt: Varicks[50] Company, in Col. McDougalls Regiment, tried by the above Court Martial, for "Mutiny"—The Court finding the prisoner guilty of the Charge, do sentence him to receive Fifteen Lashes on the bare back, for said offence.

James McDonald of Capt. Horton's[51] Company, in Col. Ritzema's Regiment, tried by the above General Court Martial for threatning the life of Lieut. Young[52] and others, of the said company, is found guilty by the Court and sentenced to be confined, eight days on bread and water, for said offence.

The General approves the foregoing sentences, and orders them to be put in execution, to morrow morning at Guard mounting.

---

[48] Capt. John Wiley, of the First New York Regiment.
[49] Capt. Anthony Sharp, of the Third New Jersey Regiment.
[50] Capt. Richard Varick, of the First New York Regiment. He was, later, aide to Schuyler; lieutenant colonel and deputy muster master general, Northern Army; aide to Arnold; and recording secretary to General Washington.
[51] Capt. Ambrose Horton, of the Third New York Regiment.
[52] Lieut. Guy(?) Young, of the Second New York Regiment.

One Colonel, and one Quarter Master, from each brigade, to attend a Committee from the Congress of this City, to morrow morning at seven o'clock, to take cognizance of the damage done to certain houses, where the Troops have been quartered— The Chairman of the Committee, will meet the Colonels at the Exchange, at the time appointed.

The General Court Martial, whereof Col Huntington was president is dissolved.

A General Court Martial of the Line, consisting of one Colonel, one Lieut. Colonel, one Major, and ten Captains, to sit to morrow morning at Ten o'Clock, to try all such prisoners as shall be brought before them. All Evidences, and persons concern'd, to attend the court.

## GENERAL ORDERS

Head Quarters, New York, May 15, 1776.
Parole Barre.   Countersign Dublin.

The Continental Congress having ordered, Friday the 17th. Instant to be observed as a day of "fasting, humiliation and prayer, humbly to supplicate the mercy of Almighty God, that it would please him to pardon all our manifold sins and transgressions, and to prosper the Arms of the United Colonies, and finally, establish the peace and freedom of America, upon a solid and lasting foundation"—The General commands all officers, and soldiers, to pay strict obedience to the Orders of the Continental Congress, and by their unfeigned, and pious observance of their religious duties, incline the Lord, and Giver of Victory, to prosper our arms.

The regiment of Artillery to be mustered, Sunday morning, at eight o'clock, upon the Common, where the Commissary General of Musters will attend.

The Company of Artillery commanded by Capt. Hamilton, to be mustered at Ten o'Clock, next Sunday morning, upon the Common, near the Laboratory.

Lieut. Howe and Ensign Kennedy[53] of Col Wards regiment, with the same non-commissioned officers, and soldiers, who were employed by the orders of the 8th. Instant in cutting picketts, are to parade at Genl. Putnams quarters, to morrow morning at sun rise, with four days provisions ready dressed to go upon the same duty as before.

The Officers of all guards, are to make their reports to the Colonel of the picquet, by nine o'clock in the morning—The Colonel of the picquet to make a report of all those reports, collected in one, to the Brigadier of the day at *10* o'clock precisely.

## To THE PRESIDENT OF CONGRESS

New York, May 15, 1776.

Sir: Since my last of the 11 Instant, which I had the honor to address you, nothing of Moment or Importance has occurred, and the principal design of this, is to communicate to Congress, the Intelligence I received from General Schuyler by a Letter of the 10th. Instant,[54] respecting the progress of our Troops in getting towards Canada, not doubting of their impatience and anxiety to hear of it, and of every thing relating to the expedition; for their more particular information and satisfaction, I have done myself the pleasure to extract the substance of his Letter on this head, which is as follows "That General Thompson with the last of his Brigade in the Morning of Tuesday

---

[53] Lieut. Baxter Howe and Lieut. John Kennedy of the Twenty-first Continental Infantry.

[54] Schuyler wrote two letters to Washington on May 10, both of which are in the *Washington Papers.*

sennight embarked at Fort George, and in the Evening of the next day, General Sullivan arrived at Albany; That he had ordered an additional Number of Carpenters to Assist in building Boats, who funishing Eight every day, would have 110 complete by the 21st. before which he was fearful the last of General Sullivan's Brigade could not embark; That they would carry 30 Men each besides the Baggage, Ammunition and Intrenching Tools; That he has given most pointed orders to restrain the licentiousness of the Troops, which was disgraceful and very Injurious in those gone on heretofore, in abusing the Inhabitants and Batteauxmen and that he had ordered Captain Romans from Canada for Trial at Albany, there being sundry complaints lodged against him. He also informs that the 60 Barrells of Powder had arrived and would be forwarded that day; That the 1st. Regiment of General Sullivan's Brigade marched that Morning and that the Intrenching Tools and about 600 Barrels of Pork were also gone on; That he could not possibly send more than half of the 300,000 Dollars into Canada being greatly in debt on the public Account and the Creditors exceedingly clamorous and Importunate for payment, which Sum he hopes will be sufficient 'till the Canadians agree to take our paper Currency, to which they are much averse, and of which he is exceedingly doubtful; That he had got the Chain and would forward it that day to General Arnold, with orders to fix it at the rapids of Richlieu. He adds that he had reviewed General Sullivan's Brigade in presence of about 260 Indians who were greatly pleased with the order and regularity of the Troops and supprized at their Number which the Tories had industriously propogated consisted only of 3 Companies and that they were kept always walking the Streets to induce them to believe their Number was much greater than it really was."

I have enclosed a copy of General Schuyler's Instructions to Jas. Price Esqr. Deputy Commissary General, for the regulation of his Conduct in that department, which I received last night and which General Schuyler requested me to forward you; I also beg leave to lay before Congress a Copy of a Letter from Samuel Stringer director of one of the Hospitals, purporting an Application for an Increase of Surgeons, Mates &ca.; an Estimate of which is also inclosed, and submit it to them what number must be sent from hence, or be got else where:[55] It is highly probable that many more will be wanted in Canada, than what are already there, on Account of the late Augmentation of the Army, but I thought it most advisable to make his requisition known to Congress, and to take their order and direction upon it: As to the Medicines I shall speak to Doctor Morgan, (not yet arrived) as soon as he comes, and order him to forward such as may be necessary and can be possibly spared. I have &ca.[56]

## To MAJOR GENERAL PHILIP SCHUYLER

New York, May 15, 1776.

Dear Sir: I received your Favours of the 3rd. and 4th. Inst. and was happy to hear of the safe Arrival of the Commissioner from Congress at St. John's, and that so many Batteaus with Troops had passed there the 29th. Ulto. 'Ere this, I hope, the Army before Quebec is considerably augmented; I am too well convinced there was great Occasion for it.

As to Money, the State of our Chest would not have justified a Loan or Supply, if Congress had not furnished you with what you received by Colo. Reid, having seldom more than will satisfy pressing Claims against myself.

[55] These documents are in the *Washington Papers*.
[56] In the writing of Robert Hanson Harrison.

As to Pork, I refer you to my Letter of the 3rd. Inst. and can only add, that the Commissary has assured me he will do all in his Power to forward a Supply.

In Respect to the Trial of Captain Romans[57] or any other, that it may be expedient to bring to Justice, I think it highly necessary, and tho' it may not be altogether so formal and regular, yet I shall most readily dispense with Ceremonies, where it will promote the public Good.

I have made Inquiry into our Stores of Lead and find that I have it in my Power to spare you about 5 Tons, which shall be sent with the Nails as soon as they can be collected; the Qr. Master having Persons out in different Places trying to procure them. I suppose whatever can be got will be forwarded To-Morrow or next Day with the utmost Expedition, as you seem to be so much in Want from your Letter of the 11th. Instant.

Your Favors of the 10th. came to Hand last Night with their several Inclosures, for which I return you my Thanks and agreeable to your Request by this Morning's Post, I transmitted to Congress a Copy of your Orders to Mr. Price with the several Letters for them.

The Letter from the Commissioners, which you were kind enough to leave open for my Perusal, describes Matters and the Situation of our Affairs in Canada, in so striking a Light, that nothing less than the most wise and vigorous Exertions of Congress, and the Army there, can promise Success to our Schemes and Plans in that Quarter. What might have been effected last Year without much Difficulty, has become an arduous and important Work. However, I hope, all Things will yet go well.[58]

---

[57] Capt. Bernard Romans, of the Pennsylvania Independent Artillery.

[58] Three commissioners—Benjamin Franklin, Samuel Chase, and Charles Carroll—were appointed by Congress (February 15) to repair to Canada. Their instructions will be found spread on the *Journals of the Continental Congress* of March 20. They were accompanied by the Rev. John Carroll, a Catholic clergyman, afterwards archbishop

I am exceedingly glad that so large a Number of Indians was present at the Review of General Sullivan's Brigade. They probably, from the Appearance of so many armed Men somewhat instructed in Discipline, may have received some favorable Impressions of our Strength sufficient to counteroperate all the ingenuous and insidious Arts of Toryism. When those arrive which you mention, I shall take proper Notice of them, and have necessary Provisions made for their Entertainment. I am, Sir, etc.

## To THE COMMITTEE OF SUFFOLK, LONG ISLAND[59]

New York, May 16, 1776.

Sir: Your favor of the 14th with an Account of the apprehending of Sundry Tories by order of your Committee and the taking of others by Capt. Harden is now before me. Your Zeal and activity upon this occasion is truly commendable, and with great pleasure I will lend any aid in my power, that shall be thought within the line of my department, to root out or secure such abominable pests of Society. But as you have neither pointed out the names or places of abode of the persons aluded to, by your Informants on long Island, I must beg the favor of a more explicit description from you; and in the mean while, will set

---

of Baltimore, whose influence with the people, on account of his religious principles and character, it was thought, would be useful.

The commissioners arrived at Montreal on April 29. But they found the state of affairs in Canada by no means such as to encourage any just hope of success to their mission. The Canadians seemed to remember the antagonism displayed by the Congress to the Quebec Act and the religious prejudice formerly displayed. Negligence, mismanagement, and a combination of unlucky incidents where the troops were concerned had produced a confusion and disorder that it was now too late to remedy. The commissioners used every effort in their power, but to little effect. Ill health caused Doctor Franklin to return in a few days. His two associates remained till after the American forces had retreated to Sorel, and were preparing to evacuate Canada.

[59] Jonathan Sturges was chairman of this committee.

on foot a proper enquiry into this matter of some Gentlemen here, acquainted with the Island, and concert some plan for defeating the designs which you think are in agitation. I shall add no more at present than that. I am, etc.

## To THE COMMITTEE OF SAFETY
## OF NEW HAMPSHIRE

New York, May 16, 1776.

Gentn: The Honorable Continental Congress having lately come to some Resolutions, respecting the Cannon and other Stores in Boston, which Interest your Colony, and the mode to be observed for paying the Militia lately called in for the defence of the lines before Boston; I do myself the honor to transmit you Copies thereof least they may not have been otherwise forwarded. and am Gentn:

## To THE MASSACHUSETTS LEGISLATURE

New York, May 16, 1776.[60]

Gentn: The Honorable Continental Congress having come to sundry resolutions, respecting the Cannon and Stores in and about Boston, and the mode of paying the Militia lately called in for the defence of the Lines before it; I do myself the honor to transmit you Copies thereof, least they may not have come to hand. I would observe, that I think it will be of advantage to you, to make your arrangements out of the Cannon, originally belonging to the Colony and those presented it by

[60] On this same day, Robert Hanson Harrison, by direction of the Commander in Chief, wrote to Maj. Gen. Artemas Ward, setting Ward aright as to the regiments on Bunker Hill and Dorchester Heights. The committee of the Massachusetts Legislature apparently had influenced Ward in regard to these regiments as Washington has noted, in silver-point, upon the letter of May 3 from the committee: "Genl. Washington would remark upon above that one of the 5 Regiments left at Boston was compleat and that the other 4 contained the average of those brought away." (See Washington's letter to the committee of the Massachusetts Legislature, May 9, 1776, *ante*.)

Congress, and not to count on those brought from Ticonderoga and which are left, tho' Congress are willing to lend them. For it is more than probable they may be wanted elsewhere, and if they should; It will derange your order and lay you under the necessity of providing others and Carriages, at a time when it may be Inconvenient and when they may be most useful. I am &c.

## GENERAL ORDERS

Head Quarters, New York, May 16, 1776.
Parole Annapolis.   Countersign Calvert.

Robert Hanson Harrison Esqr. is appointed Secretary to the Commander in Chief, in the room of Joseph Reed Esqr., whose private concerns will not permit him to continue in that office.

Any orders delivered by Caleb Gibbs, and George Lewis[61] Esquires (Officers of the General's guard) are to be attended to, in the same manner, as if sent by an Aid-de-Camp.

The Congress having given directions for the discharge of the Militia, and Minute Men in this district; the Battalion of the Militia of this City, are dismissed, accordingly; and have the Generals thanks, for their masterly manner of executing the work on Bayard's hill.

Some Errors having happened in drawing the pay of the Quarter Masters of several regiments; the mistakes are to be rectified, and they allowed their dues.

As the Troops are to be exempt from all duties of fatigue to morrow, the regiments are to parade on their regimental parades, and to be marched from thence a little before Ten, to hear divine service from their respective chaplains.

For the future, there is to be no expence of ammunition at the Interment of any officer, or soldier, of the Continental Army, unless expressly ordered by the Commander in Chief.

[61] Washington's nephew.

Uriah Chamberlain of Capt. Hamilton's Company of Artillery, tried at a late General Court Martial, whereof Colonel Huntington was president for "Desertion"—The Court find the prisoner guilty of the charge, and do sentence him to receive Thirty nine Lashes, on the bare back, for said offence.

The General approves the above sentence, and orders it to be put in execution, on Saturday morning next, at guard mounting.

## GENERAL ORDERS

Head Quarters, New York, May 17, 1776.

Parole Newcastle.   Countersign Wilmington.

Capt. Wolverton's[62] Company of New Jersey, is to join Genl. Greene's brigade—the Captain to take his orders from the General, respecting his post.

An exact return of the pikes to be made without delay; and of the state of the arms in each regiment and corps, specifying the number of each kind, wanting to compleat.

The damage done to Mr.        house yesterday by the bursting of one of the cannon, to be repaired by the Carpenters in the Continental pay.

## To THE NEW YORK LEGISLATURE

New York, May 17, 1776.

Sir: As I have no doubt of the Willingness of the Militia of this City, to Join in its defence against the attempts of the Enemies of America; It is highly necessary, in order to avoid Confusion in the time of any alarm, that the Posts of the several Regiments of Militia be fixed on, in Conjunction with those of the Continental Army, and that they be allotted to the Brigades most convenient to their several Situations; and as I am now

---

[62] Capt. Thomas Woolverton, or Wolverton, of the Sussex County Minutemen.

arranging that part of the Business of the Army, It will I presume be proper, that directions be given to the Commanding officers of the several Corps, to take the Stations that I shall Assign, and to obey the orders, they may in time of danger receive from me, or the Brigadier Generals of the Continental Army; the like measure will be equally necessary with regard to the Militia of King's County and part of Queen's County on Long Island, and also the Militia of Staten Island, and I am persuaded, that the mention of a Matter so obviously necessary will be sufficient to induce the Congress of this Province to give such directions as are proper on this occasion. I am &c.

## To MAJOR GENERAL PHILIP SCHUYLER

New York, May 17, 1776.

Dear Sir: I this Morning received your Favour of the 13th. Inst. with it's Inclosures, conveying Intelligence of the melancholy Situation of our Affairs in Canada, and am not without my Fears, I confess, that the Prospect we had of possessing that Country, of so much Importance in the present Controversy, is almost over, or at least, that it will be effected with much more Difficulty, and Effusion of Blood than were necessary, had our Exertions been timely applied. However we must not despair. A manly and spirited Opposition, can only ensure Success, and prevent the Enemy from improving the Advantage they have obtained.

I have forwarded the Letters to Congress, and their Answer to you and the Honble Commissioners, I will transmit you, as soon as they come to Hand.

I am fully sensible that this unfortunate Event has greatly deranged your Schemes, and will involve you in Difficulties only to be obviated by your Zeal and Assiduity, which I am well satisfied will not be wanting in this or any other Instance, where the Good of your Country require them.

Notwithstanding the most diligent Pains, but a small Part of the Nails you wrote for, is yet collected, nor will there be a Possibility of getting half the Quantity. The Quarter Master expects that they will be here to Day, when they will be instantly forwarded with the five Ton of Lead. I am, etc.

P. S. The Nails are embarked 27½ Casks. You have the acct. and Quality inclosed, with Thos. Warner's Receipt, and also for 5 Tons of Lead.

## To BRIGADIER GENERAL JOHN SULLIVAN

New York, May 17, 1776.

Dr. Sir: Your Favour of the 14th. Inst. I received this Morning and am exceedingly sorry for the sad Reverse of Fortune in our Affairs in Canada. They are rather alarming; but I still hope our vigorous Exertions will be attended with Success, notwithstanding the present unpromising Appearances, and that we shall yet acquire and maintain Possession of that Country, so important to us in the present Contest.

I have transmitted the Intelligence to Congress with your Orders from General Schuyler, whose Directions you must follow, 'till I send you their Determination, or my Commands to the contrary. I am, etc.

## To PHILIP VAN RENSSELAER[63]

New York, May 17, 1776.

Sir: I received your Favour of the 6th. Inst. and am of Opinion, as you have not a sufficient Number of Armourers at Albany to repair the whole of the Arms in your Possession, that whatever more you have than can be repaired in a convenient Time, had better be sent immediately to the Armourers here. This will save much Time, which would be lost were the Armourers to go from hence and return again. I am, etc.

---

[63] Commissary of military stores at Albany, N. Y.

## To THE PRESIDENT OF CONGRESS

New York, May 17, 1776.

Sir: I This moment received, by Express from Genl. Schuyler, an Account of the Melancholly prospect and reverse of our Affairs in Canada, and presuming the Letters, which accompanies this, will give Congress full information upon the Subject, I shall only add, that General Schuyler in pursuance of orders from the Honorable Commissioners, has directed General Sullivan to halt his Brigade, as a further reinforcement, on account of the scarcity of Provisions, would not relieve, but contribute greatly to destress our Troops already in Canada. Before he received these orders the whole of the Brigade, except Dayton and Wayne's Regiments had left Albany, but I suppose he will be able to stop their march.

By my Letter of the 15th. Instant, Congress will perceive the quantity of Pork already gone from hence, and the Commissary has assured me, that he will forward a further supply as soon as it can be possibly collected. I had also directed five Tons of Lead to be sent General Schuyler for the Canada expedition, before I received this unfortunate Account, which was as much as could be spared at this Time, our Stock being inconsiderable in proportion to the demand we may reasonably expect for it, and shall do everything in my power to relieve our Affairs from their present destressed and melancholy situation in that Quarter, which occur to me and appear necessary.

I am also to acknowledge the receipt of your favors of the 10th. and 13th. Instant, with their several Inclosures. The Money mentioned in the Latter came safe to the Pay Master's Hands. I have the Honor etc.[64]

---

[64]In the writing of Robert Hanson Harrison.

## GENERAL ORDERS

Head Quarters, New York, May 18, 1776.
Parole Brest.  Countersign Lee.

Lieut. Grover, of the 2nd. Regiment (commanded by Col. James Reed) having been tried by a General Court Martial, for "insulting Capt. Wilkinson, disobeying his orders, and abusive language," was found guilty of the charge, and yet mulct'd of half a month's pay only—a punishment so exceedingly disproportioned to the offence, that the General resolved to lay the whole proceeding before the Congress, and know whether they inclined to continue an officer in their service, who had misbehaved in so capital a point; but Lieut. Grover appearing to be thoroughly convinced of the error of his conduct, and having promised strict obedience to the orders of his Captain, and other superior Officers; for the time to come, the General (before any determination of Congress could be had upon the matter) ordered him to be released, and to join his regiment; but has it now in command from Congress,[65] to signify to the Army, that no promotion upon vacancies, shall take place merely by succession, without their authority, inasmuch as they have reserved, and will exercise the power; of giving Commissions to persons of merit, regardless of any claim by succession. Of this all Officers are desired to take notice, as it may serve on the one hand to prevent the dissatisfaction which have but too frequently arisen, from an idea, that all promotions should be confined to regiments, and go in regular succession; and because, on the other hand, it opens a large field for the rewarding of merit, which ought, and is hoped will be, a powerful excitement to the brave and active to signalize themselves in the noble cause they are engaged in.

---

[65] The resolves of May 10, 1776. (See *Journals of the Continental Congress.*)

This determination of Congress, the Adjutant General is to communicate to the officers commanding in different departments, that it may be published to the different Regiments, and Corps, under their respective commands.

The General has the pleasure to inform the recruiting officers of the regiments that came from the eastward (no allowance having been heretofore made them) that upon a representation of their case, Congress have been pleased to allow a Dollar and one third of a Dollar, for each good, and able bodied man, that shall be recruited, for the purpose of completing the several regiments, as a compensation for their trouble, and expence; and that the same allowance, will be made those officers, who have heretofore inlisted men, upon the new-establishment, excluding all Boys, and such men as were inlisted in Camp, out of the old regiments. The several Officers which have been employed in this service, are to settle this matter, under these exceptions, with their several Colonels, or commanding officers; and to give in Rolls of the men's names, by them respectively inlisted. The utmost care, and exactness, is recommended to the Officers claiming this allowance, as proof will be required, agreeable to the above direction.

## To THE PRESIDENT OF CONGRESS

New York, May 18, 1776.

Sir: I do myself the Honor to transmit to you the inclosed Letters and papers which I received this Morning, in the State they now are, and which contain sundry matters of Intelligence of the most Interesting nature.

As the consideration of them may lead to important consequences and the adoption of several measures in the Military Line, I have thought It advisable for General Gates to attend Congress who will follow to morrow, and satisfy and explain to them, some points they may wish to be informed of, in the course of their deliberations not having an Opportunity at this Time to submit to them my thoughts upon these Interesting Accounts.[66] I have &ca.[67]

## To RICHARD HENRY LEE

New York, May 18, 1776.

My Dear Sir: In great haste I write you a few lines to cover the enclosed,[68] they came in the manner you see them, and as explained in Captain Langdon's letter to me. I hesitated some time in determining whether I could, with propriety, select them from the rest, considering in what manner they came to my hands; but as there are some things in each which may serve to irritate, I concluded it best to send not only the one directed to you, but the other also, (to Doctor Franklin) under cover to you, as you may communicate and secrete such parts as you like. I have no time to add the necessity of vigorous exertions; they are too obvious to need any stimulus from me. Adieu, my dear Sir.[69]

---

[66] The important papers consisted of intelligence from England, and copies of the treaties made by that nation with the Duke of Brunswick, the Landgrave of Hesse Cassel, and the Count of Hanau for troops to be sent to America. The papers were referred to a committee consisting of John Adams, William Livingston, Thomas Jefferson, Richard Henry Lee, and Roger Sherman, who were directed to publish such extracts of the intelligence as they thought proper. This publication was made in the *Pennsylvania Gazette* of May 22; the *Pennsylvania Evening Post* of May 23; and the *Pennsylvania Ledger* of May 25. The treaties also appeared in the supplements of the *Pennsylvania Journal* of May 24, and *Pennsylvania Packet* of May 27. They are also printed in Force's *American Archives,* Fourth Series, vol. 6, 271–277.

[67] In the writing of Robert Hanson Harrison. It was read in Congress on May 21, the same time Washington's letters of May 19 and 20 were read.

[68] These inclosures were letters brought by George Merchant, captured at Quebec and taken a prisoner to England. He had escaped and reported to John Langdon, who forwarded the papers Merchant brought to Washington. These letters included two from Arthur Lee, dated February 13 and 14, which Burnett, in *Letters of Members of the Continental Congress,* calls mysterious. Merchant had brought copies of the treaties with the German princes. (See following letter of Washington to the President of Congress.)

[69] Text is from *Memoirs of the Life of Richard Henry Lee and His Correspondence.*

P. S. Upon second thought, knowing that Doctor Franklin is in Canada, I send you a copy only of a letter to him, (which I take to be from Doctor Lee) and the original to the Doctor.

## To THE PRESIDENT OF CONGRESS

New York, May 19, 1776.

Sir: This will be delivered you by General Gates who sets out this Morning for Congress, agreeable to my Letter of Yesterday.

I have committed to him the Heads of sundry matters to lay before Congress for their consideration, which from the Interesting Intelligence contained in my last, appears to me of the utmost Importance, and to demand their most early and serious attention.

Sensible that I have omitted to set down many things necessary and which probably when deliberating they wish to be acquainted with, and not conceiving myself at Liberty to depart my post, tho' to attend them, without their previous approbation,[70] I have requested General Gates to subjoin such hints of his own as he may apprehend material. His Military experience and intimate acquaintance with the situation of our Affairs, will enable him to give Congress the fullest satisfaction about the measures necessary to be adopted at this alarming crisis, and with his Zeal and attachment to the Cause of America, have a claim to their Notice and favors.

When Congress shall have come to a determination on the Subject of this Letter and such parts of my former Letters, as have not been determined on, you will be pleased to honor me with the result. I am &ca.[71]

---

[70] Congress had already (May 16) requested Washington's attendance.
[71] In the writing of Robert Hanson Harrison.

## To THE NEW YORK LEGISLATURE

New York, May 19, 1776.

Sir: Having reason to believe from Intelligence lately received, that the Time is not far distant when the arrival of a considerable Armament may be expected, I must again repeat my Applications on the subject of Arms, and intreat your Honble. Body to use their utmost exertions, that a supply May be obtained for the Regiments of this Colony, which in General are extremely deficient, some of them almost destitute. I trust your own feelings will readily suggest, I have sufficient cause of anxiety and concern upon this occasion, and will furnish an Apology for my so often troubling you. I have tried, I have pursued every Measure my Judgment led to, without being able to procure a sufficient Quantity; nor have I any power to apply to but you, from which I can promise myself the least prospect of Success.

I would also take the Liberty of praying your endeavours to procure a Quantity of Intrenching Tools, Vizt. Spades and Shovels; as our operations go on much slower than they would, If we had more of them; which at a crisis like this, is exceedingly alarming, when the utmost labour and Industry will not more than Compleat the Necessary Works of defence, by the time the Enemy may Attempt an Invasion. The Quarter Master Assures me that he has taken every possible method in his power to get them, but without Success, which is the reason of my requesting an exertion of your Interest. I am, etc.

## GENERAL ORDERS

Head Quarters, New York, May 19, 1776.
Parole Albany.   Countersign Schuyler.
The Brigadier Generals are desired to make their respective brigades, perfectly acquainted with the alarm posts, which

have been reported to the Commander in Chief: But in case of an Alarm, the respective regiments are to draw up, opposite to their encampments, or quarters, until they receive orders to repair to the alarm posts above referred to. The following Signals are to give the alarm, to all the Troops (as well Regulars as Militia) and the Inhabitants of the city: (viz) In the day time; two Cannon to be fired from the rampart at Fort George, and a Flag hoisted from the Top of General Washingtons, head quarters:[72] In the night time, two Cannon fired as above, from Fort George, and two lighted Lanthorns hoisted from the Top of Head Quarters, aforesaid.

The Colonels, and Officers commanding Corps, are immediately to have their men compleated with twenty-four Rounds of powder and ball, properly, and compleatly, made up into Cartridges, six rounds of which, each man is to have in his pouch, or cartridge box, for ordinary duty; the remaining eighteen, are to be wrapped up tight, in a Cloth, or coarse Paper, and mark'd with the name of the soldier to whom they belong, and carefully packed into an empty powder barrel. The Captains, or Officers commanding Companies, are to see that this is done, and to take into his own possession, the barrel, with the cartridges so packed, and to have them delivered to the men, as occasion may require: And whatsoever Soldier shall be found wasting, or embezzling, his ammunition, shall not only be made to pay for it, but be punished for so base and shameful a neglect, and disobedience of orders.

Notwithstanding the care and pains, that has been taken to provide good arms for the troops, on examination they are found to be in the most shocking situation. The Colonels, or commanding Officers of the Regiments, are requested to get the arms belonging to their Regiments, put in good order as

---

[72] Headquarters at this time were in a house (not now standing) on Pearl Street.

soon as possible, the work to be executed at the Continental Armoury, or elsewhere, so as to have them repaired in the most expeditious manner—Every man to be furnished with a good Bayonet: But all that have had Bayonets heretofore, and have lost them, to pay for the new ones—Wherever a Soldier is known to have injured his gun, on purpose, or suffered it to be injured by negligence; to be chargeable with the repairs. An Account to be rendered of the expence of those repairs, after deducting what each Individual ought to pay—A Warrant will be given the commanding Officer of the regiments, for the discharge of the same.

All Repairs that are done to the arms hereafter, except unavoidable accidents, to be paid by the men, and stopt out of their wages by the commanding officer of the regiment—An Account to be rendered to him, by the Captains, or commanding Officers of companies.

Capt. Joseph Butler of Colonel Nixons Regiment, is to be furnished with a Copy of the accusation, lodged against him by Lieut. Silas Walker, and both are to attend the next General Court Martial with their evidences.

The Lads lately picked out of Col. Nixon's, and Col. Webb's Regiments; are to be immediately discharged, and their accounts settled, and paid: In order the better to enable them to return to their respective homes—ten days provisions, and pay, is to be allowed them from this day.

John Lewis of Capt. Haronburry's[73] Company in Col. Ritzema's Regiment, tried by a late General Court Martial, whereof Col Ritzema was President "for insulting and striking Lieut. Cole of Col Wyllys's Regiment, when on command"— The Court find the prisoner guilty of the charge, and a breach of the 7th. Article of the Continental Rules and Regulations;

---

[73] Capt. Cornelius Hardenbergh, of the Third New York Regiment.

and do sentence him to be whipp'd Thirty-nine Lashes for said offences.

The General approves of the above sentence, and orders it to be put in execution to morrow morning at Guard mounting.

### *To THE PRESIDENT OF CONGRESS

New York, May 20, 1776.

Sir: Your favour of the 16th. with several resolution's of Congress, therein Inclosed, I had not the honor to receive 'till last night; before the receipt, I did not think myself at liberty to wait on Congress, altho' I wish'd to do it, and therefore, the more readily consented to General Gates's attendance; as I knew there were many matters which could be better explaind in a personal Interview than in whole Volumes of Letters. He accordingly set out for Phila. yesterday Morning, and must have been too far advancd on his journey (as he proposed expedition) to be over taken. I shall, if I can settle some matters, which are in agitation with the Provincial Congress here, follow to morrow, or next day; and therefore with every Sentiment of regard, attachment and gratitude to Congress for their kind attention to the means which they may think conducive to my health, and with particular thanks to you for the politeness of your Invitation to your House,[74] conclude Dear Sir, &ca.

### GENERAL ORDERS

Head Quarters, New York, May 20, 1776.
Parole Brunswick.   Countersign White.

The Sentries at all the batteries, where Cannon are placed, are to be increased to the number the Brigadier finds necessary;

---

[74] The invitation was not accepted by Washington.

and they are all to be doubled at night: They are not to suffer any person whatever (excepting the Rounds, or Officer of the guard) to go into the Batteries at night; nor is any person whatever, but the Generals, or Field Officers of the Army, and officers and men of the Artillery, who have real business there, to be permitted, even in the day time, to go on the platforms in the batteries, or to approach the Cannon, or to meddle with the Rammers, Spungers, or any of the Artillery Stores placed there. The Officers of every Guard, are to see that their men, are particularly alert in executing this order.

No Person whatever, belonging to the Army, is to be innoculated for the Small-Pox—those who have already undergone that operation, or who may be seized with Symptoms of that disorder, are immediately to be removed to the Hospital provided for that purpose on Montresor Island. Any disobedience to this order, will be most severely punished—As it is at present of the utmost importance, that the spreading of that distemper, in the Army and City, should be prevented

## To ROBERT MORRIS [75]

New York, May 20, 1776.

Sir: I received your favors of the 11th. and 16th. Instant; the former respecting powder for which you have inclosed the Commissary's receipt, as to the Number of Barrels, but not of the Contents, no Invoice thereof having been delivered either to me or him, which certainly should have been sent for the detection of any fraudulent practices, if any were committed.

The Commissary will expect one, and that they will always accompany such Stores as may be transmitted in Future: The latter, about Arms at Rhode Island, covering Letters for the

---

[75] Then a member of the Secret Committee of Congress.

Gentlemen in whose possession they are, having read, I have sealed and forwarded to them, with directions to send the musquets immediately, being in great want. I am &ca.

### *To BENJAMIN FRANKLIN

New York, May 20, 1776.

Dear Sir I do myself the pleasure to Transmit you the Inclosed Letter which I received yesterday with several others in the condition this is and containing similar Intelligence—the rest I forwarded to Congress immediately on receipt. They had passed thro the hands of some of the Committees in the Eastern Governments by whom they were opened.

On the morning of the 17 Inst with much concern and surprize I received the melancholy account of our Troops being Obliged to raise the Seige of Quebec with the loss of their Cannon, a number of small Arms, provisions &c.

I had hoped before this misfortune, that the Troops there wou'd have maintained their posts, and on the Arrival of the two Brigades detached from hence, consisting of Ten Regiments (the last of which was at Albany under Genl Sullivan when the account came) the Blockade bravely kept up for a long time by a handfull of men against a victorious Enemy superior in numbers, wou'd terminate in a favourable and happy Issue, the reduction of Quebec and our consequent possession of the Important Country to which It belongs—to what cause to ascribe the sad disaster, I am at loss to determine, but hence I shall know the events of War are exceedingly doubtfull, and that Capricious fortune often blasts our most flattering hopes.

I feel this important and Interesting event, not a little height-en'd by Its casting up, just on your entrance and that of the other Honorable Commissioners in that Country—tho your presence may conduce to the public good in an essential manner, yet I am certain you must experience difficulties and embarrassments of a peculiar nature—perhaps in a little Time, Things may assume a more promising appearance than the present is, and your difficulties in some degree be done away.

Wishing your Councils under the guidance of a kind providence and a tender of my respectfull Compliments to the Gentn who accompany you, I have the honor etc.[76]

## To THE PRESIDENT OF CONGRESS

New York, May 21, 1776.

Sir: The Bearer, Mr. Mersay being at Quebec when the Garrison Sallied and Obliged our Troops to an abandonment of the Siege and a precipitate retreat; I have taken the Liberty to refer him to you for examination, that Congress may have such further Information of this unfortunate Event as he possesses. I have the Honor &ca.

## To MAJOR GENERAL PHILIP SCHUYLER

New York, May 21, 1776.

Dear Sir: I have inclosed for your Perusal Copies of two Informations, and a Letter I received on Saturday last from the Committee of King's District by the Hands of a Martin Bebee, who says he is their Clerk and was sent Express.

From these you will readily discover the diabolical and insidious Arts and Schemes carrying on by the Tories and Friends to Government, to raise Distrust, Dissensions and Divisions among us.

[76] From the original in the American Philosophical Society's *Franklin Papers*. The editor is indebted to that society and to the kindness of Miss Laura E. Hanson, its librarian, for a correct copy of the text.

Having the utmost Confidence in your Integrity, and the most incontestible Proof of your great Attachment to our common Country and its Interest, I could not but look upon the Charge against you with an Eye of Disbelief, and Sentiments of Detestation and Abhorrence, nor should I have troubled you with the Matter, had I not been informed that Copies were sent to different Committees and to Governor Trumbull, which I conceived would get abroad, and that you, (should you find that I had been furnished with them) would consider my suppressing them, as an Evidence of my Belief, or at best of my Doubts of the Charges.

The Confidence and Assurance I have of the Injustice and Infamy of the Charges against the Convention, obliged me also to lay the Matter before them; least my not doing it, should be construed a Distrust by them of their Zeal, and promote the Views of the Tories; who, to excite Disorder and Confusion, judge it essential, to involve those in high Departments in a Share of the Plot, which is not unlikely to be true in some Parts, believing that our internal Enemies have many Projects in Contemplation, to subvert our Liberties.[77]

Before I conclude, I would mention that some Officers called upon me a few Days ago, having your Permit to go to Pensylvania and settle some Affairs there. This Licence, when there is really Business, is certainly countenanced by Humanity and Generosity; but nevertheless should not be indulged, and I

---

[77] Sparks enlarges on the prejudice of New England against Schuyler in his *Writings of Washington,* Appendix XV, vol. 3, but does not go into the causes thoroughly, though he prints several documents. (Ford reprints these as a footnote.) The Berkshire country was fearful of a British advance, after the Quebec defeat, and the New Hampshire Grants consulted their grievances against New York as a difficulty in addition to their fears of the British. The feeling behind this outburst against Schuyler, later merged with Gates's New England popularity and ended in Schuyler being superseded. This frontier prejudice was an outer fringe of a New England state of mind that developed later into the demonstration known as the Conway Cabal, but the Berkshire hysteria of 1776 was not, of course, connected with the cabal except through the New Hampshire Grants movement.

hope will not be granted in future, as it gives them an Opportunity of getting Intelligence of all our Operations; of forming Opinions of our Strength, the Places proper for Attack and settling a Channel of Correspondence with the disaffected, by which our Enemies may and will be furnished with full Accounts of our Designs, and every Thing that can promote their Service and injure ours. There is but little Reason to believe, nay we are certain, they will not conduct themselves upon Principles of the strictest Honour for the Favors done them but will when in their Power, exercise every Matter that can operate to our Prejudice. I am, Sir, &c.

### *To MAJOR GENERAL ISRAEL PUTNAM

Head Quarters, City of New York, May 21, 1776.

Sir: The Congress having been pleased to signify a desire that I should repair to Philadelphia, in order to advise and consult with them on the present posture of affairs, and as I am on the point of setting out accordingly; I have to desire that you will cause the different Works now in agitation to be carried on with the utmost expedition,[78] to this end I have wrote to the Provincial Congress (of this Colony) for Tools and have hopes of obtaining them. Apply therefore accordingly, takg an exact acct. of what you receive.

The Works upon Long Island should be compleated as expeditiously as possible, so should those in and about this Town, and upon Governors Island. If New Works can be carried on without detriment to the old, (for want of Tools) I would have that intended at Powles hook,[79] set abt. immediately as I

---

[78] Putnam, as senior major general, was left in command at New York.

[79] Powles Hook, now Jersey City, N. J. The spelling used by the British and all who followed their engineer maps is Paulus Hook. Washington and other Americans usually spell it Powles; the British, having only the sound of the name, spelled it phonetically. William H. Richardson, historian of the Pavonia Tercentenary Celebration, 1930, has definitely settled the point.

conceive it to be of Importance, in like manner would I have that at the Narrows begun, provided Colo. Knox, after his arrangement of the Artillery should find that there are any fit pieces of Cannon to be spared for it: otherwise, as I have no longer any dependance upon Cannon from Admiral Hopkins, it wd. be useless.

The Barriers of those Streets leading from the Water are not to be meddled with; and where they have been pull'd down are to be repaird, and [erected] nearer the Water if more advantageous.

As it does not appear to me improbable that the Enemy may attempt to run past our Batteries in, and about the Town, and Land between them and the woody grounds above Mr. Scot's, I would have you imploy as many Men as you can in throwing up Fleches at proper places, and distances within that space in order to give opposition in Landing but if there are not Tools enough to carry on the other (more essential) Works and these at the same Instant you are not to neglect the first but esteem these as secondary considerations only.

Delay not a Moment's time to have the Signals fixed for the purpose of communicating an alarm upon the first appearance of the Enemy, let them be placed in such a Manner, and at such distances, as to be easily discerned; day, or Night. If this was continued upon the long Island Shore for some distance, good consequences might result from it; as nothing can be attended with more signal advantages than having timely notice of the Enemy's approach whilst nothing can add more to the disgrace of an Officer than to be surprizd; for this reason I have to beg that the same vigilance and precaution may be used as if the Enemy were actually within sight; as a brisk Wind, and flowing tide will soon produce them when they are once on the coast, the Officers and Men therefore shd. be constantly at their

Qrs. the Guards alert and every thing in Readiness for immediate action.

As I have great reason to fear that the Fortifications in the
High lands are in a bad situation, and the Garrisons on Acct.
of Arms worse; I would have you send Brigadier Lord Stirling
with Colo. Putnam (and Colo. Knox if he can be spared) up
there, to see report and direct such alterations, as shall be judg'd
necessary for putting them into a fit, and proper posture of
defence.

Open any Letters which may come directed to me upon
Public Service whilst I am absent; and if any very Interesting
advices should be contain therein, either from the Eastward,
or Northward, forward them on to Philadelphia after regulating your conduct thereby.

I must again beg that your particular Attention may be
turnd to our Powder Magazines to see that that that valuable
Article is properly placed and Secured. I also beg that no time
or Means be neglected to make as many Musket Cartridges
as possible.

### *To MAJOR GENERAL ISRAEL PUTNAM

Head Quarters, City of New York, May 21, 1776.

Sir: I have reason to believe that the Provencial Congress of
this Colony have in Contemplation a Scheme for Siezing the
principal Tories, and disaffected Person's [in the most obnoxious parts of the Government] on Long Island, in this
City, and the Country round about;[80] and that to carry the
Scheme into Execution, they will be obliged to have recourse

---

[80] On May 19 Gouverneur Morris and John Morin Scott reported to the New York
Provincial Congress that they had interviewed General Washington on the subject of
these rumored Tory plots and found that a scheme of cooperation was on foot between the Connecticut and Long Island Tories. Measures were taken by the Congress
and several arrests were made. (See note to Washington's letter to the New York
Legislature, Aug. 11, 1776, *post*.)

to the Military power, for assistance. If this should be the case, you are hereby required, during my absence, to afford every aid which the said Congress or their secret Comee. shall apply for [(consistent with the general Plan of defence now going on) to carry these measures into execution provided it does not interfere too much with our general Plan of defence in weakening this place by].[81]

I need not recommend secrecy to you, as the success, you must be assured will depend absolutely upon precaution, and the dispatch with which the measure, when once adopted, is executed.

General Green will, tho' not in person perhaps, have a principal share in ordering the detachments from his Brigade on Long Island, of course will be a proper Person to let into the whole Plan. I wd. therefore when application is made by Congress, have you and him concert Measures with such Gentlemen as that body shall please to appoint and order the execution with as much secrecy and dispatch as possible and at the same time with the utmost decency and good order.

### To THE NEW YORK LEGISLATURE

New York, May 21, 1776.

Gentn: Congress having been pleased to request my attendance at Philadelphia, to advise with them on the Situation of affairs and being about to set out immediately; I judged it proper to give Major Genl. Putnam Instructions similar to those I have the honor to inclose you; for the regulation of his Conduct, in case you come to any determination respecting the Tories here and on Long Island and should have occasion for Military assistance, to carry it into execution. I have &ca.

---

[81] The words within brackets in this letter were stricken out by Washington in the letter sent.

## GENERAL ORDERS

Head Quarters, New York, May 21, 1776.

Parole Camden.   Countersign Liberty.

That no confusion may ensue when the Troops are called into action, the General has order'd, that all the posts and of the lines, redoubts and batteries, be so fixed and regulated, as every officer, and soldier, may know his place and duty; which will be explained to them by the Brigadiers General, according to the orders of yesterday; And further to confirm the order, and discipline of the Guards of the Army; the General orders, that the officers, and men, who are to mount guard, do parade by half past *Six* o'Clock, where they are by their Adjutants, in the presence of a Field Officer; to be reviewed, and their Arms, and Ammunition, to be examined, according to the orders of the 19th Instant—which last mentioned Officers are to see that their ammunition and accoutrements are complete, and the men dressed in a soldierlike manner. The Adjutants are then to march them to the parade of the brigade, and to deliver them over, to the Major of their respective brigade, who is very minutely to inspect and see, that the Guards are compleat in the particulars above-mention'd—The Brigade Majors are then to march them to the Grand parade in the Common, in the Artillery Park, and from thence the several out-Guards are to be relieved—On the Grand parade the Brigadier, with the Field Officers of the day, will attend to see the Guards paraded, and march'd to their several destinations—The Brigade Major of the day, is also to attend on the Grand parade, and make up the Guards, before he repairs to Head Quarters, for the purpose of reporting the same, and to receive any Orders from the Commander in Chief, to the Brigadier General of the day, and to the other Brigadiers of the line—The Brigadier General of the

day, will give his orders on the parade, to the Field Officers of
the day, at what time he would have them go the visiting, and
grand rounds.—At Reveille beating, which is to be at the dawn
of day; all the Guards are to be under Arms, at their proper
posts, and visited by the Field Officers of the picquet (who are
all esteemed Field Officers of the day) who are to see that the
Guards are properly placed, and that every thing is in good
order for defence, in case of an attack. The Brigadier General
will, on the parade, assign to each Field Officer of the day, the
posts he is to visit for this purpose.

The Artillery Guard is to parade at the same time and
place—the Matrosses and Gunners necessary, to be constant
at each battery, are with their proper implements to march off
from the Grand parade, at the head of the Guards, to be station'd
at the respective batteries.

The Field Officer who goes the Grand Rounds, is to visit the
Camp Guards, as well as the Guards stationed in the town, and
at the batteries—The other two Field Officers of the day are to
do the like, at such hours of the night, as will be assigned them
by the Brigadier of the day.

By the present demand for Flints, by some of the Troops,
the General has reason to apprehend, that due care has not been
taken of those lately deliver'd to the Soldiers, who have had no
occasion to make an extraordinary use of them—and it is well
known, that a good flint, well screw'd in, will stand the firing of
sixty rounds (after which it may still be repaired) 'tis therefore
presumed, that the men have either lost their Flints through
negligence, or abused them by that worst of practices, *Snapping their pieces continually,* which not only spoils their Lock,
softens the Hammer, and destroys the Flint, but frequently
causes the death of many a man, by the Gun being unknow-
ingly loaded—The Officers are therefore required, to pay a very

strict attention to this particular, and have their men's Flints examined when they review their Ammunition; for Men being surprized with bad flints in their Guns, may be attended with fatal consequences—The Officers are also desired to be careful, that when their men turn out to exercise, their Flints be taken out, and a wooden Snapper screw'd into their gun, until their exercise be over; when the Flint is again to be well screw'd in, and their arms immediately put in proper fighting order, after which, no man is on any account to snap his piece.

One Flint pr Man will be delivered to the Troops, and 'tis expected more care will be taken of them, than has been done heretofore.

The Sentries in Fort George, and on the Battery, are to keep a sharp look out towards the Narrows, Staten Island, Red-hook &c. to observe if any Signals are given from thence; and acquaint the officer of the guard immediately therewith.

The Officers and Men, are strictly enjoined to keep close to their quarters—No excuse will be admitted from either, for a neglect of it; and the rolls are frequently to be called over.

## GENERAL ORDERS

Head Quarters, New York, May 22, 1776.
Parole Washington.   Countersign Gates.

The following are the names of the different Batteries, in and about this City—The Battery at the South part of the Town, the *Grand Battery*—The one immediately above it, *Fort George*—The one on the left of the Grand Battery, *Whitehall Battery*. That behind his Excellency General Washington's Head Quarters, the *Oyster Battery*. The circular Battery near the Brewhouse, on the North River, The *Grenadier Battery*. That on the left of the Grenadier's Battery The *Jersey*

*Battery:* The one on Bayards-hill, *Bayard's Hill Redoubt;* The one on the hill where General Spencer's Brigade is encamped *Spencer's Redoubt,* below this Hill, on a Wharf, is a Fascine Battery called *Waterbury's Battery.* On the hill directly above it, is a Redoubt, near the Jews Burying Ground, by the name of *Badlam's Redoubt.*

Andrew O'Brien, Serjeant, and William Welch, Corporal, both of Capt. O'Hara's [82] Company, in Col Wynkoops Reg., tried by a late General Court Martial, whereof Col Ritzema was President for "assaulting, beating, and dangerously wounding, one William Irvine" are both acquitted by the Court. The General approves the sentence, and orders the prisoners to be released immediately.

## To MAJOR GENERAL PHILIP SCHUYLER

Amboy, May 22, 1776.

Dear Sir: Congress having been pleased to request my Attendance at Philadelphia, to advise with them on the Situation of our Affairs, and of such Measures as may be necessary to adopt for this Campaign, I had got thus far on my Journey, when I called to view the Ground, and such Places on Staten Island, contiguous to it, as may be proper for Works of Defence; when your Favor of the 16th. Inst. with its several Inclosures came to Hand.

I am exceedingly concerned for the Distress of our Troops in Canada, and as I informed you heretofore, have been very importunate with the Commissary to forward all the Provisions in his Power; in Consequence of which he has sent a good Deal on, and I shall again repeat my Orders, and enjoin

---

[82] Capt. Henry O'Mara, of the Fourth New York Regiment.

him to continue his Supplies as largely and expeditiously as possible.

I wrote you on the 17th. Inst. and am hopeful the 27½ Casks of Nails, which were all that could be got with the 5 Tons of Lead then sent, will have reached you, or got to Albany, from whence they will be forwarded: and in a Letter to General Putnam have directed him to examine our Stock of the latter, and to furnish you with a further Quantity, if it can be spared. At Philadelphia I will try to get a Supply. I have also directed him, to send you two Tons more of Powder and such intrenching Tools as can be possibly spared or procured from the Convention, in Consequence of an Application I made two or three Days since. We are deficient in these, not having a sufficiency to carry on the Works for the Defence of New York, with the Expedition I wish, or the Exigency of the Times demands.

In Respect to Cannon Shot and Guns for the Vessels in the Lake, I have requested him to consult with Colo. Knox, and with the Convention about Sail Cloth &c. and if any of them can be spared or procured, that they be immediately sent you.

Our situation respecting the Indians is delicate and embarrassing. They are attached to Johnson,[83] who is our Enemy. Policy and Prudence on the one Hand, suggest the Necessity of seizing him and every Friend of Government; on the other, if he is apprehended, their will be Danger of incurring their Resentment. I hope the Committee will conduct the Matter in the least exceptionable Manner, and in that Way that shall most advance the public Good.

---

[83] Sir John Johnson, son of Sir William Johnson. He declined to accept his father's Indian appointments, which were taken over by Guy Johnson, a nephew of Sir William. Sir John assembled about 300 of his Scotch tenants and marched from Johnson Hall to Canada to escape arrest. He was colonel of a British provincial regiment, and took part in the attack on Fort Stanwix, N. Y. He is accused of responsibility for the massacre at Cherry Valley, N. Y., and other frontier raids.

I observe by the Minutes of a Council of War, Genl. Thomas's Letter and that of Messrs. Carrol and Chase to Doctor Franklin, that our Troops cannot make a Stand at De Chambault as I had hoped. I wish it were practicable; For most certainly, the lower down the River we can maintain our Post, the more important will the Advantages resulting from it be. Considering all the Country below us as lost, and that there may be some Prospect of gaining that above from whence we might draw Supplies in some Degree, and have the Friendship and Assistance of the Inhabitants; it is certain we should make a stand, as low down as we can, so as not to have a Retreat cut off in Case of Necessity, or an Opportunity of receiving Provisions: but unacquainted as I am with the Country, I cannot undertake to say where it should be, not doubting and hoping that every Thing for the best will be done. I am, etc.

## To MAJOR GENERAL ISRAEL PUTNAM

Amboy, May 22, 1776.

Sir: Your Letter of the last Night with the Dispatches from Canada, came to my Hands at Woodbridge this Morning.

I wish that the Information given you by Captain Goforth,[84] respecting the Number of Prisoners taken may prove true. What he told you about the Enemy's not having sallied out, differs widely from General Thomas's Account of that Affair.

You will please to give every Assistance which General Schuyler requires, that may be in your Power, and least you may not have kept a Copy of his Letter, I will transcribe that Paragraph, which contains his Demand. "Intrenching Tools of every Kind will be wanted, more Powder, Lead, and Cannon

---

[84] Capt. William Goforth, of the First New York Regiment.

Ball, and guns for the Vessels on Lake Champlain. Rigging, Sail-Cloth, and Sail Makers to be sent up."

For intrenching Tools, Rigging, Sail Cloth, and Sail Makers, I would have you apply immediately to the Provincial Congress, who will probably be able to procure them for you. Some of the Members mentioned to me, that they could procure a Quantity of Tools, of which you will send off as many as you can spare. You must take Care not to leave yourself destitute.

I sent five Tons of Lead forward, which General Schuyler knew not of: However I would have you examine what Quantity there is in store; and if you can spare it send up two tons more.

As to the Cannon Ball and Guns, you will consult with Colo. Knox, who must judge what Sort of each is necessary, and send them up with the other Articles.

I have already spoke to the Commissary General to send off as much salt Provisions as he could; but you must urge him on this Head, as they are in very great Want, and have no other Place to depend on but what goes from New York. He must lay in all he can get, to supply the Quantity which he sends up, for he must take Care to keep up his Stock.

It was a Misfortune, indeed, that the Vessel with Powder and Arms should fall into the Enemy's Hands.

Let the Committee by all Means have the Pettiauger[85] to cruize off the Back of the Island. The sooner she is out the better, as more Vessels with these Articles may be daily expected. I am etc.

P. S. Please to forward the inclosed by the first Express; or the Post which goes to Albany. Send two Tons of Powder, which will serve until we can send a further Supply.

---

[85] The Americanization of piragua, a large flatboat, decked in at each end, propelled by oars and two demountable masts with leg-of-mutton sails. It could carry from 25 to 35 tons.

## GENERAL ORDERS[86]

New York, May 23, 1776.

Parole Amboy. Countersign York.

The Sail Makers in the different Regiments, are all to parade in front of the General's Quarters, to morrow morning at six o'clock.

A reinforcement to be immediately made to the Main Guard at the lower barracks of one Sub. two Serjt., two Corporals, one Drumr., and thirty Privates.

The order for doubling the Sentries at night to be strictly attended to.

All those men of the following Regiments (Vizt:) Colonel Persons's, Webb's, Baldwin's, Nixon's, Wyllys's and Read's, who have agreed to serve in the Whaling Boats with Lieut: Col Tupper,[87] are to repair immediately to him, and take their orders from him.

## To MAJOR GENERAL JOHN THOMAS

Philadelphia, May 24, 1776.

Sir: I received your Favor of the 8th. Inst. with it's Inclosures, confirming the melancholy Intelligence I had before heard, of your having been obliged to raise the Siege of Quebec, and to make a precipitate Retreat, with the Loss of the Cannon

---

[86] Washington arrived in Philadelphia on Thursday afternoon, May 23, about 2 o'clock.—*Ford.*

The Commander in Chief was in Philadelphia, in consultation with Congress, from May 23 to June 6. The General Orders of this period, therefore, were issued on the authority of Maj. Gen. Israel Putnam. They were entered, however, in the headquarters orderly book and copied by Varick, as General Orders, in the transcript made in 1781.

[87] Lieut. Col. Benjamin Tupper, of the Twenty-first Continental Infantry. His whaleboats were to prevent the prevalent intercourse between the inhabitants of New York City and the British ships in the harbor.

in the Batteaus, and Interception of the Powder going from General Schuyler.

This unfortunate Affair has given a sad Shock to our Schemes in that Quarter; and blasted the Hope we entertained of reducing that Fortress, and the whole of Canada to our Possession.

From your Representation, Things must have been found in great Disorder, and such as to have made a Retreat almost inevitable; but nevertheless it is hoped you will be able to make a good Stand yet, and by that Means secure a large or all the upper Part of the Country. That being a Matter of the utmost Importance in the present Contest, it is my Wish and that of Congress, that you take an advantageous Post, as far down the River as possible, so as not to preclude you from a Retreat, if it should be ever necessary, or from getting proper Supplies of Provision. The lower down you can maintain a Stand, the more advantageous will it be, as all the Country above will most probably take Part with us, and from which we may draw some Assistance and Support, and considering all below as entirely within the Power of the Enemy and of Course in their Favour.

This Misfortune must be repaired, if possible, by our more vigorous Exertions; and trusting that nothing will be wanting on your Part, or in your Power to advance our Country's Cause. I am, &c.

## GENERAL ORDERS

Head Quarters, New York, May 24, 1776.
Parole Mifflin.  Countersign Lynch.

The Brigadier Generals will settle the mode, and hours, for going the Rounds at night, every morning on the General Parade at Guard-mounting.

The following Sail Makers are to embark this day on board a Vessel, in order to proceed to Albany, and from thence to Genl: Schuyler, and receive his further orders—Vizt:

Francis Howard  
Samuel Holmes  
Ebenezer Durkee  
Daniel Van Der Pool } of Col Wards Regiment

Lewis Lamb of Col Little's Regt.  
George Lemot of Col Bailey's Regt.

They are to be furnished, with ten days provision a man. Capt. Harwood's[88] Company is to join Lieut. Col Tupper, and do duty on board the whaling boats &c, &c.

Mr. Livingston, who has hitherto supplied Col. McDougall's Regiment with provisions, having declined doing it any longer; he is to order his Quarter Master, to apply to the Commissary General for provision for the future, who is desired to supply all those Corps, which were hitherto supply'd by Mr. Abraham Livingston.

The removal of General Washington's Guard, from his Head Quarters in Town, occasions the following alterations in the detail of guards (vizt.) The seven Men lately added to the Provost, to be taken from it; and a Guard of one Serjeant, one Corporal, and fifteen Men to mount at the place where Genl. Washington's Guard was kept; who are to relieve the Sentries at his door, General Gates's, Pay Master General's &c.

### GENERAL ORDERS

May 25, 1776.

Parole Mugford.   Countersign Leonard.

Capt. Butler[89] of Col. Nixon's Regiment, tried at a late General Court Martial, on the several charges exhibited against him

---

[88] Capt. Peter Harwood, of the Third Continental Infantry.  
[89] Capt. Joseph Butler, of the Fourth Continental Infantry.

by Lieut. Walker (viz) "Defrauding his Company, defrauding the public, absenting himself from his Company when on their march, and inlisting a man unfit for the service;" is acquitted of the several charges against him.

The General approves of the sentence of the above Court Martial, and orders that Capt. Butler be released from his arrest.

John Moore and Joshua Smith, both of Col Ritzema's regiment, tried by the above Court Martial for "absenting themselves from Camp without leave, and forging a pass," are found guilty, and sentenced to receive corporal punishment (Vizt.) Moore thirty nine Lashes; Smith twenty Lashes; and both to be kept seven days confined on bread and water— The General approves of part of the above sentence, and orders the corporal punishment to be put in execution to morrow morning, at the head of the regiment, at Guard-mounting, but for several reasons, thinks proper to disapprove of the latter part of the sentence.

A working party consisting of nine hundred men, to be ordered, to morrow morning, from the different Brigades and Regiments (vizt.)

Genl. Heath's: Colonels Learned's, Bailey's, Read's, Baldwins, to go to Powles hook.

Genl. Spencer's: Colonels Parsons's, Wyllys's, to Bayard's-hill; Colonel Huntington's, to Red-hook; Colonel Arnold's, to Fort Stirling; Colonel Ward's, Fifty men with four days provisions to cut picquets. These men to be provided with Axes this day, and to parade to morrow morning at five 'OClock on the Bowling Green, the remainder of this Regiment's working party at Fort George; a party of which will be reserved to load boats.

Lord Stirling: Colonels Nixon's, Webb's, McDougall's, Ritzema's On Governours Island, every day, until further orders.

As there is great complaint of Officers not attending properly; The Majors of brigade are every evening to send an exact detail of the number of officers, and men, they furnish for fatigue, to Col. Putnam, Engineer. They are always to furnish, to every two hundred men one Field Officer—three Captains— nine subalterns—twelve Serjeants and twelve Corporals.

## GENERAL ORDERS

May 26, 1776.

Parole Hancock.   Countersign Trumbull.

In Provincial Congress, New York, May 25, 1776.

Messrs. John Berrien and Robert Harpur, two of the members of the General Committee of the City of New York, delivered in the report of the said Committee, which was read and filed, and is in the words following. (vizt.)

"Committee Chamber, May 24, 1776.

"Doctor Foster[90] appearing before the Committee says, that information was given to General Putnam, that several persons had been inoculated, at the house of one Fisher, in Stone Street, contrary to a resolve of the Provincial Congress of this Colony, he, the examinant (agreeable to Genl: Putnam's order) immediately went to the house of the above mentioned Fisher, where he discovered that Lt. Colonel Moulton,[91] Capt. Parks,[92] Doctor Hart[93] and Lieut. Brown had been inoculated by Doctor Azor Betts.

"Doctor Azor Betts being sent for, appeared before the Committee, allowed the charge against him, and offer'd in his vindication—that he had been repeatedly applied to by the officers of the Continental Army to inoculate them, that he refused, but being overpersuaded, he at last inoculated the persons above-mentioned.

"*Resolved,* That Doctor Azor Betts, be committed to the Goal of this City, and be kept in safe custody, until released by the Provincial Congress.

---

[90] Dr. Isaac Foster(?), hospital surgeon.
[91] Lieut. Col. Johnson Moulton, of the Seventh Continental Infantry.
[92] Capt. Warham Parks(?), of the Third Continental Infantry.
[93] Dr. John Hart(?), surgeon of the Seventh Continental Infantry.

"*Ordered,* That a Copy of the minutes relating to Doctor Azor Betts's case, be handed to the Provincial Congress.

"Extract from the minutes.

"Signed.     Josh. Winter Secry."

Messrs. Berrian and Harpur further inform, that the wife of Azor Betts, on her examination, says That Lieut. Seymour from Long Island had informed her, that seven persons of the Army (Officers as she understood) on Long Island, were taking mercurial preparations, and as he supposed, were inoculated, or preparing to be inoculated for the small pox.

*Ordered,* That a Copy of the report of the General Committee, to this Congress, be delivered to Major Genl. Putnam—that he give such direction to the Continental Army, for preventing the Small Pox among them on Long Island, as he may think necessary.

Extract from the minutes.

Signed.     John McKesson Secry.

The General presents his Compliments to the Honorable The Provincial Congress, and General Committee, is much obliged to them, for their Care, in endeavouring to prevent the spreading of the Small-pox (by Inoculation or any other way) in this City, or in the Continental Army, which might prove fatal to the army, if allowed of, at this critical time, when there is reason to expect they may soon be called to action; and orders that the Officers take the strictest care, to examine into the state of their respective Corps, and thereby prevent Inoculation amongst them; which, if any Soldier should presume upon, he must expect the severest punishment.

Any Officer in the Continental Army, who shall suffer himself to be inoculated, will be cashiered and turned out of the army, and have his name published in the News papers throughout the Continent, as an Enemy and Traitor to his Country.

Upon the first appearance of any eruption, the Officer discovering of it in any Soldiers, is to give information to the

RegimentalSurgeon,andtheSurgeon make report of the same, to the Director General of the hospital.

The working party from Col Nixon's Regiment, are to be orderedevery dayto Long Island,instead ofGovernoursIsland, as mentioned in yesterday's orders.

The form of a morning report (which the Captain of the lower Barrack Guard is to make every day to the Field Officer) may be had, by applying to any of the Brigade Majors; and 'tis expected this form will be duly attended to.

## GENERAL ORDERS

May 27, 1776.

Parole Killingly.   Countersign Pomfret.

Nathaniel Stanley, of the 1st. Company of Colonel Wyllys's Regiment, tried by a late General Court Martial, whereof Col Ritzema was president for "absenting himself from and refusing to join said company, after he had received a Months pay and blanket money"—The Court find the prisoner guilty of a breach of the 8th. Article of the Continental Rules and Regulations, and do sentence him to be whipped Thirty-nine Lashes on his naked back, and be confined seven days upon bread and water.

John Brown, of Capt. Scotts[94] Company in Col Wyllys's Regiment, tried by the above Court Martial for "Desertion"—The Court find the prisoner guilty of the Charge, and sentence him to be whipped Twenty Lashes on his bare back, for said offence.

The General approves the above sentences, and orders the execution of them, to morrow morning at guard mounting.

Capt. Harwood is not to take any other men more than his own company, at present, from Col Learneds Regiment, to

---

[94] Capt. Ezekiel Scott, of the Twenty-second Continental Infantry.

serve on board the whaling boats &ca—except by the consent of
Lieut. Colonel Shephard;[95] whose Consent, the General imagined Capt. Harwood had obtained, when he gave him the
order this morning.

### To MAJOR GENERAL ARTEMAS WARD

Philadelphia, May 28, 1776.

Sir: On Saturday Morning I was favoured with yours of the
17th. Inst., giving the agreeable Intelligence of the important
and valuable Prize, made by the armed Schooners in the Continental Service, and am hopeful, that if a vigilant Look out is
kept, that others not less valuable, will fall into our Hands.

Congress having passed a Resolve respecting this Cargo, as
you will see by the inclosed Copy,[96] I desire that you will immediately forward to New York, eight Hundred of the Carbines
and the Residue have put into some good and secure Place, not
to be disposed of 'till further Directions, unless the Recruits
raising to compleat the five Regiments left at Boston, should
be in Want, in which Case you may supply the Deficiency
out of them.

I also request that you will directly forward to New York,
400 Barrels of the Powder, and have the Remainder of it, sent
to some Place of Security in the Country, not too contiguous to
Boston, there to be kept under a good and trusty Guard 'till
it shall be disposed of; apprehending it imprudent that more
should remain in Boston than may be absolutely necessary for
Fear of Accidents, tho' I do not think any Attempts will be
made against it by the Enemy.

You will forward too, the Lead wrote for by General Putnam, and such Articles out of the Cargo as Colo. Knox and

---

[95] Lieut. Col. William Shepard, of the Third Continental Infantry.
[96] This was one of the supply ships from Cork, captured by the *Franklin*.

Colonel Putnam shall respectively apply for, and have the Rest properly secured.

As to the two Hundred Carbines, that are to remain at Boston, I do not mean that they are to be put into the Hands of the Recruits raising to compleat the old Regiments, but in Case of absolute Necessity, such as the Appearance of an Invasion, or the like, and that every possible Method should be used for them to procure Arms without depending on these.

I shall be glad of your returning to the Massachusetts Government the Powder they have lent the Continent; as by this fortunate Capture we are enabled to pay our Debts in that Way.[97] I am, etc.

## To MAJOR GENERAL ISRAEL PUTNAM

Philadelphia, May 28, 1776.

Sir: I received yours of the 24th. Inst. with it's several Inclosures, and the Letter and Invoice from General Ward, giving Intelligence of the fortunate Capture made by our armed Vessels, on which Event you have my Congratulations.

I have wrote Genl. Ward, as you will see by the inclosed Letter, (which having read, you will seal and send by Post) to send forward to New York Colo. Putnam's Demands, and also such Articles as Colo. Knox may apply for, out of the Cargo taken. In like Manner I have desired him to send me as soon as possible, Part of the Powder, and eight Hundred of the Carbines which will greatly assist in making up the Defficiency in this Instance. As to the Plan[98] for employing the Armed Vessels, I

---

[97] The resolve of May 25, 1776, placed the disposal of any arms and military stores captured in prizes in the hands of the Commander in Chief.

[98] The plan for using the armed vessels in the Hudson River and New York Bay accompanies Putnam's letter to Washington (May 24), which is in the *Washington Papers*. The names and stations of the various armed vessels are there given.

have no Objection to it's being adopted, provided it will not frustrate the main Design for which they were fitted out. That I would by no Means have injured, as it is a Matter of much Importance to prevent a Correspondence between the disaffected and the Enemy and the latter from getting Supplies of Provision; but if this End can be answered, and the other Advantages in the Plan mentioned, it is certainly an eligible one.

The great Variety of Business in which Congress are engaged, has prevented our settling what I was requested to attend for, tho' we have made several Attempts, and a Committee has been appointed for the Purpose Day after Day,[99] nor can I say with Precision when I shall be at Liberty to return. I must, therefore, pray your Attention and Vigilance to every necessary Work and further, if you should receive, before I come, certain Advices and such as you can rely on, of the Enemy's being on the Coast or approaching New York, that you inform me thereof by Express, as early as possible. I do not wish an Alarm to be given me without Foundation; but as soon as you are certified of their coming, that it be instantly communicated to me, and Orders given the Express who comes, to bespeak at the different necessary Stages on the Road, as many Horses, as may

---

[99] The committee was appointed on May 23 to confer with General Washington, Maj. Gen. Horatio Gates, and Brig. Gen. Thomas Mifflin, on the Canadian situation. It consisted of Benjamin Harrison, Richard Henry Lee, John Adams, James Wilson, and Edward Rutledge. May 24 Robert R. Livingston was added. May 25 a new committee of conference on a plan of campaign, consisting of Harrison, Lee, Adams, Wilson, Livingston, William Whipple, Roger Sherman, Stephen Hopkins, William Livingston, George Read, Matthew Tilghman, Joseph Hewes, Arthur Middleton, and Lyman Hall, was appointed. A report was rendered on May 29 advising the issue of an address to the inhabitants of the United States. May 30 a further report was brought in. May 31 another report was made. June 1 further consideration was given the matter, and eight battalions for Canada ordered raised by Massachusetts, Connecticut, New Hampshire, and New York. June 3 Washington was empowered to employ Indians in Canada; 13,800 militia from Massachusetts, Connecticut, New York, and New Jersey were authorized to reenforce New York; Pennsylvania, Maryland, and Delaware were to furnish 10,000 more for a flying camp, to serve until December 1. Various other measures were adopted, for which the *Journals of the Continental Congress* should be consulted. Washington was excused on June 3 and was back in New York on June 6.

be proper for facilitating my Return, and that of the Gentlemen with me, with the greatest Expedition. I am, etc.

P. S. I desire you'll speak to the several Colls., and hurry them to get their colours done.

## GENERAL ORDERS

New York, May 28, 1776.

Parole Lynn.    Countersign Salem.

Col Prescott's Regiment to be mustered at nine O'Clock, Thursday Morning, on their regimental parade.

Three men from each regiment in the three Brigades, of Genl. Heath, Spencer and Lord Stirling, together with two Subalterns and two Serjeants, to parade at Genl. Putnam's quarters, to morrow morning at six o'clock—these men are to be such as understand rowing.

The General Court Martial of which Colonel Ritzema was President, is dissolved, and the Officers to return to their ordinary duty.

A Wheelwright from each Regiment, in the three Brigades above mentioned, to parade in front of the Laboratory, at eight o'clock in the morning, and receive their orders from Mr. Hughes,[1] Assistant Quarter Master General.

### AFTER ORDERS

A Serjeant, Corporal and twelve men to be immediately detached from the upper Barrack Guard, to Powles Hook, who are to guard the works there, and secure the working tools: This detachment to be immediately replaced by a like number from any one brigade; who will be allowed their quota in to morrow's detail, from henceforward the guard at Powles-hook,

---

[1] Hugh Hughes, of New York. He served as Assistant Quartermaster General of the Continental Army until the end of the year 1781.

are to take with them four days provision, and to be relieved every fourth day, commencing to morrow.

## GENERAL ORDERS
May 29, 1776.
Parole Chamblee.   Countersign Thompson.

One Man from each Regiment, to parade to morrow morning, at six o'clock, at General Putnam's quarters, to go on board the Mifflin, armed Schooner—these men are to be such as best understand the business.

A reinforcement to be added to the upper barrack Guard, of one Serjeant, one Corporal, and twenty-four privates. The above Guard is to furnish four additional Sentries over the Laboratory, and four over the Magazine of Forage, for the placing those Sentries, and the Orders they are to receive, application is to be made to Mr. Hughes Assistant Quarter Master General.

A General Court Martial, consisting of one Colonel, one Lieut. Colonel, one Major and ten Captains, to sit to morrow morning, at nine o'clock, for the trial of all such prisoners as may be brought before them.

Col Nixon President.

| Lieut. Col Shepard. | | | Major Wells. | |
|---|---|---|---|---|
| Captains | | | Captains | |
| Genl. Heaths Bri- | | Members. | Genl. Spencers Bri- | |
| gade............4 | | | gade............4 | |
| Lord Stirling's......2 | | | .................... | |

The names of the prisoners to be tried, together with their crimes, and evidences, to be given unto the Judge Advocate this afternoon—All Evidences to give due attendance on the court.

James Grant, of Capt. Waterhouse's[2] Company, in Colonel Parsons's Regiment, tried at late General Court Martial

---

[2] Capt. Abraham Waterhouse, of the Tenth Continental Infantry.

(whereof Col Ritzema was President) for "destroying his arms, abusing the Serjeants, and insolently affronting his officers"—is found guilty, and sentenced to pay for his arms, and receive Twenty Lashes on his bare back—The General approves of the sentence, and orders the Corporal Punishment to be inflicted to morrow morning, at the head of the regiment, at guards mounting.

Daniel Kitts, of Col Ward's Regiment, and Capt. Allen's[3] Company, tried at the above Court Martial for "Stealing a shirt"—The General thinks proper to postpone his sentence 'till further orders—

Joseph Lent, of Col McDougall's regiment, and Capt. Hoyt's[4] Company, tried at the above Court Martial for "Disobedience of orders, and striking his commanding Officer, Ensign Young, when in the execution of his duty"—is found guilty of *Disobedience of orders,* and sentenced to be confined five days on bread and water, in the Provost Dungeon.

The General is not a little surprised at the Sentence of the Court, on the prisoner Joseph Lent, and thinks the punishment so inadequate to the crime, that he disapproves of the sentence—The General hopes this hint, will make future General Court Martials more particular, and severe on the *heinous crime,* of a Soldier's striking, or attempting to strike his officer, or disobey his commands.

## GENERAL ORDERS

Head Quarters, New York, May 31, 1776.

Parole Portsmouth.    Countersign Georgia.

The Provost Marshal to make a report in writing, every morning, at Head Quarters, of the prisoners he has in charge, specifying their names, regiments, companies, by whom confined, crimes, number of nights confined, tried or not tried.

---

[3] Capt. Jonathan Allen, of Ward's Twenty-first Continental Infantry.
[4] This name is also given as Hyatt in some of the returns. There was a Capt. Ezekiel Hyatt in the Westchester County, N. Y., Militia.

Edmund Britt of Capt. Butler's[5] Company, and Col Nixon's Regiment, tried at the General Court Martial whereof Col Nixon is President for "Desertion"—is found guilty, and sentenced to receive Thirty-nine lashes.

Ahimaas Sherwin of Capt. Butler's Company, of Col Nixon's Regiment, tried at the above Court Martial for "Desertion" is also found guilty, and sentenced to receive Thirty-nine lashes.

The General approves of the sentence, on the above two prisoners, and orders it to be put in execution, to morrow morning, at guard mounting.

AFTER ORDERS

Genl Washington has wrote to Genl. Putnam, desiring him in the most pressing terms, to give positive orders to all the Colonels, to have Colours immediately completed for their respective regiments.

## *To JOHN AUGUSTINE WASHINGTON

Philadelphia, May 31, 1776.

Dear Brother: Since my arrival at this place, where I came at the request of Congress, to settle some matters relative to the ensuing Campaign I have received your Letter of the 18th. from Williamsburg, and think I stand indebted to you for another, which came to hand some time ago, in New York.

I am very glad to find that the Virginia Convention have passed so noble a vote, and with so much unanimity,[6] things

---

[5] Capt. Joseph Butler, of the Fourth Continental Infantry.

[6] On Wednesday, May 15, the Virginia Convention, consisting of 112 members, resolved unanimously to instruct their delegates in the Continental Congress to propose "to that respectable body to declare the Colonies free and independent States, absolved from all allegiance to, or dependence upon, the Crown or Parliament of Great Britain," pledging their support to such a declaration, and "to whatever measures may be thought proper and necessary by the Congress for forming foreign alliances, and a confederation of the colonies, at such time, and in the manner, as to them shall seem best: Provided, that the power of forming government for, and the regulation of the internal concerns of each colony, be left to the respective colonial legislatures." These instructions were carried out by the Virginia delegates in Richard Henry Lee's motion of June 7, which precipitated the debate that ended in the passage of the Resolution of Independence on July 2, and the adoption of the Declaration of Independence on July 4.

have come to that pass now, as to convince us, that we have nothing more to expect from the justice of G. Britain; also, that she is capable of the most delusive Arts, for I am satisfied that no Commissioners ever were design'd, except Hessians and other Foreigners; and that the Idea was only to deceive, and throw us off our guard; the first it has too effectually accomplished, as many Members of Congress, in short, the representation of whole Provences, are still feeding themselves upon the dainty food of reconciliation; and tho' they will not allow that the expectation of it has any influence upon their judgments (with respect to their preparations for defence) it is but too obvious that it has an operation upon every part of their conduct and is a clog to their proceedings, it is not in the nature of things to be otherwise, for no Man, that entertains a hope of seeing this dispute speedily, and equitably adjusted by Commissioners, will go to the same expence and run the same hazards to prepare for the worst event as he who believes that he must conquer, or submit to unconditional terms, and its concomitants, such as Confiscation, hanging, &c., &c.

To form a new Government, requires infinite care, and unbounded attention; for if the foundation is badly laid the superstructure must be bad, too much time therefore, cannot be bestowed in weighing and digesting matters well. We have, no doubt, some good parts in our present constitution; many bad ones we know we have, wherefore no time can be misspent that is imployed in seperating the Wheat from the Tares. My fear is, that you will all get tired and homesick, the consequence of which will be, that you will patch up some kind of Constitution as defective as the present; this should be avoided, every Man should consider, that he is lending his aid to frame a Constitution which is to render Million's happy, or Miserable, and that a matter of such moment cannot be the Work of a day.

I am in hopes to hear some good Accts from No. Carolina. If Clinton has only part of his force there, and not strongly Intrenched, I should think Genl. Lee will be able to give a very good acct. of those at Cape Fare. Surely Administration must intend more than 5000 Men for the Southern district, otherwise they must have a very contemptable opinion of those Colonies, or have great expectation of assistance from the Indians, Slaves, and Tories. We expect a very bloody Summer of it at New York and Canada, as it is there I expect the grand efforts of the Enemy will be aim'd; and I am sorry to say that we are not, either in Men, or Arms, prepared for it; however, it is to be hoped, that if our cause is just, as I do most religiously believe it to be, the same Providence which has in many Instances appear'd for us, will still go on to afford its aid.

Your Convention is acting very wisely in removing the disaffected, Stock, &ca., from the Counties of Princess Anne and Norfolk; and are much to be commended for their attention to the Manufacture of Salt, Salt Petre, Powder &ca. No time, nor expense should be spared to accomplish these things.

Mrs. Washington is now under Innoculation in this City; and will, I expect, have the Small pox favourably, this is the 13th day, and she has very few Pustules; she would have wrote to my Sister but thought it prudent not to do so, notwithstanding there could be but little danger in conveying the Infection in this manner. She joins me in love to you, her, and all the little ones. I am, with every Sentiment of regard, etc.

### GENERAL ORDERS
Head Quarters, New York, June 1, 1776.
Parole Jay.   Countersign Alsop.

A Serjeant, Corporal and twelve men, to march to morrow morning, at Six OClock, at which time they will be directed where to march to. they are to be furnished with six days provisions pr man.

Eight men (that understand making Cartridges) from each of the five Regiments, in General Spencer's Brigade, and from Col Nixons and Col Webb's Regiments, to parade to morrow morning at Six OClock, at the Bowling Green, before Col Knox's door, and receive their further orders from him.

## GENERAL ORDERS

Head Quarters, New York, June 2, 1776.

Parole Fitch.    Countersign Babcock.

General Greene to order all arms in his brigade which want repairs to be immediately brought in to the Armourers shop, where they will be fitted up properly after which, all repairs will be stopped out of the men's wages.

Capt. Oliver Soaper of the 13th. or Colonel Read's Regiment, tried at the General Court Martial, whereof Col Nixon is President) On Complaint of Lieut. Thomas Williams of said Company, for "defrauding the public, in knowingly and willingly drawing pay, for more men than he had belonging to his company"—The Court are of opinion, that Capt. Soper is not guilty of the charge brought against him, therefore do acquit him.

The General approves of the proceedings of the above Court Martial, and orders, that Capt. Soper be immediately released from his arrest.

Lieut. Thomas Williams of Capt. Soper's Company, and Col Reads Regiment, also tried at the above Court Martial, for "Impeaching and falsly asserting that Capt. Soper of the said Regiment, had knowingly and designedly defrauded the public, in making up, and drawing pay, for more men than he had in his company: Also for signing Returns of the Company expressly against the orders of Capt. Soper—Also for refusing to repair to his Tent, when ordered by Capt. Soper." The Court are of opinion, that the prisoner is guilty of the charge brought against him, and unanimously adjudge that he be *cashiered* for the said offence.

The General approves of the sentence of the above Court Martial, and orders that Mr. Williams, late a Lieutenant in Col Reed's Regiment, immediately depart the Camp by the way of Kingsbridge, or on board a vessel going up the sound.

John Quinn, of Capt. Allen's[7] Company and Col Ward's Regiment, tried at the above Court Martial, for "Desertion"— is found guilty, and sentenced to receive Thirty-nine Lashes, on his bare back for said offence.

John Suby and James Johnston, both of Captain King's[8] Company, and Col Ward's Regiment, tried severally at the above Court Martial, for "Desertion"—are each found guilty, and sentenced severally, to be whipped Thirty-nine Lashes, on their bare back.

The General approves of the several Sentences above, and orders them to be put in execution, to morrow morning at Guard mounting.

Hugh Killbreath, of Capt. Rosse's[9] Company, in Col Hand's Regiment, tried at the above Court Martial, for "Assaulting, beating and wounding Assa Baker, and David Avery, of the Artillery"—is found guilty of the Charge, brought against him, and sentenced to be whipped Thirty-nine Lashes on his bare back.

The General approves of the above sentence, and orders the prisoner to be transmitted to his Corps, and that the punishment be inflicted on him at the head of the regiment at Guard mounting, on the first morning the Commanding Officer shall find suitable for the purpose.

---

[7] Capt. Samuel Allen, of the Twenty-first Continental Infantry.
[8] Capt. William King, of the Twenty-first Continental Infantry.
[9] Capt. James Ross, of Hand's Pennsylvania Regiment.

## To THE PRESIDENT OF CONGRESS

Philadelphia, June 3, 1776.

Sir: I have perused the Petition preferred by the Independent Corps of Boston and beg leave to Inform Congress, that the Five Regiments there are extremely deficient in Arms, as are many other Regiments in Continental pay, and submit to their consideration, whether any part of the Arms lately taken, under these circumstances should be delivered to the Gentlemen applying for them, determining at the same time whatever decision Congress may come to, respecting them, will be agreeable to me and be litterally complied with. I have &ca.[10]

## To MAJOR GENERAL ISRAEL PUTNAM

Philadelphia, June 3, 1776.

Dear Sir: I received your Favor by Yesterday Evening's Express with the several Letters and Intelligence from General Schuyler and am much concerned for the further Misfortunes that have attended our Arms in Canada. I have laid the whole before Congress, who had before resolved to send a considerable Augmentation to our Army there and doubt not that General Schuyler may receive Assistance from the Militias most convenient to him, for securing the different Passes and Communications 'till they can be releived.

As to sending a Reinforcement from New York, neither Policy or Prudence will justify it, as we have the strongest Reasons to believe the Day not far distant when a large Armament will arrive; and vigorously attempt an Impression there; to oppose which the Forces we have will not be more than equal, if sufficient.

---

[10] In the writing of Robert Hanson Harrison.

Congress have determined on building sundry Gondolas and
Fire Rafts, to prevent the Men of War and Enemy's Ships from
coming into the New York Bay or Narrows.[11] I must therefore
request, that you make Inquiry after Carpenters, and procure
all you can, with Materials necessary for building them, that
they may go on with all possible Expedition, as soon as the
Person arrives from hence, whom I have employed to superintend the Work. He will be there in a Day or two. I am &c.

## GENERAL ORDERS

Head Quarters, New York, June 3, 1776.
Parole Hartford.   Countersign Wethersfield.
Col. Learned's and Col. Webb's regiments to be mustered
Wednesday Morning at nine o'clock.

## GENERAL ORDERS

Head Quarters, New York, June 4, 1776.
Parole Brunswick.   Countersign Stratford.
Col. Reads Regiment to be mustered to morrow morning, at
nine o'clock; and not Col Webb's, as was mentioned in the
orders of yesterday.

## To COLONEL LACHLIN McINTOSH

Philadelphia, June 4, 1776.
Sir: I received your Favor of the 16th. of Feby.[12] by Yesterday's Post, with it's Inclosure, for which and the Information
respecting the State of your Province, I return you my Thanks.

---

[11] On May 30 Congress resolved that the Commander in Chief should build all fire
rafts, boats, row galleys, etc., needed for the defense of New York.
[12] McIntosh's letter, dated Feb. 16, 1776, at Savannah, Ga., is in the *Washington
Papers*. It is printed in Sparks's *Letters to Washington*, vol. 1, p. 148.

I am exceedingly sorry for the Difficulties you have had to encounter, and that they are not yet all at an End; but I am hopeful, by your Perseverance and Activity, they will be surmounted, and that Things will assume a more pleasing Appearance.

Being far removed from the Department you are in, it will be impossible for me to know or transmit the Orders necessary for regulating your Battallion. I must, therefore, refer you to Majr. Genl. Lee, who has been appointed to command in the southern District, and to Brigr. Genl. Armstrong[13] in South Carolina, who are more immediately over you. They will give you, from Time to Time, such Instructions as appear to them necessary, proper, and likely to advance the public Good, which you must make the Rule of your Conduct.

You will be particular and punctual in making your Returns to these Gentlemen, who will forward them to me; and trusting that every Thing in your Power, will be done to promote the Common Cause and Interest of the United Colonies. I am etc.

## GENERAL ORDERS

Head Quarters, New York, June 5, 1776.

Parole Esopus.    Countersign Albany.

Lieut. John Riggs of Capt. McFarland's[14] Company, and Col Nixon's Regiment, tried at the General Court Martial, whereof Col. Nixon is President, for "Counterfeiting, and assuming the character of a Field Officer, and under pretence of being Field Officer of the day, ordering out one of the principal Guards, in the army; imposing upon Capt. Sumner[15] commanding the upper Barrack Guard; and behaving herein

---

[13] Brig. Gen. John Armstrong, of Pennsylvania.

[14] Capt. Moses McFarland, of the Fourth Continental Infantry. He was wounded at Bunker Hill; transferred to the Invalid Regiment in March, 1779; served to close of the war; mustered out with the brevet rank of major.

[15] Capt. Ebenezer Sumner, of the Twenty-second Continental Infantry.

unbecoming the Character of an Officer, acting in subversion of military order, &c., is found guilty of the several charges brought against him, and sentenced by the Court to be *cashiered* for the same.

The General approves of the sentence of the Court, and orders that Mr. John Riggs, late Lieutenant in Col Nixon's Regiment do depart the Army, City and Encampment immediately.

George Cottingen and Daniel Dunevil, both of Captain Van Wyck's[16] Company, of Col. McDougall's Regiment, tried at the above Court Martial, for "Desertion"—are severally found guilty of the same, and sentenced to be whipped Thirty-nine Lashes each, on their bare backs.

The General approves the above sentence, and orders it to be put in execution to morrow morning, at guard mounting, at the head of the regiment.

### GENERAL ORDERS

Head Quarters, New York, June 6, 1776.
Parole Woodstock.   Countersign Dudley.

The Brigadiers of each Brigade, are to send to the Quarter-Master-General's to morrow at Ten O'Clock for the spears.[17]

The Colonel of each Regiment wanting Arms, are to draw on Mr. Cheever, Commissary of Stores for thirteen, and give their receipts.

One Captain, two Subs., two Serjeants, two Corporals and fifty Privates from Colonel Webb's[18] Regiment, to parade to morrow morning at six o'Clock at White-hall Slip—these men

---

[16] Capt. Abraham Van Wyke, of the First New York Infantry. He was killed by lightning in August, 1776.

[17] Spears were used by the light horse, or dragoons, as lances, and sometimes by the Infantry in lieu of bayonets. Some of the spears had jointed handles, or staffs, so they could be folded for convenience in transportation.

[18] Col. Charles Webb, of the Nineteenth Continental Infantry.

to be furnished with five days provision—and each man an Ax to cut picketts: Axes and Provisions to be got ready this day, they are not to bring their fire-arms.

This party to be deducted from their usual detail.

The Guard of one Sub: one Serjeant, one Corporal, and twenty-four Privates from the fourth Brigade, with six days provisions, is to be posted at Kingsbridge, to prevent any Soldiers of the army passing that way, unless they have leave in writing from the Commanding Officer of their respective Corps: This Guard is to be relieved every Wednesday 'till further orders: All Masters of Vessels and Ferrymen, are strictly enjoined not to carry off any Soldiers of the Army without leave in writing from their Commanding officer.

Each of the three brigades in the Grand Camp, are to furnish a Patrole every two hours in the day time, consisting of a serjeant and six men, who are to patrole at least two miles to the northward of their respective Camps, and to take up all Soldiers, whom they find with Fire-Arms out of Camp, and endeavour to prevent their committing any disorders whatever; and in particular to seize and confine, all who shall fire a gun.

The 4th. Brigade is to furnish a Guard, consisting of one subaltern, one Serjeant, one Corporal, one Drum, and twenty Privates to guard the works on Bayard's-hill and be relieved every day.

George Edgel of Capt. Hobby's[19] Company, and Colonel Ritzema's Regiment, tried at the General Court Martial whereof Colonel Nixon is President, for "leaving his guard, getting drunk, and damning the Officer of the guard," is found guilty, and sentenced to be whipped Thirty-nine Lashes on his bare back.

---

[19] Capt. David Hobby, of the Third New York Regiment.

John O'Brien of Capt. Varick's Company, and Col McDougall's Regiment, tried at the above Court Martial for "sleeping on his post when Sentry," is found guilty, and sentenced to be whipped Twenty Lashes on his bare back.

Benjamin Richards of Capt. Mighill's[20] Company and Col Baldwin's Regiment, tried at the above Court Martial for "publishing the Countersign, and openly proclaiming it in a public house after Taptoo Beating"—is found guilty, and sentenced to be whipped Twenty Lashes, on his bare back, for said offence.

John Sinnet of Capt. Johnson's[21] Company, and Colo. McDougall's Regiment, tried at the above Court Martial for "Desertion" is found guilty of the same, and sentenced to be whipped Twenty Lashes, on his bare back for said offence.

The General approves of all the foregoing Sentences, and orders that they be put in execution at the usual time and place.

## To MAJOR GENERAL PHILIP SCHUYLER

New York, June 7, 1776.

Dear Sir: I have not Time to answer your two last Favours minutely, but only to acknowledge the Receipt of them; being just returned from Philadelphia, and the Post about to depart this Morning.

The Situation of our Affairs in Canada is truly alarming, and I greatly fear, from the Intelligence transmitted from thence by Capt. Wilkinson[22] to General Greene, that 'ere this we have sustained further and greater Misfortunes, than what happened when you wrote. I have inclosed you a Copy of his Letter, by which you will see I have too much Ground for my Concern,

---

[20] Capt. Thomas Mighill, of the Twenty-sixth Continental Infantry.
[21] Capt. John Johnson, of the First New York Regiment.
[22] Capt. James Wilkinson. As this time he was an aide to Arnold; later he was an aide to Gates.

and I sincerely wish the next Letters from the Northward,may not contain melancholy Advices of General Arnold's Defeat and the Loss of Montreal.

The most vigorous Exertions will be necessary, to retrieve our Circumstances there and I am hopeful you will strain every Nerve for that Purpose. Unless it can be now done Canada will be lost for ever; the fatal Consequences of which every one must feel.

I have inclosed you a Copy of a Resolve of Congress for reinforcing the Army in Canada, and keeping up the Communication with that Province. I hope the several Colonies will immediately furnish their Quotas of Men, which, or as many of them as may be necessary, I should imagine had better be employed at the Communications, and all the inlisted Soldiers sent forward to Canada.

You have also another Resolution for employing and engaging a Number of Indians in the Service.[23] Tho' Congress have not particularised the Mode for raising and engaging them, I would have you,and the Commissioners appointd. for Indian Affairs, pursue such Measures for the Purpose, as to you may seem best for securing their Friendship and Service. If a smaller Number than 2000 will do I would not advise more to be embodied than may be necessary.

If your Presence or Direction at St. John's or any Post in Canada could be of Service and tend to put our Affairs in a better Channel than they now are, I would wish you to go; as General Thomas is down in the small Pox; but I do not mean to direct or request you to do it, if you think by remaining where you are,

---

[23] As before noted, Congress had voted the raising of Indians for the Canada service. The number authorized was 2,000. General Schuyler, when informed, very naturally inquired where they were to be found, and added that, instead of raising this number for the American cause, he thought that if they could be prevented from joining the enemy it was more than could be expected. Schuyler did, however, succeed in negotiating a treaty with the western New York Indians at German Flats shortly after this.

or not going, will be of more public Advantage, or that the Cause will be injured by doing it. You will be governed by such Measures as appear to you best, and the Circumstances of our Affairs under your Management, and those in Canada, with which you must be much better acquainted than I am, or can possibly be, at this Distance.

It is probable your Presence may be necessary and wanted at the Negotiation with the Indians, which will be one Cause to prevent your going. I am, Sir, &c.

## To THE NEW YORK LEGISLATURE

New York, June 7, 1776.

Gentn.: I suppose you have received from the Congress two Resolutions, for the reinforcement of our Army in Canada; but, least you should not be apprized of them, I take the liberty to inclose you a Copy. I most earnestly request, you will exert every endeavour, to furnish the Quota expected from your Province, as speedily as possible. General Schuyler is extremely importunate for a Supply of Men, and it is altogether out of my power to afford them from the Troops here; as they by no means exceed the Number requisite for the defence of this Place. I have the honor to be, etc.

## To THE PRESIDENT OF CONGRESS

New York, June 7, 1776.

Sir: I do myself the honor to inform Congress, that I arrived here yesterday afternoon about one O'Clock and found all in a state of Peace and quiet. I had not time to view the works which were carrying on and those ordered to be begun when I went away, but have reason to beleive, from the reports of such of the General and other officers I had the pleasure to see, that they have been prosecuted and forwarded, with all possible diligence and dispatch.

I am much concerned for the situation of our Affairs in Canada and am fearful 'ere this, It is much worse than was first reported at Philadelphia. The Intelligence from thence in a Letter from Captain Wilkinson of the 2d Regiment, to General Greene, is truly alarming; it not only confirms the Account of Col. Bedel and Major Sherburne's defeat, but seems to forebode General Arnold's with the Loss of Montreal I have Inclosed a Copy of the Letter, which will but too well shew that there is foundation for my apprehensions.

On Wednesday Evening, I received an Express from General Schuyler, with sundry papers respecting Sir John Johnson, which I have not time to copy as the post is just going off, but will do myself the honor of transmitting you them as soon as I possibly can.[24]

Before I left Philadelphia, I employed a person to superintend the Building the Gondolas which Congress had resolved on for this place; he is arrived and all things seem to be in a proper Channel for facilitating the work; but when they are done, we shall be in much want of Guns, having never received any of

---

[24] Sir John Johnson resided at Johnstown, in Tryon County, about 40 miles north-west of Albany, N. Y., and possessed large patrimonial estates in that neighborhood. Adhering to the Royal cause, and having many of the Indians in his influence, as well as two or three hundred Highlanders, who were his tenants, an eye was kept upon his conduct. In January he had given his parole that he would take no part against the Colonies. General Schuyler received such intelligence as convinced him that Sir John was secretly instigating the Indians, by which he had virtually broken his parole, and was likely to produce much mischief on the frontiers. To prevent this he thought it advisable to secure Sir John and quell the rising spirit of hostility which he was fomenting among the inhabitants and Indians in that quarter. Col. Elias Dayton, with a part of his regiment, was sent to make the arrest. But Sir John escaped to the westward and sought security with the Indians and a small British force on the Lakes. Sir John's papers were examined by Colonel Dayton, in compliance with his orders, and Lady Johnson was removed to Albany, where she was retained as a kind of hostage for the peaceable conduct of her husband. In the January following Sir John Johnson found his way to New York City, then in possession of the British Army.—*Sparks*.

those taken by Commodore Hopkins. Be pleased to remember me to Congress with the utmost respect; and I am etc.

P. S. I this minute received your favor of the 5th Inst. I am in need of Commissions and beg Congress to point out precisely the line I am to pursue in filling them up. this I mentioned in my Letter of the 11 Ulto. I am much pleased at the fortunate Captures and the generous conduct of the owners and masters for the tender of the money to Congress.

## GENERAL ORDERS

Head Quarters, New York, June 7, 1776.
Parole Gates.   Countersign Mifflin.

The Honorable The Continental Congress, have been pleased to appoint Horatio Gates Esqr. Major General; and Thomas Mifflin Esqr. Brigadier General in the Army of the United Colonies: They are to be obeyed as such.

The Honorable The Continental Congress have been pleased to appoint Stephen Moylan Esqr. to be Quarter-Master-General, in the room of Thomas Mifflin Esqr. preferr'd; and to be obeyed as such.

Walter Stewart and Isaac Peirce Esquires are appointed Aid-de-Camps to Major General Gates; All orders written, or verbal, deliver'd by either of them, are to be considered as coming from the Major General, and obeyed as such.

### AFTER ORDERS

The Adjutants of each regiment to give in immediately at Head Quarters, a Return of what number of Pikes are fit for service, and what number wanting, to complete in each regiment.

## GENERAL ORDERS

Head Quarters, New York, June 8, 1776.

Parole York. Countersign Hudson.

The Quarter-Master-General is to return the number of Spears, and intrenching Tools in his store.

The Brigadiers are to see that an exact return of the Spears, in their respective Brigades, and Posts, is also given in; and that a Report be fortwith made of the deficiencies of Arms and Accoutrements, wanting in each Regiment, distinguishing the kinds—These several returns are expected without delay.

The Colonels and commanding Officers of Regiments and Corps, are to make out pay-abstracts for the month of April. These are to be carefully examined by the Brigadier under whom they serve, and the Pay Master-General before they are brought to the Commander in Chief [to] sign the warrants.

The Brigadier of the day is to make a report to the Commander in Chief in writing, so soon as his tour of duty is ended, of the Guards, and all remarkable occurrences.

The charges made by Capt. Butler,[25] against Lieut. Silas Walker, of Col Nixon's Regiment, are to be laid before the General-Court-Martial now sitting, and the parties to attend with their Evidences when called for by the court.

Lieut. Van-Hook[26] of Colonel McDougall's Regiment, charged with "Disobedience of orders"—to be tried by the General Court Martial now sitting. Also

Lieut. Ezekiel Oakley of Colonel McDougall's Regiment, charged with "beating Sally Paterson, an Inhabitant of this town, on the head with a stick," to be tried by the General Court Martial now sitting.

The different Charges against the several persons above mentioned, to be tried, to be given in immediately to the Judge

---

[25] Capt. Joseph Butler, of the Fourth Continental Infantry.
[26] Lieut. Arant Van Hook, of the First New York Regiment.

Advocate, together with the names of the evidences—All Evidences are to give due attendance.

Colonels—Nixon's, Varnum's, Parsons's, Little's, Huntington's, Webb's and Arnolds Regiments, have never given a Return of their Arms and Accoutrements, altho' ordered near a month since, 'tis expected they will be more particular in future—And as an alteration in the state of the arms and accoutrements, may have happened in some of the Regiments, who have sent in their Returns, by purchases of arms &c. since; those Regiments are desired to furnish a fresh return, agreeable to the General Order above—specifying *good, bad* and *wanting.*

### To THE PRESIDENT OF CONGRESS

New York, June 8, 1776.

Sir: In my Letter of Yesterday, which I had the honor of addressing you and which was designed to have come by Post but was prevented by his Departure before the usual time, I mentioned my having received by Express a Letter and sundry Papers from General Schuyler respecting Sir John Johnston, Copies of which I herewith transmit for your Inspection and Perusal, they will shew you what Measures were planned and attempted for apprehending him and securing the Highlanders in Tryon County.

Having heard that the Troops at Boston are extremely uneasy and almost mutinous for want of Pay (several Months of which are now due), I must take the Liberty to repeat a Question contained in my Letter of the 5th Ulto., What mode is to be adopted respecting it, Whether is Money to be sent from hence by the Pay Master General, or some Person, subordinate to him, to be appointed there for that Purpose? I expected some direction would have been given in this instance long 'ere this, from what was contained in yours accompanying, or about the time of the last remittance. I presume it has been omitted by reason of the Multiplicity of important Business before the Congress.

In perusing the several Resolves you honored me with when at Philadelphia, and since my return, I find one allowing a Chief Engineer for the Army in a seperate Department. The Service requiring many of them, I wish Congress, if they know any Persons skilled in the Business, would appoint them. General Schuyler has frequently applied and suggested the Necessity of having some in Canada. I myself know of none.

I also find there is a resolve of the third of June for taking Indians into service which if litterally pursued confines them to that in Canada. Is that the meaning of Congress, or that the Commander in Chief may order their Service to any place he may think necessary?

In respect to establishing Expresses between the several Continental Posts, Who is to do it? The Resolve does not say. Is it expected by Congress that I should? Whoever the Work is assigned to, I think should execute it with the utmost dispatch. The late imperfect and contradictory Accounts respecting our Defeat at the Cedars [27] strongly point out the Necessity there is for it. No Intelligence is yet come from any Officer in command there, and most probably for want of a proper Channel to convey it, though this Misfortune happened so long ago. When I had the Honor of being in Congress, If I mistake not, I heard a Resolve read, or was told of one, allowing the New York Troops the same pay of others in the Continental Service. This, if any such I do not find, and, if there is not such a one, I shall be under some Embarrassment, how to pay the Militia to be provided by this Province.

---

[27] Col. Timothy Bedel, of New Hampshire, had been sent by Arnold to hold a narrow pass known as The Cedars, about 45 miles above Montreal. An English force appearing, Bedel went to Montreal for reenforcements, and on May 19 Maj. Isaac Butterfield, whom he had left in charge, surrendered almost without a show of fighting. Some reinforcements from Arnold, under the command of Maj. Henry Sherburne, were met and routed.—*Ford.*

The Resolve providing them says, "they are to be paid whilst in service as other Troops here" but if those enlisted heretofore in this Province, are to receive according to the first Establishment, it is a matter of Doubt what the Militia are to have.[28]

Before this comes to hand, a hand Bill, containing an Account of a Victory gained by General Arnold over the Party that had defeated Colonel Bedel and Major Sherburne will most probably have reached you; I have enquired into the Authenticity of this fortunate report, and have found there is no Dependence to be put in it, nor do I believe it deserving of the least Credit; I shall be happy not to hear the Reverse.[29]

P. S. If Congress have come to any resolution about an allowance to induce men to reinlist, you will please to favor me with it, as the Time the Rifle Regiment is engaged for is just expired. As the Militia will be coming in, and they will be in much need of covering, please to have all the Tents and the Cloth proper for making them that can be procured, forwarded as soon as possible.

### To BENJAMIN HARRISON, JOHN ADAMS AND WILLIAM WHIPPLE[30]

New York, June 8, 1776.

Gentlemen: In Answer to your Favor of the 14th. instant in which you request me to employ proper Persons to survey the

---

[28] Resolved, "That the pay of the continental troops, in the middle department, be henceforth the same as that of the troops in the eastern." (See *Journals of the Continental Congress,* June 10, 1776.) The pay of the eastern forces being higher than that allowed those of New York, it was found that many from New York were enlisting in the regiments of New England. The Congress of New York, upon receiving a requisition from the Continental Congress for more troops, sent Gouverneur Morris to Philadelphia to determine, if possible, this "odious discrimination," with the above result.—*Ford.*

[29] Arnold had marched against the British with the object of regaining by force the 470 Americans captured in the two engagements at The Cedars, but the British officer asserted that a massacre must ensue upon such an attempt, and Arnold was forced to be content with obtaining the Americans (save four officers retained as hostages) on the condition of returning an equal number of British prisoners. This agreement was set aside by Congress.—*Ford.* (See *Journals of the Continental Congress,* July 10, 1776.)

[30] A committee of Congress.

Harbour, Fortifications &ca. of Cape Ann, and of New London, I informed you of my writing to Colonel Richard Gridley and Colonel Henry Knox, to undertake the Business and promised to transmit you their report, as soon as it should come to hand.[31] I accordingly have the Pleasure to enclose you Colonel Gridley's report of the Harbour and Works of New London, with the several Plans he has taken, which appears to be accurate and well done. I have the Honor to be, etc.

### GENERAL ORDERS

Head Quarters, New York, June 9, 1776.

Parole Amboy. Countersign Brunswick.

It is strongly recommended to the officers of the different regiments, to practice the *Salute* with the Fusee, and to fall upon a method of being uniform therein; so as that all may acquire one and the same mode: And The General desires, that when the line is turned out at any encampment, all the officers keep their arms advanced, and salute only by taking off their hats, until they have attained a more correct method of saluting with their arms.

A Guard of one Serjeant, one Corporal, and ten Men, to mount to morrow morning, at Murray's Magazine—Mr. Norward will give directions for placing the Sentries &c.

Lieut. Jacob Zanck of Col. Hands Regiment, tried at the General Court Martial whereof Col. Nixon is President, for "Insulting and abusing Lieut. Zeigler,[32] Adjutant of said regiment, and for behaving in an infamous, scandalous manner, unbecoming the officer and gentleman"—The Court are of opinion that the prisoner is guilty of publickly insulting Lieut. Zeigler on the regimental parade; and adjudge that Lieut. Zanck, ask

---

[31] See Washington's letter to Benjamin Harrison, John Adams, and William Whipple, Apr. 22, 1776, *ante*.

[32] Lieut. David Zeigler, of the Fourth Continental Infantry.

pardon of Lieut. Zeigler, in presence of the officers of the Battalion, and be reprimanded by the Commanding officer of the regiment—The General approves the above sentence.

Giles Burrow, of Capt. Barns's[33] Company, Col Nixon's Regiment, tried at the above Court Martial for "Desertion and forging a Discharge from the Continental Service"—is found guilty of the same, and sentenced to receive Thirty-nine Lashes on his bare back.

John Monney of Capt. Stenrods[34] Company Col McDougall Regt. tried at the General Court for "Desertion," is found guilty but unfairness had been used in inlisting the prisoner, and his being very ignorant, judge him to be confined seven days on bread and water.

Gustus Seely of Capt. Hull's[35] Company Col Webb's regiment, tried at the above Court Martial for "being drunk and disobedience of orders and insulting Mr. Webb[36] A. D. C. to General Putnam," is found guilty and sentenced to be whipped Thirty Lashes on his bare back.

The General approves of the above sentences and orders them to be put in execution at the usual time and place.

## To THE PRESIDENT OF CONGRESS

New York, June 9, 1776.

Sir: I was honored Yesterday, with your favor of the 7th. instant with its inclosures. When Doctor Potts[37] arrives, I shall

---

[33] Capt. Thomas Barnes, of the Fourth Continental Infantry.

[34] Capt. Cornelius Steenrod, of the First New York Regiment.

[35] Capt. William Hull, of the Nineteenth Continental Infantry. He rose to rank of major, lieutenant colonel, and brigadier general in the United States Army. He was cashiered Apr. 25, 1812, for surrendering Detroit to the British.

[36] Maj. Samuel Blatchley Webb. He, later, became lieutenant colonel and aide to Washington; was colonel of one of the 16 Additional Continental regiments; was taken prisoner on an expedition against Long Island, N. Y., in December, 1777; exchanged in 1780, and transferred to the Third Connecticut Regiment. He held the rank of brevet brigadier general at the close of the war. Major Webb was wounded at Bunker Hill, Mass., at White Plains, N. Y., and again at Trenton, N. J.

[37] Dr. Jonathan Potts. He was deputy director general of the Northern Hospital, of which Dr. Samuel Stringer was director general.

order him to Canada or Lake George, as may appear most proper. It is certainly necessary that he or Doctor Stringer should go to the former. The resolve respecting General Wooster's recall, I will immediately transmit him with Directions to repair hither without delay.[38]

The Situation of our Affairs in Canada, as reported by the Honorable Commissioners, is truly alarming, and I am sorry that my Opinion of the ill consequences resulting from the short Inlistment of the Army should be but too well confirmed by the experience they have had of the want of Discipline and Order in our Soldiery there this induces me again to wish Congress to determine on a liberal allowance to engage the Troops already in service to reinlist for a longer Period or during the continuance of the War; nor can I forbear expressing my Opinion of the Propriety of keeping the Military Chest always supplied with Money; as Evils of the most interesting Nature are often produced by want of a regular Payment of Troops,—the neglect makes them impatient and uneasy.

I am much surprized at the scarcity of Provisions there, particularly of Flour, as from several Accounts I had received from thence, I was led to expect that considerable supplies of that Article could be procured there. That our misfortunes may not become greater, I have wrote the Commissary to forward more Provisions in Addition to those already sent. An Adjutant and Quarter Master General are indispensibly necessary with Assistants, the Money saved the Continent by their non-appointment, will be but small and trifling, when put in competition with the

---

[38] On June 6 Congress took action on the recall of Wooster. The President wrote to Washington (June 7) describing the situation in Canada as reported by the commissioners, and Washington wrote to Wooster a 4-line note ordering him to repair to headquarters in New York City. Wooster requested an inquiry into his conduct, and a committee report absolved him of blame. (See *Journals of the Continental Congress*, Aug. 17, 1776.) He resigned and was appointed major general of militia by the State of Connecticut. Washington's note to Wooster, dated June 9, 1776, is in the *Washington Papers*.

Loss for want of them. Colonel Fleming[39] who acted in the former capacity under General Montgomery is now here, but his Indisposition is such, as to render him unfit at this Time for the Post. It is an important one, and requires Vigour and Activity to discharge the Duties of it; he will be of much service to Colonel Reed,[40] the Business of whose Office will be considerably increased by the Augmentation of the Army. it will be necessary too that the Commissary and Quarter Master General in Canada should have several Assistants and Clerks; nor do I think a precise Number can be fixed on; as a variety of circumstances may and must occur to render the Number essential for doing the Business in these Departments greater, or less, at different Times: it will be better I apprehend to leave it indefinite and with Power to the Commanding Officer to allow such as may be wanted. I am still in the Dark, how the unfortunate Affair ended at the Cedars, or on what Terms the Surrender was made, as the last letter from the Commissioners, has reference to a former, and mentions an Agreement entered into which I have not seen; but I know of it more than I would wish.

I have received from Providence, in consequence of Mr. Morris's order as Chairman of the secret Committee of Congress, 234 Musketts in part of the 244 directed to be sent. the enclosed Copy of a Letter from Mr. Brown[41] will account for the deficiency.

I shall be much Obliged by your ordering a Quantity of Lead and Flints to be immediately forwarded. our demands are and will be very pressing. There are also wanted some particular and necessary medicines, to complete our Hospital Chests, of

---

[39] Col. Edward Fleming. He resigned June 15, 1776.

[40] Col. Joseph Reed. He was Adjutant General of the Continental Army from June 5, 1776, to Jan. 22, 1777, when he resigned. Subsequently, he was offered a brigadier's commission, but declined; became President of Pennsylvania.

[41] Nicholas Brown's letter is dated May 27 from Providence, R. I. A copy by Caleb Gibbs is in the *Papers of the Continental Congress*.

which I will get Doctor Morgan to furnish the Congress with a List, when he writes or waits on them about some other matters necessary to be fixed in his Department.

As General Wooster in all Probability will be here in a little time, in Compliance with the Resolve of Congress and my order transmitted him, I wish to know what I am to do with him when he comes. General Schuyler in his Letter of the 31st. Ulto., of which I transmitted you a Copy yesterday, mentions that sundry Persons had a design to seize him, as a Tory, and probably still have, and wishes Congress to give him some Public mark of their approbation, if they are convinced of his Zeal and Attachment to the Cause of his Country. Whether he intended, that I should communicate his Desire to them or not, I am not certain; but supposing that he did, I must beg leave to request that you lay the Paragraph before them, that they may do in the instance of his Requisition, whatever they may judge necessary. I have the Honour &ca.

P. S. If Congress have agreed to the Report of the Committee, for allowing the Indians 5 *pounds* for every Prisoner they shall take at Niagara &ca it is material I should be informed of it. this will be a proper Opportunity for them to embrace to gain Possession of Detroit and the other Posts whilst the Enemy are engaged toward Montreal &ca.[42]

---

[42] In the writing of Robert Hanson Harrison.

In Provincial Congress, New York, June 8, 1776.

Resolved, That the thanks of the Congress be presented to his Excellency, General Washington, for the important services he has rendered to the United Colonies, and for the attention he has paid to the interest and civil authority of this colony; and that he be assured of the readiness of this Congress, to afford him all the aid in their power to enable him to execute the important trust reposed in him.

Ordered, That the President wait upon General Washington and communicate the said resolution to him.

June 9.

The President informed the Congress that, pursuant to the order of yesterday he waited upon his Excellency, General Washington, and communicated to him the resolve therein mentioned; that his Excellency was pleased to return the following answer, and requested the President to communicate the same to Congress:

"Gentlemen: I am extremely obliged for the high sense you entertain of my services, and for your promises of every possible assistance in the discharge of my important

## To MAJOR GENERAL PHILIP SCHUYLER

New York, June 9, 1776.

Dear Sir: I am now to acknowledge the Receipt of your several Favors of the 21st, 24th, 26th, and 26th, 27th, 28th and 31st Ulto. with the several Papers inclosed. The whole of them except the last I communicated to Congress when at Philadelphia; That I did not get 'till my Return; but have since transmitted them a Copy of it, and of the Papers respecting Sir J. Johnson.

In Regard to a further Remittance to Canada the Commissioners have wrote Congress fully on the Subject, and I presume they will forward such a Supply of Money immediately as they think necessary.

As there is but too much Probability that Sir J. Johnson may attempt to ravage the Frontier Counties, and to excite the disaffected to take Arms against us, I think it will be adviseable that Colo. Dayton should remain as you request, as long as you apprehend a Necessity for it.

It is not in my Power to spare any more Men from hence, either for the Communication, or to assist in repairing Ticonderoga. The Detachments already gone to Canada have weakened the Force necessary for the Defence of this Place, considering its Importance, more perhaps than Policy will justify. Be that as it may, the Reinforcement which Congress have resolved to send to Canada, for keeping open the Communication between that Country and it's Colonies, as you will see by the Copy inclosed in my Letter of the 7th, would supersede the Necessity of Men going from this Camp, provided they could be spared. I should suppose, that Van Schaick's and Wynkoop's Regiments, exclusive of any other Men would nearly suffice for the Purposes

duty. You may rest assured, that my attention to the happiness of this Colony shall not be wanting, nor my regard to the civil authority remitted, while I am honored with the command I now hold."

mentioned in your several Letters; or that very few Men more, in Addition to them certainly would, if they were compleat, and properly employed; but I am informed by a Letter from General Sullivan of the 18th. Ulto., dated at Albany, that these Regiments were not to be found on the strictest Inquiry he could make; that Colo. Van Schaick[43] who was there, never furnished a single Man for Guard, or any other Duty, after he got there, and that Lieut. Colo. Courtland[44] of Wynkoop's Regt., when he applied for Pay for two Companies said to be in Tryon County, to keep the Tories in Order, informed him they had neither Arms nor Ammunition; that in some Companies there was not a Man present fit for Duty; and that in others there was not more than eleven and in some less. He also complains of the great Waste of Pork, by the Waggoners drawing out the Brine to lighten the Carriage, and in his Letter two Days before, charges the Batteaux Men, and the Waggon Master with Indolence and a Strange Neglect of Duty.

I well know, my dear Sir, that the Multiplicity of Matters you are engaged in, will necessarily put in the Power of those who are not influenced by Principles of Honesty and Justice, to practise many Impositions; but I must beg you will turn your Attention as much as possible to these Things, and reform such Abuses as have already happened, or prevent them in future.

I am very doubtful, whether the Flour you seem to think may be had in Canada can be got. The Commissioners Letters as late as the 28th. Ulto. seem to preclude every such Hope.

I esteem it a Matter of Importance, not only to fortify, and secure Ticonderoga; but every other Post on the communication: and that you should garrison them with Men under judicious

---

[43] Col. Gooze (or Gozen) Van Schaick, of the Second New York Regiment, and, later, of the First New York Regiment.

[44] Lieut. Col. Philip Van Cortlandt, of the Fourth New York Regiment. Later he was colonel of the Second New York Regiment.

and spirited Officers, to be fixed there, who might be called to Account for Misconduct, which is difficult to do, where they are shifting and changing continually, and who would esteem it their indispensible Duty to carry on and maintain the Works against any Surprizes or Attacks that may be attempted.

I have wrote to Congress to appoint Engineers, if they can fix upon proper Persons for the Office. If you know of any, you had better employ them. I am confident Congress will allow them the usual Pay.

When I came from Philadelphia I left the Indians there and doubt not but Congress will use their Endeavours to prevent them returning for some Time. I have shewed them what you said upon the Subject.

I have spoken to the Qr. Master, about a proper Person to superintend the Building of Gondolas but he knows of none. There is a Man who came to direct the Building of some here; and if any of the Carpenters shall be deemed qualified after seeing the Model, I will send you one.

I have wrote to Philadelphia for a Supply of Flints, which shall be forwarded you as soon as possible, and will give Direction that you be furnished with a Quantity of necessary Medicines.

With Respect to St. Luke Lecorne, Major Campbell and the other Prisoners at Esopus, I think it will be prudent for you to remove them, or such of them as you apprehend dangerous, to some other secure Place, and they should be under a suitable and trusty Guard.

Your continuing to build Batteaux appears a necessary Measure; as a sufficient Number should be had to transport our Troops going to Canada or coming from thence; if they should ever be under the disagreeable Necessity of evacuating the Possession they now have to the Enemy; an Event, I sincerely wish not to happen; but which from the melancholy Complexion of Things in that Quarter, I conceive possible.

I have been much surprised at not receiving more perfect and explicit Account of the Defeat of Colo. Bedel and his Party at the Cedars. I should have thought some of the Officers in Command there would and ought to have transmitted it immediately; but as they have not, it is probable I should have long remained in Doubt as to the Event, had not the Commissioners called on me to Day. Nor should I consider my not having a Return of the Army, Stores, &c. in Canada, a Matter of less Wonder had I not been accustomed to the Neglect. If it is not become too inveterate, I wish it could be got the better of. It is certainly of much Importance, and necessary to be known frequently.

Since mine of the 21st. and yours of the 31st. Ulto. Captains Swan[45] and Dundee[46] with three Privates have been here, having a Permit to go to Philadelphia. They came down the North River from Albany (I believe) to this Place, where I make no Doubt they reconnoitre all our Works, and in their Passage, those at the Highlands. This Indulgence, I conceive of such infinite Prejudice to our Cause, for the Reasons I have assigned and many more that may be added, that I hope, it will never be granted again.

I wish you to notify the several Committees in the Neighbourhood of Albany, having the Care of Prisoners, of the injurious Consequences which must necessarily result from such a License, to prevent their allowing it to any on future Applications.

As Congress have resolved on a large Augmentation to the Army in Canada, as you will see by the Copy of their Vote transmitted in my last; it seems material that you should advise with the Commissary in that Department, and Mr. Trumbull here and concert a Plan for their Subsistence. If they cannot be supplied plentifully with Provisions, their going will be of more Injury than Benefit, and encrease the Distress of the whole.

---

[45] Capt. Rowland Swan, of the Twenty-sixth Foot, British Army.
[46] Capt. Peter Dundee, of the Seventh Foot, British Army.

In your Favor of the 20th. you are desirous that a Court of Inquiry should be ordered respecting the Charge contained in the Informations I inclosed you in mine of the 21st.; If you conceive it necessary, I will do it with Pleasure, if you will point out the Mode to be pursued, to me. The Matters objected to [by] you, appear so uncertain, vague, and incredible, that there is nothing to found the Proceedings on, were there the most distant Necessity for the Scrutiny. By Reason of a Paragraph in your Letter of the 31st., I mentioned the Matter to Congress, to whom I had the Honor of writing this Day, and when at Philadelphia communicated it to some of them, on their reading your first Letter, in which Mention was made of the Subject. In doing this and giving you the Information I had received, I consider myself as having only discharged the Duties of Justice and of Friendship.

I am sorry for the Attack you have had of the Ague and wishing you a perfect Recovery. I am, etc.

### To JOSEPH TRUMBULL

Head Quarters, New York, June 9, 1776.

Sir: I herewith transmit you the Resolutions of Congress for several Augmentations of the Army.

With Respect to Canada, I must inform you, that the last Accounts abound with Complaints of the deplorable Scarcity of Provisions which our Men labour under and mention the Impossibility of procuring Relief in that Colony. You will, therefore, with all Expedition, forward a Supply of Meat and Flour (particularly of the latter) to Albany.

As there is a Reinforcement of six Thousand Men shortly to be sent to Canada, there is a Prospect of the Want of Necessaries being still increased; in making Provision for the Troops already there, you must have a View to the Augmentation, which, I fear, will be sent before any Preparation can be made for them, by Mr. Price.

As to the flying Camp, it is probable, it's first Station will be in the Neighbourhood of Amboy. I am &c.

P. S. I am informed, that several Merchants are about to purchase Salt Pork for Exportation, and I would recommend it to you, immediately to apply to the Provincial Congress to take some Measures to prevent them; as there is not only a Probability that it may fall into the Hands of the Enemy, but we may ere long experience the Want of it ourselves.

### *To THE PRESIDENT OF CONGRESS

New York, June 10, 1776.

Sir: Since I did myself the honor of Writing to you Yesterday, I have had the satisfaction of seeing, (and for a few Minutes conversing) with Mr. Chase and Mr. Carroll from Canada; their Acct. of our Troops, and the situation of our Affairs in that department cannot possibly surprize you more than it has done me; but I need not touch upon a Subject which you will be so well informd of from the fountain head; nor shou'd I have given you the trouble of a Letter by this days Post but for the distraction which seems to prevail in the Commissary's department (as well as others in that Quarter) the Necessity of having it under one general direction; and the dissatisfaction of Col. Trumbell at the allowance made him by Congress (as an equivalent for his trouble). With respect to this particular matter, I can only say that I think he is a Man well cut out for the business; and that where a Shilling is saved in the Pay, a pound may be lost by Mismanagement in the Office; and that his resignation at this time (I mean this Campaign) may possibly, be attended with fatal Consequences; I therefore humbly submit to Congress the propriety of handsomely rewarding those Gentlemen who hold such very important, troublesome, and hazardous Offices, as Commissary and Quarter Master.[47]

In speaking to the former about the Supplies necessary for the Troops to be raiz'd; he informd me that the quantity of Salt Provisions, which was Shipping from hence might render his attempts to do it, precarious; in consequence of which I desired him to lay the matter before the Convention of this Colony, which he will do this day; but in the mean while desired Congress might be informd of the matter which I cannot better do than in his own Words, Inclosed, and submit the consideration of it to the Wisdom of that honourable body.

To Congress I also submit the Propriety of keeping the two Continental Battalions (under the Comd. of Colonels Shae[48] and McGaw[49]) at Philadelphia, when there is the greatest probability of a speedy attack upon this place from the Kings Troops; the Incouragements given by Gov. Tryon to the disaffected, which are circulated, no one can well tell how; the Movements of these kind of People which are more easy to perceive than describe; the confident report which is said to have come immediately from Govr. Tryon, and brought by a Frigate from Hallifax that the Troops at that place were Imbarking for this, added to a thousand Incidental Circumstances, trivial in themselves, but strong from comparison, leaves not a doubt upon my Mind but that Troops are hourly expected at the Hook.

I had no doubt when I left this City, for Philadelphia, but that some measures would have been taken to secure the suspected, and dangerous Persons of this Government before now,

---

[47] A copy of Trumbull's letter to Congress on the subject of his pay and suggesting a commission on his purchases is in the *Papers of the Continental Congress*. Instead of the commission, Congress raised his pay to $150 a month. (See *Journals of the Continental Congress*, June 17, 1776.)

[48] Col. John Shee, of the Third Pennsylvania Regiment.

[49] Col. Robert Magaw, of the Fifth Pennsylvania Regiment.

and left Orders for the Military to give every aid to the Civil Power: But, the Subject is delicate, and nothing is done in it: we may therefore have Internal, as well as external Enemies to contend with. I have the honor, etc.

### To JAMES BOWDOIN

New York, June 10, 1776.

Sir: Congress having requested my attendance in Philadelphia, I was in that City when your letter of the 11th. ulto. came to this place; this day's post therefore affords me the first opportunity of acknowledging the receipt of it.

I am hopeful that you applied to General Ward and have received all the assistance that Mr. Machin[50] could give in determining upon the practicability of cutting a canal between Barnstable and Buzzards Bay ere this, as the great demand we have for engineers in this department, Canada &c. has obliged me to order Mr. Machin hither to assist in that branch of business.

I thank you most heartily for your kind congratulations on the departure of the troops from Boston and am, etc.[51]

### To MAJOR PETER SCHUYLER[52]

Head Quarters, New York, June 10, 1776.

Sir: Immediately upon Receipt of this Order, you are to repair to Long Island, and take upon you the Command of three Companies belonging to your Regiment, posted towards the East End thereof, for the Defence of the Inhabitants, Protection of the Stock &c. To effect these Ends, you are to use every Means in your Power; as it is of great Importance to prevent the Enemy

---

[50] Lieut. Thomas Machin, of Knox's artillery. He was, later, captain-lieutenant and captain, Second Continental Artillery.

[51] The text is from the Toner Transcripts in the Library of Congress.

[52] Major of the Third New York Regiment.

from obtaining Supplies of fresh Provisions, and other Necessaries. You are also to prevent, as far as in your Power lies, all Kind of Correspondence and Intercourse between the Inhabitants and the Enemy, seizing upon and carrying before the Committees of Safety for Trial all those who shall be detected in such infamous Practices.

You are to see, that your Men are kept close to their Duty, and not suffered under any Pretence to be absent on Furlough, but in Cases of great and real Necessity, and then, that not more than two at a Time from each Company, be indulged.

You are to view the Men and inspect their Arms so soon as you arrive at their respective Posts, and make exact Return thereof.

Make your Quarters as centrical as you can and advise me from Time to Time of all remarkable Occurrences.

## *To WILLIAM BEDLOW, AND THE OTHER COMMISSIONERS AT THE FORTS MONTGOMERY AND CONSTITUTION[53]

June, 10, 1776.

Gentn: Unacquainted as I am with the Situation of the Posts in the Highlands, I can do no more than desire you will pursue, and with as much Dispatch as possible, the Plan of Work pointed out in the within Directions. I am, Gentn., etc.

## To GOVERNOR JONATHAN TRUMBULL

New York, June 10, 1776.

Sir: Before this, I expect you have received the Resolve of Congress for augmenting our Army here, and in Canada, with their requisition for the Quota of Men to be furnished by your

---

[53] The commissioners had been appointed by the New York Provincial Congress. They were William Bedlow and Jonathan Lawrence at Fort Constitution and Thomas Palmer and Gilbert Livingston at Fort Montgomery. They had written Washington (June 9) asking for decisions on a number of questions. A copy of their letter is in the *Washington Papers,* but the directions referred to in his letter are not found.

Colony; I must beg leave to add, that, from intelligence I have just received, and a Variety of Circumstances combining to Confirm it, Genl. Howe, with the Fleet from Halifax, or some other Armament, is hourly expected at the Hook, with designs, doubtless, to make an Impression here, and possess themselves of this Colony, of the last Importance to us, in the present controversy. Our Works are extensive and many, and the Troops here but few for their defence; being greatly reduced by the Regiments detached on the Canada Expedition. In this critical conjuncture of Affairs, the Experience I have had, of your Zeal and readiness to assist the Common cause, induces me to request the most speedy and early Succour, that can be obtained from your Colony, and that the Militia be forwarded one Battalion after another, as fast as they can possibly be raised; without waiting to make up the whole complement to be furnished for this Place, before any of them March. I would advise, that they come properly provided with Field and other officers, and that the person appointed by the Colony to Command the whole, be here a day or two before them, to receive his Orders, and be in readiness to take the Command on their Arrival. It will be proper too, that Notice be sent a day or two before their Coming, that provision may be made for furnishing and disposing of them in proper places.

I have wrote a Similar Letter to the Jersey Convention, praying Aid from them. I am, &c.

## GENERAL ORDERS

Head Quarters, New York, June 10, 1776.
Parole Bedford.    Countersign Cumberland.

The Brigadier Generals are requested to make their different Brigades, perfectly acquainted with their several alarm posts, and that they pay particular attention to the men's arms, and see that they are in perfect good fighting order.

The Colonels, or commanding Officers of Regiments, from which men were taken, to compose His Excellency The Commander in Chief's guard, are not to include them in their future Returns, or Abstracts, after the month of March, they being consider'd as a distinct Corps

### GENERAL ORDERS
Head Quarters, New York, June 11, 1776.
Parole Cambridge.   Countersign Dorchester.

A working party of fifty men, to attend at the Laboratory, to morrow morning, at Six o'Clock; The Asst. Qr. Mr. General will direct them where to work.

Daniel Claflin of Capt. Bolsters[54] Company in Col Learneds Regt. tried at the General Court Martial whereof Col Nixon is President, for "Desertion" is found guilty and sentenced to be whipped Thirty-nine Lashes on his bare back for the same.

William Camp of Capt. Moores[55] Company, in Col Prescot's Regt. tried at the above Court Martial for "Desertion" is found guilty and sentenced to be whipped Thirty-nine Lashes on his bare back.

Ebenezer Sawyer of Capt. Moore's Company, in Col Prescots Regiment, tried at the above Court Martial for Desertion, is found guilty and sentenced to be whipped Twenty Lashes on his bare back for the same.

The General approves of the above Sentences, and orders them severally to be put in execution, at the usual time and place.

### GENERAL ORDERS
Head Quarters, New York, June 12, 1776.
Parole Dublin.   Countersign Essex.

Colonel Nixon President, of the present sitting General Court Martial, being to be called upon to give Evidence against a

---

[54] Capt. Isaac Bolster, of the Third Continental Infantry.
[55] Capt. Joseph Moore, of the Seventh Continental Infantry.

prisoner, to be tried this day, at said Court, is therefore discharged from his duty as President of said Court, and Colonel Parsons (the next Colonel in rotation) is to succeed him as President of said General Court Martial.

Col Nixon, Col Varnum, and some other Colonels, in consequence of the orders of the 17th. ultimo, having given in a Return of their Arms to the Adjutant General's office about the time General Gates, set off for Philadelphia; and the same having been lost, or overlooked, were called upon the 8th. Instant for neglect in this particular, the mistake therefore being cleared up; The General does with pleasure acquit them of a breach of duty, in this instance, and feels a satisfaction in finding those Gentlemen unwilling to labour under a suspicion of neglect of their duty, as nothing but an attentive observance of orders, can enable the Commander in Chief to govern Troops, and preserve that regularity and discipline, which is necessary to distinguish a well conducted army, from an unruly Rabble.

'Tis therefore hoped and expected, that officers of every Rank and Denomination, will pride themselves in the execution of the orders which falls within their department to obey.

No sick person is to have leave of absence from Camp, 'till the Director General of the Hospital certifies the necessity of it (and the lenght of time requisite for such absence) to the Brigadier of the Brigade he belongs to, who in that case is to grant the permission. All persons absent otherwise than this, will be considered as deserters; and those now out to be recalled.

## To LUND WASHINGTON

New York, June 12, 1776.

(Forged Letter) [56]

---

[56] The first of the "Spurious Letters." They were published in London in 1776 by J. Bew in a small pamphlet under the title of "Letters from General Washington, to several of his Friends in the year 1776," etc. Handbills of one of the letters therefrom to Mrs. Washington were struck off by Rivington, in New York, as soon as the

## To THE PRESIDENT OF CONGRESS

Head Quarters, June 13, 1776.

Sir: I have the Honor of transmitting to Congress, a Letter which came by Express last Night from General Schuyler inclosing the Copy of a Letter to him from Colonel Kirkland.[57] I have likewise inclosed the Copy of one directed to General Putnam or the Commanding Officer at New York.

The Representation contained in these Letters have induced me, without waiting the determination of Congress, to direct General Schuyler, immediately to commence a Treaty with the Six Nations, and to engage them in our Interest, upon the best Terms he and his Colleagues in commission can procure, and, I trust the Urgency of the Occasion will justify my Proceedings to the Congress. The necessity for decision and dispatch in all our Measures, in my Opinion, becomes every day more and more apparent.

The Express Mr. Bennet,[58] was overtaken at Albany by General Schuyler, who had received Intelligence at Fort George, that a considerable Body of Indians were coming Down the

pamphlet reached America. A photostat copy of one of these bills is in the Library of Congress (Manuscripts Division). A complete reprint of the London pamphlet was also issued in America in 1778, and Hildeburn claims it as a Philadelphia imprint. The letters were plainly political propaganda put out by the London publisher, as much, it seems, for profit as for mischief-making, though the influences behind the move have not been traced. In America the reprint was made in the hope of creating discord between the New England and Southern Colonies. Washington attributed them to John Randolph, the last royalist attorney general of Virginia. The English magazines of 1776 expressed doubt of the authenticity of the letters and their hoped-for effect fell flat. In 1796 these letters were printed again, in New York, under the title "Epistles, Domestic, Confidential and Official from General Washington," to injure Washington's political standing, and he then took the trouble to refute their authenticity in a letter to Timothy Pickering, pointing out their discrepancies at some length. (See Mar. 3, 1797, *post.*)

The various letters will be noted under their dates, as above, to clear up the matter for the many people who often are misled about these epistles. As full an explanation as can be made will be found in The George Washington Scandals, by John C. Fitzpatrick, in *Scribner's Magazine* for April, 1927, and reprinted by the Washington Society of Alexandria, 1929.

[57] Lieut. Col. Peter Kirkland, of the New York Militia.
[58] Elijah Bennett, a trusted express rider of Congress.

Mohawk River under the conduct of Sir John Johnson, the General's extreme hurry would not allow him to write; but it seems his Intention is to collect at Albany a sufficient Force to oppose Sir John. I have given him my Opinion, that Col. Dayton's Regiment[59] should be employed in that service and to secure the Post, where Fort Stanwix formerly stood.

In consequence of an Information that several Merchants were exporting salted Beef and Pork from this place, I requested the Commissary General to make Application to the Provincial Congress for a restraint to be laid on the Exportation of these Articles, as I apprehended not only that the Enemy might receive supplies by the Capture of our Vessels, but that our People might shortly experience a scarcity; The Provincial Congress have accordingly made a Resolution, (a copy of which is inclosed) to stop Exportation for fourteen Days; they expect Congress will, in the meantime, frame some general Regulations on this Head; they are unwilling they say to subject their constituents to partial Restraint.

I once mentioned to Congress, that I thought a War Office extremely necessary, and they seemed inclined to institute one for our Army, but the Affair seems to have been since dropt; give me leave again to insist on the Utility and Importance of such an Establishment; the more I reflect upon the Subject, the more I am convinced of its necessity, and that Affairs can never properly be conducted without it.[60]

---

[59] Col. Elias Dayton's Third New Jersey regiment.

[60] "The establishing a War Office is a new and great event in the History of America, and will doubtless be attended with essential Advantages when properly conducted and inspected. I hope the Committee will be ready, in a few days to enter upon the Execution of their Duty."—*Hancock to Washington*, June 14, 1776. Hancock's letter is in the *Washington Papers*.

The membership of the Board of War was, at first, John Adams, Roger Sherman, Benjamin Harrison, James Wilson, and Edward Rutledge. Richard Peters, of Pennsylvania, was appointed secretary of the board. (See *Journals of the Continental Congress*, June 12 and 13, 1776.)

T'is with Pleasure I receive the Resolve inclosed, in your favor of the 11th. instant; one considerable Ground of Dissatisfaction in the Army is thereby removed.

I have employed Persons in Building the Gondolas and Rafts, which the Congress thought necessary for the defence of this Place, and in conjunction with the Provincial Congress, have determined to sink Cheveaux de Frizes one of which is already begun. I am, etc.[61]

## To SAMUEL CHASE

Head Quarters, New York, June 13, 1776.

Sir: I am to inform you that Colonel Nicholson,[62] of whose Character and Conduct you have received an unfavorable Impression, is in Town; he comes for the purpose of raising Recruits for a New York Battalion, to the Command of which he has been nominated. When I intimated to him, that from certain representations I had received, I judged him very unfit for the Employment, he insisted upon a Court of Enquiry to manifest his Innocence, and clear his reputation. Now Sir, as I am not well apprized of any particular charge to be exhibited against him, I must request you to acquaint me with what you know of the matter, and what persons it will be proper to call in as Witnesses; he may otherwise be acquited by the Court (when there are just Grounds of Accusation) merely for want of Testimony. I am, etc.

## To MAJOR GENERAL PHILIP SCHUYLER

New York, June 13,[63] 1776.

Dear Sir: I last Night received by Mr. Bennet, your Favor of the 8th. Inst., addressed to General Putnam, or the Officer

---

[61] In the writing of Alexander Contee Hanson.
[62] Col. John Nicholson. He was colonel of a New York regiment and, according to Heitman, colonel of a Continental regiment from March to November, 1776. His petition, dated June 12, 1776, is in the *Washington Papers*.
[63] Ford prints this letter under date of June 17.

commanding here, covering one for Congress, with a Copy of Colo. Kirkland's to you, both of which I shall immediately forward to Philadelphia.

In Consequence of your former Letters, the Commissary has been directed to continue Supplies of Provisions. I shall repeat the Direction, and doubt not of his Exertions in this Instance. If it's Arrival at Albany ceased for a Time, it might be owing to the Accounts received, that a good Deal, particularly Flour, might be had in Canada. I will speak to him about the Expenditure of Pork here, and request that no more be used than he may find necessary, that there may be a larger Quantity for the Canada Department.

I will also speak to the Qr. Mr. Genl. to provide and forward all the Clothing he can get, as soon as possible.

As to intrenching Tools, they are extremely scarce, and what we have, far too few for the Works carrying, and proper to be carried on for the Defence of this Place. However I will try to furnish you with a few more, and wish your Endeavours to purchase what you can from the Country People. Many of them perhaps will part with a Spade or Pick Ax, and some with both, and though many may not be collected in that Way; what are, will be of great Service.

If the Accounts of Colo. Bedel's and Major Butterfield's Conduct be true, they have certainly acted a Part deserving the most exemplary Notice. I hope you will take proper Measures and have good Courts appointed to bring them, and every other Officer that has been or shall be guilty of Mal-Conduct, to Trial, that they may be punished according to their Offences. Our Misfortunes at the Cedars were occasioned, as it is said, intirely by their base and cowardly Behaviour, and cannot be ascribed to any other Cause.

In my Letter of the 7th. which will have reached you ere this, I inclosed a Resolve of Congress for engaging the Indians, not more than two Thousand, in our Service. This will indicate to you, their Opinion, and knowing their Sentiments fully upon this Head, I cannot but advise, that you forthwith hold a Conference with the six Nations, and any others, you with your Brother Commissioner, may think necessary; and form with them an Alliance on such Terms and Conditions, as shall seem most likely to secure their Interest and Friendship, without waiting the further Directions of Congress. The Situation of our Affairs will not suffer the Delay, and I am persuaded your Conduct, and the Speech you intend to deliver the Sachems, will meet their Approbation and Thanks. I think that Part of it which mentions the Time and Place of our taking Post, might be omitted; but this I leave to you. I shall inform Congress of what I have wrote you on this Subject, and of the verbal Intelligence you sent me by Bennet from Albany, when you overtook him, respecting the Indians coming down the Mohawk River under Sir John Johnson, and of your preparing to resist them. I sincerely wish you Success and that their first Incursions and Attempts against us may be attended with their intire Defeat. It will be necessary to employ Colonel Dayton and his Regiment in this Service and in securing a Post where Fort Stanwix formerly stood, which I esteem of much Importance; But I submit it to you, who are much better acquainted with that Country than I am; whether, previous to that, it will not be necessary and essential that a Post be established lower down, somewhere about the Falls below the German Flatts, to secure our Communication with that Garrison. Should this not be done, will it not be in the Power of the Savages to come between that and our Frontiers and intercept all Supplies of Men and Provisions going thither.

I observe you esteem the Ground opposite to Ticonderoga to be more advantageous for a Post against the Enemy. Messrs. Chase and Carroll had told me the same. I should think, therefore, that the Place most capable of Defence, and having the greatest Advantages, should be improved and necessary Works thrown up, with the utmost Dispatch. But will not both be best? Cannot Ticonderoga be kept and this improved and maintained at the same Time? I must submit this to you, and refer you to my Letter of the 9th. upon the Subject of fortifying all the Posts, and about the Engineers. If you know of any Persons who can be of Service in that Way, do employ them. I know of none myself or have I one that I can possibly spare.

I have been applied to by Colo. Nicholson, (who says he was appointed by Congress to the Command of a Regiment to be raised out of two Battalions of York Troops that were in Canada last Year), for Instructions for that Purpose. As this concerns the Department more immediately under your Directions, and with which you must be much better acquainted than I am, I did not think it right to give him any Direction about it, but if the Fact is so, desire that you will give him such Orders, that the Views of Congress may be carried into Execution, as you judge necessary.

In like Manner, I have had several Applications from Officers coming from the Canada Department, for Pay that became due there, which I did not conceive myself at Liberty to comply with; being ignorant of their Appointments or Services, and as they will perhaps apply to you for Certificates to lay before me, I wish you to be very explicit, as to the Time of their being in Office and from which their Pay is due. I am, etc.

## To BRIGADIER GENERAL JOHN SULLIVAN

New York, June 13, 1776.

Dear Sir: Having received Intelligence of the unfortunate Death of General Thomas, occasioned by the small Pox he had taken, the Command of the Army in Canada devolves on you.

I am therefore, to request your most strenuous Exertions to retrieve our Circumstances in that Quarter, from the melancholy Situation they are now in, and for performing the arduous Task of bringing Order out of Confusion. I confess there is more Room for Enterprize and Activity than I could wish; but then you will remember that you and your Colleagues will be entitled to the grateful Thanks of your Country, in Proportion to the Services you render.

Being extremely hurried in sending Dispatches to Congress and General Schuyler, I have not Time to write you so fully, as I could wish and therefore shall only add my Request, that you from Time to Time make me regular Returns of the Strength of the Army, military Stores, and any material Occurrence, and wishing you and your Brothers, under the Direction of a gracious Providence, to lead your Army to Conquest and Victory. I am, etc.

## To THE NEW YORK LEGISLATURE

Head Quarters, New York, June 13, 1776.

Sirs: I am informed that a Number of persons on Long Island (by character not the most friendly to the cause of the United Colonies) have in their hands considerable Quantities of Pork and other provisions; which they refuse to part with for Continental Bills they may have other reasons for their Conduct, still more detrimental and therefore I must beg the Interposition of your Congress in this Matter, so as to prevent the evils which are much to be apprehended. The Commissary General will purchase all their Provisions, at good prices and give them Continental Bills in pay; Gold and Silver he has none. The provisions are wanted for the Army, and those who are wellwishers to the Cause, and live in exposed Situations, will undoubtedly be glad to dispose of them; the disadvantages which may result to the Public, by leaving them in the

Hands of Men of a different complexion, are too obvious to need animadversion.[64]

I have your report respecting the obstruction of the navigation of the Hudson's River under Consideration, and am pursuing measures to carry it into Execution, with all possible Dispatch. With great Respect, I am &c.

## GENERAL ORDERS

Head Quarters, New York, June 13, 1776.
Parole Epsom.    Countersign Falmouth.

The party at Kingsbridge to be reinforced with one Serjeant, one Corporal and twenty men, and a guard from the above party is to be mounted over the Cannon beyond Kingsbridge, who are to be exceedingly careful that no damage is done them.

## GENERAL ORDERS

Head Quarters, New York, June 14, 1776.
Parole Falkland.    Countersign Georgia.

The great extensiveness of the Fortifications and works, requiring a greater number of Artillery-men than are at present in the Artillery Regiment, The General, in order to remedy the deficiency, and forward the service, directs, that four able bodied, active men be pitched upon, in each Company of every Battalion, now here (the Riflemen excepted) for the purpose above mentioned.

These men are to have their Arms, Ammunition and accoutrements; in the several Regiments they go from, to supply the deficiency, in each company—they are to join the Artillery

---

[64] The legislature answered (June 15) that it depended on the Commissary General to obtain the provisions desired and that it had "in contemplation some general and effectual measures for securing the live stock in certain parts of the Colony for the benefit of the Army." Its letter is in the *Washington Papers*.

Regiment and do duty in that Corps under the Command of Col Knox, but are to be continued upon the pay and Muster Rolls of their respective regiments.

These additional Artillery men, are to be delivered to Col Knox with their necessaries at the Bowling-Green on Sunday morning at Six o'clock—The Adjutants of the different Regiments are to attend with the men and a Roll of their names at the hour above-mentioned.

The Engineers are to take an exact account of all the intrenching Tools (not in the Quarter Masters Store) in and about New York, on Long Island, Governors Island, Powles-hook and Horns-hook—they are then to proportion the tools to the different works, and take the overlooker at each place, his receipt for the number deliver'd, calling upon him once a week regularly, to account for them; the overlooker is to receive and deliver the tools regularly, every evening and morning, as he will be made accountable for them.

The Engineers are to consider this as a standing order and invariably to pursue it.

All the Carpenters, Ship-Carpenters and Joiners, in the first, second and fourth Brigades, with a proportion of officers, to parade to morrow morning at Six oClock, before the Deputy Quarter-Master General's Office, near the Liberty-pole in the Common; and there take their orders from the Quarter-Master-General.

One Capt. and fifty good ax-men, with four days provision to parade at the same time and place; and to take their orders also from the Q. M. General.

Lieut. Chapman[65] of Col Webb's Regiment, under an Arrest for "refusing to do his duty" is to be tried by the General Court Martial now sitting—The Adjutant of that Regiment and the other evidences are to attend the court.

---

[65] Lieut. Alpheus Chapman, of the Nineteenth Continental Infantry.

The five Companies of Col Wayne's Regiment, on Long Island are to be mustered to morrow afternoon at four o'clock near General Greene's Head Quarters.

## To THE PRESIDENT OF THE CONGRESS

New York, June 14, 1776.

Sir: I herewith transmit you copies of a Letter from General Schuyler and of its several Inclosures, which I received since I had the honor of addressing you Yesterday. From these you will learn General Thomas died the 2d. Instant and the Apprehensions of our Frontier friends in this Colony, that our Savage Foes are meditating an Attack against them.

I must beg leave to refer you to a paragraph in the copy of General Schuyler's letter to General Putnam or the commanding officer here, inclosed in mine of the 13th. Instt. where he requests a supply of Clothing to be sent for the Army in Canada. As there is but little or no probability of getting it here, I shall be glad to know whether there will be any chance of procuring it in Philadelphia, and if it should be sent thro' the hands of the Quarter Master here, to what account it is to be charged.

I was last evening favored with yours of the 11th. inst., and hope the two Battalions which Congress have ordered from Philadelphia to the defence of this place, will come provided with Arms: If they do not, they will be of no service, as there are more Troops here already than are Armed.

From General Schuyler's Letter, he has in View the taking post where Fort Stanwix formerly stood. I wrote him I thought it prudent, previous to that, to secure a post lower down about the Falls below the German Flats least the Savages should possess themselves of the Country thereabouts, and prevent such supplies of Men and Money as may be necessary to send there in future.—he says he is in want of Cannon and Ammunition, but has expressed himself so ambiguously, that I am at a loss to know, whether he meant what he has said as an Application or not, this being the only Intelligence on the Subject, and the first mention of his wants. I have desired him to explain the matter, and in his future requisitions for necessaries, to be more certain and explicit. In the mean time I shall send some Intrenching Tools, and enquire whether any Cannon can be spared from hence. I am &ca.[66]

## To MAJOR GENERAL PHILIP SCHUYLER

New York, June 14, 1776.

Dear Sir: I was favoured with yours of the 10th. Inst.[67] with its Inclosures by last Night's Post. The Stroke meditating by the Indians against our Frontier Inhabitants, is what I have long thought would happen, as they were not engaged in our Interest. But I am in full Hopes you will be able to repel their hostile Designs, and convince them of their Imprudence in joining our Enemies, without the least Cause of Quarrel.

As to intrenching Tools, I shall direct the Qr. Master to send up some, as early as possible; but in Respect to what you say about Cannon and Ammunition, I am at a Loss whether it is intended as an Application or not. I do not know, that any of the former have been requested, but for the armed Vessels in the Lakes; or of the latter, but what has been sent for the Canada Expedition. I wish you to explain the Matter, and that your Requisitions for Necessaries may be always certain and explicit, as to Quantity and Quality.

As the Militia to reinforce the Army in Canada, and for keeping open our Communication with that Province or a Part of them, will probably be on their March before long. I think it

---

[66] In the writing of Robert Hanson Harrison.
[67] Schuyler's letter, dated June 10, 1776, is in the *Washington Papers*.

will be advisable for you to write the different Governors furnishing them, of the Routs they should take, and of the Places proper for, their Rendezvous.

I wrote you Yesterday and on the 9th. Inst. to which I refer you for full Answer to all yours between the 21st. Ulto. and your last. I am, &c.

## To COLONEL JAMES CLINTON

Head Quarters, New York, June 14, 1776.

Sir: You are to repair to Fort Montgomery and take upon you the Command of the Posts in the Highlands. Use every Means in your Power to provide your Regiment with Arms fit for Service; As one Step towards which, endeavour to employ an Armourer or two, or more, as the Case may require.

Use every possible Diligence in forwarding the Works at Forts Montgomery and Constitution, agreeable to late Directions given to Mr. Bedlow, who will furnish you with the same: as it is proposed by the Provincial Congress of New York to recall their Commissioners from those Posts, and leave the Care of them altogether to the Commanding Officer of the Continental Forces and his Order.

As these are or may become Posts of infinite Importance, especially the lower one; I cannot sufficiently impress upon you the Necessity of putting them into a fit Posture of Defence, without Delay. I have desired that a Battalion or at least five Hundred of the York Militia, may be ordered to reinforce those Garrisons, as well for the Purpose of Defence, as to assist in the Work. These are also to be under your Command. The whole are to be kept close to Duty, and not suffered to be absent on Furlough, but in Case of real Necessity, and then not more than two at a Time are to be absent from a Company at once.

Review the Men, inspect the Arms &c. and make a Report of the State of Things, so soon as you get to these Posts. Your Lieutt. Colo. Livingston[68] is to be sent to this Place, in Order to proceed to Long Island, to take Charge of the Remainder of your Regiment, posted toward the East End thereof.

Inform me, if there are Barracks or Houses convenient to the Forts Montgomery and Constitution, in which the Militia ordered there, can be lodged.

Make Weekly Returns of your Strength, and advise me regularly of all Occurrences of any Kind, of Importance.

## To JOSHUA WENTWORTH

New York, June 15, 1776.

Sir: I received yours of the 1st. Inst. and am to inform you, your Letters of the 15th. and 22nd. of April, advising of the Capture of the Brig Elizabeth by Commodore Manley, were put into the Hands of Mr. Moylan to answer; but by some Means or other were not; nor can they be found. It will be, therefore, necessary to acquaint me again with the Contents, if you esteem my Answer to them material.

I have, agreeable to your Request, transmitted you Copies of such Resolves of Congress respecting your Department as are in my Hands. They will point out the Line of Conduct to be observed in general Cases, which I apprehend must be pursued. But if there is any Thing particular in the Capture you mention, which is not provided for, it will be proper that it should be forwarded me, in Order to my referring it to Congress for their Opinion.

It is likely the Memorial you mention, if presented, has already occasioned them to determine upon the Matter. If they have not,

---

[68] Lieut. Col. Henry Beekman Livingston.

and I find it necessary, I shall transmit them such a Representation of the Circumstances of this Capture, as you may send me, not intending myself to point out any Rule of Decision not authorized by Congress. I am, etc.

## GENERAL ORDERS

Head Quarters, New York, June 16, 1776.
Parole Hanover.  Countersign Ireland.

The Continental Congress have been pleased to come to the following Resolution:

"In Congress, June 10, 1776.

"Resolved: That the pay of the Continental Troops, in the middle department be henceforth the same, as that of the Troops in the Eastern departments."

The General therefore directs, that when the Pay Abstracts for any of the Corps of the middle Department are made out, that the Colonels, or commanding Officers thereof, will take care that the pay of the men, from the 10th. of June, be the same as those of the Eastern Regiment.

The Brigadiers are to make themselves well acquainted with the nature, and situation of the Grounds, on the North and East Rivers, for some considerable distance about the City, with the best approaches to them, that they may know how to occupy these grounds, to the best advantage if occasion should require, and they are to cause the same to be done by their respective officers in turn.

Great and crying Complaints being made against the Armourers, not only for their Idleness, but the deceitful manner in which their work is executed—The General does in explicit terms assure them, that if any further Complaint of either should be exhibited, he will punish them in a most examplary manner; of this the Superintendent of that branch of business is desired, to make them fully acquainted.

Lieut. Walker[69] of Col Nixon's Regiment, tried at the General Court-Martial, whereof Col Parsons is president, on a charge exhibited against him by Capt. Butler of said Regiment for "maliciously and falsly accusing him of high Crimes and misdemeanours, and in consequence of which, procuring him, the said Capt. Butler, to be arrested and tried at a late General Court-Martial, by which he was honorably acquitted."

The Court after mature consideration are of opinion, that Lieut. Walker had sufficient grounds for exhibiting a Complaint against Capt. Butler, and that he is not guilty of maliciously, and falsely accusing Capt. Butler, and therefore do acquit the prisoner of the charge against him.

The General approves of the above sentence past against Lieut. Walker, and orders him released from his arrest.

Bowers Laybourn, and Thomas Perry, both of Capt. Van Wyck's Company, and Col McDougall's Regiment, tried at the above Court-Martial for "Desertion," are found guilty and sentenced severally, to be whipped Thirty-nine Lashes each on his bare back, for their respective offences.

Henry Davis of Capt. Johnson's Company, Col. McDougall's Regiment tried at the above Court Martial for "Desertion" is found guilty of the same and sentenced to be whipped Thirty-Lashes on his bare back for said offence.

The General approves of the above sentences, and orders the corporal punishment to be executed at the usual time and place.

Lieut. Elijah Oakly of Capt. Stenrods Company, in Col. McDougall's Regiment, tried at the General Court Martial, whereof Col Nixon was President, for "assaulting and beating, without provocation, one Miss Patterson, an Inhabitant of the City of New York" The Court are of opinion that Lieut. Oakley is guilty of the charge brot. against him, and that he has behaved unworthy the character of a Gentleman and Officer; and the

---

[69] Lieut. Silas Walker, of the Fourth Continental Infantry.

Court adjudge that he, Lieut. Oakley, be cashiered for said offence, and further orders, that Twenty Dollars be stopped out of the prisoner Lieut. Oakley's pay (if so much be due to him) and be paid by way of damage to Miss Patterson.

The General approves of the sentence of the Court and orders that the Late Lieut. Oakley do immediately depart the camp.

Lieut. Chapman of Capt. Hale's[70] Company, and Col Webb's Regiment, tried at the General Court Martial whereof Col Parsons is President, for "Disobedience of orders, and refusing to do his duty"—The Court are of opinion that the charge is fully supported against the prisoner Lieut. Chapman, and adjudge that he be dismissed the Continental Army for said offence.

The General approves of the sentence of the Court Martial, against Lieut. Chapman, and orders that he be dismissed the Service, and depart the camp.

## To THE PRESIDENT OF CONGRESS

New York, June 16, 1776.

Sir: I do myself the honor to transmit Congress, a Copy of a Letter covering Copies of other Letters which I received Yesterday Evening from General Sullivan.

The Intelligence communicated by him is pleasing and Interesting, and such as may afford the greatest satisfaction; If the conduct the Canadians have discovered since his arrival among them is Ingenious and sincere. This Account is contradicted by General Arnold's Letter to General Schuyler, of which a Copy is also Transmitted.

General Sullivan mentions his having given Commissions to some of the Canadians, as a measure founded in necessity and requests my approbation of it; but not considering myself impowered to say any thing upon the Subject, it may not be

---

[70] Capt. Nathan Hale, of the Nineteenth Continental Infantry. He was captured by the British and hanged as a spy Sept. 22, 1776.

improper for Congress to give him their Opinion in this Instance. I have also inclosed Copies of General Schuyler's Letters, received at the same time. they contain Accounts respecting the Indians, variant from what were reported by Mr. Kirkland, but amounting to the same thing, the probability of the Savages attacking our Frontiers. By last night's post, I had information of a Capture made by our Armed Vessels, of one of the Transports, with a Company of Highlanders on board bound to Boston; The inclosed extract of Genl. Wards letter to me will give you the Intelligence more particularly. There are Accounts in the City mentioning other valuable prizes, but as General Ward has said nothing of them, I fear they want Authenticity.

I beg leave to mention that a further sum of Money will be wanted for our Military Chest by the time it can be sent; the inclosed Note from the Pay Master General shews the necessity for it and I may add, besides his estimate of Drafts to be made, there are the claims of the Eastern Troops at Boston, for three or four Month's pay not included, and now due.

Col: McGaw is arrived with part of his Battalion and by Wednesday Evening the whole, both of his and Col: Shee's will be here as I am told.

As it is and may be of great Importance, to have a Communication with the Jerseys and Long Island, I have had several Flat Bottom Boats built for the purpose, and have thoughts of getting more for Passaic and Hackensack Rivers where they may be equally Necessary for the Transporting our Army, or part of it occasionally, or succours coming to or going from it. I am etc.[71]

## To MAJOR GENERAL ARTEMAS WARD

New York, June 16, 1776.

Sir: I am now to acknowledge the Receipt of your Favors of the 27th. Ulto. and of the 3rd. and 6th. Inst., and in Answer to

---

[71] In the writing of Robert Hanson Harrison.

the First, think you was right in your Direction to Mr. Bartlett, about the Brigantine Hannah, as Mr. Morris had wrote for one.

The two Schooners, considering their Force and Number of Men, certainly behaved extremely well in repelling the Attack, made by such a Number of Boats, and it is only to be lamented that the Affair was attended with the Death of Captain Mugford. He seemed to deserve a better Fate.[72]

The Determination of the Court of Inquiry upon Colonel Varnum's Complaint, transmitted in that of the 3rd., is very different from what he expected, or I imagined it would be, from his State of the Case. Whether it is right or wrong, it is not in my Power to determine, as the Evidence which was before them is not inserted in the Proceedings, which ought to have been, as I at this Distance can have no other Means to warrant me, either in confirming, or rejecting the Sentence. I cannot but add that it seems extraordinary to me and exceedingly strange, that Captain Lane[73] should have been at so much Trouble and Expence to get the Men, without having a Right to them. For which Reason, to discountenance a Practice extremely pernicious in its Nature, of one Officer's trying to take away, and seduce the Men of another, and on Account of the Imperfection in the Proceedings, in not stating the Matter fully and the whole Evidence. The Complaint should be reheard, and every thing appertaining to it, the Manner of Inlistment &c. particularly specified for me to found my Judgment on.

---

[72] Capt. Thomas Mugford, of the armed schooner *Franklin*.

"The intrepid Captain Mugford fell a little before the Enemy left his Schooner, he was ran through with a lance while he was cutting off the hands of the Pirates as they were attempting to board him; and it is said that with his own hands he cut off five pair of theirs; no other Man was either killed or wounded on board the Franklin."— *Artemas Ward to Washington*, May 20, 1776. This letter is in the *Washington Papers*.

[73] Capt. John Lane, of the Ninth Continental Infantry. On June 26 a court of inquiry sat on his complaint against Lieut. Daniel Merrill, of the Eighteenth Continental Infantry, charged with improperly enlisting men. A court of inquiry had already been held on Merrill (May 24) on a similar complaint from Varnum. The proceedings of both courts are in the *Washington Papers*, but Col. James Mitchell Varnum's petition has not been found.

The Arms &c. which you sent to Norwich as mentioned in the Invoice, contained in that of the 6th., are not arrived. The Number of Carbines is only half of what General Putnam wrote for, as I have been informed, and it is less by three Hundred, than I directed to be sent in my Letter from Philadelphia, of the 28th. Ulto. This, I suppose had not come to Hand, when you wrote, as you have not acknowledged the Receipt of it.

I have inclosed two Letters for Major Small and Charles Proctor Esqr. supposed to be at Hallifax; which being wrote with a Design to procure the Inlargement of Captn. Proctor, a Prisoner on Board the Mercury Man of War, or induce them to intercede for a more humane Treatment to be shewn him, I request you to forward by the first Opportunity, by Way of Nova Scotia.

I am this Moment favoured with yours of the 9th. Inst., advising me of the Capture made by the armed Vessels, of one of the Transports with a Company of Highlanders on Board, and I flatter myself if our Vessels keep a good Lookout, as the whole Fleet are bound to Boston which sailed with her, that more of them will fall into our Hands. This is a further Proof, that Government expected General Howe was still in Boston.

I am extremely sorry that your Health is more and more impaired, and having heard by a Letter from Colo. Hancock, that Mr. Whitcombe, Colo. Whitcomb's Brother, is appointed a Brigr. General,[74] I shall order him to relieve you, as soon as I am informed that he accept his Commission; and if he does, you may immediately call him to your Assistance before I am certified of his Acceptance. This will ease you of some Trouble, 'till I can regulate a few Matters of Importance here, which I hope to do in a little Time. I am, etc.

---

[74] John Whitcomb, brother of Col. Asa Whitcomb, of the Sixth Continental Infantry. At this time he was major general of Massachusetts Militia. He declined the offered brigadier general's commission in the Continental Army.

## To MAJOR GENERAL PHILIP SCHUYLER

New York, June 16, 1776.

Dear Sir: I received your several Favours of the 11th. continued to the 12th. and 12th. with a Copy of General Arnold's Letter.

The Return delivered you by General Wooster you have forgot to inclose.

The Account of Mr. Dean,[75] is variant from Colo. Kirklands; but yet they seem both to agree in the most material Points; vizt. That some Parts of our Frontiers are to feel the Effects of the Savage Resentment, which the Friends of Government have been industriously trying to call forth against us. You have done well in your Message to the six Nations. The sooner a Conference can be held the better, and I think the most vigorous Exertions necessary to secure a Post, as you mention where Fort Stanwix formerly stood, and below that as I intimated in my last. If you can effect these, I am hopeful all their Attempts in that Quarter will be unavailing.

I have ordered a Ton of Powder, half a Ton of Lead, five Thousand Flints, some Cannon, intrenching Tools, and a Dozen whip Saws and Files, to be immediately sent you; which you will receive in two or three Days, with a List of them and every other Article sent from hence at this Time.

I have inclosed you a Copy of an Invoice of Goods now in the Hands of Mr. Robert Henry, which he offered the Qr. Mr. Genl. this Week, on moderate Terms as the Qr. Master informs me. It will certainly be proper, that you purchase them or such of them as will suit the Army in Canada; and it will be less troublesome and expensive, than sending Articles from hence, supposing they can be procured. I wish you to get every Thing

---

[75] James Dean, or Deane, agent and interpreter for Indian affairs in the Northern Department.

you want, and that can be had, either in Albany, or it's Vicinity, rather than to send here for them, for I am really so immersed in Business, and have such a Variety of Things to attend to, that I scarcely know which Way to turn myself. Perhaps if you make strict Inquiry you may obtain not only more Goods but other Necessaries.

The Indians are here, just returned from Philadelphia. I will communicate to them your Wishes for their Return, and give Direction, that every Mark of Respect be shown them by those who go with Them.

I have requested the Pay-Master to procure, if possible, as much hard Money as will discharge Mr. Black's Claim. How he will succeed, I cannot tell. If he can get it, it shall be forwarded, as soon as a proper Conveyance can be had.

In Regard to a Person to superintend the Building of Gondolas, and other Carpenters to carry on the Work, I refer you to my Letter of the 9th. and shall only add, that they cannot be now had, every one qualified for the Business, being employed here.

The Intelligence contained in General Sullivan's Letter is extremely pleasing, and I sincerely wish his most sanguine Hopes may be more than answered. If the Affection of the Canadians can be engaged, and he seems to have no Doubt of it, it will be of much Importance, and probably the Means of our retrieving our Misfortunes in that Quarter.[76]

I find by General Arnolds Letter to General Sullivan; Colo. Bedel, Major Butterfield; and Captn. Young,[77] are gone to the Sorrel for Trial. If their Conduct was as base and infamous

---

[76] Considering the actual state of affairs in Canada, General Sullivan's letter was extraordinary. He described the situation in a most favorable light; yet 12 days afterwards the whole American army was driven out of the Province, which all the officers on the spot, except General Sullivan, had foreseen and predicted. This letter, dated June 5–6, 1776, is in the *Washington Papers*. It is printed in Sparks's *Letters to Washington*, vol. 1, p. 211.

[77] Capt. Samuel(?) Young, of Bedel's Rangers.

as represented, it will surely meet with an exemplary Punishment. Men who will not discharge the Duty they owe their Country from Principle, must be influenced to it by other Motives; or at least, be prevented from betraying our most valuable Rights by a cowardly and disgraceful Behaviour.

Inclosed you have an Extract of a Letter I received by last Night's Post from General Ward, from which we may reasonably conjecture, that the Rest of the Transports which sailed with the one taken, will not be long before they arrive. It seems evident they expected to find General Howe at Boston, and I am hopeful some others, under this Idea, will fall into our Hands.

There are also Accounts in Town of two or three valuable Prizes more, being taken to the Eastward, one with several light Cannon, another a West Indiaman homeward bound with a Quantity of Dollars and Sugars. But, I fear, tho' the Accounts seem particular, that they want Confirmation, as General Ward mentions nothing of them. I am, etc.

P. S. The Whip Saws, I fear, can't be got. The Qr. Master says he has tried without Success.

## To BRIGADIER GENERAL JOHN SULLIVAN

New York, June 16, 1776.

Dear Sir: I was favoured with yours of the 5th. and 6th. Inst. by Express Yesterday Evening from General Schuyler; and am exceedingly happy on Account of the agreeable and interesting Intelligence it contains. Before it came to Hand, I almost dreaded to hear from Canada, as my Advices seemed to promise nothing favourable, but rather our farther Misfortunes. But I am now hopeful, our Affairs, from the confused, distracted and almost forlorn State, in which you found them, will emerge and assume an Aspect of Order and Success. I am convinced many of our Misfortunes are to be attributed to a Want of Discipline, and a proper Regard to the Conduct of the

Soldiery. Hence it was, and from our feeble Effects to protect the Canadians, that they had almost joined, and taken Part against us. As you are fully apprised of this and conceive them well disposed towards us, with Confidence I trust, you will take every Step in your Power to conciliate and secure their Friendship. If this can be effected, and of which you seem to have no Doubt, I see no Objection to our indulging a Hope that this Country, of such Importance in the present Controversy, may yet be added to and compleat our Union. I confess, this interesting Work is now more difficult than it would have been heretofore had Matters been properly conducted; but yet, I flatter myself it may be accomplished by a wise, prudent and animated Behaviour in the Officers and Men engaged in it; especially if assisted by the friendly Disposition of the Inhabitants. I think every Mark of Friendship and Favour should be shewn them, to encourage their Zeal and Attachment to our Cause, and from which, if they once heartily embark, we shall derive innumerable Benefits.

Your Conduct in pushing and securing Posts low down the Country, is certainly judicious, and of the utmost Advantage. The farther down we can take and maintain Posts, the greater will our Possession of the Country be; observing at the same Time the Necessity of having a safe Retreat left, if you should be obliged to abandon them by a superior Force. I am hopeful and shall anxiously wait to hear of General Thompson's making a successful Attack upon the Party intrenching at the three Rivers. Their Defeat will be of the most essential Service. It will chagrin them and disconcert their Schemes on the one Hand, and animate our Men and give Life to our Canadian Friends on the other, and efface from their Minds the unfavorable Impressions our late Conduct has made.

It will be of material Consequence, in your Advances down the Country, to secure the several important Posts as you go; at

which you may, in Case you should be obliged to decline the
main Object you have in View, make a vigorous and successful
Stand, in your Retreat. I concur with you in Opinion in thinking it not of material Moment to keep a very large Number of
Men at Lachine or the upper Posts. There should be no more
than will be necessary to repel such Attacks and Attempts as
may be made by the Savages, and the Regular Troops above
you, allowing for such a Number of disaffected Canadians as
may join them. But then there should be a sufficient Number
for that Purpose, as our further Misfortunes there, might be
of the most injurious Consequences. If they can be maintained,
the disaffected above will dwindle away and the Insurrection
promise nothing disastrous.

It is impossible for me at this Distance, and not acquainted
with the Situation of Affairs as well as you, who are on the Spot,
to give any particular Directions for your Conduct and Operations. I, therefore, have only to request that you with your Officers will in every Instance, pursue such Measures as the Exigency
of our Affairs may seem to require, and as to you shall appear
most likely to advance and promote the Interest and Happiness
of your Country.

The Return which you mention to have inclosed, was not in
your Letter. You probably thro' Hurry forgot to put it in, or
General Schuyler may have omitted it, when in his Hands. I
wrote you on the 13th. on this Subject, and must again enjoin
a particular Attention to this Part of your Duty, it being of
the utmost Importance to be frequently certified of our whole
Strength and Stores.

In Compliance with your Request, I shall transmit a Copy of
your Letter to Congress, by To-Morrow's Post. It will give them
sensible Pleasure, and such as they had no good Reason to expect,
at least so soon.

I have inclosed you an Extract of a Letter from General Ward. From the Capture mentioned in it, there is Reason to expect the other Transports that sailed with her are not far off the Coast.

In Regard to your giving Commissions, it is a Measure that I can neither approve or disapprove, having no Authority to act in this Instance myself. The Propriety of it, must depend upon the Powers and Practice of your Predecessors in Command. If they had none, it will be judged of, most probably, by the good or bad Consequences it may produce. Congress from your Letter will see you have exercised such a Power, and when they write you, will either confirm or refuse it, in all Probability.

Least you should conceive that I do not think Lachine, or the Cedars, Posts of Importance and whose Defence are not very material; I must here add, that I esteem them of much Consequence, but only mean that more Men need not be employed than what will be equal to any probable Attack, that may be made against them.

I would observe, before I have done, that it is my most earnest Request, that Harmony, a good Understanding, and a free Communication of Sentiments, may prevail and be preserved between the General and Field Officers, particularly the former. Nothing can produce greater Benefits than this, nor tend more to promote your military Operations. Whereas History and Observation, do sufficiently evince (they abound with numberless Examples) the fatal Consequences, which have ever resulted, from Distrust, Jealousy, and Disagreement among Officers of these Ranks.

Wishing, therefore, your Counsels and Efforts to be founded in a happy Union, and to meet the Smiles of a kind Providence. I am, etc.

P. S. Knowing your great Zeal for the Cause of your Country, and desire to render her every possible Service, I must caution you not to put too much to the Hazard in your Exertions to establish her Rights, and to receive with a proper Degree of Caution, the Professions the Canadians may make. They have the Character of an ingenuous, artful People, and very capable of Finesse and Cunning. Therefore my Advice is, that you put not too much in their Power; but seem to trust them, rather than do it too far. I would also have you to keep all your Posts as you go well secured, to guard against any treacherous Conduct.

## *To THE PRESIDENT OF CONGRESS

New York, June 17, 1776.

Sir: The Inclosed came to my hands, as a private Letter from General Sullivan. As a private Letter, I lay it before Congress.[78] The tendency (for it requires no explanation) will account for the contrast between it and the Letter of Genl. Arnold.

That the former is aiming at the Command in Canada, is obvious. Whether he merits it or not, is a matter to be considered; and that it may be considered with propriety I think it my duty to observe, as of my own knowlege, that he is active, spirited, and Zealously attach'd to the Cause; that he does not want Abilities, many Members of Congress, as well as myself, can testify. But he has his wants, and he has his foibles. The latter are manifested in a little tincture of vanity, and in an over desire of being popular, which now and then leads him into some embarrassments. His wants are common to us all; the want of experience to move upon a large Scale; for the limited, and contracted knowledge which any of us have in Military Matters stands in very little stead; and is greatly over balanced by sound judgment, and some knowledge of Men and Books; especially when accompanied by an enterprizing genius, which I must do Genl. Sullivan the justice to say, I think he possesses; but

---

[78] Sullivan's letter, dated June 7, 1776, is in the *Papers of the Continental Congress.* Washington, apparently, kept no copy of it. It is printed in Force's *American Archives,* Fourth Series, vol. 6, 938.

as the Security of Canada is of the last Importance to the well being of these Colonies, I should like to know the Sentiments of Congress, respecting the Nomination of any Officer to that Command. The Character I have drawn of Genl. Sullivan is just, according to my Ideas of him. Congress will be pleased therefore to determine upon the propriety of continuing him in Canada, or sending another, as they shall see fit. Whether Genl. Sullivan knew of the promotion of Genl. Gates (at the time of his Writing) and that he had quitted the department he left him in, when he Marchd his Brigade from hence to Canada I cannot undertake to say, nor can I determine whether his wish to be recalled would be chang'd by it if he did. I shall add no more than my respectful Complimts to Congress, and that I have the Honour to be &ca.

### To THE PRESIDENT OF CONGRESS

New York, June 17, 1776.

Sir: I beg leave to inform Congress, that General Wooster has repaired to Head Quarters in obedience to their resolve transmitted him, and shall be extreamly glad If they will give me such further direction about him, as they may conceive necessary; he is desirous of seeing his Family in Connecticut, as I am informed, having been a good while from it. I shall wait their Instructions as to his future Employment. I am &ca.[79]

### To THE COMMITTEE OF SAFETY OF PENNSYLVANIA

New York, June 17, 1776.

Sir: I was this Evening honoured with yours of the 15 Inst, and It is with no small degree of pain that I am under the necessity of Informing you It is out of my power at this time to comply with the request made by your Honourable body. The many

---

[79] In the writing of Robert Hanson Harrison.

Important works carrying on for the defence of this place[80] against which there is the highest probability of an Attack being made in a little time, will not allow me to spare from hence any person who has the least skill in the business of an Engineer nor have I but one on whose Judgment I would wish to depend in laying out any work of the least consequence. Congress well know my wants in this Instance, and several of my late Letters to them, have pressed the appointment of Gentlemen qualified for this business; added to this, on account of the deficiency, I have not been able to secure or Improve Two posts in the Highlands, esteemed of the utmost Importance to prevent the Enemy from passing up the North River and getting into the Interior parts of this Colony, should our attempts to stop them here prove ineffectual. But I beg you to be assured Sir and to Inform the Committee, that as soon as It is in my power, I shall with infinite pleasure direct a person to attend them for two or three days. If the service will not admit of a longer absence, in order to trace out such works and plans for carrying them on, as shall appear necessary and wishing you to ascribe my non-compliance, to want of ability and not of inclination to perform your request. I have the honor, etc.[81]

[P.H.S.]

## To THE COMMITTEE OF ESSEX COUNTY, NEW JERSEY[82]

New York, June 17, 1776.

Gentn.: The absolute necessity of preventing all corespondence between the Inhabitants of this Country and our Enemies,

---

[80] Congress had authorized the Committee of Safety in Philadelphia to erect a redoubt at Billingsport and throw obstructions across the Delaware at that place, for the purpose of opposing the progress of the enemy's ships up the river, and had agreed that the same should be constructed at the Continental expense. The committee had requested the Commander in Chief to send them an engineer to plan and superintend these works.—*Sparks.*

[81] In the writing of Robert Hanson Harrison.

[82] Dr. William Burnet was chairman of the committee.

obliges me to every degree of Intelligence, that lead to the Channel of such Intercourse. Doctor William Burnet of New Ark can inform you of certain Insinuations and charges against part of the Army under my Command, as if they were liable to bribery and Corruption, in permitting persons to go from Staten Island to the Men of War at or near Sandy Hook, and as the Person from whom he has received his Intelligence, resides at New Ark, within the district of your Committee, I must request it, as a Matter of great importance, that your Committee will as soon as possible call on David Ogden Esqr., to declare who the person was, who informed him, that he had engaged the guard of the Rifle men at Staten Island, to carry him on Board the Men of War; with all the circumstances within his knowledge; and also that you do call on the person whom he points out, to be his Informant, to declare every Circumstance within his knowledge, relative to the Matter. I am &c.

## GENERAL ORDERS

Head Quarters, New York, June 17, 1776.
Parole Philadelphia.  Countersign Lancaster.

A Detachment consisting of one Major, three Capts. Six Subs. nine Serjeants, nine Corporals, three Drummers and Fifers and one hundred and twenty Privates to parade this evening at six o'clock at the Bowling-Green, there to receive further orders from Major Brooks[83] of Col Webb's Regiment, who is to take the command of this party.

Especial care is to be taken that the mens arms, and ammunition are in good order—each man to have his Twenty-four rounds of powder and ball, and to be furnished with seven days provisions.

---

[83] Maj. John Brooks, of the Nineteenth Continental Infantry.

## GENERAL ORDERS

Head Quarters, New York, June 18, 1776.

Parole Hancock.    Countersign Johnson.

Joseph Reed Esqr. is appointed Adjutant General of all the Continental Forces with the Rank of Colonel, and is to be regarded and obeyed accordingly.

Capts. Post[84] and Pollard[85] are to make Returns every evening to Col. Putnam of the service of the men under their command, shewing when, and how they are employed—And on Saturday to make a Weekly Return of their Companies to the Adjutant General.

The Colonels of every Regiment are to see that their Drums are put in good Order, at the public Expence, after which they are to be kept so at the charge of the Drummers, who have extra-pay on that account; from which deductions will be made if necessary: But in case of unavoidable accidents, the charge of repair will be borne as heretofore.

Peter Meredith and Peter Bickerstaff of Capt. Ledyards[86] Company in Col McDougall's Regiment, having been tried by a General Court Martial whereof Col Parsons was President for "Desertion," are found guilty and sentenced to receive Thirty Lashes each, which sentence the General confirms and orders to be executed at the usual time and place.

In addition to the orders of the 14th. Instant, made to prevent the embezzlement of the public tools, the Quarter-Master General shall cause all the Tools, of every kind, belonging to the United Colonies, or at any time purchased for them, to be marked, with the following brand or stamp: <u>Cxiii</u>.

---

[84] Capt. Anthony Post of the Artillery artificers.
[85] Capt. Benjamin Pollard, of the Artillery artificers.
[86] Capt. Benjamin Ledyard, of the First New York Regiment.

The Engineers to provide Stores for securing the Tools, under their Care, and such Sentries placed over them, as they shall find necessary: All officers commanding a party, or detachment from any Regiment on the works, to be accountable for the Tools he receives from the overseers, as he will be obliged to pay for all lost while under his care, and the Soldiers who shall lose, or purposely destroy, any of the Tools delivered him to work with, shall not only have the price thereof stoped out of his next pay, but be punished according to the nature of his offence; and in order that the public works may not be retarded by the several overseers, attending to deliver the Tools, to every Regiment, before they set any of them to work, (which may be the case in some instances) therefore the Chief Engineer, has leave, when he finds the case requisite, to take suitable persons from any of the Battalions, to attend the Stores and deliver and receive the Tools; and when any Tools are out of repair, or become useless, they may be changed at the Quarter-Master-General's store, for others which are good, and in case other Tools are not wanted, or not to be had in the store, The Quarter Master General shall receive the defective tools, and discharge the Engineer of so many tools as they do receive.

## To JOHN PARKE CUSTIS

June 18, 1776.

(Forged letter)[87]

## GENERAL ORDERS

Head Quarters, New York, June 19, 1776.
Parole London.   Countersign Montgomery.
A working party consisting of nine hundred men properly officered to parade to morrow morning at Six O'Clock near the

---

[87] See note to letter to Lund Washington, June 12, 1776, *ante.*

Artillery park—Those of Bailey's and Read's Regiments to go to Powle's-hook—Wyllys's to Governor's Island—All of the other Regiments to parade at the Laboratory, and there receive orders from the Chief Engineer.

The whole of the above men to be furnished with one days provision, except Parsons's and Arnold's, who will return to their respective encampments to dinner.

Brigadier General Greene and Col Prescott, will furnish, one hundred and fifty men each, as a working party on Governor's Island.

On the present emergency, all working parties to work 'till Six o'Clock in the afternoon, except such as go by water, who will be allowed to leave work sooner, if the Wind and Tide make it necessary.

### GENERAL ORDERS

Head Quarters, New York, June 20, 1776.

Parole Gates.   Countersign Canada.

Fifty men, one Capt. two Subs. three Serjts—three Corporals and one Drum to parade to morrow morning nine oclock at the Assitant Quarter-Master Hughes with one weeks provision and there receive their orders from him.

Five Carpenters to be nominated by the Quarter Master General out of Col. Reeds, Col. Bailey's and Col Learneds Regiments to be sent to assist the Wheelwrights.

Nathaniel Powers of Capt. Bowlton's[88] Company and Col. Sheppards[89] Regiment having been tried by a Court Martial whereof Col Parsons was President for "Desertion" was found guilty and sentenced to receive Thirty-nine Lashes. The General approves the sentence and orders it to be put in execution at the usual time and place.

---

[88] Capt. Isaac Bolster.
[89] Lieut. Col. William Shepard commanded the Third Continental Infantry at this time.

## To THE PRESIDENT OF CONGRESS

New York, June 20, 1776.

Sir: I am now to acknowledge the receipt of your Favours of the 14th and 18th. instant, and the interesting resolves contained in them, with which I have been honored.

The several matters recommended to my attention, shall be particularly regarded, and the directions of Congress, and your requests complied with, in every instance, as far as is in my power.

The Institution of a War Office is certainly an Event of great importance, and in all probability will be recorded as such in the Historic Page. The Benefits derived from it, I flatter myself will be considerable tho' the plan, upon which it is first formed may not be entirely perfect. This like other great Works in its first Edition, may not be entirely free from Error. Time will discover its Defects and experience suggest the Remedy, and such further Improvements as may be necessary; but it was right to give it a Beginning.[90]

The Recommendation to the Convention of New York for restraining and punishing disaffected Persons, I am hopeful will be attended with salutary consequences, and the prohibition against exporting Provisions appears to have been a measure founded in sound Policy, lest proper supplies should be wanted wherewith to subsist our Armies.

I have transmitted General Schuyler, the resolves about the Indians, and the others on which he is to act, and have requested his strict attention and exertions in order to their being carried into Execution with all possible Dispatch.

I note your request respecting Mr. Hancock;[91] he shall have such Directions as may be necessary for conducting his Office

---

[90] The duties of the board are described in the resolves of Congress of June 12 and 13. (See note to Washington's letter to the President of Congress, June 13, 1776, *ante*.)

[91] Ebenezer Hancock, Deputy Paymaster General of the Continental Army.

and I am happy he will have so early a remittance for paying the Troops in his Department.

The Silver and Paper Money designed for Canada will be highly serviceable, and I hope will be the means of reestablishing our Credit there in some degree with the Canadians, and also encourage our Men, who have complained in this Instance; when it arrives, I will send it forward under a proper Guard.

I have communicated to General Gates the Resolve of Congress for him to repair to Canada, and directed him to view Point au Fere,[92] that a Fortress may be erected if he shall judge it necessary; he is preparing for his command and in a few days will take his Departure for it: I would, fain hope his arrival there will give our Affairs, a complexion different from what they have worn for a long Time past, and that many essential Benefits will result from it.

The kind attention Congress have shewn to afford the Commander in Chief here every assistance, by resolving that recommendatory Letters be written to the conventions of New Jersey, New York and the Assembly of Connecticut, to Authorize him to call in the militias in cases of exigency, claims my thankful acknowledgments and I trust, if carried into execution, will produce many advantages, in case It may be expedient to call in early reinforcements; the delays Incident to the ordinary mode may frequently render their aid too late and prove exceedingly Injurious.

I this Evening received Intelligence of the 19th. instt. from Captn. Pond[93] of the Armed Sloop Schuyler, of his having taken, about 50 miles from this on the South side of Long Island, a Ship and a Sloop bound to Sandy Hook: The Ship from Glasgow with a Company of the 22d Regiment, had been taken

---

[92] A point of land on the western shore of Lake Champlain between Isle aux Noix and Isle la Motte.

[93] Capt. Charles Pond. His letter is in the *Washington Papers*.

before by one of Commodore Hopkins Fleet, who took the Soldiers out and ordered her to Rhode Island, after which she was retaken by the Cerberus and put under the convoy of the Sloop. As Captain Pond informs, there were five Commissioned Officers, Two Ladies and four Privates on board; they are not yet arrived at Head Quarters; inclosed is an Invoice of what they have on Board.

General Wooster having expressed an inclination and wish to wait on Congress, I have given him permission, not having any occasion for him here. he sets out this morning.

I have been up to view the grounds about Kings Bridge, and find them to admit of many Places well calculated for defence, and esteeming it a Pass of the utmost importance have ordered Works to be laid out and shall direct part of the two Battalions from Pennsylvania, to set about the erection immediately, and will add to their Numbers several of the Militia, when they come, in to expedite them with all possible Dispatch;[94] their consequences, as they will keep open the Communication with the Country, requires the most speedy completion of them.[95] I have the Honor to be &c.

## *To COLONEL JAMES CLINTON

New York, June 20, 1776.

Sir: On the Execution of the Inclosed Warrant with expedition, care and exactness, much may depend; I therefore desire you will perform the Service therein required, yourself.[96] In the

---

[94] These works embraced the fort on an eminence near the Hudson River, called Fort Washington, the redoubts at Jeffreys Point, and on the hills north and east of Fort Washington, breastworks at Kings Bridge, and Fort Independence, on the north side of Harlem Creek near its junction with the Hudson.

[95] This letter was read in Congress on June 24, and instances the functioning of the new Board of War in being referred to it.

[96] The individual to be arrested was Fletcher Matthews.

Instant he is siezed (and his Papers) inform him that there are indubitable Evidence of his being concerned in a Scheme of Inlisting Men for the Kings Service, and note his answers. Communicate this matter to no Person living till you perform the Office required of you. I am, etc.[97]

## To MAJOR GENERAL PHILIP SCHUYLER

New York, June 20, 1776.

Dear Sir: I herewith transmit you, sundry Resolves of Congress respecting the Indians, the fortifying Fort Stanwix &c. and for rendering more easy and commodious, our Passes into Canada. As the Resolves are of an interesting, and important Nature, I must request your particular Attention to them and most active Exertions for accomplishing, and carrying the whole into Execution with all possible Dispatch.

I am hopeful the Bounty Congress have agreed to allow, as you will perceive by the last Resolve, will prove a powerful Inducement to engage the Indians in our Service, and their Endeavours to make Prisoners of all the Kings Troops they possibly can.[98] You will use every Method you shall judge necessary, to conciliate their Favour, and to this End, are authorised to promise them a punctual Payment, of the Allowance Congress have determined on for such Officers and Privates belonging to the King's Army, as they may captivate and deliver us.

June 21, 1776.

I have this Moment received your Favours of the 15th. and 17th. and the Post being about to depart have not Time to

---

[97] The editor is indebted to Dr. A. S. W. Rosenbach for the text of this letter.

[98] The resolves of June 17, 1776, were a part of the report of the Committee of the Whole upon measures to be taken. Apparently Gates, Schuyler, and Washington contributed ideas. This particular resolve authorized General Washington to employ such Indians as he should take into the service in any place where he should think they would be most useful and to offer them a reward of $100 for every commissioned officer and $30 for every private soldier of the King's troops that they should capture in the Indian country or on the frontiers of the Colonies.

answer them fully. I shall only add that Lady Johnson[99] may remain at Albany, 'till further Directions. I am, Sir, etc.

### To THE PRESIDENT OF CONGRESS

New York, June 21, 1776.

Sir: I was this morning honored with your favor of the 19th Instant, with sundry resolves of Congress, which came to hand after I had closed mine of the 20th. I shall appoint a Deputy Muster Master General, as soon as I can fix upon a proper person for the Office, and direct him immediately to repair to Canada.

Mr. Bennet the Bearer of this, delivered me a Letter to day from General Schuyler, inclosing the Proceedings of the commissioners of Indians affairs, at a meeting at Albany, in consequence of the Resolution of Congress (as they say) which I transmitted the 7th Instant, for engaging the Indians in our service. The Gentlemen appear to me to have widely mistaken the views of Congress in this Instance, and to have formed a plan for engaging such Indians, as were not in contemplation. I cannot Account upon what principles they have gone, as a part of their proceedings shew they are about to hold a conference with the Six Nations. I suppose they esteemed what they have done, a necessary measure, a Copy of which I have the Honor to inclose you.

I shall now beg leave to lay before Congress, a proposition made by Captain Leary[1] of this City in behalf of a body of men who are desirous of being employed in the Continental Service, as a Troop of Horse, and at the same time to offer my Opinion that such a Corps may be extremely useful in many respects. In a march they may be of the utmost service, in reconnoitring the Enemy and gaining Intelligence, and have it

---

[99] Mary, Lady Johnson, wife of Sir John.
[1] Capt. John Leary, jr. His proposal was for a troop of horse 40 strong (both officers and men) at 8 shillings per day, the men to find themselves and furnish their own horses and equipment. This document is in the *Papers of the Continental Congress.*

in their power to render many other Important benefits. The Terms on which they are willing to engage are inclosed, which seems to me moderate and reasonable. I am also Informed, that another Company, might be readily made up and most probably upon the same Terms. I would therefore submit the propriety and expediency of the measure to the consideration of Congress, and wish their Opinion, whether it will be agreeable to them that both or either of them should be formed, and incorporated in this Army, on the Terms proposed by Captain Leary if it can be done. I have the Honor to be &ca.[2]

## To THE PRESIDENT OF CONGRESS

Head Quarters, June 21, 1776.

Sir: This will be delivered you by the Chevalier de Kermorvan and Monsieur de Vermenet; they are French Gentlemen just arrived in this Place, who have made Application to me, to be received into the Continental Service. They bring Letters to Dr. Franklin and some other Gentlemen of the Congress. I suppose it will better appear from these Letters, than from any Information I can give, whether it will be proper to employ them in the Capacity they are desirous of. I am, etc.[3]

## GENERAL ORDERS

Head Quarters, New York, June 21, 1776.

Parole Albany.    Countersign Bedford.

All officers, or soldiers, belonging to either of the Regiments, serving in Canada, are to apply immediately to Major General Gates, who will give them orders for repairing to their respective detachments.

---

[2] In the writing of Alexander Contee Hanson.

[3] In the writing of Alexander Contee Hanson. The letter was read in Congress on June 26 and read before the Board of War on June 27, and referred "for further consideration."

The General has been pleased to appoint Richard Cary and Samuel Webb Esquires, his Aid-du-Camps—and Alexander Counter Harrison[4] Esqr. assistant Secretary, who are to be obeyed and regarded as such.

The Honorable Continental Congress have been pleased to give the Rank of Lieutenant Colonel, to the Aids-du-Camp of the Commander in Chief, and to his principal Secretary. Also the Rank of Major to the Aids-du-Camp of the Majors General.

The Honorable Continental Congress have resolvd that no officer shall suttle, or sell, to the Soldiers, on penalty of being fined one Months pay and dismissed the service with infamy.

The same Hon. Body have also resolved, that all sales of arms, ammunition, cloathing and accoutrements, made by any Soldier of the Continental Army, shall be void—Also, That the Baggage of officers and soldiers, shall be regulated conformably to the Rules and Customs of the British Army.

The General requires and expects, a most exact and punctual obedience, to each of the above resolves.

### GENERAL ORDERS

Head Quarters, New York, June 22, 1776.
Parole Brunswick.    Countersign Cumberland.

Aaron Burr Esqr.[5] is appointed Aide-du-Camp to Genl. Putnam in the room of Major Webb promoted. He is to be obeyed and regarded as such.

The Quarter Masters having in many late Instances, neglected to see detachments, and working parties, furnished with

---

[4]Richard Cary, of Virginia; Samuel Blatchley Webb, of Connecticut; and Alexander Contee Hanson, of Maryland. The spelling of these names by John Stagg, Assistant Adjutant General, is but one of numerous instances either of his inability to read the writing of Joseph Reed, Adjutant General of the Continental Army, or carelessness due to rapid transcribing. There is, of course, the possibility that the Adjutant General himself was weak in spelling names.

[5]Aaron Burr served as a volunteer on the Canadian expedition of 1775; was lieutenant colonel of Malcolm's Additional Continental regiment in January, 1777; resigned in March, 1779; Vice President of the United States 1801–1805; died in 1836.

the necessary quantity of provisions, The General requires greater punctuality in future and if any further neglect appears in this respect, such Quarter Master will be severely punished.

## GENERAL ORDERS

Head Quarters, New York, June 23, 1776.
Parole Cambridge.    Countersign Dorchester.

Mutual Complaints having been made by the Armourers, and Soldiers, respecting the repairing of Arms; The Officers of the several Regiments, are earnestly called upon, to examine their Men, and turn out all those who can work to any advantage in the Armourers Shop, though they should not be complete workmen; and to prevent further uneasiness, the several Captains are to inspect the arms of their Companies, and either themselves, or by some persons for whom they will be answerable, have the defective Arms sent to the Armourers when the Master Workman will give a Receipt for them—the same officer in like manner attending to the return of the arms and to make report if the Armourers fail in their work—The Honor and Safety of the army depends so much upon a strict attention, to the state of the arms, that the General hopes no pains will be spared upon this head.

A Detachment consisting of one Lieut. Colonel, one Major, six Captains, twelve Subalterns, eighteen Serjeants, eighteen Corporals, six Drums and Fifers, and three hundred Privates to parade to morrow morning, at the Grand parade, at eight OClock with their arms, ammunition and blankets, to have four days provisions, there to receive their orders from Genl. Putnam—Lieut. Col Jacobs,[6] and Major Colbourne[7] to be the Field Officers of the above detachment.

---

[6] Lieut. Col. John Jacobs, of the Twenty-third Continental Infantry.
[7] Maj. Andrew Colburn, of the Fourth Continental Infantry. He was wounded at Harlem Heights, N. Y., in October, 1776; lieutenant colonel of the Third New Hampshire Regiment; died of wounds received at Stillwater, N. Y., Sept. 19, 1777.

The Sentries at the Laboratory and Artillery Park to be doubled every night 'till further orders[8]—The Brigade Majors will strengthen these Guards with an addition of men for that purpose.

Major Trumbull[9] being promoted, Adjutant Peck[10] of Col. Huntingtons Regiment, to act as Brigade Major to General Spencers brigade, 'till further appointment is made.

### To THE PRESIDENT OF CONGRESS

New York, June 23, 1776.

Sir: I herewith transmit you an extract of a Letter from General Ward which came to hand by last night's post, containing the agreeable Intelligence of their having Obliged the Kings Ships to leave Nantasket Road, and of two Transports more being taken by our Armed Vessels with Two hundred and ten Highland Troops on board.[11]

I sincerely wish the like success had attended our Arms in another Quarter, but it has not. In Canada the situation of our Affairs is truly alarming. The inclosed Copies of Generals Schuyler, Sullivan, and Arnold's Letters will inform you, that General Thompson has met with a repulse at three Rivers and

---

[8] This action was taken as a result of the discovery of the so-called Hickey Plot.

[9] Maj. John Trumbull (the artist). He had been brigade major to Spencer; was promoted to deputy adjutant general, Northern Department, in June, 1776; resigned Apr. 19, 1777, and went to England to study under Benjamin West. There he was arrested and imprisoned, but soon released.

[10] Adjt. William Peck. He was brigade major and aide to Spencer from August, 1776, to January, 1778; also deputy adjutant general of Rhode Island troops, 1777–1781, when he resigned.

[11] Several British armed ships had kept possession of Nantasket Road from the time Boston was evacuated. On June 13, in the evening, General Ward ordered 500 men and a detachment of the train of artillery with a 13-inch mortar, two 18-pounders, and some small cannon, under the command of Colonel Whitcomb, to take post on Long Island and annoy the British ships. The necessary works were thrown up in the night, and the next morning the cannon and mortar opened a fire, and soon drove the vessels out of the harbor. The fleet, 13 in number, consisted of the *Renown,* of 50 guns, several smaller ships of war, and transports with Highland troops on board. They blew up the lighthouse as they went off, and put to sea.—*Sparks.*

is now a Prisoner in the hands of General Burgoyne, who, these Accounts say is arrived with a considerable Army;[12] nor do they seem to promise an end of our misfortunes here; It is greatly to be feared that the next advices from thence will be, that our shattered, divided and broken Army, as you will see by the return, has been obliged to abandon that Country and retreat to avoid a greater Calamity, that of being cut off, or becoming Prisoners. I will be done upon the Subject and leave you to draw such conclusions, as you conceive from the state of Facts, are most likely to result, only ading my apprehensions that one of the latter events, either that they are cut off, or become Prisoners, has already happened, If they did not retreat while they had an opportunity.

General Schuyler and General Arnold seem to think it extremely probable, and if it has taken place, It will not be easy to describe all the fatal consequences that may flow from it. at least our utmost exertions will be necessary, to prevent their Improving the advantages they have gained to our greater misfortunes. General Gates will certainly set out to morrow and would have gone before now, had he not expected to receive some particular Instructions from Congress and which Col. Braxton[13] said, he imagined would be transmitted here.

Inclosed is a Copy of a Letter from Genl. Arnold, respecting some of the Indian Tribes to General Schuyler and of a talk had at Albany with thirteen of the Oneidas; they seemed then to entertain a friendly disposition towards us, which I wish may not be changed by the misfortunes we have sustained in Canada. I am &ca.[14]

---

[12] Thompson had been ordered against Three Rivers by Sullivan. Schuyler's, Sullivan's, and Arnold's letters are in the *Washington Papers*. Arnold's, dated June 13, 1776, is addressed to Schuyler and is printed in Sparks's *Letters to Washington*, vol. 1, p. 529.

[13] Carter Braxton, a Delegate to Congress from Virginia.

[14] In the writing of Robert Hanson Harrison.

## To MAJOR GENERAL ARTEMAS WARD

New York, June 23, 1776.

Sir: By last Night's Post I was favoured with yours of the 16th. Inst., containing the interesting Intelligence of your having obliged the King's Ships to quit their Stations, and of the further Captures of two Vessels from Glascow, with Highland Troops on Board. These Events are extremely pleasing, and I flatter myself the former will be attended with salutary Consequences. It will give our little Squadron, a better Opportunity of safely bringing in such Prizes, as they may have the Fortune to take, and be the Means of more Transports, and other of their Vessels falling in our Hands in all Probability. The scheme of a Decoy Ship may answer many good Purposes, and if we get a few more of the thirty two Transports in Addition to those we have already, the Highland Corps will be pretty well broken and disconcerted.

With Respect to a Paymaster and Payment of the Troops, Congress have informed me in a Letter of the 14th. Inst. that they have appointed Ebezr. Hancock Esqr. to that Office, and that the Day after, Money would be sent him for paying the Troops in the eastern Department. I hope it will arrive in a few Days, that their Claims may be discharged, and the Grounds of their Dissatisfaction removed.

The Invalids you mention, may be turned over to other Regiments 'till further Orders, taking Notice of the Time, and a List of their Names, and transmitting them to the Colonels, or Commanding Officers of the respective Regiments to which they belonged; that they may not be included in their Abstracts after that Time, and double Pay be drawn for them.

I have inclosed you Copies of sundry Resolves of Congress, which I request you to communicate to the Persons they respect, that they may govern themselves accordingly. That, about Vessels taken, which sailed from Boston with Effects while the King's Troops possessed it, you will transmit to the different Agents for the Continental armed Vessels, and that respecting Ordinance Stores, to Commodore Manley. I have sent the original Invoice of them and do appoint          to act in Behalf of the Continent, in Conjunction with such Person, as the Commodore shall choose, for ascertaining their Value. This you will please to notify him of. They must be qualified as the Resolve directs, and pursue the Mode pointed out by it. When the Valuation is made, they will annex the Report under their Hands, to the Invoice, and deliver them to you, in Order to their being forwarded to me. The Report may mention that they were sworn and by whom. I am, Sir, etc.

### To COLONEL JAMES CLINTON

Head Quarters, New York, June 23, 1776.

Sir: Yours of the 20th. and 22nd. Inst. are both safe to Hand. The Person you was to seize by Warrant, you are immediately to send with the Papers to this Place in Charge of an Officer you can confide in. In this no Time is to be lost.[15]

It is out of my Power to assist you in procuring Arms; I must, therefore, urge you to make Application to the Convention, Committees &c. who, I hope, will supply you.

Your Letter of the 20th. I shall answer the first Opportunity, and am, in Haste, etc.

### To MAJOR GENERAL PHILIP SCHUYLER

New York, June 24, 1776.

Dear Sir: On the 20th. Inst. I received your two Favors of the 15th. and 17th. by Bennet, and Yesterday Evening that of the

---

[15] Fletcher Matthews, a New York loyalist. He was suspected of complicity in the so-called Hickey Plot.

19th. continued to the 20th. with General Sullivan's Letter and Return, and the several Copies you inclosed.

The Accounts transmitted by General Sullivan are truly alarming, and I confess, I am not without Apprehension least the next Advices should be, that the unfortunate Defeat, and taking of General Thompson, has been succeeded by an Event still more unfortunate; the Destruction of a large Part, if not the whole of our Army in that Quarter. The weak, divided, and disheartened State in which General Sullivan represents it to be, does not seem to promise any Thing much more favourable, and is what General Arnold appears to be suspicious of. From the whole of the Accounts, supposing the Facts all true, there was nothing left to prevent their Ruin, but a Retreat. That, I hope, has been made as the only Means of saving themselves, and rendering their Country the least Service. By Reason of the Succession of Ills that has attended us there of late, and this last one, I fear we must give up all Hopes of possessing that Country of such Importance in the present Controversy, and that our Views and utmost Exertions must be turned, to prevent the Incursions of the Enemy into our Colonies. To this End, I must pray your strictest Attention and request that you use all the Means in your Power, to fortify and secure every Post and Place of Importance on the Communication. You are as much impressed with the Necessity of the Measure, as any Man can be, and with Confidence I trust, that nothing you can do, will be wanting to effect it. If the Troops have retreated they will in a little Time, I am hopeful, compleat such Works on the Passes, as to bid Defiance to the most vigorous Efforts of the Enemy, to penetrate our Country; especially when you are assisted by the Militia, which most probably are on their March ere now. Had this unfortunate Defeat not happened, the Militia were designed, not only to reinforce the Army in

Canada, but to keep up the Communication with that Province, as you will see by recurring to the Resolve directing them to be employed.

Major General Gates, whom Congress had appointed to command after General Thomas's Death, will set out To-Morrow, and take with him one Hundred Barrells of Powder; out of which the Supplies necessary for the different Posts must be drawn. I have also directed Colo. Knox to send up the Cannon you wrote for, if they can be possibly spared from hence, with some Artillerists, a proper Quantity of Ball and other Necessaries for them and will in every Instance afford you all the Assistance I can. At the same Time I wish, if there are any Cannon at Ticonderoga or other Necessaries there or elsewhere, that you may want, and which can be spared from any other Post or Purpose, that you would get them in Preference to any here; as the Number we have, is not more than sufficient for the extensive and important Works, necessary to be maintained for the Defence of this Place.

In Respect to the Proceedings of the Commissioners for raising two Companies of the Mohikander and Connecticut Indians, they appear to me not to answer the Views of Congress, as I presume they live within the Government of Connecticut and are to be considered in the same Light with it's Inhabitants and that their Design was extended to those who were not Livers among us, and were of hostile Character or doubtful Friendship, but in this I may be mistaken, and there may be a Necessity of engaging those you have to secure their Interest.

As to your Doubts about the Officer commanding in Canada, his Right to punish capitally; I should suppose, that a Necessity, independent of any Thing else, would justify the Exercise of such an Authority; but Congress having determined, that the Commanding Officer there, should inflict exemplary Punishment on those who violate the military Regulations established by them, has put the Matter out of Question, and I apprehend every Commander there, has such Power, and of Right may, and should exercise it.

As Colonel Parsons has requested you to send the Person who is supposed to have murdered his Brother, I have no Objection to your doing it, if you judge it necessary. He, from what I have been told, designs to apply to Congress, for instituting some Mode of Trial for the Offence. I am, etc.

## To MAJOR GENERAL HORATIO GATES

New York, June 24, 1776.

Sir: The Honourable the Continental Congress, reposing the greatest Confidence in your Wisdom, and Experience, have directed me to appoint you, to the very important Command of the Troops of the United Colonies in Canada, with a Power to appoint a Deputy Adjt. Genl., a Depy. Qr. Mr. Genl., a Depy. Muster Mr. Genl. and such other Officers as you shall find necessary for the good of the Service.[16] You are also empowered to fill up all Vacancies in the Army in Canada, and notify the same to Congress for their Approbation.

You are also authorized until the 1st. of October next, to suspend any Officers, and fill up all Vacancies, transmitting to the Honorable Congress such Order and Suspension, giving your Reasons therefore, and specifying the special Charge made against such Officer.

---

[16] Gates had made himself exceedingly popular with the Massachusetts element during the siege of Boston, and Richard Henry Lee, of Virginia, was ever ready to follow the Massachusetts lead. He wrote to Washington (June 13): "It is more than probable, that Congress will order our friend Gates to Canada. His great abilities and virtue will be absolutely necessary to restore things there, and his recommendations will always be readily complied with. You will find that great powers are given to the Commander in that distant department. The system for Canada, adopted since the arrival of the Commissioners here, will, I hope, be of essential service to our affairs. All good men pray most heartily for your health, happiness, and success, and none more than your affectionate friend." Had not Thomas died, the New England influence would, probably, have sent Gates to command at Boston. Lee's letter is in the *Washington Papers.*

You are directed, previous to your Departure, to consult with the Commissary General, and concert with him the most effectual Measures for continuing proper Supplies of Provisions for that Department.

You are in like Manner to consult with Colonel Knox about the Artillery which may be wanted, and what may probably be procured there; and whether any Brass or Iron Field Pieces can be spared from hence for that Service.

Upon your Arrival at Albany, you will consult with General Schuyler, with Respect to the present State of Provisions, Stores &c., and fix upon some certain Means of forwarding the regular Supplies in future from that Place. At the same Time endeavour to learn whether Supplies heretofore sent, have not reached that Department, and by what Means such Failures have happened, that a proper Remedy may be provided. From General Schuyler you will also receive such Advice and Information respecting the Operations of the Campaign as may be useful and necessary. You are to direct all the General Officers, Depy. Qr. Master General, local Commissaries, Paymaster in Canada, and all other Persons there, or on the Communication without Delay to render their Accounts and settle them. No General Officer on such Settlement, receiving Pay as Colonel of a Regiment, or any Field Officer as Captain of a Company.

Upon your taking the Command of the Troops, you will give particular Orders agreeable to a Rule of Congress that no Officer suttle or sell to the Soldiers, on Penalty of being fined one Month's Pay, and dismissed the Service with Infamy.

That all Sales of Arms, Cloathing, Ammunition, and Accoutrements made by Soldiers, are to be deemed void. That the Baggage of Officers and Soldiers is hereafter to be regulated conformably to the Rules of the British Armies.

By a like Resolve no Troops in Canada are to be disbanded there; but all Soldiers in that Country ordered to be disbanded, or

whose Times of Inlistment being expired, shall refuse to reinlist, shall be sent under proper Officers to Ticonderoga, or such
other Posts on the Lakes, as you shall direct, where they are to be
mustered, and the Arms, Accoutrements, Blankets, and Utensils
which they may have belonging to the Public, shall be delivered
up and deposited in the public Store.

You will as soon as possible make as accurate a Return as you
can procure of the Troops, Artillery, Arms, Ammunition, Provision, and Stores, which you find in Canada, or upon the Communication with Albany distinguishing where stationed, and in
what Magazines; and if possible transmit such a Return to the
Honorable Continental Congress, and to me, once a Fortnight.

The Distance of the Scene, and the frequent Changes which
have happened in the State of our Affairs in Canada, do not
allow me to be more particular in my Instructions. The Command is important, the Service difficult, but honourable; and
I most devoutly pray that Providence may crown your Arms
with abundant Success. Given under my Hand, etc.

### To MARTHA WASHINGTON

June 24, 1776.

(Forged letter)[17]

### GENERAL ORDERS

Head Quarters, New York, June 24, 1776.

Parole Dedham.   Countersign Essex.

The Guard on the prisoners at the City-hall is to be strenghtned
every night as the last, so as to make up one hundred men forty
being required from the several brigades.

---

[17] See note to letter to Lund Washington, June 12, 1776, *ante.* This particular letter
was published in the *Gentleman's Magazine* (1777), which also prints immediately
thereafter two alleged resolves of Congress of Aug. 28, 1777, respecting imprisonment
of Quakers, which are correct as to names of the Quakers but highly imaginary in
every other particular.

The General Court Martial now sitting to assemble at the house where the Provost is kept till further orders—

## GENERAL ORDERS

Head Quarters, New York, June 25, 1776.
Parole Epsom.   Countersign Falkland.

The Militia Officers of the adjoining provinces who are to reinforce this army, are upon their arrival with their troops, to make report immediately, to the Brigadier General, or the officer commanding their respective Corps, who is to make report once in two days to the Commander in Chief—

The Adjutant General's Office will be removed this afternoon to a small brick house, one of the offices belonging to Head Quarters—The Brigade Majors are requested to attend there punctually hereafter, at eleven o'clock, except those at a distance, who may send an Adjutant, but the orders will not be given to any person of less rank in future.

## To COLONEL JAMES CLINTON

New York, June 25, 1776.

Sir: I received yours of the 20th Inst. and in Answer thereto, request you to draw out of your Regiment, all the Armourers, in it and set them immediately to Work. They will receive the same Pay as the Armourers here do, under the like Circumstances. You must endeavour to engage the one you mention, upon the same Terms that are given here; but if you cannot do better, you must continue him on those contained in your letter.

In Respect to keeping two of the Commissioners, if it is absolutely necessary, it must be done, till you are provided with an Engineer, or so long as they may be wanted. Will not one be sufficient? If it will, two need not be retained.

It being impossible to procure a sufficient Number of Tents for the whole Army, it will be necessary for you to procure a

Quantity of thin Boards, which you must have put up in a close Manner to answer the Purpose. This is now doing for General Scott's Militia Brigade,[18] and will do exceedingly well.

I cannot but consider the Pay of the Carpenters enormous and extravagant; nor can I suggest any good Reason, why they should receive more than those employed here; some of which, for Instance, Captain Bruen's Company from the Jerseys, are compleat Workmen, and can execute almost any Kind of Work in the best Manner. I desire you will endeavour to lessen their Pay, and to prevail on them to receive no more than what is given here.

The Pay Rolls will be settled by the Provincial Congress up to the last of April inclusive, as has been done with the other Troops raised in this Colony. The Abstracts after that Time, will be taken in, and paid by me as others are.

I observe by the Returns, that your Regiment is still greatly deficient in Arms, which is a Circumstance highly distressing at this Time. As I have no Prospect of getting any, that I know of; I request you to have no Dependence on me for a Supply, and that you will use every possible Method you can to procure what you want from the Country People, or wheresoever they can be had by purchasing. I am, etc.

P. S. The Powder of the Province in your Hands, and which is made up in Cartridges, you must not spare by any Means; But repay the Quantity of it out of continental Stock, if any.

### To LIEUTENANT COLONEL JACOB BAYLEY

New York, June 25, 1776.

Sir: I this Morning received yours of the 28th Ulto., and approve the Measures you had adopted for opening the Road to St. John's, which may be still proper to pursue; but as our Army in Canada, since their Retreat from Quebec has met

---

[18] Brig. Gen. John Morin Scott, of the New York Militia.

with further Misfortunes, and there is the strongest Reason to believe they will be obliged to abandon the Possession of that Country, if they have not already done it; I would advise you, to consider well the Advantages and Disadvantages that will result from compleating the Work. If the Enemy will be thereby afforded an easy Pass to make Incursions into our Colonies and to commit Depredations, and the Advantages we shall derive from it, will not greatly overballance these Inconveniences, it will be improper to carry it on. The Change which has taken Place in our Affairs in that Quarter, may render now, what was extremely right to be done some Time ago, very inexpedient and unadvisable. As you are well acquainted with the Country thro' which the Communication was designed to be made, and I am not, I shall submit the Propriety of compleating it to you, under the Circumstances I have mentiond, not meaning to direct you to one Thing or another.

I presume you received my Letter of the 29th. of April, and the two Hundred and fifty Pounds I sent by Mr. Wallace. You have not mentioned it. I am, etc.

## To HENRY BROMFIELD

New York, June 25, 1776.

Sir: The Honble Congress having determined a Valuation shall be made of the Ordinance Stores taken last Fall by Captain Manley, and directed me to appoint a Person in Behalf of the Continent to do it, in Conjunction with one to be chosen by Captain Manley, as you will perceive by the inclosed Resolve, I must request the Favour of you to undertake the Business.

I have transmitted the original Invoice to Major General Ward upon which you are to act.

It will be necessary to qualify, as the Resolve directs, and after the Estimate is made, to annex it to the Invoice under your Hands.

General Ward will forward it to me when it is finished, and praying your Excuse for this Trouble and Liberty.[19] I am, etc.

## To LIEUTENANT COLONEL BENJAMIN TUPPER

New York, June 25, 1776.

Sir: I this Morning received Information, that one or more Boats have passed through the Narrows in Defiance of the Fire from the Rifle Men, who had no Boats to pursue them. This Passage I had Reason to suppose was properly guarded, by the whale Boats under your Command, and am not a little surprised on hearing the contrary.

I do expect you will for the Future have them rowing across the Narrows from Dusk of the Evening to Day Light in the Morning, giving Orders to each Boat to keep the strictest Lookout; as there is no Doubt our inveterate Enemies who have had a Hand in the late horrid Plot, will try every Method in their Power to escape from the Hands of Justice.[20] I am, etc.

## To MAJOR GENERAL ARTEMAS WARD

New York, June 26, 1776.

Sir: Being in the greatest Distress here for Arms, without the most distant Prospect of obtaining a Supply, and as several have been lately brought into Boston, belonging to the Highlanders that have been taken, I request that you will immediately forward the remaining two Hundred Carbines (which in my Letter of the 28th. Ulto. I directed to be kept at Boston) to the Person at Norwich to whose Care the others were intrusted, with Orders to send them here with all possible Dispatch; together with the three Hundred mentioned in your Letter of the 9th. Inst., remaining Part of my former Order, which have not yet arrived here. You will direct him to send the whole by Land

---

[19] The same letter was sent to Commodore John Manley.
[20] The so-called Hickey Plot. (See note to General Orders, June 27, 1776, *post*.)

in Waggons without Delay, if when they arrive there, there shall appear the least Risk in their coming by Water.

The Places of these last two Hundred can be supplied out of the Arms lately taken, an exact Return of which with the Amount of the Prisoners and Stores if any, I shall be glad to have transmitted me. I am etc.

## GENERAL ORDERS

Head Quarters, New York, June 26, 1776.
Parole Falmouth.    Countersign Georgia.

Agreeable to a Resolve of the Honorable the Continental Congress, no Certificates of Expences are to be given in future by any but Brigadiers, Quarter Masters and their Deputies, or a Field Officer on a march, or officer commanding at a detached post.

The remainder of Col Wayne's [21] Regiment under Command of Lieut. Col Johnston [22] are to embark for Albany on Saturday next—The Quarter Master General is to provide Vessels, and the Commissary General, Provisions for their passage—Col Johnston will apply to the Adjutant General for particular Instructions, and for an order on Genl. Schuyler, for arms, when he arrives at Albany.

Col Johnston is to appoint one or more (as the case may require) diligent Officers of his Corps to take charge of such men as are now here belonging to the Regiment in Canada who are to take them and deliver them to their several Colonels or commanding Officers; passage and provisions to be furnished as above.

The commanding Officers of the several Regiments, whether in Camp, or detached Posts are as soon as possible to return into

---

[21] Col. Anthony Wayne, of the Fourth Pennsylvania Regiment. He was, late, brigadier general and major general in the Continental Army.
[22] Lieut. Col. Francis Johnston, of the Fourth Pennsylvania Regiment.

the Adjutant General's Office the names of their several officers; their Ranks and the Dates of their respective Commissions—in order that the same may be forwarded to Congress.

Joseph Hulbert of Capt Park's[23] Company and Late Col Learneds Regiment and Nathaniel Thompson of Capt. Peters Company Col Reads Regiment having been tried by a Court Martial whereof Col Parsons was president, and found guilty of Desertion, are sentenced to receive Thirty-nine Lashes each on their bare backs; which Sentence the General confirms and orders to be executed at the usual time and place.

## To LIEUTENANT COLONEL HENRY BEEKMAN LIVINGSTON

### Head Quarters in New York, June 26, 1776.

Sir: Immediately upon Receipt of this Order * * *[24] You will be furnished with the Sum of twenty pounds to enable you to purchase intrenching Tools, as none can be spared from the Quarter Master General's Store, and you will cause such works to be thrown up as you shall judge necessary for your Security. By applying to the Commissary of Ordnance Stores you will receive two Barrels of Powder for the use of the Men under your Command.[25]

## GENERAL ORDERS

### Head Quarters, New York, June 27, 1776.

Parole Halifax. Countersign Ireland.

Several persons having been detained by Sentries, notwithstanding their having given the Countersign at night, and others

---

[23] Capt. Warham Parks, of the Thirteenth Continental Infantry. He was, later, major of the Fourth Massachusetts Regiment; wounded at Saratoga, N. Y., in 1777.

[24] The omitted portion is identical with that of Washington's letter to Maj. Peter Schuyler, June 10, 1776, *q. v.*

[25] In the writing of Horatio Gates. The original is in the *House of Representatives Collection* in the Library of Congress.

in the day time on the wharves on a pretence of their not having passes—The General forbids such practices, and any Soldier convicted of them in future will be punished—Officers and guards to be careful, in posting their Sentries, to make them acquainted with this order.

### AFTER ORDERS

Thomas Hickey[26] belonging to the Generals Guard having been convicted by a General Court Martial whereof Col Parsons was President of the crimes of "Sedition and mutiny, and also of holding a treacherous correspondence with the enemy, for the most horrid and detestable purposes," is sentenced to suffer *death*. The General approves the sentence, and orders that he be hanged to morrow at Eleven OClock.

All the officers and men off duty, belonging to Genl. Heath's, Spencer's, Lord Stirling's and Genl. Scott's Brigades, to be under arms, on their respective parades, at Ten o'Clock to morrow morning, to march from thence to the Ground, between Genl. Spencer's and Lord Stirling's encampments, to attend the execution of the above sentence.

The Provost Marshal immediately to make the necessary preparations, and to attend on that duty to morrow—

---

[26] Hickey was court-martialed for sedition, mutiny, enlisting men for and receiving pay from the enemy, and convicted of activities designed to enlist soldiers from the Continental Army into the British service. The royalist mayor, David Matthews, was accused of complicity with the plot, which was clumsily directed toward an uprising, or outbreak, when the British Army arrived at New York. Such evidence as has survived shows the plot to have been the usual stupid maneuvers of ignorant marplots. The tension in New York City, however, owing to the large Tory element, created a dangerous situation that called for prompt and energetic handling. Many wild rumors filled the air, after the arrest of Hickey, who was charged, in these tales, with the intended assassination of Washington and his generals. No such charge is found in the court-martial proceedings. Washington went to the length of submitting (June 27) the sentence of the court-martial to a council of general officers consisting of himself, Heath, Spencer, Greene, Stirling, Mifflin, and Scott, and he was unanimously advised to approve the sentence and order it executed the next day.

The court-martial proceedings, dated June 26, 1776, are in the *Washington Papers*. The warrant for Hickey's execution, with the return of fulfillment indorsed thereon by Provost Marshal Marony, is also in the *Washington Papers*.

Each of the Brigade Majors to furnish the Provost Marshal, with twenty men, from each Brigade, with good arms and bayonets, as a guard on the prisoner to and at the place of execution.

## To THE PRESIDENT OF CONGRESS

New York, June 27, 1776.

Sir: I this morning received by express, Letters from Generals Schuyler and Arnold, with a copy of one from General Sullivan to the former, and also, of others to General Sullivan, of all which I do myself the Honor to transmit you Copies. They will give you further account of the Melancholly situation of our Affairs in Canada and shew there is nothing left to save our Army there, but evacuating the country. I am hopeful General Sullivan would retreat from the Isle a Noix without waiting for previous orders for that purpose, as from Generals Schuyler and Arnold's Letters, it is much to be feared by remaining there any considerable time, his retreat would be cut off, or at best be a matter of extreme difficulty. I would observe to Congress, that it is not in my power to send any Carpenters from hence to build the Gondolas and Gallies General Arnold mentions, without taking them from a Work equally necessary if not more so, here, of the same kind and submit it to them, whether It may not be advisable, as it is of great Importance to us to have a number of these Vessels on the Lake, to prevent the Enemy passing, to withdraw the Carpenters for the present from the Frigates building up the North River and detach them immediately, with all that can be got at Philadelphia, for that purpose.

I have the pleasure to inform you of another capture made by our Armed Vessels of a Transport on the 19th. instant with a Company of Highland Grenadiers on board; The Inclosed Extract of a letter from General Ward by last night's post, contains the particulars, to which I beg leave to refer you.

I have been honored with your favors of the 21st. and 25th. instant, in due order, with their Important Inclosures, to which I shall particularly attend. I have transmitted General Schuyler a Copy of the Resolve of Congress respecting the Mohickan and Stockbridge Indians, and directed him to put an immediate Stop to the raising the two Companies.[27]

The Quarter Master General has been called upon, for stopping the Tents designed for Massachusetts Bay and ordered to forward them immediately; he means to write Congress upon the Subject and hopes his conduct will not appear to deserve their reprehension; of this they will Judge from his relation of the matter.

Being extremely desirous to forward Intelligence from Canada to Congress, well knowing their anxiety about our Affairs there, I must defer writing upon some other matters I want to lay before them, till the next Opportunity, which I hope will be to morrow, when I will inform them fully upon the Subject of Rations, having desired the Commissary General to furnish me with some things necessary in that Instance. I have the Honor &ca.

## To THE PRESIDENT OF CONGRESS

New York, June 27, 1776.

Sir: Upon Information that Major Rodgers[28] was travelling thro' the Country under suspicious circumstances, I thought it necessary to have him secured. I therefore sent after him. He was taken at South Amboy and brought up to New York. Upon examination, he informed me, that he came from New Hampshire, the Country of his usual abode and pretended he

---

[27] Hancock's letter to Washington, dated June 25, 1776, directing that a stop be put to raising a force of Mohican and Stockbridge Indians, is in the *Washington Papers*.

[28] Maj. Robert Rogers. Congress resolved (July 6): "That Major Rogers be sent to New Hampshire, to be disposed of as the government of that State shall judge best."

was destined for Philadelphia on business with Congress, where he had left his family. As by his own confession he had crossed Hudson's River at New Windsor and was taken so far out of his proper and direct rout to Philadelphia, this consideration added to the length of Time he had taken to perform his Journey; his being found in so suspicious a place as Amboy; his unnecessary stay there on pretence of getting some baggage from New York, and an expectation of receiving money from a person here of bad Character and in no circumstances to furnish him out of his own Stock; the Major's reputation and his being an half pay Officer encreased my Jealousies about him.

The Business which he informs me he has with Congress, is a secret offer of his services, to the end that in case it should be rejected, he might have his way left open to an employment in the East Indies to which he is assigned and in that case he flatters himself he will obtain leave of Congress to go to Great Britain.

As he had been put upon his parole by Congress, I thought it would be improper to stay his progress to Philadelphia, should he be in fact destined thither. I therefore send him forward; but to prevent imposition, under the care of an Officer, with Letters found upon him, which from their Tenor seem calculated to recommend him to Congress.

I submit it to their consideration whether it would not be dangerous to accept the offer of his services. I have &ca.

## To MAJOR GENERAL PHILIP SCHUYLER

New York, June 27, 1776.

Dear Sir: Congress having disapproved the Proceedings of the Commissioners at Albany on the 13th. Inst., transmitted them in my Letter of the 21st., so far as they relate to raising two Companies of Mohekan and Stockbridge Indians. In Compliance with their Resolve, a Copy of which is inclosed, I am to request you to put the most early and speedy stop to the same.

The Honble President observes in his Letter, that the Resolve for employing Indians, is conceived in such Terms as to give, at first View, a Latitude of Construction as to the Place in which they are to be raised, and the Commissioners must have understood it so, which led to the Mistake. I am, etc.

## To BRIGADIER GENERAL JAMES WADSWORTH

New York, June 27, 1776.

Sir: Having received Information of your being appointed to command the Militia, to be furnished by your Colony for the Defence of this Place, I entreat you to give Notice to the Officers who are principally concerned in raising them, that their March be expedited as much as possible, or the Assistance they are meant to afford may come too late; as, in all Probability the Enemy, immediately on their Arrival, will make their grand Push, especially if they are apprized of our weak State.

It will be indispensibly necessary for the Men to come provided with Arms, as it will not be in my Power to furnish them with one; having many here already unarmed: nor will it contribute to the Service in the least Degree, if they do not. I, therefore, request the utmost Attention to this Matter, of the last Importance and that none come without.

As it will be proper that an Arrangement should be formed, and regular Orders given as to their Disposition, previous to their coming, to prevent Disorder and Confusion; I desire, as soon as you have notified your principal Officers, of what I have said about forwarding the Troops, and bringing Arms, that you repair here yourself, to receive your Instructions, and to be in Readiness to give such Directions to them as may be necessary for these Purposes. I am etc.

## To THE NEW YORK LEGISLATURE

Head Quarters, New York, June 27, 1776.

Sir: The necessity of the most Vigorous and decisive Measures in our present Circumstances, will I doubt not justify to your Honorable Body, the removal of the Stock of Cattle and Horses, from those parts of the Coast most exposed to the Enemy; after a long and fatiguing Voyage they will need Refreshment of this Nature and there is no doubt they will have them, if Possible on any Terms. Common prudence therefore and a regard to our own safety, strongly evince the necessity of depriving them of such supplies, as will enable them to act with more Vigour and Spirit against us; Tho' painful and disagreeable, it seems to be a measure which the great Law of self preservation now requires. Inclosed I transmit the unanimous Resolution of a Council of Genl Officers,[29] advising such removal without delay, in which it is proposed to pay a suitable regard to the necessities of the People. I flatter myself that in a Matter of such Importance and difficulty, The Honble. Body over which you preside, will approve of the proposal and carry it into execution, or co-operate with me in the most effectual Steps for the purpose. I have the Honor to be etc.

## To THE MASSACHUSETTS LEGISLATURE OR, IN THEIR RECESS, THE COMMITTEE OF SAFETY

New York, June 28, 1776.

Gentn.: By certain Advices just received I am informed that a Fleet consisting of 130 Sail left Halifax the 9th Instant, bound for this place and am well assured, that General Howe is already

---

[29] This council was held on June 27 and was attended by Brig. Gens. William Heath, Joseph Spencer, Nathanael Greene, and Lord Stirling. The original proceedings are in the *Washington Papers*.

arrived at the Hook in the Greyhound; I do therefore, in the most pressing manner request, that you would not lose a moment's time in sending forward the Militia of your Province, as the Enemy will undoubtedly attack us in our Weak state, as soon as a Sufficient force arrives, to enable them to attempt it, with the least probability of Success; and altho' I cannot expect, by reason of the distance, that your Quota of Troops will reach this so seasonably, as to afford assistance upon the first attack of the Enemy, yet I promise myself it will not occasion any delay in their March. Relying on your using all possible dispatch in this Business, I remain, etc.[30]

## To MAJOR GENERAL PHILIP SCHUYLER

New York, June 28, 1776.

Dear Sir: Your Favour of the 25th and it's Inclosures with General Arnold's of the same Date, I received by Yesterday Morning's Express. That of the 24th came by this Day's Post.

I am sorry General Sullivan, in the Situation our Affairs were in, should have stop'd at the Isle Aux Noix, till he could obtain Orders for retreating further, thereby hazarding his Army, without a Prospect of Success, and rendering his Retreat liable to an Interception, or at least difficult, in Case the Enemy were in a Condition to pursue their Victory. For these Reasons I cannot but approve your Directions, and am hopeful they would arrive in Time, if he had not before left the Isle Aux Noix, by the Advice of his Counsel of War, and joint Intercession of his Officers.

My Letter of the 24th would shew you, had it been received, that from his Representation of Matters, I thought a Retreat the only Means left for the security of his Army, and doing the least essential service to their Country. If he gets off, I shall

---

[30] Practically the same letter was sent to Gov. Jonathan Trumbull and to Brig. Gen. James Wadsworth, of the Connecticut Militia, at Dunham, this same day.

be happy that our Loss was so inconsiderable in Numbers, tho'
I regret much the Captivity of General Thompson.

I have wrote Congress about Carpenters on General Arnold's
Letter, and having none to spare from hence, have pointed out
the Necessity of their sending some from Philadelphia, if not
there, withdrawing for the present those employed up the North
River, deeming it a Matter of infinite Importance to have a
considerable Number of Gondolas on the Lakes, to prevent the
Enemy from passing.

I have directed the Qr. Mr. General to procure and forward
you the Anchors and Cables, Mill Saws and Files, if to be had.
I have also requested Colo. Knox to examine, whether some
more Field Pieces cannot be sent up, and I design to order a
further Quantity of Powder to be forwarded you, to answer
two Purposes; one that you may have proper supplies for the
several Posts, and every Contingency, the other, because I do
not wish to keep a larger Stock here than may be necessary,
least any unfortunate Event should cast up, and we be deprived
of more than we are yet able to loose.

I would have you make ready every Thing necessary for taking Post at Fort Stanwix, and when you are prepared, to use
your utmost Industry for erecting and compleating the Work.
Our most vigorous Exertions will be required in every Instance.
I am convinced our Enemies will strain their every Nerve
against us this Campaign, and try to injure us wherever we
may be unprovided.

It will be extremely proper to forward on the Militia, for reinforcing the several Garrisons on the Communication, and
securing the different Passes. I wish they were not so slow in
repairing to the Places of Rendezvous; but I would fain apprehend they will be in Time, to prevent any attempts our
Enemies may have in View.

I am extremely sorry for your Indisposition and that you should be so harrassed by the Ague and Fever, and wishing you a perfect Recovery from it and a speedy one, I am, etc.

P. S. Congress by a Letter I received from the President last Night, have resolved upon four Thousand Men more to augment the Army in the Northern Department, and recommended the Colonies of New Hampshire immediately to send one Regiment of Militia, Massachusetts two, and Connecticut one.

They have also resolved on a Bounty of ten Dollars for every Soldier that will inlist for three Years, and requested the several Governments who are to furnish Militia to do it with all possible Expedition.

Our armed Vessels at the Eastward, have taken some valuable Prizes, and also three more Transports safely brought in with about 320 or 30 Highland Troops well accoutred. Captain Bedel,[31] one of Commodore Hopkins's Fleet took two also with about 150 more. He put all the Prisoners on Board one of the Prizes: we fear she is retaken. The Arms he took into his own Vessel. The other Prize was retaken and again taken by another of our Vessels. * * *[32]

The Militia, ordered for the Defence of this Place, come in slowly. Not more than a Thousand are yet arrived. Our Force by no Means so strong as it should be.

It is said, and I beleive with Authority, that twenty Tons of Powder, and £2000 Sterlg. worth of Goods have got into Providence. I am, etc.


To THE PRESIDENT OF CONGRESS

New York, June 28, 1776.

Sir: In compliance with the request of Congress, contained in your favor of the 25th. instant and my promise of Yesterday,

---

[31] Capt. Nicholas Biddle(?).
[32] The omitted paragraph is the same as that in Washington's letter to the Massachusetts Legislature, June 28, 1776, *q. v.*

I do myself the Honor to inform you that the Cost of a Ration according to the Commissary General's estimate, from the 1st. of July to the 1st. of December will be from 8d. to 8½ York currency.[33]

Having discharged the Obligation I was under in this Instance and finding that many applications have been made for victualling the Flying Camp. I would with all possible deference, wish Congress to consider the matter well before they come to any determination upon it.—Who the Gentlemen are, that have made offers upon this Occasion I know not, consequently my Objections to their appointment cannot proceed from personal dislike, nor have I it in view to serve Mr. Trumbull the Commissary General, by wishing him to have the directions of the whole supplies for his Emolument; because what ever Rations are taking from him, save him the Trouble of supplying provisions to the amount without diminishing his pay, that being fixed and certain; But what influences me, is a regard to the Public good. I am morally certain if the Business is taken out of Mr. Trumbull's hands and put into another, that it may, and will in all probability be attended with great and many Inconveniences. It is likely, during the continuance of the War between us and great Britain, that the Army here or part of it, and the Troops composing the Flying Camp, will be frequently Joined, and under the necessity of affording each other mutual aid: If this Event is probable and most certainly it is, the same confusion and disorder will result, from having two Commissaries or one Commissary and one Contractor in the same Army and department, as did between Mr. Trumbull and Mr. Livingston, on the coming of the former to New York. I cannot discriminate between the two cases, and not foreseeing any good consequences will flow from the measure, but that many bad

---

[33] Each colony had its own currency. By York, Washington meant the New York money. The rate of exchange varied between the different Colonies.

ones will, such as a clashing of Interest, a Contention for Stores, Carriages and many other things that might be mentioned, I confess I cannot perceive the propriety of appointing a different person or any but the Commissary. I would also add, few Armies, if any, have been better and more plentifully supplied than the Troops under Mr. Trumbull's care in this Instance, which I should suppose ought to have considerable weight; especially, as we have strong reasons to induce us to believe, that a large share of the Misfortunes our Arms have sustained in Canada, sprang from a want of proper and necessary supplies of Provisions. Mr. Trumbull too I am informed, has already made provision in New Jersey for the Flying Camp which will be stationed there and employed proper persons in that Colony to transact the business. Incident to his departments in obedience to my orders and his full confidence that It was to come under his management. My great desire to see the Affairs of this Important post, on which so much depend, go on in, an easy, smooth, uninterrupted course has led me to say thus much upon the Subject and will I hope, If I am unhappy enough to differ in opinion with Congress, plead my excuse for the Liberty I have taken.

I would also beg leave to mention to Congress, the necessity there is of some new regulations being entered into respecting the Chaplains of the Army. They will remember, that application was made to increase their pay, which was conceived too low for their support. It was proposed that if, It could not be done for the whole, the number should be lessened and one, Chaplain be appointed to two Regiments and an additional allowance made them on that Account. The Latter expedient was adopted, which, at that time and while the Army continued altogether at one Encampment, answered or at least did not produce any Capital inconveniences; But the Army now being differently circumstanced from what it then was, part here, part at Boston, and a third part detached to Canada, has Introduced much confusion and disorder in this Instance. nor do I know how it is possible to remedy the Evil, but by affixing one to each Regiment, with a salary competent to their support; no Shifting, no Change from one Regiment to another, can answer the purpose, and in many cases it could not be done, tho' the Regiments should consent, as where detachments are composed of unequal numbers, or Ordered from different Posts. Many more Inconveniences might be pointed out, but these it is presumed will sufficiently shew the defect of the present establishment and the propriety of an alteration. What that Alteration shall be Congress will please to determine.

Congress, I doubt not, will have heard of the Plot that was forming among many disaffected persons in this City and Government for aiding the Kings Troops on their arrival. The matter I am in hopes, by a timely discovery, will be suppressed, and put a stop to, many Citizens and others, among whom is the Mayor, are now in confinement. It has been traced up to Governor Tryon, and the Mayor appears to have been a principal Agent, or go between him and the persons concerned in it. The plot had been communicated to some of the Army and part of my Guard engaged in it. Thomas Hicky, one of them, has been tried and by the unanimous opinion of a Court Martial, is sentenced to die having inlisted himself and engaged others. The Sentence, by the advice of the whole Council of General Officers, will be put in execution to day at 11 O'Clock. The others are not tried. I am hopeful this example will produce many salutary consequences and deter others from entering into the like traiterous practices. The inclosed Copy of a resolve of the Provincial Congress will shew that some of the disaffected on Long Island, have taken up Arms. I have agreeable to their request, sent a party after them, but have not been able to apprehend them, having concealed themselves in a difficult Wood and morass.

General Gates set out on Tuesday with fine Wind, which has been fair ever since and would soon arrive at Albany.

I this moment received a Letter from Lieut. Davison of the Schuyler Armed Sloop, a copy of which I have inclosed and to which I beg leave to refer you for the Intelligence communicated by him.[34] I could wish General Howe and his Armament not to arrive yet, as not more than a 1000 Militia have yet come in, and our whole force, including the Troops at all the detached posts and on board the Armed Vessels, which are comprized in our returns, is but small and inconsiderable when compared to the extensive lines they are to defend and most probably the Army he brings. I have no further Intelligence about him than what the Lieut. mentions, but it is extremely probable the Accounts and conjectures are true. I have &ca.

P. S: I have inclosed you a General Return of the Army.[35] The Accounts from the Lieutenant are certainly to be depended on, as some of the Prisoners in the retaken prizes were on board the Grey Hound and saw General Howe.[36]

## GENERAL ORDERS

Head Quarters, New York, June 28, 1776.

Parole Kendal.     Countersign Lebanon.

The unhappy Fate of Thomas Hickey, executed this day for Mutiny, Sedition and Treachery, the General hopes will be a

[34] Lieut. Joseph Davidson. His report (June 27) was that Howe's fleet of 130 sail had left Halifax for New York on June 9. General Howe arrived on the 25th, and the main body of his fleet on the 29th, the troops being immediately disembarked on Staten Island. Davidson's letter is in the *Washington Papers.*

[35] According to this return, dated June 28, the strength of the Army was 7,389 present and fit for duty, 744 sick, 231 absent sick, 1,931 on command, and 73 on furlough, a total of 10,368 rank and file, with 575 sergeants and 295 drums and fifes. The commissioned officers numbered 594. The regiment of artillery, not included in the above, had 365 officers and enlisted men fit for duty, with 185 on command and 34 sick.

[36] In the writing of Robert Hanson Harrison.

warning to every Soldier, in the Army, to avoid those crimes, and all others, so disgraceful to the character of a Soldier, and pernicious to his country, whose pay he receives and Bread he eats—And in order to avoid those Crimes the most certain method is to keep out of the temptation of them, and particularly to avoid lewd Women, who, by the dying Confession of this poor Criminal, first led him into practices which ended in an untimely and ignominious Death.

Officers are without delay to inspect the State of the Ammunition which the men have and get their Arms in good order for service and strongly to inculcate upon all Sentries especially on night duty the greatest vigilance and attention. The Soldiers on their part to be very attentive, and obedient to these orders, as a carelessness and neglect may be of the most fatal consequence.

No Persons to be permitted to inspect the works without leave in writing.

The General requests the Colonels of the several Regiments, not to depend wholly upon their Officers, in complying with the above order, respecting the arms and ammunition of the soldiers, but to pay particular attention to the matter themselves it being at this Juncture of the greatest importance.

#### AFTER ORDERS

It is not from any distrust of the vigilance, or spirit of the inferior Officers, (as he has the greatest confidence in them) that the General recommends to the Colonels, an attention to the arms and ammunition of their respective Regiments, but that every officer from the highest to the lowest, when the hour of attack seems fast approaching, may exert himself in this necessary duty and it is particularly recommended from the Brigadier Generals to the Ensigns to give it the utmost attention.

## GENERAL ORDERS

Head Quarters, New York, June 29, 1776.
Parole Manchester.   Countersign Norfolk.

Ensign Miller[37] of Col Wyllys's Regiment under Arrest for leaving his guard at the City Hall and suffering a prisoner to be absent from thence, to be immediately tried by a General Court Martial—Notice to be given to the witnesses to attend.

### AFTER ORDERS

'Till the reinforcement intended for this department arrives, and some general regulations takes place; Brigadier Genl. Mifflin is to take charge of the two Battalions from Pennsylvania, commanded by Colonels Shee and Magaw, but is to remain in the City of New York 'till further orders; before him all prisoners and all deserters are to be carried for examination, the former he will order to be escorted to such places as the Provincial Congress, or Committee of safety for New York, shall assign, and the latter to have removed to a distance from the army—reporting to the General all extraordinaries—General Mifflin will also turn his attention in a particular manner to the Gundoloes, Fire-Rafts &c—causing the work to advance with all possible dispatch and seeing that nothing is omitted which can complete and forward them. Jonathan Mifflin Esqr. is appointed Brigade Major to General Mifflin, and is to be obeyed as such.

The commanding officers of the Militia, from the several Counties, are to see that each private is furnished with Twenty four Rounds of Powder and Ball by applying to Commissary Cheever as fast as they arrive and to form them into Battalions as early as possible.

---

[37] Ensign Charles Miller, of the Twenty-second Continental Infantry. He rose to rank of first lieutenant and served to end of the war.

EVENING ORDERS

As many useful men belonging to the Army have been drafted, and others have been hired, for the different works of the Camp, and as their assistance may be wanted to repel the enemy; Such Carpenters, Armourers, Smiths and other Artificers, as are now under the directions of Capts. Post, Pollard, Brewin, Ford and Bacon,[88] are forthwith to be formed into a distinct Corps, under the Command of Col Jonathan Brewer, and Mr. Parke[39] Assist. Qr. Mr. General, who are to act, (pro-tempore) as their Colonel and Lieut. Colonel—Mr. Parke to parade them on the Common near the Park of Artillery, at Ten O'Clock, to morrow morning—he is to order an account to be taken of their Arms and Accoutrements, and to form them into Companies of fifty, and then report to the General, who will nominate such temporary officers, as will be necessary, to complete the several companies; this Corps to continue during the present exigency; after which they will return to their former employments; at the same time they are not to be exempted from their ordinary duty, while under the present Arrangement, except while they are arranging, or called out to action.

The Quarter Master General to deliver to Genl. Putnam's order, all the Sand-Bags in his possession—he is also to engage such a number of Cart Horses, in the City, as Col Knox shall think sufficient for the use of the Train of Artillery, and with the assistance of Col. Knox, to arrange them in such a manner as will prevent confusion in time of service, and best answer the design of employing them; he is to produce as many sound, empty Hogsheads as he can, and deliver them to Genl. Putnams order, he is to procure all the Row Boats and light

---

[88] Capts. Anthony Post, Benjamin Pollard, Jeremiah Bruen, John(?) Ford, and William Bacon.

[39] John Parke.

Pettiaugers, in and near this City; and is to station them with all other boats, belonging to the Army, and not in use, in the dock between the Exchange Slip and Albany pier.

The Commissary General to lodge a fortnight's provision on Governor's Island, Powles-hook, and in all the detached posts; to enable him to do this with precision, Genl. Putnam will furnish him with a List of the men in the several posts—

The General expects that all Soldiers, who are intrusted with the defence of any work, will behave with great coolness and bravery, and will be particularly careful not to throw away their fire—he recommends to them to load for their first fire, with one musket ball and four or eight buck Shot, according to the size and strenght of their pieces; if the enemy is received with such a fire at not more than twenty or thirty yards distance, he has no doubt of their being repulsed.

The Brigadier Generals to order Cheveaux-de-Frizes and Fascines, sufficient to shut up the Sally-ports of their respective works, to be immediately provided and lodged near the works.

## To BRIGADIER GENERAL WILLIAM LIVINGSTON[40]

New York, June 29, 1776.

Dear Sir: Since Colo. Reed[41] left this, I have received certain Information from the Hook, that about forty of the Enemy's Fleet have arrived there, and others now in Sight, that there cannot be a Doubt, but the whole Fleet will be in this Day, and To-Morrow. I beg not a Moment's Time may be lost in sending forward such Parts of the Militia, as Colonel Reed shall mention.

We are so very weak at this Post, that I must beg you to order the three Companies, which I mentioned in my last for Staten

---

[40] Commander in chief of the New Jersey Militia stationed at Elizabethtown. Later he became governor of the State.

[41] Joseph Reed, Adjutant General of the Continental Army.

Island, immediately to this City. If Colo. Herd[42] is the Commanding Officer, I must request you will lay my several Letters wrote to you before him without Delay. I am, Sir, etc.

## To THE PRESIDENT OF CONGRESS

New York, June 29, 1776.

Sir: I was last night honoured with your favor of the 26th. instant, and agreeable to your request, shall pay proper attention to the resolves it inclosed.

I observe the Augmentation Congress have resolved to make to the forces destined for the Northern department and the bounty to be allowed such Soldiers as will inlist for three Years. I hope many good consequences will result from these measures, and that from the Latter a considerable Number of Men may be induced to engage in the Service.

I should esteem myself extremely happy, to afford the least assistance to the Canada Department, in compliance with the desire of Congress and your requisition were it in my power; but it is not. The Return I transmitted Yesterday, will but too well convince Congress of my incapacity in this Instance, and point out to them, that the force I now have is trifling, considering the many and important posts that are necessary and must be supported if possible. But few Militia have yet come in; the whole being about Twelve hundred, including the two Battalions of this City and one Company from the Jerseys. I wish the delay may not be attended with disagreeable circumstances and their aid may not come too late, or, when it may not be wanted. I have wrote; I have done every thing in my power to call them in, but they have not come, tho' I am told that they are generally willing.

---

[42] Col. Nathaniel Heard. At this date he was brigadier general of New Jersey Militia.

The Accounts communicated yesterday thro' Lieut. Davison's Letter are partly confirmed, and I dare say will turn out to be true in the whole. For two or three days past three or four Ships have been droping in and I just now received an Express from an Officer appointed to keep a look out on Staten Island, that forty five arrived at the Hook to day, some say more, and I suppose the whole fleet will be in within a day or two. I am hopeful before they are prepared to attack, that I shall get some reinforcements but be that as it may, I shall attempt to make the best disposition I can for our Troops, in order to give them a proper reception, and to prevent the ruin and destruction they are meditating against us.

As soon as the Express arrived last Night, I sent the Letters for the Northern Colonies to the Quartr. Master General, with orders to forward them immediately.

When Monsr. Wiebert[43] comes, (I have not yet seen him) I shall employ him as Congress have directed. The Terms upon which he offers his service, seem to promise something from him.[44] I wish he may answer, and be skilled in the business he professes to know. I have &ca.[45]

## To THE BOARD OF WAR AND ORDNANCE

New York, June 29, 1776.

Gentlemen: I am now to acknowledge the receipt of your favor of the 21st. Inst.,[46] and the proceedings of Congress, with which you have been pleased to honor me. I must beg pardon for not having answered it before and trust the multiplicity of

---

[43] Antoine Felix Wiebert, a French engineer, was commissioned by Congress a lieutenant colonel of Engineers on June 24.

[44] Wiebert was captured by the British and, because he did not have this commission with him and refused to enter the British service, was confined in the provost in New York City and rigorously treated. After his exchange he returned to France and served as a volunteer on the *Bon Homme Richard*. John Paul Jones placed him in charge of the sick, wounded, and prisoners of that expedition on an island in the Texel.

[45] In the writing of Robert Hanson Harrison.

[46] It called for returns of the entire Army and the establishment of a regular correspondence with the Commander in Chief. This letter is in the *Washington Papers*.

War Office Philadᵃ. 21ˢᵗ June 1776

Sir

The Congress having thought proper to appoint us to the Board of War & Ordinance, we do ourselves the Honour to transmit you the foregoing Extracts from their Proceedings establishing a War Office for the more speedy & effectual Dispatch of military Business. You will perceive, on Perusal of the Extracts, that it will be necessary for you forthwith to furnish the Board with an exact State of the Army under your Command & every thing relative thereto. You will therefore be pleased, as speedily as possible, to give the necessary Directions for true & accurate Returns to be made to you, so as to enable you to give the Board the proper Information. As much depends on reducing into Method the Business recommended to our Notice, we beg you will forward all Measures conducive to this desirable Purpose by every Means in your Power. It is expected that in future monthly Returns be regularly transmitted to the War Office that Congress may frequently have a full & general Knowledge of the true Situation of their military Affairs without which it will be impossible to conduct them with Propriety & Success. We must further request that you will keep up a constant & regular Correspondence with us that we may cooperate with you in such Measures as may tend to advance the Interest of America in general & the particular Department committed to your Care. You will be pleased in the Returns of the several Regiments to mention the Colonies in which they were raised, the Times when & the Periods for which the Men were enlisted as it will be necessary for us to have sufficient Notice of these Matters that Congress may keep up the Army to its full Compliment

We are your Excellency's most obedient & most
    humble Servants

    John Adams
    Roger Sherman
    Benj Harrison
    James Wilson
    Edward Rutledge

His Excellency Genl. Washington

FIRST LETTER FROM THE BOARD OF WAR TO WASHINGTON
JUNE 21, 1776

Business in which I have been engaged, since it came to hand, will apologize for the neglect. I shall particularly regard the several Important matters contained therein, and as far as opportunity and the Situation of Affairs will permit, use every means in my power to comply with your requisitions, and the Duties enjoined on me; sensible that our joint opperations will contribute greatly to advance the Interest of America in General, and the particular department committed to my care. You may rest assured that I shall be happy to keep up a regular Correspondence, and will not fail to transmit you the most early Accounts of every measure, haveing the least tendency to this desirable end. I am, etc.

### To COLONEL JAMES CLINTON
New York, June 29, 1776.

Sir: The Committee inform me that no Evidence has appeared against Fletcher Matthews, and desire his Papers may be delivered to him, which I would have you comply with, likewise of the Request of the Committees of Newburgh and New Windsor.

I have to inform you of the Arrival of about 50 Sail this Day at the Hook. This is a Part of a Fleet of 130 which left Hallifax under General Howe the 9th. Inst.

I would have you make all possible Preparation in Case the Enemy should have in View to push some of their Frigates up the North River, to give them a proper Reception. I am, etc.

### To THE PRESIDENT OF CONGRESS
New York, June 30, 1776.

Sir: I had the pleasure of receiving your favor of the 29th. early this morning, with which you have been pleased to honor me, together with the resolves for further Augmenting our Army.

The Battalion of Germans, which Congress have ordered to be raised, will be a Corps of much service and I am hopeful that such persons will be appointed officers, as will complete their Inlistments with all possible expedition.

I shall communicate to Colonel Stevenson and one of his Field Officers, what you have requested and desire them to repair Immediately to Philadelphia. It is an unlucky circumstance, that the Term of Inlistment of these three Companies and of the Rifle Battalion, should expire at this time, when a hot Campaign is in all probability about to commence.[47]

Canada, it is certain would have been an Important acquisition, and well worth the Expences incurred in the pursuit of it. But as we could not reduce it to our possession, the retreat of our Army with so little loss under such a variety of Distresses must be esteemed a most fortunate event. It is true the Accounts we have received, do not fully Authorize us to say, that we have sustained no loss but they hold forth a probable Ground for such conclusions. I am anxious to hear it confirmed.[48]

I have the honor of transmitting you an extract of a letter received last Night from General Ward. If the Scheme the Privateers had in view, and the measures he had planned, had been carried into Execution, the Highland Corps will be tolerably well disposed of, but I fear the fortunate event has not taken place. In General Ward's Letter[49] was inclosed one from Lieut. Col. Campbell[50] who was made Prisoner, with the Highland Troops: I have transmitted you a Copy. This will give you a full and exact Account of the Number of Prisoners that were on board the four Transports, and will prove beyond a

---

[47] By resolve of June 27 Congress directed that four companies of Germans should be raised in Pennsylvania and four companies in Maryland. They also resolved that six companies of riflemen should be enlisted, four of them in Virginia and two in Maryland, to serve for three years, and be formed into a regiment with three companies already raised in New York. Capt. Hugh Stephenson was appointed colonel of this regiment.

[48] Brig. Gen. John Sullivan's letter to Washington gives the account of the retreat from Canada. This letter is in the *Washington Papers* and is printed in Sparks's *Letters to Washington*, vol. 1, p. 231.

[49] Ward's letter of June 20 expresses his desire to be relieved of command. This letter is in the *Washington Papers*.

[50] Lieut. Col. Archibald Campbell, of the Seventy-first Foot, British Army.

possibility of doubt, that the evacuation of Boston by the British Troops, was a matter neither known or expected when he received his Orders. Indeed so many facts had concurred before to settle the matter, that no additional proofs were necessary.

When I had the Honor of addressing you Yesterday, I had only been Informed of the arrival of Forty five of the Fleet in the Morning; since that I have received Authentic Intelligence from sundry persons, among them from General Greene, that one hundred and ten sail came in before Night, that were counted, and that more were seen about dusk in the offing. I have no doubt, but the whole that sailed from Hallifax, are now at the Hook.

Just as I was about to conclude my Letter, I received one from a Gentleman, upon the Subject of calling the five Regiments from Boston to the defence of Canada, or New York, and to have Militia raised in their lieu. I have sent you a Copy, and shall only observe, that I know the Author well, his hand writing is quite familiar to me: he is a Member of the General Court, very sensible, of great Influence, and a warm and Zealous friend to the cause of America. The Expedient proposed by him is submitted to Congress.[51] I am &ca.[52]

## To THE COMMITTEE OF ESSEX COUNTY, NEW JERSEY

New York, June 30, 1776.

Sir: I received you favor by Mr. Treat, and cannot but consider the officer of Mr. Franklin's Guard extremely blameable, for his conduct; It is certainly his Indispensible duty, to conduct Mr. Franklin to the place the Convention have ordered

---

[51] Joseph Hawley. Extracts of his letters of May 21 and 27 suggesting that the troops at Boston be drawn to New York and their place supplied by militia are printed by Sparks, who prints the entire letter of May 21 in his *Letters to Washington*, vol. 1, p. 229. The May 21 letter is in the *Washington Papers;* that of May 27 is not.
[52] In the writing of Robert Hanson Harrison.

without delay. The Circumstances you represent, his Letter to his Lady and the whole complexion of the case, afford a strong presumption; nay, much more, full evidence, that he means to escape if possible. he says in his Letter, "that, during his respite, the time between his writing and getting an Answer from Congress, something may turn up to make his removal improper, and at any rate to gain time will be of advantage."

I have wrote to the Captain of his guard upon the subject, and as Mr. Franklin has evidenced a most unfriendly disposition to our Cause—As the Colony Convention have ordered him to Connecticut, for refusing to Comply with such terms, as they deemed necessary and proper for him to enter into, to procure his Liberty[53]—As he does not propose to sign the Parole which they formed, but has proposed several alterations; I am of opinion, your Committee should interfere in the matter and give immediate orders to the officer of the Guard, to proceed with him, in execution of the duty wherewith he is charged; and, further, that, if you apprehend there is the least danger of his being rescued, or of the Guard, appointed to escort him, being remiss in their duty, that your Committee should appoint a strong escort for the purpose, and direct them to assist in performing the Views of the Convention, and conduct him securely to the place fixed upon to receive him.

I have inclosed the Letter for the officer of the guard, which having read, you will seal and transmit him. I am &c.

## To THE CAPTAIN OF GOVERNOR FRANKLIN'S GUARD

Head Quarters, New York, June 30, 1776.

Sir: I understand that the Convention of New Jersey did resolve that Governor Franklin was an Enemy to the Liberties

---

[53] Gov. William Franklin, royalist Governor of New Jersey, was the natural son of Dr. Benjamin Franklin. He was a strong loyalist and had been arrested as a public enemy; he was confined in Connecticut. After his exchange he became the president of the Associated Loyalists.

of America, and that he should be conducted under a safe
Guard into Connecticut, and for that Purpose he was committed
to your Charge. I have this Morning received Information, that
you have halted with him at Hackensack. I would enjoin it
upon you to set off immediately, and carry the Resolve of Convention into Execution. Delays are dangerous, and should any
Accident happen, you never could answer your Neglect to our
much injured Country. I would therefore again repeat to you,
that it is my Advice, immediately on Receipt of this, to set forward on your Journey with Governor Franklin, and make all
possible Dispatch for the Place you are ordered to. Governor
Franklin, once had his Choice, and chose Connecticut; and
it is not for you to hesitate on frivolous Pretences; but do
your utmost to execute the Orders you have received in every
Particular. I am, etc.

## GENERAL ORDERS

Head Quarters, New York, June 30, 1776.
Parole Philadelphia.    Countersign Holland.

The Brigadiers are to order the officers and men belonging
to their several Brigades (not on duty) to march from their respective Regimental parade to their alarm posts at least once
every day that they may become well acquainted therewith,
they are to march by such Routes as are least exposed to a fire
from the shipping and it is expected that all officers from the
highest to the lowest, will make themselves well acquainted
with the ground, that they may at any time be able to make
advantage of it.

Upon the Signal for the enemies approach, or upon any alarm,
all fatigue parties are immediately to repair to their respective
Corps, with their arms, ammunition and accoutrements ready
for instant action; the working parties in no other instance are
to be interrupted; the finishing of our Lines of defence and

other works expeditiously, is a matter of so much consequence, that the General is persuaded from the known Zeal of the troops, that officers and men will stand in no need of arguments, to stimulate them upon common exertion upon the occasion, his anxiety for the Honor of the American Arms, and the noble cause we are engaged in, not a distrust in the officers care, induces him once more, and while time will allow it, to recommend a thorough Inspection in the men's arms and ammunition, to see that every Soldier is completed to Twenty-four Rounds, and has a good Flint, well fixed into the lock; in short to be well prepared for an engagement is, under God, (whose divine Aid it behoves us to supplicate) more than one half the battle.

The General desires that each Colonel, or commanding officer of the established Regiments, will furnish him with a list of the vacancies therein, and that the Field Officers of those Regiments would recommend proper persons, to fill them—The commanding officer for the time being, of such Militia as shall arrive in this City from New Jersey, Connecticut and Massachusetts bay, is to give in Returns thereof to the Adjutant General of the parties as they arrive, he is immediately to discharge every man who comes without Arms, and is to see that all the others are completed with their Twenty-four Rounds pr man, and that they do their proportion of all duties, as well fatigue as other duty.

Capt. Josiah Fay [54] of Col. Ward's Regiment to act as Major of the said regiment, 'till further orders, he is to be obeyed as such.

### AFTER ORDERS

Twenty six thousand Musket Cartridges to be sent Col. Prescott on Governor's Island with some flints.

---

[54] Of the Twenty-first Continental Infantry. He died Aug. 8, 1776.

The Brigadiers to order a circle to be marked round the several Redoubts, by which their officers are to be directed, in giving orders for the first discharge—Small brush may be set up to make the line more distinct and familiar to the men, who are by no means to be ordered to fire before the enemy arrive at the circle.

The Countersign in future to be delivered by the Adjutant General, to the Brigade Majors, and Adjutant of Artillery, at Six oClock P.M; who are to send the same sealed to their respective Brigades, and to the Field Officers of their respective brigades, if required by the latter and to no others—

Capt. Stephen Brown[55] of Col Durkee's Regiment, to go immediately to New-Ark, and apply for assistance in procuring and fixing boats, near the ferries, for facilitating the passage of the Troops from Jersey to New York.

Genl. Heath to order the house and barn on Governors Island, to be consumed.

## GENERAL ORDERS

Head Quarters, New York, July 1, 1776.
Parole Jersey.   Countersign Militia.

The General Court Martial whereof Col Parsons is President is dissolved—A General Court Martial of the lines consisting of one Colonel, one Lieut. Colonel, one Major and ten Captains to sit to morrow morning at Ten O'Clock to try all such prisoners as shall be brought before them—All Witnesses and other persons concerned to attend the Court—Field Officers for the above General Court Martial Col Read[56] President, Lieut. Col Clark[57] and Major Sprout.[58]

---

[55] Of the Twentieth Continental Infantry.
[56] Col. Joseph Read, of the Thirteenth Continental Infantry.
[57] Lieut. Col. Joel Clark, of the Seventeenth Continental Infantry.
[58] Maj. Ebenezer Sprout, of the Third Continental Infantry.

John Lynch of Capt. Benezets Company[59] and Col. Magaw's Regiment convicted by a General Court Martial of "striking and wounding an officer of Col Shee's Battalion"; and Richd. Neal and James Higgins of Capt. Stevenson's Independent Company of Rifle Men being convicted by the same Court Martial whereof Col Parsons was President, of "striking and abusing several officers of the 20th. Regt."—were sentenced by the Court to receive Thirty-nine Lashes each—The General approves the sentences, and orders them to be put in execution, at such time and place, as the commanding officer of their respective Corps shall direct.

A working party of nine hundred men from General Heath's, Spencer's and Lord Stirling's Brigades and the same proportion from General Scott's to turn out at five oClock A. M.—Huntington's, Ward's, Nixon's and Webb's Regiments to work at the Redoubts on Jews-hill plain, and Bayards-hill, to be allowed one hour for breakfast—three for dinner and to work 'till sunset—Parson's Regiment to work on the Well under Capt. Chapman's[60] directions—Learneds, Wyllys's and Bailey's Regiments go to Governors Island: Learneds to take Axes from the Laboratory: Prescott's Regiment to work as Huntingtons, and turn out the whole off duty, the picquet not excepted, Prescott's Regiment is required to be more attentive to duty, not having furnished their compliment at the works for two Weeks 'till yesterday—Baldwins Regiment to work at Red hook, and take tools from the Laboratory—Genl. Scotts Brigade, McDougall's, Ritzema's and Reeds Regiments, to receive Orders at the Laboratory in the morning—All working parties to work 'till sunset, and those Regiments not otherwise directed, to parade by Six oClock A: M:

---

[59] Capt. Samuel Benezet, of the Fifth Pennsylvania Regiment.

[60] Capt. James Chapman, of the Tenth Continental Infantry. He was promoted to major in August and killed Sept. 15, 1776, in the retreat to Harlem.

The Troops in rotation to be allowed to fire two Cartridges pr Man, in such a manner, and at such time, as the respective Brigadiers may direct: The Brigadiers to give notice to the General of their several determinations on this head.

William Hurly of Capt. Parks Company, and of the Regiment late Learned's tried by the above Court Martial for firing on and wounding without cause one Peter Child a Citizen was acquitted—The General approves thereof and orders him to be discharged.

### AFTER ORDERS

The whole Army to be under Arms to morrow morning at day light, on their Regimental parades, with their full Ammunition ready for action: The Militia of the City will parade at their usual places, and take their orders from the Brigadier General commanding in that quarter. The Artificers and such Militia or other Troops as are arrived in Town, and have no other destination are to parade on the Common in the front of the Park of Artillery, and take their orders from Brigadier General Lord Stirling—Colonel Nixon with his regiment, is to proceed, as soon as possible, in the morning, to Governors Island, and take the command there.

### To MAJOR GENERAL ARTEMAS WARD

New York, July 1, 1776.

Sir: I received your Favours of the 20th. and 23rd. Ulto. and am happy to hear of the further Success of our armed Vessels in the Capture of the Transport with the Highland Grenadiers. If they have been fortunate enough to take the 11. Ships mentioned in your last, I suppose we are in Possession of a large Share of the Highlanders ordered against us.

I am extremely sorry for your Indisposition and wish to afford you all the Relief in my Power, and that the Situation of Things will admit of it. It is particularly unlucky that Mr. Whitcomb[61] should refuse his Commission at this Crisis.

A Fleet has arrived at the Hook, which we suppose to be General Howe's, having received authentic Intelligence of his sailing from Hallifax on the 9th Ulto., with 132 Sail. One Hundred and ten came in on Saturday, more were in the Offing and a few had got in two or three Days before. We expect he will make an Attack, as soon as possible, and I am making every Preparation to receive him.

As we are extremely deficient in Arms here, and in great Distress for Want of them; I shall be glad if you will send all of those taken from the Highlanders, which you conceive can be possibly spared. Let them be sent immediately to Norwich, to the Persons there who were entrusted with the others, with Directions to forward them without Delay by Water, if there shall be no Risk; if there is, by Land.

You will observe, that the new Regiments to be raised in the Massachusetts, are to furnish their own; before they are received or can be taken into Pay. I am, etc.

P. S. It is not in my Power to send a General Officer now. I have but one Major General, and not Brigadiers more than are absolutely necessary nor so many. I have heard nothing more of the other three Hundred Carbines. They are not yet arrived.

### GENERAL ORDERS

Head Quarters, New York, July 2, 1776.

Parole Armstrong.   Countersign Lee.

Genl. Mifflin is to repair to the post near Kingsbridge and use his utmost endeavours to forward the works there—General Scott in the mean time to perform the duty required of General Mifflin in the orders of the 29th of June.

---

[61] Maj. Gen. John Whitcomb, of the Massachusetts Militia. He declined an appointment of brigadier general in the Continental Army.

No Sentries are to stop or molest the Country people coming to Market or going from it but to be very vigilant in preventing Soldiers leaving the army.

Col Cortland[62] of the New-Jersey Brigade is to send over five-hundred of the Militia under his command to reinforce General Greene's Brigade; these troops are to be distinguished from the old Militia in future by being called New-Levies— The Quarter Master General to furnish them with Tents: The detachment from General Spencers Brigade to return when these get over. The Militia not under the immediate Command of General Heard[63] are to be under that of Genl. Mercer[64] until the arrival of their own General Officer.

The time is now near at hand which must probably determine, whether Americans are to be, Freemen, or Slaves; whether they are to have any property they can call their own; whether their Houses, and Farms, are to be pillaged and destroyed, and they consigned to a State of Wretchedness from which no human efforts will probably deliver them. The fate of unborn Millions will now depend, under God, on the Courage and Conduct of this army—Our cruel and unrelenting Enemy leaves us no choice but a brave resistance, or the most abject submission; this is all we can expect—We have therefore to resolve to conquer or die: Our own Country's Honor, all call upon us for a vigorous and manly exertion, and if we now shamefully fail, we shall become infamous to the whole world. Let us therefore rely upon the goodness of the Cause, and the aid of the supreme Being, in whose hands Victory is, to animate and encourage us to great and noble Actions—The Eyes of all our Countrymen are now upon us, and we shall have their blessings, and praises, if happily we are the instruments of saving them from the

---

[62] Col. Philip Van Cortlandt, of the New York Militia. He seems to have been detailed to the New Jersey brigade of General Heard; his name appears on one of Heard's returns later in 1776.

[63] Brig. Gen. Nathaniel Heard.

[64] Brig. Gen. Hugh Mercer. He died of wounds received at Princeton, N. J.

Tyranny meditated against them. Let us therefore animate and encourage each other, and shew the whole world, that a Freeman contending for LIBERTY on his own ground is superior to any slavish mercenary on earth.

The General recommends to the officers great coolness in time of action, and to the soldiers a strict attention and obedience with a becoming firmness and spirit.

Any officer, or soldier, or any particular Corps, distinguishing themselves by any acts of bravery, and courage, will assuredly meet with notice and rewards; and on the other hand, those who behave ill, will as certainly be exposed and punished— The General being resolved, as well for the Honor and Safety of the Country, as Army, to shew no favour to such as refuse, or neglect their duty at so important a crisis.

The General expressly orders that no officer, or soldier, on any pretence whatever, without leave in writing, from the commanding officer of the regiment, do leave the parade, so as to be out of drum-call, in case of an alarm, which may be hourly expected—The Regiments are immediately to be under Arms on their respective parades, and should any be absent they will be severely punished—The whole Army to be at their Alarm posts completely equipped to morrow, a little before day—

Ensign Charles Miller, Capt Wrisst's[65] Company, and Colonel Wyllys's Regiment, charged with "absenting himself from his Guard" tried by a General Court Martial and acquitted—The General approves the sentence, and orders him to be dismissed from his arrest.

As there is a probability of Rain, the General strongly recommends to the officers, to pay particular attention, to their Men's arms and ammunition, that neither may be damaged—

---

[65] Capt. Samuel Wright, of the Twenty-second Continental Infantry.

Lieut. Col Clark who was ordered to sit on General Court Martial in the orders of yesterday being absent on command, Lieut. Col Tyler [66] is to sit in Court.

### EVENING ORDERS

'Tis the General's desire that the men lay upon their Arms in their tents and quarters, ready to turn out at a moments warning, as their is the greatest likelihood of it.

## GENERAL ORDERS

Head Quarters, New York, July 3, 1776.
Parole Brunswick.  Countersign Princeton.

The Director General of the Hospital having laid before the General, a plan of conduct for the Surgeons and Mates of the Regiments, by which, in case of action, they will do their duty with greater ease and benefit to the service: And the General much approving thereof; they are to attend the Director General and each take a Copy of said plan, to which they are strictly to conform—The Adjutants of the several Regiments to make this order particularly known, to each Surgeon and Mate, without delay.

A working party to morrow consisting of 800 men properly officered from Genl. Heaths, Spencers, Lord Stirling's and Scott's Brigades—Spencers at Bayards-hill plain, and Jones's hill, Capt. Chapman to direct them. The others to apply at the Engine Store for tools, and directions (at the west end of the upper barrack)—Scotts brigade in particular not to depart the store 'till they have a director, as it will relieve the Engineer from much intricateness; they being unacquainted, did not find the

---

[66] Lieut. Col. John Tyler, of the Tenth Continental Infantry. He was colonel of the Tenth from August to December, 1776; brigadier general of Connecticut Militia, 1777–78.

place destined for them yesterday by which means the works at the Bomb-Battery was entirely omitted.

### AFTER ORDERS

That the several Brigades and Troops be at their Alarm posts every morning at day break, as ordered this morning and hold themselves in constant readiness in case of an alarm.

### To THE PRESIDENT OF CONGRESS

New York, July 3, 1776.

Sir: Since I had the honor of addressing you and on the same day several Ships more arrived within the Hook; making the number that came in them, 110, and there remains no doubt of the whole of the Fleet from Hallifax being now here. Yesterday Evening 50 of them came into the Bay and Anchored on the Staten Island side.[67] Their views I cannot precisely determine, but am extremely apprehensive, as a part of them only came, that they mean to surround the Island and secure the whole stock upon it. I had consulted with a committee of the Provincial Congress on the Subject, and a person was appointed to superintend the business and to drive the Stock off. I also wrote to Brigadier General Herd[68] and directed him to the Measure, lest it might be neglected, but am fearful it has not been effected.

Our reinforcements of Militia are but small yet: Their amount I cannot ascertain, having not been able to procure a return. However, I trust, if the Enemy make an Attack, they will meet with a repulse, as I have the pleasure to inform you, that an

---

[67] Howe's intention, as noted in his letter to Lord George Germain (July 7), was to land at Gravesend Bay, Long Island; but he became doubtful of the safety of it and began disembarking on Staten Island before July 4. The last ships of the fleet did not arrive until August 12. The strength of the British was in the neighborhood of 32,000 men.

[68] Brig. Gen. Nathaniel Heard. The letter, dated June 29, 1776, was written and signed by Robert Hanson Harrison by Washington's direction. It is in the *Washington Papers*.

agreeable Spirit and willingness for Action, seems to Animate and prevade the whole of our Troops.

As it is difficult to determine what Objects the Enemy may have in contemplation, and whether they may not detach some part of their force to Amboy and to ravage that part of the Country if not to extend their views farther;

I submit it to Congress whether it may not be expedient for them to repeat and press home their requests to the different Governments, that are to provide men for the Flying Camp, to furnish their quotas with all possible dispatch.[69] It is a matter of great Importance and will be of serious consequence to have the Camp established in case the Enemy should be able to possess themselves of this River and cut off the supplies of Troops that might be necessary, on certain emergencies, to be sent from hence

I must entreat your attention to an application I made some time ago for Flints; we are extremely deficient in this necessary Article and shall be greatly distressed, If we cannot obtain a supply. Of Lead we have a sufficient Quantity for the whole Campaign, taken off the Houses here.

Esteeming it of Infinite Importance, to prevent the Enemy from getting fresh Provisions and Horses for their Waggons, Artillery &ca. I gave orders to a party of our Men on Staten Island, since writing General Herd, to drive the Stock off without waiting for the assistance or direction of the Committee there, lest their slow mode of transacting business might produce too much delay, and have sent this morning to know what they have done. I am this Minute informed by a Gentleman that the Committee of Elizabeth Town, sent their Company

---

[69] Congress had, by a resolve of June 3, ordered the formation of a Flying Camp. It was to be 10,000 strong and was designed to protect New Jersey and to prevent a sudden move by the British against Philadelphia while Washington's army was held in New York. After that city was evacuated and the army thus set free for field maneuvering the purpose of the camp merged with that of the main force, and the organization was not continued after the year 1776.

of Light Horse, on Monday to effect it, and that some of their Militia was to give their aid Yesterday; he adds he was credibly told last Night, by part of the Militia coming to this place, that Yesterday Evening they saw a good many stock driving of the Island and crossing to the Jerseys. If the business is not executed ere now, It will be impossible to do it. I have the Honor &ca.

## To THE PRESIDENT OF CONGRESS

New York, July 4, 1776.

Sir: This will be handed you by Colo: Stevenson whom I have ordered, with the Captains of the two Rifle Companies from Maryland to wait on Congress. They will point out such measures as they conceive most likely to advance the raising of the New Battalion and the Persons they think worthy of promotion that have served with them, agreeable to the inclosed List: I am not acquainted with them, but from their report and recommendation, which I doubt not is just, and if Congress will please to enquire of them, they will mention other proper persons for officers.

Only about 40 of the three Old Companies have reinlisted, which I shall form into one for the present and place under an Officer or two, 'till a further and complete Arrangement is made, of the whole Battalion. I have the Honor &ca.[70]

### A LIST OF OFFICERS RECOMMENDED

To serve in Captain Hugh Stephensons Company of Rifle Men: Abraham Shepherd, Captain; Samuel Finlay, first Lieutenant; William Kelly, 2nd. Lt; Henry Bedinger, 3rd. Lt.

To serve in Captain Rawlings Company: Richard Davis, Captain; Daniel Cresap, first Lieut; Nieman Tannehill, 2nd. Lt; Rezin Davis, 3rd. Lt. not at Present in the Company.

---

[70] In the writing of Robert Hanson Harrison; the list of names of those recommended for appointment is in that of John Fitzgerald.

To Serve in Captain Williams's Company: Philemon Griffith, Captain; Thomas Hussey Luckett, first Lieutt; Adamson Tannehill, 2nd. Lieut; Henry Hardman, 3rd. Lieut. not at Present in the Co.

## To MAJOR GENERAL ARTEMAS WARD

New York, July 4, 1776.

Sir: The distress we are in for want of Arms induces me again to urge your sending on all such as can possibly be spared with the greatest expedition. The enemy have landed under cover of their Ships and have taken possession of Staten Island, from which in all probability they will soon make a descent upon us. The Arms would have to be sent to Norwich and from there by Water to this place provided there is no risque; otherwise by land. Wishing you better Health, I am, etc.[71]

## To BRIGADIER GENERAL HUGH MERCER

Head Quarters, 9 OClock P. M., July 4, 1776.

Dear Sir: I am to acknowledge the Receipt of your Favours of Yesterday and this Morning, and approve much of the Steps you have taken for securing the Ferries, as well as quieting the Apprehensions of the Inhabitants of New-Ark, by stationing some Troops there.

Upon full Consideration of all Circumstances, I have concluded to send the Militia Home, except 500, to guard Bergen Neck, which I deem an important Post, and capable of being used very much to our Prejudice. I am also of Opinion that a Body about Woodbridge and Amboy would be very useful. I propose to retain the Morris County Militia for the first Purpose, and leave it to General Livingston, to order the Security of the other Places. As to the Militia who have marched from

---

[71] The editor is indebted to the kindness of Thomas F. Madigan, of New York, for the text of this letter.

distant Parts, I suppose like all others, they are impatient to return to their Farms and Business; and as others are discharged, it will be difficult to keep them. However, that I leave to General Livingston, who, if he thinks they are necessary for the Defence of the Province, will give them his Orders; but I do not require their Service any longer.

I cannot spare Captain Burr any Swivels, the row Gallies requiring all I have.

I would by all Means recommend to you, to place a Guard at the two Ferries, Hackinsack, and Passaic. I shall send over an Engineer To-Morrow, to erect some Works for the Security of these Places. The Militia of distant Parts are better in such Cases, than the Militia of the Neighbourhood.

In detaining Troops, you will please to distinguish, and inculcate upon others, the Distinction between the New Levies, and Militia. Every Man of the former, I expect with all Expedition. I am etc.

### GENERAL ORDERS

Head Quarters, New York, July 4, 1776.

Parole Alexandria. Countersign ———

The Colonels and commanding officers of Regiments, are to make out Pay-Abstracts, for the Month of May; these are to be carefully examined by the Brigadiers under whom they serve, and by the Pay Master General, before the Warrants are brought to be signed by the General, they are then to deliver them in and receive payment.

### To THE PRESIDENT OF CONGRESS

New York, July 4, 1776.

Sir: When I had the honor to address you on the 30th. Ulto., I transmitted a copy of a Letter I had received from a Gentleman a Member of the Honorable General Court of

Massachusetts Bay, suggesting the improbability, of succours coming from thence in any reasonable Time, either for the defence of this place, or to reinforce our Troops engaged in the Canada expedition. I am sorry to inform you, that from a variety of Intelligence his apprehensions appear to be just, and to be fully confirmed. Nor have I reason to expect, but that the supplies from the other two Governments, Connecticut and New Hampshire, will be extremely slow and greatly deficient in number. As it now seems beyond Question, and clear to demonstration, that the Enemy mean to direct their Operations and bend their most vigorous Efforts against this Colony and will attempt to Unite their two Armies, that under General Burgoyne, and the one arrived here. I cannot but think the expedient proposed by that Gentleman is exceedingly just and that the Continental Regiments now in Massachusetts Bay, should be immediately called from thence and be employed, where there is the strongest reason to believe their aid will be indispensably necessary.[72] The expediency of the Measure I shall submit to the consideration of Congress, and will only observe as my Opinion, that there is not the most distant prospect of an attempt being made where they now are, by the Enemy, and if there should, that the Militia that can be assembled upon the shortest Notice, will be more than equal to repel it; They are well armed, resolute and determined, and will instantly oppose any Invasion that may be made in their own Colony.

I shall also take the Liberty again to request Congress, to Interest themselves in having the Militia raised and forwarded with all possible expedition, as fast as any considerable number of them can be collected, that are to compose the Flying Camp.[73]

---

[72] On July 8, on report of the Board of War, the Commander in Chief was vested with discretionary power to call to New York such of the Continental regiments in Massachusetts as had not already been ordered to Ticonderoga. The militia were to supply their place at Boston. (See *Journals of the Continental Congress*.)

[73] The 10,000 men for the Flying Camp were to be furnished from the militia of Pennsylvania, Delaware, and Maryland. They were to be, of course, in Continental pay.

This I mentioned in my Letter of Yesterday, but think proper to repeat it, being more and more convinced of the necessity. The Camp will be in the Neighbourhood of Amboy, and I shall be glad, the Conventions or Committees of Safety of those Governments from whence they come, may be requested to give me previous notice of their marching, that I may form some plan, and direct Provision to be made for their reception. The disaffection of the People at that place and others not far off, is exceedingly great, and unless it is checked and overawed, it may become more general and be very alarming. The arrival of the Enemy will encourage it.

They or at least a part of them are already landed on Staten Island, which is quite contiguous and about 4000 were marching about it yesterday, as I have been advised and are leaving no Acts unessayed, to gain the Inhabitants to their side, who seem but too favourably disposed. It is not unlikely that in a little time they may attempt to cross to the Jersey side, and induce many to join them, either from motives of Interest or fear, unless there is a force to oppose them.[74]

As we are fully convinced that the ministerial Army we shall have to oppose this Campaign, will be great and numerous and well know, that the utmost Industry will be used, as it already has been, to excite the Savages and every body of People to Arms against us whom they can Influence, It certainly behooves us to strain every nerve to Counteract their designs: I would therefore submit it to Congress whether, especially as our Schemes for employing the Western Indians do not seem

---

[74] "The enemy's fleet is now come up within twelve miles of us; and yesterday a large body of men, with Cortlandt Skinner at their head, landed on Staten Island, and dividing themselves into three bodies, traversed the whole Island, with a view of collecting stock and vegetables. The villainy and treachery of many of the inhabitants will give them some supplies; for though the General took every method to get off the stock, (force excepted,) they contrived by some means or other to evade it."— *Joseph Reed to Esther Reed (his wife)*, July 4, 1776. This letter is from Reed's *Life and Correspondence of Joseph Reed*.

to be attended with any great prospect of success from General Schuyler's Accounts, It may not be advisable to take measures to engage those of the Eastward, the St. Johns, Nova Scotia, Penobscot &ca. in our favor. I have been told that several might be got, perhaps five or six hundred or more, readily to Join us. If they can, I should imagine, It ought to be done. It will prevent our Enemies from securing their friendship, and further, they will be of infinite service, in annoying and harrassing them should they ever attempt to penetrate the Country. Congress will be pleased to consider the measure and if they determine to adopt it, I conceive it will be necessary to Authorize and request the General Court of the Massachusetts Bay to carry it into Execution.

Their situation and advantages will enable them to Negotiate a Treaty and an Alliance better than it can be done by any persons else.[75]

I have been honored with your two favors of the 1st. instant, and agreeable to the wishes of Congress, shall put Monsieur Wiebert in the best place I can, to prove his Abilities in the Art he professes. I shall send him up immediately to the Works erecting towards Kings Bridge under the direction of General Mifflin, whom I shall request to employ him.

I this Moment received a Letter from General Greene, an extract of which I have inclosed. The Intelligence it contains is of the most Important nature, and evinces the necessity of the most spirited and Vigorous exertions on our part.[76] The

---

[75] On July 8 Congress resolved: " That General Washington have permission to call forth and engage in the service of the United States so many Indians of the St. Johns, Nova Scotia and Penobscot tribes, as he shall judge necessary, and that he be desired to write to the general court of the Massachusetts bay, requesting their aid in this business, and informing them that Congress will reimburse such expences as may be necessarily incurred." (See *Journals of the Continental Congress.*)

[76] The extract, in the writing of George Lewis, is from Greene's letter of July 4, which is not found in the *Washington Papers*. The extract is filed with Washington's letter in the *Papers of the Continental Congress.*

expectation of the Fleet under Admiral Howe,[77] is certainly the reason the Army already come, have not begun their Hostile operations. when that arrives we may look for the most interesting events and such as in all probability will have considerable weight in the present Contest. It behoves us to be prepared in the best manner, and I submit it again to Congress whether the Accounts given by these prisoners do not shew the propriety of calling the several Continental Regiments from the Massachusetts Bay Government, raising the flying Camp with all possible dispatch and engaging the Eastern Indians.

July 5.

General Mercer arrived here on Tuesday and the next morning was ordered to Powles Hook to make some Arrangement of the Militia, as they come in, and the best disposition he could to prevent the Enemy crossing from Staten Island, if they should have any such Views.

The distressed situation of the Inhabitants of Elizabeth Town and New Ark, has since induced me upon their application, to give up all the Militia from the Jerseys, except those engaged for Six Months. I am hopeful they will be able to repell any Incursions that may be attempted. Generals Mercer and Livingston[78] are concerting plans for that purpose. By a Letter from the Latter last night, I am informed the Enemy are throwing up small Works at all the passes on the North side of Staten Island, which it is probable they mean to secure. None of the Connecticut Militia are yet arrived, so that the reinforcement we have received, is very inconsiderable.

A Letter from General Schuyler with sundry inclosures, of which No. 1, 2. and 3. are exact Copies, this Moment came to hand and will no doubt claim as It ought to do the immediate

---

[77] Richard, Lord Howe, rear admiral and commander in chief of the British Fleet in North America.
[78] Gen. William Livingston.

attention of Congress. The evils which must inevitably follow a disputed Command are too obvious and alarming to admit a Moments delay, in your decision thereupon.[79] And altho' I do not presume to advise, in a matter now of this delicacy, Yet as it appears evident that the Northern Army has retreated to Crown Point and mean to act upon the defensive only, I cannot help giving it as my Opinion, that one of the Major Generals in that Quarter would be more usefully employed here, or in the flying Camp, than there; for it becomes my duty to observe. If another experienced Officer, is taken from hence in order to command the flying Camp, that your Grand Army will be entirely stripped of Generals who have seen service, being in a manner already destitute of such. My Distress on this Account; the Appointment of General Whitcomb[80] to the Eastern Regiments; a conviction in my own breast, that no Troops would be sent to Boston and the certainty of a number coming to this place, occasioned my postponing from time to time sending any General Officer from hence to the Eastward heretofore, and now I shall wait the Sentiments of Congress relative to the five Regiments in Massachusetts Bay, before I do anything in this matter.

The Commissary General has been with me this Morning concerning the other matter contained in General Schuyler's Letters respecting the Business of that department. He has I believe in order to remove difficulties recalled Mr. Avery; but seems to think it necessary in that case, that Mr. Livingston should be left to himself, as he cannot be responsable for persons not of his own Appointment. This matter should also be clearly

---

[79] By the time Gates's leisurely movements had carried him toward his Canadian command the army had retreated from Canada and had fallen down to Ticonderoga. Gates claimed the supreme command, but Schuyler demurred on the ground that Gates was to command in Canada only. The matter was submitted to Congress and, as Gates's influence was not yet as great with that body as it afterwards became, the decision (July 8) was against Gates. Hancock wrote him urging cordial cooperation with Schuyler. (See *Journals of the Continental Congress.*)

[80] Gen. Jonathan Whitcomb.

defined by Congress. I have already given my Opinion of the necessity of these Matters, being under one General direction, in so full and clear a manner, that I shall not take up the Time of Congress to repeat it in this place.[81] I am &c.[82]

### GENERAL ORDERS

Head Quarters, New York, July 5, 1776.
Parole Cambridge.   Countersign Durham.

Those Regiments who have not made a Return of their officers, their ranks and dates of their Commissions, agreeable to a former order are now called on to do it without delay and to mention in such Returns the Colony in which such Regiment was raised, the time when and period in which they inlisted, together with the vacancies in their respective regiments.

### To BRIGADIER GENERAL WILLIAM LIVINGSTON

Head Quarters, July 5, 1776.

Sir: Your Favour of the 4th. came safely to Hand. The situation of New Jersey is such, and the Apprehensions of the Inhabitants so justly excited, that I have concluded to discharg, the Militia from this Place, except those from Morris County, whose internal Situation is such, as to leave them nothing to fear from the Enemy. These I have posted in Bergen in Order to prevent any Communication, and to give the Enemy Obstruction in Case they should attempt to land in that Quarter, which with the Assistance of the Continental Troops posted there, I hope, they will be able effectually to do. The Remainder of the Militia I have dismissed, as I have Reason to believe

---

[81] Elisha Avery and Walter Livingstone's dispute over command of the commissary department of the Northern Army was an outcome of the Gates-Schuyler controversy. Schuyler's letter to Washington, dated July 1, 1776, outlining the matter, is in the *Washington Papers*. It is printed in Sparks's *Letters to Washington*, vol. 1, p. 247.
[82] In the writing of Robert Hanson Harrison.

the Enemy is waiting for the European Fleet, and will not make a general Attack until it arrives; but we have not yet one Man from Connecticut. You will observe, I have dismissed the Militia from hence; but have not discharged them: as I am of Opinion a Part of them may be usefully employed in the immediate Defence of the Province. In this View they fall properly under your Command, and I would suggest to you the Propriety of stationing them in proper Places along the Shore, opposite to Staten Island, so as to relieve the Inhabitants from the Apprehensions they are under of being plundered, as well as preventing any Communication with the Enemy. There are a Number of People in Amboy who will undoubtedly open a Correspondence with them immediately and endeavour to excite Disafection thro' the Province, now they feel themselves under some Kind of Protection. If it is practicable in the present Situation of Things, I am of Opinion, those Officers of Government, and the notoriously disaffected there, should be removed with all possible Expedition to less dangerous Places. That the Cattle and Sheep, and Horses on the Shores contiguous to Staten Island should be immediately drove back, the Ferries carefully attended to, and all Boats watched that pass or attempt so to do. The Number of Men necessary for these Services, you will be able to ascertain better than I can; but in such Emergency it is better to exceed than fall Short.

As to Provisions for the Men, I presume, while the Militia are employed in the immediate Defence of the Province, the Expence, at least in the first Instance, will fall upon the Colony. How far the Continent will reimburse the Province, I can not determine; but the Necessity of some Supplies being collected, is so evident, that I make no Doubt the Convention will immediately go into it. In the mean Time I should think no Person could run any Risk, in doing what is immediately necessary, under your Appointment.

I have been the more induced to dismiss the Militia, that the New Levies (or six Months Men) may be forwarded as soon as possible; and I must request your Exertion for this purpose, as it is my Intention to have them here without a Moments Delay.

Since this Letter was begun another of your Favors came to my Hands, informing me, that the Enemy have thrown up two small Breast Works on the Cause Way from the Point.

You also request some experienced Officers to be sent over, which I would gladly comply with, if in my Power; but I have few of that Character, and those are so necessarily engaged here, that for the present I must refer you to General Mercer, whose Judgement and Experience may be depended upon. I have wrote him that I should endeavour to send over an Engineer as soon as possible.

From all Accounts we receive, I cannot think they have any serious Intentions at present, beyond making themselves Masters of Staten Island, guarding against any Attack from us, and collecting what Stock they can; but at the same Time it is highly prudent for you, to be in the best Posture of Defence you can. I am, Sir, etc.

## To BRIGADIER GENERAL WILLIAM LIVINGSTON

Head Quarters,
New York, 5 O'Clock P. M., July 6, 1776.

Sir: Your Favour of this Date, inclosing Major Duychinck's[83] Letter, was this Moment received. The known Disaffection of the People of Amboy, and the Treachery of those of Staten Island, who, after the fairest Professions, have shewn themselves our most inveterate Enemies, have induced me to give Directions that all Persons of known Enmity or doubtful Character,

---

[83] Maj. John Duychinck, who seemed to have been a lieutenant colonel of Jersey Militia at this date. He deserted to the British. (See Washington's letter to Maj. Gen. John Sullivan, Feb. 22, 1777, *post.*) A copy of Duychinck's letter, dated July 5, 1776, informing of British troop movements, is in the *Washington Papers.*

should be removed from Places, where they might enter into a Correspondence with the Enemy, and aid them in their Schemes. For this End, General Herd has Directions to apprehend such Persons, as from their Conduct had shewn themselves inimical, or whose Situations, Connections, or Offices, gave just Cause of Suspicion. I have no Knowledge of the Persons apprehended; but suppose General Herd had good Reason for taking hold of them. However, if there are any, whom, from your personal Knowledge and Opinion, you think may be permitted to return, I have no Objection, and sending the others to Provincial Congress for their Disposal. But as to the former, I would suggest to you, that my Tenderness has been often abused, and I have had Reason to repent the Indulgence shewn them. I would shew them all possible Humanity and Kindness, consistent with our own Safety; but Matters are now too far advanced to sacrifice any Thing to Punctilios.

I have given Direction to forward you a Supply of Ammunition; but must beg you to inculcate the utmost Frugality and Care of it, as we have no Superfluity. This Supply consists of Cartridges, some loose Powder and Lead. If you have any Occasion for Ammunition for Field Pieces, which the latter will not supply, I will endeavour to assist you; but I would wish you to make no more Draughts than are absolutely necessary.

General Mercer has just set off for Jersey. In his Experience and Judgment you may repose great Confidence. He will proceed to Amboy after conferring with you.

You will please to keep me constantly informed of the Proceedings of the Enemy, and be assured of every Assistance and Attention. [84] I am, etc.

---

[84] General Howe's headquarters were now at Staten Island. In a letter to Lord George Germain (July 7) he wrote: "I have the satisfaction to inform your Lordship, that there is great reason to expect a numerous body of the inhabitants to join the army from the provinces of New York, the Jerseys, and Connecticut, who in this time of universal apprehension only wait for opportunities to give proofs of their loyalty and zeal for government. Sixty men came over a few days ago with a few

## To COLONEL GOLD SELLECK SILLIMAN[85]

New York, July 6, 1776.

Sir: Governor Trumbull having informed me in a Letter of the 3rd. Inst., that he had ordered three Regiments of the Militia light Horse to march to the Defence of this Place, under the Command of Lieutt. Colo. Seymour,[86] least the other Troops from your Colony should not arrive in Time for succour; and at the same Time requesting, if their Service is unnecessary or can be dispensed with, that I would signify it to you. I must take this Opportunity to acquaint you, that the Intelligence we have received from three or four Prisoners, that have fallen in our Hands within a few Days past, leads me to conclude, that no Force that can be collected, will be too great to ward off the Blow that our Enemies mean to strike in a little Time. They say (the Prisoners), Genl. Howe has already 10,000 Men here, being joined by some Regiments from the West Indies, and Part of the Highland Troops in his Passage and that he is in daily Expectation of the Arrival of Admiral Howe, with a large Fleet of 150 Sail, with Troops on Board; That before he left Hallifax, a Packet had arrived there, giving Intelligence that he would be met here by this Fleet in a very little Time, and that the Expectation of them, is the only Reason why the Enemy have not begun their Operations. From these Accounts, you will readily conceive the Necessity of our most vigorous and

---

arms from the neighborhood of Shrewsbury in Jersey, who are all desirous to serve; and I understand there are five hundred more in that quarter ready to follow their example. This disposition among the people makes me impatient for the arrival of Lord Howe, concluding the powers with which he is furnished will have the best effect at this critical time; but I am still of the opinion, that peace will not be restored in America until the rebel army is defeated."

[85] Colonel Silliman was at Fairfield, Conn., in command of a Connecticut State regiment. He became a brigadier general of Connecticut Militia in 1777.

[86] Col. Thomas Seymour, commandant of Volunteer Connecticut Light Horse.

spirited Exertions and that there is Occasion here for all the Men that can be possibly got. But what to do with the Horses of this Reinforcement, I am at a Loss to determine: It will be impossible to support them, and if it could be done, the Expence would be enormous. I cannot think myself at Liberty to consent to the Horses coming; at the same Time, I must request your Exertions to prevail on the Men. They may have it in their Power to dismiss their Horses, perhaps after bringing them almost here. The Exigency of our Affairs calls aloud for their Assistance, and more especially, as there is almost a moral Certainty that the Battalions which are intended for this Place, will be some Time before they all arrive and when they do, will not be more than half compleat.

Recommending to your and their Notice what I have said; and the alarming Consequences that may result, from not having sufficient and timely succour to repel the Enemy. I am Sir, etc.

## GENERAL ORDERS

Head Quarters, New York, July 6, 1776.
Parole Essex.   Countersign France.

The Quarter-Master-General to have all the empty Casks, which have been collected, filled with fresh Water, to be changed occasionally.

The General hopes the officers and soldiers will improve this opportunity, to get their Arms in the best Order for service— as they cannot tell how soon, or how suddenly, they may be called forth.

Two hundred men properly officered (exclusive of the number ordered the 3rd. Instant) to parade to morrow morng, five OClock at the Laboratory, with four days provisions—they will receive tools and directions from the chief Engineer.

## GENERAL ORDERS

Head Quarters, New York, July 7, 1776.
Parole Goshen.    Countersign Hartford.

A working party of one hundred and fifty men properly officered to go to Kingsbridge to morrow, to march at six OClock from the parade; they are to take two days provision with them, after which they will draw out of the Stores there—to take their arms and tents with them and when they get there Genl. Mifflin will give them orders.

As the enemy may make an attack early in the morning, when there may not be time for the soldiers to fill their Canteens; The General directs that they be filled every evening— The officers to take care that it is not neglected, as it is a matter of much consequence at this season.

James Johnson a Soldier in Capt. Hides [87] Company, and Col Wyllys's Regiment, tried at a General Court Martial whereof Col Read is President for "*Desertion*" is found guilty and sentenced to be whipped Thirty-nine Lashes on his naked back— Serjt. George Douglass, John Davis, John Cooper, Robt. Sawyer and George Clarkson, all of Capt. Van Wycks Company, Col McDougalls Regiment, tried at the same Court Martial for "Mutiny and Sedition": Serjt. George Douglass is acquitted, the others severally found guilty and sentenced, Davis to be whipped Thirty-nine Lashes, Cooper, Thirty Lashes; Sawyer and Clarkson be whipped each Twenty Lashes, on their bare backs for said offence. The General approves of the foregoing Sentences, and orders them put in execution at the usual time and place.

Some persons having barbarously wounded, and maimed some Cattle belonging to Leonard Lispenard Esqr. on Friday last; the General hopes no Soldier in the Army is concerned in

---

[87] Capt. Jedediah Hyde, of the Twenty-second Continental Infantry.

so base, and scandalous an action, but if it should appear otherwise such person may depend on the severest punishment; any person who can give any information in the matter will be well rewarded.

### To MAJOR GENERAL ARTEMAS WARD

New York, July 7, 1776.[88]

Sir: I received your Favour of the 30th. Ulto., and doubt not but the Powder claimed by the Assembly of New Hampshire was lent the Continent. The exposed Situation of their Frontiers renders every Precaution necessary for their Defence.

I think it would be proper, to send a Quantity of it to some safe Place on the Communication betwixt this and Boston, there to be ready in Case of Accident; or if it should be wanted. I therefore wish you to lodge at Norwich, which I suppose will be as secure as any other Place, from three to four Hundred Barrels.

In my Letter of the 1st., I desired you to send a Quantity of the Highlander's Musquets that were taken. I pray your Attention to my Request, and that they may come with all possible Expedition. The Deficiency here, in this essential Article is greatly alarming. I am extremely sorry, that your Indisposition has increased, and I hope in a little Time you will be relieved.

It is now before Congress to determine, whether the Continental Regiments at Boston, should not be ordered from thence; as there is almost a moral Certainty, that the Enemy mean not to make an Attack there, but to bend their whole Force against this Province.

[88] On this day Washington wrote to the Massachusetts Legislature: "I was yesterday honored with your favor of the 2d Inst: with the proceedings you have adopted in Compliance with the requisition of Congress and my application since, for which, and your kind wishes for my success, I beg your Acceptance of my most hearty thanks." This letter is in the *Washington Papers*.

Four Prisoners, that fell into our Hands last Week, on a seperate Examination agree, that General Howe being joined by some Regiments from the West Indies, and Part of the Scotch Highlanders in his Passage hither, has now about 10,000 Men; That a few Days before they left Hallifax an Express Packet arrived, ordering him to come to this Place, where he would be joined by Admiral Howe with a Fleet of 150 Sail, with Troops on Board, which was about to sail when the Packet did; That they are daily expected, which has been the Reason nothing has been yet attempted.

If Congress withdraw the Regiments, you will be instantly relieved; and if they do not, I must send (inconvenient as it is, to spare a General Officer at this critical Time) one to take the Command. I expect to know the Result of their Deliberations, in a Day or two.

It will be right to comply with the Order of the Board of War and Ordinance, and a List may be transmitted of the Persons you have judg'd most proper to fill the Vacancies. I am, Sir, with my best Wishes for your Recovery, etc.


### To COLONEL JAMES CLINTON

Head Quarters, New York, July 7, 1776.

Sir: I received yours by Major Rensselaer[89] and am pleased to find you are making the necessary Preperations to repel the Enemy in Case of an Attack.

I hope you will be able to get Arms sufficient for the Men under your Command who are destitute; but if not, you are to dismiss all those whom you cannot equip. I mean to confine myself to the Militia wholly, as it is equally absurd and unjust, to keep Men in continental Pay, who will be of no Service in Time of Action, for Want of Arms. It is, in Fact, amusing

---

[89] Maj. John Van Rensselaer, of the New York Militia.

ourselves with the Appearance of strength, when at the same Time we want the Reality.

Colonel Knox informs me, he has no Carriages to spare; but you can have the Carriage Wheels, which with the Iron will be delivered to the Care of Major Rensselaer.

As to the Ball for the small Arms, they should be sent, if the Sizes could be ascertained, so as to fit the Musquets exactly; but as that cannot be done, I shall order a sufficient Quantity of Lead to be sent up, which you will direct to be cast into Balls suitable for your Purpose. You must furnish the Bullet Moulds in the best Manner you can, as there are none here.

With Regard to the Appointment of Doctor Tappen,[90] I would just mention, that as it is a Matter transacted between you and the Provincial Congress, with which I am quite unconnected, I would choose it should continue so. However, by renewing your Application to the Congress, you will doubtless receive a satisfactory Answer. I am, etc.

## To WILLIAM WATSON

New York, July 7, 1776.

Sir: I received yours of the 19th. Ulto., and directed the Papers you wrote for to be transmitted you; but find upon Inquiry, they are not among any in my Possession now. Colonel Moylan, who used generally to receive and examine the Papers appertaining to the Prizes, being called upon, says, that previous to his Departure from Cambridge, he made up all the Prizes Papers and put them in such a Channel as he thought most likely to convey them to the different Agents. He supposes these were with the Rest. He cannot recollect to whom they were delivered. If they cannot be got, you must try the Legality of the Captures, upon

---

[90] Peter Tappan. He had been a lieutenant of New York Militia in 1775, and was at this date a surgeon's mate in the Continental Hospital.

such Evidence, as you can collect from the Men who were in the Vessels when they were taken, and from other Circumstances.

If they were going to Nova Scotia, for the Purpose mentioned by the Claimants, I presume, it will not be difficult for them to prove it by Witnesses. I am, Sir, etc.

## To GOVERNOR JONATHAN TRUMBULL

New York, July 7, 1776.

Sir: I have been honored with your favors of the 3d. and 4th. Inst. and return you my sincere thanks for your kind intention to afford me every assistance in your power, at this truly Critical and alarming period. The situation of our affairs calls aloud for the most vigorous exertions and nothing less will be sufficient to avert the impending blow. From four Prisoners taken the other day, we are Informed Genl. Howe has Already about Ten thousand Men, being joined by the Regiments from the West Indies and some of the Highland Troops in his passage hither; that he is in daily expectation of the arrival of Admiral Howe and that nothing would be attempted till he came, having some from Halifax, in Consequence of Advices received a few days before, from England; that the Admiral was ready to Sail with a Fleet of one hundred and fifty Ships, with a large reinforcement to join him here, these Armies when United, you will readily conceive will be extremely Formidable and such as will require a large and Numerous one on our part, to oppose them. But yet I have been under the necessity of informing Colo. Silliman, that it will be impossible to Subsist the Horse of the three Regiments Ordered, and if it could be done, the Expence would be enormous and what I do not apprehend I have authority to Assent to. At the same time, knowing the Important Advantages that may result from their Aid, I have intreated his exertions to prevail on the Men to come themselves. I hope, on the one hand they will see the propriety of my objecting to their Horses and on the other the Necessity there is of coming themselves. My Anxiety leads me to request a Continuance of your good offices in forwarding the Battalions Ordered with all possible dispatch. The Interest of America is now in the Ballance, and it behoves all Attached to her Sacred Cause and the rights of Humanity, to hold forth their Utmost and most speedy Aid. I am Convinced nothing will be wanting in your power to Effect.

The situation of the Northern Army is certainly distressing, but no relief can be afforded by me; this I am persuaded you will readily agree to. I should Suppose, If proper precautions are taken, the Small pox may be prevented from spreading. this was done at Cambridge, and I trust will be contrived by Generals Schuyler and Gates, who are well apprized of the fatal Consequences that may attend Its infecting the whole Army; but a small part of the Forces here have had it and were it not the case, neither policy or prudence would allow me to send any more from hence, that have seen the least of Service.— too many have been already detached; to part with more, would be to put all to the Hazard.

The retreat of the Army from Canada, I doubt not will occasion a General Alarm to the Frontier Inhabitants, and our Enemies, without question, will use every means they can suggest, to Excite the Savages against them. But I would feign hope, their Incursions will be prevented and repelled without much difficulty. The first opportunity I have, I will transmit a Copy of your Letter to Congress upon this Subject and request their attention to it. I am, etc.

### To LUND WASHINGTON
### (Forged Letter)[91]

July 8, 1776.

---

[91] See note to letter to Lund Washington, June 12, 1776, *ante*.

## GENERAL ORDERS

Head Quarters, New York, July 8, 1776.

Parole Johnston.   Countersign Lebanon.

The new Levies from Connecticut, and New Jersey, daily arriving—a Report is to be made every day to the General of the Number arriving by the commanding officer of each corps, in order that proper arrangements may be made.

All officers are required to be careful that their men are acquainted with orders, that they may not plead ignorance.

## To COLONEL THOMAS SEYMOUR

Head Quarters, New York, July 8, 1776.

Sir: By a letter from his Honor Govr. Trumbull received on the 5th. Inst. I was informed he had ordered three Regiments of Horse on to this place (under your command) with all possible dispatch, and was desired in case they were not wanted to inform Colo. Silliman thereof, accordingly I wrote Colo. Silliman acquainting him, it was my desire the Men might come on provided they could leave or send back their Horses, which letter did not go forward so soon as I intended.  Majr. Starr[92] this morning waited on me informing of his arrival with 50 of the troop, and that the rest were on their March.  I have ordered him to find some pasture for his horse this day, and immediately ride forward and acquaint You, that there is not more forage on hand or to be had than is absolutely necessary for the Use of our Working and Artillery Horses, and that it is my desire your Men may be halted some way in the Rear of this place, and their Horses sent back, otherways the Men can only be a stop and check to the service, as they cannot act as Horse

---

[92] Maj. Thomas Starr.

Men in case of Action, or if they could forage would not be found to support them. I think it absolutely necessary the Men should be here 'till the New Levies all arrive, but for the above reasons shall be necessitated to order their return unless they can be persuaded to come on without their Horses. I would not be supposed by this to discourage the troops of Horse from being in constant readiness in the different States, as I am fully persuaded they will be much more useful than the Militia to throw in succours to a place on an Emergency. I am pleased to see with what chearfullness and alacrity the troops from your Province step forward to the assistance of their Countrymen when ever call'd, and doubt not it will continue. Majr. Starr will be able to inform you fully from what I have mentioned to him the absolute necessity for the Men, and the utter impossibility of keeping the Horses. Baggage Waggons may be hired to bring on Baggage &c. for your Men, from any place they leave their Horses. I am, etc.[93]

## To THE PRESIDENT OF CONGRESS

New York, July 8, 1776.

Sir: Congress having resolved to raise a Regiment of Germans, to counteract the designs of our Enemies, I must beg leave to recommend to their Notice John David Woelpert,[94] now a first Lieutenant in Colonel Shee's Battalion, to the Office of Captain in said Regiment.

I am personally acquainted with him and know that he joined the Virginia forces under my command in the Year

---

[93] The text is from the *Magazine of American History*, vol. 6, p. 135.

[94] John David Woelper (Wilper). He was commissioned first lieutenant, Third Pennsylvania Regiment, in January, 1776; captain July 17, 1776; transferred to the Invalid Regiment June 11, 1778; served to April, 1783. On July 16, 1776, Congress resolved that another company be added to the German battalion and that Woelper be appointed to command it.

1754, and continued in service the whole War, during which he conducted himself as an active, vigilant and brave Officer. He is a German and his Merit as a Soldier entitles him much to the Office he wishes for. I have &c.[95]

### To THE BOARD OF WAR AND ORDNANCE

New York, July 9, 1776.

Gentlemen: In Answer to your request communicated by Mr. Peters's[96] Letter of the 6th. Instant, I am to inform you that no Provision has yet been made in the Continental Army in the instances of your Inquiry, tho' I have been frequently applied to.

In respect to the Serjeant Majors and Quarter Master Serjeants, they have been exempted from common duties, which has been complained of by the rest. As to Drum and Fife Majors, in the British Army, their pay is generally made up out of Stoppages from that of the Drummers and Fifers, but it cannot be well done in ours, all stoppages being attended with difficulty and giving uneasiness. I would therefore propose, that an additional allowance of a Dollar per month should be made to their several pays as now established, as a sufficient compensation and satisfaction, for any extraordinary trouble attending their Offices. I have the Honor &ca.

### To THE MASSACHUSETTS LEGISLATURE OR COMMITTEE OF SAFETY OF THE STATE

New York, July 9, 1776.

Gentn.: You will perceive by the inclosed Declaration, which I have the honor to transmit you, that Congress of late have been

---

[95] In the writing of Robert Hanson Harrison. Washington also wrote, this same day, practically the same letter to the Pennsylvania Committee of Safety recommending Woelper. This letter is printed in Force's *American Archives*.

[96] Richard Peters, secretary to the Board of War. The letter (July 6) asked if any allowances had been made for sergeant majors, drum and fife majors, and quartermaster sergeants, and, if none, what allowances ought to be made. His letter is in the *Washington Papers*.

employed in deliberating on Matters of the utmost Importance. Impelled by Necessity and a Repetition of Injuries unsufferable, without the most distant prospect of relief, they have asserted the Claims of the American Colonies to the rights of Humanity and declared them, Free and Independent States.[97]

Judging from a variety of circumstances, that the British Arms are meant to be directed this Campaign against the State of New York, to effect Its reduction; they have empowred to order the three fullest Regiments of their Troops in the Massachusetts Bay, to reinforce our Northern Army, as you will see, by a Copy of their Resolve which I have inclosed; I have accordingly requested General Ward to detach them with all possible expedition, to join that Army and prevent the fatal and alarming consequences that would result from the Enemies passing the Lakes and making an impression on our Frontiers. I am almost morally certain, that no attempts will be made on the Massachusetts Bay; and if there should, they must prove abortive and ineffectual. The Militia, Independent of other Troops, being more than competent to all the purposes of defensive War; However should it be deemed expedient by your Honble Body, Congress have Authorised you to embody and take into pay a Number of Militia, equal to the Regiments to be detached. I have etc.

## To GOVERNOR NICHOLAS COOKE

*Head Quarters, New York, July 9, 1776.*

Sir: By a Letter received by Congress from Mr. Thomas Greene, Copy of which they did me the Honor to inclose, I have the Pleasure to hear of the Arrival of Capt. Chase with a Valuable Cargo at Providence. and As that Honbl. Body have been pleased to order the Flints at Rhode Island, belonging to the Continent, to be sent me here, (as pr. their Resolution

---

[97] Whether Washington inclosed one of the John Dunlap broadsides of the Declaration of Independence or a manuscript copy is not known to the editor.

Inclosed) I would therefore request, you would cause it to be done without the smallest delay, together with the small Arms which came in the Vessel. As to the Duck, if it is of the kind suitable for Tents, either the whole or part, I should be greatly obliged to you if you would order them made up as fast as possible, and forwarded to Norwich: but if it is Coarse and Stubborn, and of a Quality unfit for the above purpose, it will be unnecessary to give yourself any trouble about the Matter.

I am very sorry I cannot spare you a General officer, agreeable to your desire, to take the Command of the Forces belonging to Rhode Island, but in the present Critical juncture, it is utterly out of my power, to comply with your request. General Mercer is the only Officer who has no Brigade assign'd him, and at a time when we are in constant expectation of some important movement of the Enemy; his presence is so necessary here, that it cannot possibly be dispensed with.—The best expedient that can be fallen upon, I presume, would be to give the Command to the Senior Officer of the Troops till a Brigadier is appointed. I have only to add, that I am with much respect.

## To GOVERNOR JONATHAN TRUMBULL

Head Quarters, New York, July 9, 1776.

Sir: Your's, of the      Inst., is safely come to hand. Col. Seymour arrived yesterday with a few of his Men, when I sent for and acquainted him, it would be impossible for me to have his Horses remain here; Forrage is not to be procured; and, if it could, it would only be a great expence, without a single Advantage arising from it. The Men are absolutely necessary, till the arrival of the New Levies;—Colo. Seymour is to propose the Matter to them this Morning and return me an Answer. We have intelligence, that may be relied on, of Lord Howe's being on his passage for this place with a large Fleet and about 15,000 Men, and is hourly expected. By several deserters from Staten Island and the Ships of War, whose Accounts all agree;—that Genl. Howe proposes no Attempt on us, till the Arrival of this reinforcement, when, it is said, with a part of his Army, he will make a descent on the Jersey side, while the Fleet and the other part of the Army in Conjunction, attack this City. To oppose this force, in which the Ministry put so much Confidence, I think it necessary to exert our every Nerve, and, by defeating their Views this Campaign, be enabled to meet them with double advantage the next; should they think proper to pursue their unwarrantable measures, I hope the good people of your Colony, or State, will be ready, on all occasions, to fly to our assistance, if needed; I have a Confidence in and doubt not they will be ready and willing.

To prevent the Enemy from obtaining fresh provisions, is a Matter highly necessary to be attended to. I am informed that there are great Quantities on the Islands in the Neighbourhood of New-London, Vizt: Fishers, Block, Plumb and Elizabeth Islands and Martha's Vineyard; these are accessible to Ships of force, and no doubt, they will soon be on a plundering Voyage. I could wish your Attention to this Matter, that the Stock might all be removed quite out of reach of the Enemy. The East end of Long Island, I am told, is not less exposed than the others; I think effectual steps will be taken in regard to that, as I have had a Conference with the Convention of this Province, and an order has gone out for driving all the Stock from the Sea Coasts.

In conference, of a full Board of General Officers yesterday, it was recommended, I should apply to your Honor for the three Row Gallies, being now at New London, or in the River;

together with as many heavy Cannon as you can possibly spare, they are what will be much wanted here; and, if you find it consistent, would beg you to forward them on as soon as possible.[98]

I would not have it understood, from what I said above in regard to the *Horse,* that I think it a wrong step their coming forward. I think it a Step, which was highly advisable; and am much pleased to see, with what chearfulness and dispatch your Orders were executed. This Body of Horse, provided they are well Arm'd with good Muskets, must always be of greater Service, on sudden emergencies; to throw in succours when call'd for than the Militia. I have the honor to be, etc.

## To MAJOR GENERAL ARTEMAS WARD

New York, July 9, 1776.

Sir: The inclosed Declaration will shew you, that Congress at Length, impelled by Necessity, have dissolved the Connection between the American Colonies, and Great Britain, and declared them *free* and *independent States;* and in Compliance with their Order, I am to request you will cause this Declaration to be immediately proclaimed at the Head of the Continental Regiments in the Massachusetts Bay.

It being evident, from a Variety of concurring Circumstances, that the British Armies mean to direct their most vigorous Operations this Campaign against the State of New York, to penetrate into it by Way of the Lakes, and the North River and to unite their Attacks. The Importance of it, has induced Congress to take further Measures, for baffling their Designs, and rendering it more secure. You will see by the Resolves now transmitted, that the northern Army is to be augmented by

---

[98] The sinking of hulks at Tappan Bay to block the passage up the river; using the Connecticut volunteer troop of horse, but sending the horses back to Connecticut; and ordering three regiments from Boston to Canada were decided upon. The proceedings of this conference (July 8), in the writing of Joseph Reed, are in the *Washington Papers.*

Part of the Troops under your Command; and I do desire that you will immediately detach for that Purpose, three of the fullest Regiments forthwith to march to Ticonderoga, or such other Place as the said Army may be at, and put themselves under the Order and Directions of the General Officer commanding the same.

You will also perceive, that Congress have resolved, that the Arms taken in the Scotch Transports should be sent here. The President informs me, he has wrote to the Agents respecting them; but as I presume they are in your Possession, or in some of the Stores by your Order, you will have the Whole of them forwarded with all possible Dispatch, in the usual Rout and with necessary Directions.

Congress have made some Alteration in the Establishment of Chaplains, and advanced their Pay; as they have that of the regimental Surgeons, as you will see by their Proceedings, Copies of which in these Instances are also transmitted.

You will be particularly attentive to hastening the March of the three Regiments, and give proper Orders for their Rout, and to the Commissary and Quarter Masters, that every Thing necessary for the same may be immediately provided. Their Aid is much wanted, and may be of the utmost Importance. When they have marched, you will be pleased to put the remaining Regiments under the Command of the oldest Colonel, with such Instructions as you may judge necessary and then retire, if it shall be agreeable to you, for the Recovery of your Health, as I cannot possibly request you longer to continue, and wishing you a speedy Restoration of it, I am, etc.

P. S. I would have you consult with proper Persons and some of the Members of the General Court, respecting the Route of the three Regiments to be detached to the northern Army, and if they shall be of Opinion, that they may probably arrive there as soon, if they come to Norwich, and embark from thence for

Albany, I should think that would be most preferable for two Reasons, First, it will ease the Troops of much Fatigue and second, they might, if there was a Necessity for it, afford Succour here as they passed. I do not mean to give any Direction in the Matter, nor do I wish this Mode to be adopted, unless there appears a Probability of their arriving where they are intended to be sent by Congress, as early as if they pursued their March by Land and across the Country.

## GENERAL ORDERS

Head Quarters, New York, July 9, 1776.

Parole Manchester.    Countersign Norfolk.

John Evans of Capt. Ledyards Company Col McDougall's Regiment—Hopkins Rice of Capt. Pierce's[99] Company Col Ritzema's Regiment having been tried by a General Court Martial whereof Col. Read was President and found guilty of "Desertion," were sentenced to receive each Thirty-nine Lashes. The General approves the Sentences and orders them to be executed at the usual time and place.

Passes to go from the City are hereafter to be granted by John Berrien, Henry Wilmot and John Ray Junr. a Committee of the City appointed for that purpose—Officers of the Guards at the Ferries and Wharves, to be careful in making this regulation known to the Sentries, who are to see that the passes are signed by one of the above persons, and to be careful no Soldier goes over the Ferry without a pass from a General officer.

The North River Guard to be removed to the Market House near the Ferry-Stairs, as soon as it is fitted up.

The Hon. Continental Congress having been pleased to allow a Chaplain to each Regiment, with the pay of Thirty-three

---

[99] Capt. Jonathan Pearsee(?). There was a Capt. William Perce of the Dutchess County, N. Y., Minutemen and a Captain Pierce (first name not given) in the Seventh Regiment of Dutchess County Militia.

Dollars and one third pr month—The Colonels or commanding officers of each regiment are directed to procure Chaplains
accordingly; persons of good Characters and exemplary lives—
To see that all inferior officers and soldiers pay them a suitable
respect and attend carefully upon religious exercises. The
blessing and protection of Heaven are at all times necessary but
especially so in times of public distress and danger—The General hopes and trusts, that every officer and man, will endeavour
so to live, and act, as becomes a Christian Soldier defending the
dearest Rights and Liberties of his country.

The Hon. The Continental Congress, impelled by the dic-
tates of duty, policy and necessity, having been pleased to
dissolve the Connection which subsisted between this Country,
and Great Britain, and to declare the United Colonies of North
America, free and independent STATES: The several brigades
are to be drawn up this evening on their respective Parades, at
Six OClock, when the declaration of Congress, shewing the
grounds and reasons of this measure, is to be read with an
audible voice.

The General hopes this important Event will serve as a fresh
incentive to every officer, and soldier, to act with Fidelity and
Courage, as knowing that now the peace and safety of his
Country depends (under God) solely on the success of our
arms: And that he is now in the service of a State, possessed
of sufficient power to reward his merit, and advance him to the
highest Honors of a free Country.

The Brigade Majors are to receive, at the Adjutant Generals
Office, several of the Declarations to be delivered to the Brigadiers General, and the Colonels of Regiments.

The Brigade Majors are to be excused from farther attendance at Head Quarters, except to receive the Orders of the day,
that their time and attention may be withdrawn as little as
possible, from the duties of their respective brigades.

## GENERAL ORDERS

Head Quarters, New York, July 10, 1776.

Parole Ogden.    Countersign Philadelphia.

A working party of one hundred and fifty men, properly officered, to parade to morrow morning with their Arms, near the Laboratory, at Six OClock; to take three days provisions. The Commanding Officer to come to Head Quarters for his orders—The Quarter Master General to provide tents.

Genl. Heaths Brigade instead of repairing to their Alarm post to morrow morning to hold themselves in readiness to march—they will receive their Orders from the Brigadier General on the parade at four OClock—The Brigadier will attend at Head Quarters this afternoon for the Orders.

John Butler of Capt. Bridgham's[1] Company, Col Baileys[2] Regiment having been tried by a General Court Martial whereof Col Read was president; found guilty of "Desertion" and sentenced to receive Thirty Lashes—The General confirms the sentence and orders it to be executed at the usual time and place.

'Tho the General doubts not the persons, who pulled down and mutilated the Statue,[3] in the Broadway, last night, were actuated by Zeal in the public cause; yet it has so much the appearance of riot, and want of order, in the Army, that he disapproves the manner, and directs that in future these things shall be avoided by the Soldiery, and left to be executed by proper authority.

### AFTER ORDERS

Col Drake,[4] who was ordered in the orders of yesterday for picquet, this day, being unable to mount, Colonel Bailey is to

---

[1] Capt. John Bridgham, of the Twenty-third Continental Infantry.

[2] Col. John Bailey, of the Twenty-third Continental Infantry.

[3] The gilded leaden statue of King George III. Col. John Montresor secured the head after the British took New York and sent it to Lord Townshend. Most of the statue was carried to Litchfield, Conn., and melted into bullets for the American troops.

[4] Col. Samuel Drake, of the New York Militia.

mount picquet this day in his stead; Likewise Lieut. Col Stoutenburgh[5] is sick, Lieut. Col Sheppard is to succeed in his place to morrow.

## To THE PRESIDENT OF CONGRESS

New York, July 10, 1776.

Sir: I am now to acknowledge the receipt of your two favors of the 4th and 6th instants, which came duly to hand, with their important inclosures. I perceive that Congress have been employed in deliberating on measures of the most interesting Nature. It is certain that it is not with us to determine in many instances what consequences will flow from our Counsels, but yet it behoves us to adopt such, as under the smiles of a Gracious and all kind Providence will be most likely to promote our happiness; I trust the late decisive part they have taken, is calculated for that end, and will secure us that freedom and those priviledges, which have been, and are refused us, contrary to the voice of Nature and the British Constitution. Agreeable to the request of Congress I caused the Declaration to be proclaimed before all the Army under my immediate Command, and have the pleasure to inform them, that the measure seemed to have their most hearty assent; the Expressions and behaviour both of Officers and Men testifying their warmest approbation of it. I have transmitted a Copy to General Ward at Boston, requesting him to have it proclaimed to the Continental Troops in that Department.

It is with great pleasure that I hear the Militia from Maryland, the Delaware Government and Pennsylvania, will be in Motion every Day to form the Flying Camp. It is of great importance and should be accomplished with all possible dispatch. The readiness and alacrity with which the Committee of Safety of Pennsylvania and the other conferrees have acted in order to

---

[5] Lieut. Col. Isaac Stoughtenburg, later of Malcolm's Additional Continental regiment.

forward the Associated Militia of that State, to the Jerseys for service 'till the Men to compose the Flying Camp arrive, strongly evidence their regard to the Common Cause, and that nothing on their part will be wanting to support it. I hope and I doubt not, that the Associated Militia, impressed with the expediency of the Measure, will immediately carry it into execution and furnish in this instance a proof of the continuance of that Zeal which has so eminently marked their conduct. I have directed the Commissary to make necessary provision for their reception, who will also supply the Army for the Flying Camp with Rations. A proper Officer will be appointed to command it.[6]

In pursuance of the power given me by Congress and the advice of my General Officers, I have wrote to General Ward and desired him forthwith to detach three of the fullest Regiments from the Massachusetts Bay, to join the Northern Army, esteeming it a matter of the greatest importance to have a sufficient force there, to prevent the Enemy passing the Lake and making an impression in that Quarter. The Gondolas and Gallies will be of great service, and I am hopeful the Carpenters you have sent from Philadelphia, and that will go from the Eastward, on your application, will be able to build a sufficient number in time to answer every Exigency.[7] I have requested Governor Cook if the Duck mentioned in Mr. Greene's Letter is proper for Tents, to have it made up as early as possible and forwarded here. I have also desired him to send the Flints and small Arms, as I have General Ward those of the latter that were taken out of the Scotch Transports; our deficiency in these necessary Articles being still great.

---

[6] The resolve of July 3 authorized Washington to make this appointment, which he conferred on Brig. Gen. Hugh Mercer.

[7] On July 5 Congress had asked Governor Cooke to send 50 ship carpenters to Albany. On July 6, 50 carpenters from Philadelphia under the lead of Captain Cardrop started for camp.—*Ford*.

Observing that Congress have particularly mentioned a bounty of Ten Dollars to be paid to Men of some Corps directed to be raised in two or three instances, since their Resolve of the 26th. of June, allowing such Bounty, I have been led to doubt how that Resolve is to be construed, whether it is a general Regulation and extends to all Men that will engage for three Years; for instance, the Soldiers of the present Army, if they will Inlist for that service:[8] If it is, and extends to them, it will be necessary to forward a large sum of Money; many perhaps would engage. I also observe by their Resolve of the 25th. of June, for raising four Regiments of Militia in the Eastern Governments, to augment the Troops in the Northern Department, that the Assemblies of those Governments are empowered to appoint Pay Masters to the said Regiments. This appears to me a regulation of great use, and I could wish that it was made general and one allowed to every Regiment in the Service, many advantages would result from it.

The Connecticut Militia begin to come in, but from every Account the Battalions will be very incomplete, owing they say to the busy season of the Year.

That Government, least any inconvenience might result from their Militia not being here in time, ordered three Regiments of their Light Horse to my Assistance, part of which have arrived, but not having the means to support them, and if it could be done, the expence would be enormous, I have thanked the Gentlemen for their Zeal and the Attachment they have manifested upon this Occasion, and informed them that I cannot consent to their keeping their Horses, at the same time wishing them to stay themselves. I am told that they, or part of them mean to do so.

---

[8] On July 16 Congress resolved that General Washington be informed that the bounty granted June 26 was a general regulation, to extend to all men now in the service and all others who may enlist for a term of three years.

General Mercer is now in the Jerseys for the purpose of receiving and ordering the Militia coming for the Flying Camp, and I have sent over our chief Engineer to view the Ground within the Neighbourhood of Amboy, and lay out some necessary Works for the Encampment, and such as may be proper at the different passes in Bergen Neck, and other places on the Jersey Shore opposite Staten Island, to prevent the Enemy making impressions and committing depredations on the Property of the Inhabitants. The Intelligence we have from a few Deserters that have come over to us, and from others, is, that General Howe has between 9. and 10.000 Men, who are chiefly landed on the Island, posted in different parts, and securing the several communications from the Jerseys with small Works and Intrenchments, to prevent our people paying them a visit; that the Islanders have all joined them, seem well disposed to favor their Cause and have agreed to take up Arms in their behalf. They look for Admiral Howe's arrival every day, with his Fleet and a large Reinforcement, are in high Spirits, and talk confidently of Success and carrying all before them when he comes. I trust through Divine Favor and our own Exertions they will be disappointed in their Views, and at all Events, any advantages they may gain will cost them very dear. If our Troops will behave well, which I hope will be the case, having every thing to contend for that Freemen hold dear, they will have to wade thro' much Blood and Slaughter before they can carry any part of our Works, if they carry them at all; and at best be in possession of a Melancholly and Mournfull Victory. May the Sacredness of our cause inspire our Soldiery with Sentiments of Heroism, and lead them to the performance of the noblest Exploits. With this Wish, I have the honor to be, etc.[9]

---

[9] In the writing of Robert Hanson Harrison.

## To THE PRESIDENT OF CONGRESS

New York, July 11, 1776.

Sir: I was honored with your favor of the 8th. inst. by Yesterday morning's Post, with the several Resolves to which you referred my attention; I shall duly regard them, and attempt their execution as far as I am able.

By Virtue of the discretionary powers that Congress were pleased to vest me with, and by advice of such of my General Officers, as I have had an Opportunity of consulting, I have ordered the two remaining Continental Regiments in the Massachusetts Bay, to march immediately for the defence of this place, in full confidence that nothing Hostile will be attempted against that State in the present Campaign.

I have wrote to the General Court of Massachusetts Bay, and transmitted a Copy of the Resolve for employing the Eastern Indians, entreating their good Offices in this Instance, and their exertions to have them forthwith engaged and marched to join this Army. I have desired five or Six hundred of them, to be Inlisted for two or three years if they will consent to it, subject to an earlier discharge, if it shall be thought necessary and upon the same Terms of the Continental Troops, If better cannot be had, though I am hopeful they may.

In my Letter of Yesterday, I mentioned the Arrival of part of the Connecticut Light Horse, to assist in the defence of this place and my Objection to their Horses being kept; Four or Five hundred of them are now come in, and in Justice to their Zeal and laudable attachment to the Cause of their Country, I am to inform you they have consented to stay as long as occasion may require, though they should be at the expence of maintaining their Horses themselves, they have pastured them out about the neighbourhood of Kings Bridge, being unwilling to send them away, at the rate of half a Dollar per Week each, meaning to leave it intirely with Congress either to allow, or refuse it, as they shall Judge proper: I promised to make this Representation, and thought it my duty and will only observe the motives which induced them at first to set out, were good and praise worthy, and were to afford the most speedy and early succour which they apprehended would be wanted before the Militia arrived; their services may be extremely Important, being most of them, if not all, Men of Reputation and of property.

The Subject of the inclosed copy of a Letter from Governor Trumbull, I beg leave to submit to the Consideration of Congress. They will perceive from his representation, the disquieting apprehensions that have seized on the minds of the people, since the retreat of the Northern Army, and how exposed the Northern frontiers of New York and New Hampshire are to the Ravages and Incursions of the Indians. How far it may be expedient to raise the Battalion he conceives necessary to prevent the Calamities and distresses he points out, they will determine upon what he has said, and the necessity that may appear to them for the Measure,[10] what I have done, being only meant to lay the matter before them in Compliance with his wishes. I have also Inclosed a Memorial from the Surgeons Mates, setting forth the Inadequacy of their pay to their Services and

---

[10] Governor Trumbull had written (July 4): "The Retreat of the Northern Army and its present Situation, have spread a general Alarm. . . . The prevalence of the small pox among them [the troops] is every way unhappy; our people in general have not had that Distemper. Fear of the Infection operates strongly to prevent Soldiers from engageing in the Service, and the Battalions ordered to be raised in this Colony fill up slowly: are there no Measures may be taken to remove the Impediment? . . . The retreat of the Army from Canada exposes the Northern Frontiers of New York and New Hampshire to the Ravages of the Indians, who will doubtless be spirited up to fall upon them; some of the Settlements on Onion River, I am informed, are breaking up and removing, and the whole are filled with the most disquieting Apprehension. . . . I could therefore wish, that your Excellency might think proper to recommend to the continental Congress to order a Battalion to be raised and stationed there for the defence of those Settlements." His letter is in the *Washington Papers*.

maintainance, and praying that it may be increased. I shall observe that they have a long time complained in this Instance, and that some additional allowance may not be unnecessary.

As I am truly sensible the time of Congress is much taken up with a variety of Important matters, It is with unwillingness and pain I ever repeat a request after having once made it, or take the Liberty of enforcing any Opinion of mine after it is once given, but as the establishing some Office for Auditing Accounts is a matter of exceeding importance to the Public Interest, I would beg leave once more to call the attention of Congress to an appointment competent to the purposes: two motives induce me to urge the matter; first, a conviction of the utility of the measure; Secondly, that I may stand exculpated, if hereafter it should appear that money has been improperly expended, and the Expences for the Army obtained upon unreasonable Terms.

For me, whose time is employed from the hour of my rising 'till I retire to bed again, to go into an examination of the Accounts of such an Army as this, with any degree of precission and exactness, without neglecting other matters of equal Importance, is utterly Impracticable; All that I have ever been able to do, and that in fact was doing nothing, was when the Commissary and Quarter Master and Director General of the Hospital (for it is to these the great advances are made), applyed for Warrants, to make them at times produce a General Account of their expenditures, but this answers no valuable purpose, it is the Minutiæ that must be gone into, the propriety of each Charge examined, the Vouchers looked into; and with respect to the Commissary General, his victualling returns and expenditures of Provisions should be compared with his purchases, otherways a person in this department, if he was inclined to be knavish, might purchase large quantities with the

Public Money and sell one half of it again for private emolument and yet his Accounts upon paper would appear fair and be supported with Vouchers for every Charge.

I do not urge this matter from a Suspicion of any unfair practices in either of the departments before mentioned, and sorry should I be if this Construction was put upon it, having a high Opinion of the Honor and Integrity of these Gentlemen, but there should nevertheless be some control, as well upon their discretion as honesty; to which may be added that accounts become perplexed and confused by long standing and the errors therein not so discovered as if they underwent an early revision and examination.

I am well apprized, that a Treasury Office of Accounts has been resolved upon and an Auditor General for settling all public Accounts; but with all deference and Submission to the Opinion of Congress, these Institutions are not calculated to prevent the Inconveniences I have mentioned, nor can they be competent to the purposes, circumstanced as they are.[11]

We have intelligence from a deserter that came to us, that on Wednesday Morning, the Asia, Chatham and Greyhound Men of War weighed Anchor, and it was said, intended to pass up the North River above the City to prevent the communication with the Jerseys, they did not attempt it, nor does he know what prevented them.

A Prisoner belonging to the 10th. Regt. taken Yesterday, informs that they hourly expect Admiral Howe and his Fleet, he adds that a Vessel has arrived from them and the prevailing Opinion is, that an Attack will be made immediately on their Arrival.

By a Letter from General Ward I am informed that the Small Pox has broke out at Boston and infested some of the Troops. I

---

[11] Auditors for handling the accounts of the main army were not appointed until January, 1778.

have wrote him to place the Invalids under an Officer to remain 'till they are well and to use every possible precaution to prevent the Troops coming from thence, bringing the Infection.

The distresses and Calamities we have already suffered by this disorder in one part of our Army, I hope will excite his utmost care, that they may not be increased. I have the Honor to be &ca.[12]

## To MAJOR GENERAL ARTEMAS WARD

New York, July 11, 1776.

Sir: Since writing you on the 9th. Inst., I have been "honoured" with a Letter from Congress inclosing a Resolve, a Copy of which you have transmitted herewith, impowering me to call to the Assistance of the Army here, the other two Regiments of Continental Troops, now in the Massachusetts Government, and not ordered in my last, to be detached to join the northern Army. I am now to request, by Advice of my General Officers, that you will give immediate Orders not only to them, but the three destined for the Northward, to repair with all possible Dispatch to Norwich, where they will embark; it being the Opinion of all the Officers, that it will be better for the whole, as well the three intended for the Northward, as those to reinforce the Troops here, to take this Rout in Preference of any other. It may turn out the most expeditious, and it is certain the Men will be eased from the Fatigues of a long and disagreeable March at this hot and uncomfortable Season. It will be necessary, that you should write Mr. Huntingdon[13] at Norwich, to prepare as many Vessels as will bring the whole of them. The Qr. Master and Commissary, you will give proper Orders to, that they may provide, in each of their Departments, such Supplies of Necessaries for the Rout, as may be wanted.

---

[12] In the writing of Robert Hanson Harrison and sent unsigned.
[13] Joshua Huntington.

I have just now received your Favour of the 4th. Inst. with its several Inclosures. It is extremely unlucky, that the small Pox should prevail in the Army at this Time; but such is the Necessity, that every possible Succour should be given to the Troops here and those at the Northward, at this critical Period, that it is the Sentiment of myself and other General Officers, that the whole of the Regiments, that are not infected with the Disorder, should be instantly forwarded. The Calamities that would flow from its being communicated to the whole Army are too obvious to need Mention. You will, therefore, direct the utmost Care and Attention to be used to prevent those that are well from taking the Infection, and for this End, that they may be kept seperate, and apart from those that have the Disorder. Every Precaution will not be more than necessary, to prevent the fatal Consequences, that will attend their bringing and spreading it at this Time, and I trust, that nothing in your Power to prevent it will be wanting. Such of the Men who are down with it, and those you may suspect have received the Infection, you will put under a proper Officer or Officers, to whom you will give Orders, to proceed with them to this Place, as early as possible after they are well and clear of the Infection. The Company or such Part of the Train of Artillery as are there must remain, in Case they should be wanted.

I request that you will have an accurate and exact Return made of all the military and other Stores belonging to the Continent, that I may be enabled to transmit it to the Board of War, and Ordinance, agreeable to their Order.

You will charge the Commissary or Conductor with the Care of them, and that he will remain and guard them in a safe and secure Manner. He must be active and vigilant in his Duty, that nothing may be lost or injured. I am, etc.

## To MAJOR GENERAL PHILIP SCHUYLER

New York, July 11, 1776.

Dear Sir: I received your Favour of the 1st. and 2nd. Inst. and agreeable to your Request transmitted Congress, a Copy of the former and of its several Inclosures. The important Subject referred to them, have met with their Attention, and the Letter accompanying this, will inform you and General Gates, of the Result of their Deliberations. I hope that Harmony, and a good Agreement will subsist between you, as the most likely Means to advance the Interest of the Cause you both wish to promote.[14]

They have determined the Matter between Mr. Trumbull and Mr. Livingston, and the Right of supplying the Northern Army, and appointing Persons for that Purpose, to be in the former.

I gave Orders immediately on Receipt of your Favour, for the several Articles you wrote for to be sent you, if they could be had. Ball or Buck Shot could not be spared from hence, and I directed a Quantity of Lead to be sent you, out of which you must attempt to have them made.[15]

---

[14] Gates's claim to command the Northern Department, when his instructions from Congress were explicit and definitely allotted him the command in Canada, would hardly have been advanced and pushed by him had he not been well aware of the New England influence in Congress in his favor. Despite the decision of Congress against him, his ambitions were sustained by such encouragement as Elbridge Gerry's letter of August 2, 1776: "We want very much to see you with the sole command in the northern department, but hope you will not relinquish your exertions, until a favorable opportunity shall effect it." This to a character like Gates was *carte blanche* to maneuver for the command, regardless of the effect of such actions upon the affairs of the Northern Department.

[15] "What will become of our affairs in Canada, or rather in this Province in the Northern Department? Our General has more trouble and concern with that Department than his own, and after every step taken and supply sent, we are told of great necessities and wants arising from incredible *waste*. If Mr. Schuyler is so good a quarter-master and commissary, why is there such incredible waste? In short, my dear Sir, if some speedy and decisive measure is not taken in this matter, in my opinion that army will waste and disperse, leaving the enemy an easy passage into the heart of these Colonies."—*Joseph Reed to Robert Morris*, July 18, 1776. This letter is from Reed's *Life and Correspondence of Joseph Reed*.

"Such scenes of mismanagement, misconduct, and ill success as have been exhibited in that quarter, ever since the loss of the brave Montgomery, have no parallel."—*Morris to Reed*, July 20, 1776. This letter is from Reed's *Life and Correspondence of Joseph Reed*.

I have not heard any Thing of the Money mentioned by Mr. Duane;[16] I imagine it has not been sent. If any Accident had befallen it, the Matter would have been known ere now.

Since my last, General Howe's Fleet from Hallifax has arrived; in Number about 130 Sail. His Army is between nine and ten Thousand, being joined by some of the Regiments from the West Indies, and having fallen in with Part of the Highland Troops, in his Passage. He has landed his Men on Staten Island, which they mean to secure, and is in daily Expectation of the Arrival of Lord Howe, with one Hundred and fifty Ships, with a large and powerful Reinforcement. This we have from four Prisoners which fell into our Hands and some Deserters; That an Advice Packet arrived at Hallifax before they left it, informing that he was ready to sail when they came from England, to join Genl. Howe here, in Consequence of which he came with the present Armament. They add, that nothing will be attempted 'till his Arrival. Their Intelligence, I have no Doubt, is well founded; indeed the Enemy, having done nothing yet affords Proof beyond Question, that they are waiting for more Troops. We are strengthening ourselves as much as possible, and deem their staying out so long, a fortunate Circumstance; as it not only gives us an Opportunity of advancing our Works; but of getting some Relief from the neighbouring Provinces. From every Appearance, they mean to make a most vigorous Push, to subdue us this Campaign; and for this Purpose to possess themselves of this Colony, if possible, as a Step leading to it. Our utmost Exertions must be used, and I trust, thro' the Favour of divine Providence, they will be disappointed in their Views.

As, having a large Number of Gondolas and Gallies on the Lakes, will be of great Importance, Mr. Hancock informs me in

---

[16] James Duane, a New York Delegate to the Continental Congress.

his Letter of the 6th. Inst., that fifty Carpenters were gone from Philadelphia, in Order to build them; and that he had wrote to Governor Cooke, to engage and forward the same Complement. I am advised by Governor Trumbull, in a Letter just received, that he has procured two Companies of twenty five each, who were about to set out. When they arrive, they will be able I am in Hopes, to turn several of the Stocks in a little Time.

It being evident, that an Attempt will be made by General Burgoyne to penetrate and make an Impression into the Colonies, by Way of the Lakes, unless their is a sufficient Force to oppose him; I have exercised a discretionary Power, with which I was honoured by Congress, and ordered three of the fullest continental Regiments, that were stationed in the Massachusetts Government, to march immediately on receiving my Orders, to join the northern Army. I have directed them to come to Norwich and there embark for Albany, hoping they will arrive as expeditiously in this Way, and with much less Fatigue, than if they had pursued their Rout by Land altogether, at this hot uncomfortable Season. These, with such Militia as may be furnished from the several Colonies required to provide them, and the Troops that were under General Sullivan in Canada, I flatter myself will be able and more than equal, to repel any Invasion that may be attempted from that Quarter. It will be some Time, before their Aid can be had, having never had the Authority of Congress to order them, 'till within this Week.

You will perceive by the inclosed Declaration, that Congress of late have been deliberating on Matters of the utmost Importance. Impelled by Necessity and a Repetition of Injuries no longer sufferable, without the most distant Prospect of Relief, they have asserted the Claims of the Colonies to the Rights of Humanity, absolved them from all Allegiance to the British Crown, and declared them *free* and *independent States.* In

Obedience to their Order, the same must be proclaimed throughout the northern Army.

A Prisoner taken Yesterday, belonging to the 10th. Regiment, informs that Admiral Howe is hourly expected. He adds, that a Vessel has arrived from his Fleet. I am etc.

## To GOVERNOR JONATHAN TRUMBULL

New York, July 11, 1776.

Sir: I duly received your favor of the 6th. Instant; and return you my best thanks for the attention you have shewn at this Crisis, in preparing the several Regiments of Militia, which are nearest this Place, to be ready for Marching when Ordered. Some of the Troops have arrived, and I hope the rest will follow without loss of time. In my Letter of the 9th. Inst. I wrote you fully relative to the Light Horse; which have arrived, to the number of between 4 and 500; and have the happiness to acquaint you, the Officers and Men of that Corps, have manifested so firm an attachment to the Cause we are engaged in, that they have consented to remain here, till such a Body of Troops are marched from your Colony, as will be a Sufficient Reinforcement, so as to admit of their leaving this City with safety. I mention this Matter with greater pleasure, as they have the additional Merit of determining to stay, even if they are obliged to maintain their Horses at their own expence. I have also wrote you with regard to sending any Troops from hence to the Northward, to be replaced by the Militia from your Province, and have stated the injudiciousness, of adopting such a Measure. It is indeed a great misfortune, that the small Pox is so prevalent in our Northern Army; but I conceive it would be highly impolitic at this important period, to send away Troops who have been a considerable time in the Service, and to have their places supplied by Men of much less experience, who belong to the Militia. I have only to add, that I am with much esteem, Sir etc.

P. S. I must refer you to my Letter above mentioned, for my Sentiments with respect to removing the Cattle from the different places specified. As to the Cattle on Montauk Point, I can only say, some method must be devised, to answer the purpose of preventing the Inhabitants of East Hampton from Suffering on the one hand, and the Supply of the Enemy with any Stock on the other.

## To THE MASSACHUSETTS LEGISLATURE OR, IN ITS RECESS, THE COMMITTEE OF SAFETY

Head Quarters, New York, July 11, 1776.

Gentn.: At a Crisis like the present, when our Enemies are prosecuting a War with unexampled severity; when they have call'd upon foreign Mercenaries and have excited Slaves and Savages to Arms against us; a regard to our own Security and happiness, calls upon us to adopt every possible expedient to avert the Blow and prevent the meditated ruin.

Impressed with this Sentiment and impelled by Necessity, the Congress have been pleased to impower me, as you will perceive by the inclosed Copy of their Resolve, which I have the Honor of transmitting you; to call to our Aid so many of the St. Johns, Nova Scotia, and Penobscott Indians, as I might judge necessary; at the same time they have desired, that I should request the Assistance of your Honble. Body, in carrying their Views into execution, and to assure you, that whatever expences you may necessarily incur in doing it, and as incident to it, they will reimburse. Esteeming this Service of such Importance; particularly, if the Enemy should attempt an Impression into the Interior parts of the Country; I must intreat your kind Offices upon this occasion, and your friendly exertions immediately to engage on the best terms you can, five or Six hundred Men of these Tribes and have them marched with all possible expedition to join the Army here.

Having professed a strong Inclination to take part with us in the present Contest, It is probable they may be engaged for less pay and on better terms than the Continental Troops; but, if they cannot, they must be allowed it; The Term of their inlistment should be for two or three Years, unless sooner discharged (the right of which should be reserved us) if they will engage for so long a time; if not, for such time as they will agree to, provided it is not too short; and it must be part of the treaty, and enjoined upon them, to bring every Man his firelock, if it can be possibly effected. As the Services they may render will probably depend on their early and timely arrival, It is unnecessary to suggest to you, the necessity of the utmost dispatch in the Matter.

I well know the execution of the Work will be attended with some trouble and Inconvenience; but a consideration of the Benefits that may arise from employing them and your Zeal for the Common Cause, I am persuaded will surmount every Obstacle, and apologize for my requisition; especially as it comes recommended and supported by Authority of Congress. I have the Honor etc.

P.S. Since I had the honor of addressing you on the 9th Inst., I have received a Resolve from Congress, for calling the other two Continental Regiments from the Mass. Bay, to join the Army here, a Copy of which I have inclosed, and by the advice of my General Officers, have wrote General Ward, to detach them immediately; the Accounts we have all agreeing, that Lord Howe is every day expected with 150 Transports with 15,000 Men at least, in addition to those already here.

## GENERAL ORDERS

Head Quarters, New York, July 11, 1776.

Parole Quebec.   Countersign Roxborough.

General Spencers Brigade, instead of repairing to their Alarm post, to hold themselves in readiness to march to morrow morning at four O'Clock. The Brigadier General will attend at Head Quarters, this evening for orders which he will deliver on the parade, to morrow morning to the brigade.

As the weather is very warm, there will be the greatest danger of the Troops growing unhealthy, unless both officers and men are attentive to cleanliness, in their persons and quarters, The officers are required to visit the men frequently in their quarters to impress on them the necessity of frequently changing their linnen, cleaning their persons, and wherever it can be avoided not to cook their victuals in the same room where they sleep. If any of the officers apprehend themselves crowded in their quarters they are to represent it to the Barrack Master who is ordered to accommodate them in such a manner as to be most conducive to health and convenience. The good of the service, the comfort of the men, and the merit of the officers will be so much advanced, by keeping the troops as neat and clean as possible, that the General hopes that there will be an emulation upon this head; and as a scrutiny will soon be made, those who shall be found negligent will be punished, and the deserving rewarded.

## GENERAL ORDERS

Head Quarters, New York, July 12, 1776.

Parole Somerset.   Countersign Tunbridge.

Thomas Blunfield of Capt. Darrow's[17] Company, Col. Parson's Regiment, tried by a General Court Martial whereof

---

[17] Capt. Christopher Darrow, of the Tenth Continental Infantry.

Colonel Read was President, was found guilty of "Desertion" and sentenced to receive Thirty-nine Lashes. The General approves the Sentence and orders it to be executed at the usual time and place.

Lord Stirling's Brigade to be on the parade at four OClock to morrow morning, with their Arms and Accoutrements, ready to march; they will receive their orders from their Brigadier at the parade.

## To THE PRESIDENT OF CONGRESS

New York, July 12, 1776.

Sir: The design of this is to inform Congress that at about half after three O'Clock this Evening, two of the Enemy's Ships of War, one of 40 and the other of 20 Guns with three Tenders weighed Anchor in the Bay opposite Staten Island and availing themselves of a brisk and favourable breeze, with a flowing Tide, run past our Batteries up the North River, without receiving any certain damage that I could perceive, notwithstanding a heavy and incessant Cannonade was kept up from our several Batteries here as well as from that at Paulus Hook. They on their part returned and continued the fire as they run by. I dispatched an Express to Brigadier General Mifflin, at our Encampment towards the upper end of the Island, but have not heard whether they have got by or received any Damage.

The Account transmitted by this Morning's Post respecting the arrival of one of the Fleet, seems to be confirmed. Several Ships have come in to day. among them, one this Evening with a St. George's Flag at her Fore topmast head which we conclude to be Admiral Howe, from the circumstance of the Flag and the several and General Salutes, that were paid. It is probable they will all arrive in a Day or two and immediately begin their operations.

As it will be extremely necessary, that the flying Camp should be well provided with Powder and Ball, and it may be impracticable to send supplies from hence on Account of our hurry and engagements, besides the Communication may be uncertain. I must beg the attention of Congress to this matter, and request that they will forward with all possible expedition, such a Quantity of Musket powder and Lead. If Balls of different Sizes can not be had, as will be sufficient for the Militia to compose that Camp.

By an Express this minute from General Mifflin the Ships have past his Works. I am in haste, etc.[18]

## To BRIGADIER GENERAL GEORGE CLINTON

Head Quarters, New York, July 12, 1776.[19]

Sir: Two Ships of Force with their Tenders have sailed up Hudson's River.[20] I am apprehensive, that they design to seize the Passes in the Highlands by Land, which I am informed may be done by a small Body of Men. I must, therefore request you, instantly to desire General Ten Broeck,[21] to march down

---

[18] In the writing of Robert Hanson Harrison.

[19] On July 12 Washington proposed to a council of war the question of a general attack on the enemy's quarters on Staten Island, but it was unanimously agreed that such a step was not advisable. "To alarm the Enemy and encourage our own Troops, who seem generally desirous something should be done," the Commander in Chief then proposed "That Major Knowlton who is stationed at Bergen and has reconnoitred the Island do confer with General Mercer thereon, and if they upon Consideration shall deem such a Surprise practicable and that the Retreat of the Men can be secured, the General be advised to prosecute it. That this Enterprise be accompanied with a Cannonade upon the fleet from Bergen Point if the Distance will admit." The council consisted of the Commander in Chief, Maj. Gen. Israel Putnam, and Brig. Gens. William Heath, Joseph Spencer, Nathanael Greene, Lord Stirling, John Morin Scott, James Wadsworth, and Nathaniel Heard. The proceedings of the council, in the writing of Joseph Reed, are in the *Washington Papers*. Lord Stirling's plan for attacking Staten Island, dated July, 1776, is in the *Washington Papers*.

[20] The *Phoenix*, of 40 guns, and the *Rose*, of 20, with three tenders, were sent up the Hudson to cut off supplies which came down the river to New York. They anchored in Tappan Bay. Clinton had already stationed regiments at Fort Constitution, Fort Montgomery, and Newburgh, and ordered a chain of craft to be ready to act as fireboats at the Narrows at Fort Constitution.

[21] Brig. Gen. Petrus Ten Broeck, of the New York Militia.

as great a Force as he can collect to secure them, particularly the Post where the Road runs over Anthony's Nose.

Send off an Express directly (if you please) to the West Parts of Connecticut, desiring them to collect all their Force at the same Point, since I have the highest Reason to believe, it will be absolutely necessary, if it was only to prevent an Insurrection of your own Tories. I am, etc.

P. S. A Return must be immediately made to me of the Number of Men you collect.[22]

### To THE SECRET COMMITTEE
### OF THE NEW YORK LEGISLATURE[23]

Head Quarters, July 13, 1776.

Gentn: A mutiplicity of engagements, and a Continual pressure of other Concerns, has prevented proceeding in the case of the Soldiers confined for seditious and treasonable practices; but as soon as time will admit, a proper attention will be paid to it: In the mean time, I beg leave to suggest the propriety of the Authority of the Province, taking some steps, with regard to those persons confined by them for the same offences. They certainly are to be deemed the principals, and Justice to the inferior Agents, while the others pass unnoticed, I observe, only

---

[22] Precisely this same letter was sent to the Dutchess County, N. Y., Committee on July 13.

[23] The New York Congress had appointed a committee in May, 1776, to deal with "intestine enemies." A standing committee of five was appointed May 27, 1776, and later increased to nine members, with enlarged powers, to function until the committee was dissolved by the Congress. In September, 1776, this committee was given a perfected organization, to which the county committees became subordinate. This organization was dissolved in February, 1777, and was succeeded by a legislative committee of three, soon after increased to five, and, in August, 1778, again enlarged to nine members, who became known as the Commissioners for Detecting and Defeating Conspiracies. As the British held New York City from 1776 to the end of the war, this committee moved from place to place in exercisng its functions. The whole system in New York is comprehensively treated in Flick's *Loyalism in New York during the American Revolution* (New York: 1901) (*Columbia University Studies in History, etc.*, vol. 14, p. 1). At the date of this letter the personnel of the committee was: Robert Yates, John Jay, Robert R. Livingston, Christopher Tappan, and Gilbert Livingston.

excites compassion and censure. I am very sensible, it is a case full of difficulty and perplexity, and well deserving your most serious deliberations; nor do I entertain a doubt, but the result will be such, as will conduce to the Public good. I have, some time ago, mentioned to the Body, of which you are a Committee, the Necessity of falling upon some Measure to remove, from this City and its Environs, Persons of known disaffection and Enmity to the Cause of America. The safety of the Army, the Success of every Enterprize, and the Security of all, depends so much on adopting the most Speedy and effectual Steps for the purpose, that I beg leave again to repeat it; and do most earnestly intreat you to fall upon some plan for this purpose, or give me your Assistance so to do, as to remove those disquieting and discouraging apprehensions, which pervade the whole Army on this Subject. A suspicion, that there are many Ministerial Agents among us, would justly alarm Soldiers of more experience and discipline than ours; and I foresee very dangerous Consequences, in many respects, if a Remedy to the evil is not soon and efficaciously applied.

The removal of the Tory Prisoners, confined in the Gaol of this City, is a matter to which I would Solicit your attention, in every View it appears dangerous and improper. In case of an Attack and Alarm, there can be no doubt what part they will take and none can tell what Influence they might have. You will, Gentlemen, do me the justice to believe, that nothing but the Importance and necessity of the Case, could induce me thus to urge these matters, in which you have also an immediate and Common Interest.[24] The Gentlemen appointed to give passes to persons leaving the City, I am informed decline acting. Great

---

[24] Sparks notes that this representation had its effect. Thirteen Tory prisoners, including the persons most obnoxious for their principles and conduct, were speedily removed by order of the convention to the jail at Litchfield in Connecticut. Two lists of loyalist prisoners confined in the city hall, New York, are in the *Washington Papers,* under the assigned date of July 1, 1776.

Inconvenience will ensue to the Citizens, if this Business should be Committed to Officers of the Army, who from their ignorance of the Inhabitants, as well as other reasons are wholly improper for the management of it. I should be glad if your Committee will take this Matter also into their Consideration. I am etc.

## To CAPTAIN PATRICK DENNIS [25]

Head Quarters, July 13, 1776.

Sir: Mr. Duer informs me, that there are two or three Vessels lying at the Dock of Mr. Beverley Robinson in the Highlands. As it is probable, the Men of War which sailed up the River Yesterday, may have anchored to the northward of those Ships, I think it absolutely necessary that an Attempt should be made to secure those Vessels for future Service. I have, therefore to desire the Favour of you, to procure proper Persons to bring these Vessels down the River, and to anchor them under the Fort where General Mifflin commands.

It is absolutely necessary, that this Matter should be conducted with the utmost Secrecy, and Dispatch, and as I am of Opinion that you possess these Requisites, I have thought proper to apply to you, for your Services in this Matter. I am, etc.

## GENERAL ORDERS

Head Quarters, New York, July 13, 1776.

Parole Ulster.   Countersign Winchester.

The Guard at Fort George to be reinforced with a Field Officer, two Captains, four Subalterns, six Serjeants, six Corporals and seventy Privates.

The General was sorry to observe Yesterday that many of the officers and a number of men instead of attending to their duty

---

[25] A sea captain and New York Bay pilot.

at the Beat of the Drum; continued along the banks of the North River, gazing at the Ships; such unsoldierly Conduct must grieve every good officer, and give the enemy a *mean* opinion of the Army, as nothing shews the brave and good Soldier more than in case of Alarms, cooly and calmly repairing to his post, and there waiting his orders; whereas a weak curiosity at such a time makes a man look mean and contemptible.

A well dress'd orderly Serjeant, from Genls. Scotts, Wadsworth's and Heard's Brigades, to attend at Head Quarters every day.

The Majors of the New Brigades, and all other officers of those Corps, are directed to look over the Orderly Books, before they come into Camp, and acquaint themselves well with former Orders; they are also to be very careful that the daily orders are delivered so, as that neither officer, or soldier, may plead Ignorance, as in that case they will be deemed answerable.

A party of eight hundred men properly officered, to parade to morrow morning—Learneds and Wyllys's Regiments to receive tools for making Fascines; they are to take their dinner with them; Ensign Field of Learneds Regiment to attend this party— All the other Regiments to attend at the Engineer's Store for tools, and orders; three hours allowed for dinner, and to work till Seven, and so continue till further orders—All who have tools belonging to the Engineer's Store, to return them immediately.

If any Brigade, or Regiment, are exempted from fatigue at any time, the Brigade Majors to inform the Engineer thereof (except it be in General Orders) that he may proportion what are sent accordingly.

The safety and success of the army depends so much upon having the works, in all possible forwardness, that the General is much concerned to find the Brigade Majors represented as deficient in their part of the duty: Only five Regiments; Learneds—

Reads—Bailey's—Parson's and Wyllys's Regiments have turned out their working parties this day—The General hopes this is the last time he shall have occasion to take notice of any such neglect.

## GENERAL ORDERS

Head Quarters, New York, July 14, 1776.

Parole Andover.     Countersign Bristol.

A Court of enquiry to sit to morrow morning to examine into the conduct of Col. Ritzema,[26] who stands charged with practices contrary to the rules and discipline of the Army.

Brigadier General Heath President.

| Col Wyllys. | Col Malcom.[27] |
| Lt. Col Johnston. | Lt. Col Brearly.[28] |

The Judge Advocate General and Witnesses, to attend the Court, at Mr. Montagnies Tavern, in the fields, ten OClock.

The Regiment of Artificers under command of Col Parke, to join Lord Stirling's brigade; they will receive orders from the Brigadier with respect to their Alarm Posts, Arrangement and duty in case of action.

The Regimental Surgeons to meet on Tuesday next at nine o'clock A: M: at the Coffee House, on business of importance: The Adjutants of the several Regiments to give them special notice.

The Majors of brigade, and Adjutants of Generals Scotts, Heards and Wadsworths Brigades are to send into the Adjutant

---

[26] Col. Rudolphus Ritzema, of the Third New York Regiment. He deserted to the British.

[27] Col. William Malcolm, of a New York regiment.

[28] Lieut. Col. David Brearley, of the Fourth New Jersey Regiment.

[29] Abraham Montagne's Tavern (spelled also Montaigne), on Broadway, near Murray Street, was a favorite resort of the Sons of Liberty. In January, 1770, it was the scene of a riot when soldiers of the Sixteenth Foot, British Army, attempted to destroy the "liberty pole" which the Sons had erected in front of the building. The citizens were driven into the tavern, the windows demolished, and furniture broken. In all there appear to have been five "liberty poles" erected in the neighborhood at different times. (See I. N. Phelps Stokes's *Iconography of Manhattan Island*, vol. 4, pp. 805-7.)

General's Office, a daily report of every Regiment, or Company, belonging to their several Brigades as they join the Army in order that proper Arrangement may be made while time will admit: The Majors of brigade are to be answerable for obedience to this order; and if the Adjutants refuse or neglect their duty they are to be put in Arrest immediately.

All the Brigade Majors, and Adjutants are again reminded, that the Weekly Returns (as well Brigade as Regimental ones) are to be brought in every Saturday, at Orderly time, to the Adjutant Generals office; and as Inaccuracy and Neglect in their Returns will create difficulties in the payment of their men: The Colonels, or Officers commanding, should carefully examine the Returns, compare them with those of the preceeding week, and have all the alterations accounted for. The General strongly recommends it to the Soldiers, to be careful of their arms and ammunition, at all times, but more especially in rainy weather; An enterprising enemy depending upon neglect in this article, often makes an attack, and too frequently with success—Officers will also be very attentive to this order and see it complied with.

John Andrews, Jeremiah Williams, William Cary late belonging to Genl. Lee's Guard, to join Capt. Fords[80] Company of Artificers.

The Chief Engineer was mistaken in his report yesterday, as to Col Baldwin, Col Huntington and Ward's Regt.—neglect of fatigue, and takes the first opportunity to rectify it.

### To THE PRESIDENT OF CONGRESS

New York, July 14, 1776.

Sir: My last of Friday evening which I had the Honor of addressing you, advised that two of the Enemy's Ships of War

---

[80] Capt. John Ford, of the Massachusetts Artificers.

and three Tenders had run above our Batteries here and the Works at the upper end of the Island.

I am now to inform you, that Yesterday forenoon, receiving Intelligence from General Mifflin that they had past the Tappan Sea and were trying to proceed higher up; by advice of R. R. Livingston Esqr. and other Gentlemen, I dispatched expresses to General Clinton, of Ulster and the Committee of Safety for Dutchess County, to take Measures for securing the passes in the Highlands, least they might have designs of seizing them and have a force concealed for the purpose.

I wrote the Evening before to the commanding Officer of the Two Garrisons there, to be vigilant and prepared against any attempts they or any disaffected persons might make against them and to forward Expresses all the way to Albany that Provision and other Vessels might be secured and prevented falling into their Hands. The information given General Mifflin was rather premature as to their having gone past the Sea. A Letter from the Committee of Orange County, which came to hand this Morning says they were there Yesterday, and that a Regiment of their Militia was under Arms, to prevent their Landing and making an Incursion.

The Messenger who brought it, and to whom it refers for particulars, adds "that a party of them in two or three boats, had approached the Shore, but were forced back by our people firing at them." Since the manuvre of Friday, there have been no other movements in the Fleet.

General Sullivan in a letter of the 2d. Inst. informs me of his arrival with the Army at Crown Point, where he is fortifying and throwing up Works; he adds, that he has secured all the Stores, except three Cannon left at Chamblee, which in part is made up by taking a fine Twelve pounder out of the Lake; The Army is sickly, many with the small pox, and he is apprehensive the

Militia ordered to join them will not escape the Infection; An Officer he had sent to reconnoitre, had reported, that he saw at St. Johns about 150 Tents, 20 at St. Roys, and 15 at Chamblee, and works at the first were busily carrying on.

I have inclosed a General return of the Army here which will shew the whole of our Strength. All the detached posts are included.[31]

A Letter from the Eastward by last night's post, to Mr. Hazard[32] Post Master in this City, advises that two Ships has been taken and carried into Cape Ann; one from Antigua, consigned to General Howe with 439 Puncheons of Rum. The other a Jamaicaman with 400 Hogsheads of Sugar, 200 puncheons of Rum, 39 Bales of Cotton, Pimento, Fustick, etc., etc. Each mounted 2 Guns; Six Pounders.

About 3. O'Clock this afternoon I was informed that a Flag from Lord Howe was coming up and waited with two of our Whale Boats untill directions should be given. I immediately convened such of the General Officers, as were not upon other duty, who agreed in Opinion that I ought not to receive any Letter directed to me as a private Gentleman; but if otherwise and the Officer desired to come up to deliver the Letter himself, as was suggested, he should come under a safe conduct: Upon this I directed Col. Reed to go down and manage the Affair under the above general Instruction: On his return he informed me, after the common civilities the Officer acquainted him, that he had a Letter from Lord Howe to Mr. Washington, which he shewed under a superscription *"to George Washington Esquire."* Col. Reed replied there was no such person in the Army, and that a Letter Intended for the General could not

---

[31] This return, dated July 13, showed a strength of 10,319 rank and file present and fit for duty, with 963 officers. There were nearly 1,500 sick and nearly 2,000 on command. The artillery regiment was 426 strong, with 54 officers.

[32] Ebenezer Hazard. He was, later, Postmaster General of the United States.

be received under such a direction. The Officer expressed great concern, said it was a Letter rather of a Civil than Military Nature; That Lord Howe regretted he had not arrived sooner; That he (Lord Howe) had great Powers. The anxiety to have the Letter received was very evident, tho' the Officer disclaimed all Knowledge of its Contents; However Col. Reeds Instructions being positive, they parted. After they had got some distance, the Officer with the Flag, again put about and asked under what direction Mr. Washington chose to be addressed,[33] to which Col. Reed answered his station was well known, and that certainly they could be at no Loss how to direct to him. The Officer said they knew It and lamented It, and again repeated his wish that the Letter could be received. Col. Reed told him, a proper direction would obviate all difficulties, and that this was no new Matter. This Subject having been fully discussed in the course of the last year of which Lord Howe could not be ignorant, upon which they parted.

I would not upon any occasion sacrifice Essentials to Punctilio, but in this Instance the Opinion of others, concurring with my own, I deemed it a duty to my Country and my Appointment, to insist upon that respect, which in any other than a public view I would willingly have waived. Nor do I doubt but from the supposed nature of the Message and the anxiety expressed, they will either repeat their Flag, or fall upon some mode to communicate the Import and consequence of It.[34]

---

[33] "He [Lieutenant Brown of the *Eagle*] then asked me under what title General,— but catching himself, Mr. Washington chose to be addressed."—*Reed to Pettit*, July 15, 1776. This letter is from Reed's *Life and Correspondence of Joseph Reed.*

[34] On July 17 Congress passed the following resolution: "That General Washington, in refusing to receive a letter said to be sent from Lord Howe, and addressed to 'George Washington, Esqr.' acted with a dignity becoming his station; and, therefore, this Congress do highly approve the same, and do direct, that no letter or message be received, on any occasion whatsoever from the enemy, by the commander in chief, or other, the commanders of the American army, but such as shall be directed to them in the characters they respectively sustain. Ordered, That the above be published."

I have been duly honoured with your two Letters, that of the 10th. by Mr. Anderson, and the 11th. with its inclosures. I have directed the Quarter Master to provide him with every thing he wants to carry his scheme into Execution. It is an Important one, and I wish it success, but I am doubtfull that it will be better in Theory than practice.[35]

The passage of the Ships of War and Tenders up the River, is a matter of great importance, and has excited much conjecture and speculation; to me two things have occurred as leading them to this proceeding; first, a design to seize on the narrow passes on both Sides the River, giving almost the only Land Communication with Albany, and of consequence with our northern Army, and for which purpose they might have Troops concealed on board, which they deemed competent of themselves as the defiles are narrow, or that they would be joined by many disaffected Persons in that Quarter; others have added a probability of their haveing a large Quantity of Arms on board, to be in readiness to put into the hands of the Tories immediately on the arrival of the Fleet, or rather at the Time they intend to make their attack: The second, is to cut off entirely all Intercourse between this and Albany by Water and the upper Country, and to prevent Supplies of every kind going and coming. These matters are truly Alarming and of such Importance, that I have wrote to the Provincial Congress of New York and recommended to their serious consideration, the adoption of every possible expedient, to guard against the two first, and have suggested the propriety of their employing the Militia or such part of them in the Counties in which these defiles are to keep the

---

[35] Ephraim Anderson proposed to destroy the British Fleet at New York. Hancock had written to Washington (July 10): "The Congress are willing to give him an opportunity of trying the experiment, and have therefore thought proper to refer him to you." Anderson had made an attempt of this kind at Quebec; but the enemy received intelligence of it and, stretching a cable across the mouth of the harbor, rendered entrance impossible. He was adjutant to the Second Jersey Battalion.—*Ford.*

Enemy from possessing them till further Provision can be made, and to write to the several leading Persons on our side, in that Quarter, to be attentive to all the Movements of the Ships and the Disaffected in order to discover and frustrate whatever pernicious Schemes they have in view.[36]

In respect to the second conjecture of my own and which seems to be generally adopted, I have the Pleasure to inform Congress, That If their design is to keep the Armies from Provision, that the Commissary has told me upon Inquiry he has forwarded supplies to Albany, now there and above it, sufficient for 10,000 Men for four Months. That he has a sufficiency here for 20,000 Men for three Months and an Abundant Quantity secured in different parts of the Jersey for the flying Camp, besides having 4,000 Barrells of Flour in some Neighbouring part of Connecticut.

Upon this head there is but little occasion for any apprehensions, at least for a Considerable Time. I have &ca.

P. S. I have sent orders to the Commanding Officer of the Pennsylvania Militia to March to Amboy as there remaining at Trenton can be of no good Service.[37]

## To THE NEW YORK LEGISLATURE

Head Quarters, July 14, 1776.

Gentn.: The passage of the Enemy up the North River, is a point big with many Consequences to the Public Interest; one particularly occurs to me well deserving your attention, and to prevent which, I shall gladly give every assistance in my

---

[36] The ships passed all the batteries without receiving any apparent injury. The decks were guarded with ramparts of sandbags, which protected the men from small shot, and the motion of the vessels was so rapid that they remained but a very short time within the range of the heavy guns. They ascended to the broad part of the river called Haverstraw Bay and anchored so far from shore on either side as to be out of danger. Their boats were daily sent out to take soundings. When they occasionally attempted to land they were beaten back by the militia, who watched them narrowly on both sides of the river.—*Sparks.*

[37] In the writing of Robert Hanson Harrison.

power, consistent with the Safety of the Army. I am informed, there are several passes on each side the River, upon which the Communication with Albany depends, of so commanding a Nature, that an inconsiderable Body of Men may defend them against the largest Numbers. It may be, that on Board these Ships there may be Troops for this purpose, who expecting to be joined by the disaffected in that Quarter, or Confiding in their own Strength, may endeavour to seize those defiles in which case the intercourse between the two Armies, both by land and Water, will be wholly cut off; than which a greater Misfortune could hardly befall the Service and Army, I must intreat you, to take the measure into Consideration and if possible provide against an Evil so much to be apprehended. I should hope the Militia of those Counties, might be used on such an Emergency until further provision was made; I have also thought it very probable, those Ships may have carried up Arms and Ammunition, to be dealt out to those who may favor their Cause and cooperate with them at a prefix'd time. I would, to guard against this submit to your Consideration, the propriety of writing to the leading Men on our Side in these Counties, to be very vigilant in observing any movements of this kind, in order that so dangerous a Scheme may be nipped in the Bud. For that purpose to keep the utmost attention to the Conduct of the principle Tories in those parts; any attempts of intercourse with the Ships and all other Circumstances which may lead to a discovery of their Schemes and the Destruction of their Measures. I am Gentn. &c.

## To THE COMMITTEE OF ORANGE COUNTY, NEW YORK

Head Quarters, New York, July 14, 1776.

Gentn: Nothing can be more pleasing, than on all occasions, to see the People ready to fly to the protection of any part of the

Country where there is any danger from the Enemy; but at this extreme busy Season, I cannot recommend your keeping the Regiment embodied. It would be well to notify them all to be ready at a Moments Warning, to Assemble at any place they may be call'd to. Every precaution ought to be taken to prevent the Men of War from getting any Supplies of fresh Provisions, or keeping up any intercourse or Correspondence with the disaffected Inhabitants. I shall be much obliged for timely Information of every Manœuvre of the Ships and Tenders up the River, and hope that every necessary Step will be taken, to prevent any of our Vessels falling into their hands. I am, etc.

## To THE OFFICER COMMANDING THE PENNSYL- VANIA TROOPS AT TRENTON OR ELSEWHERE IN NEW JERSEY

Head Quarters, New York, July 14, 1776.

Sir: From sundry Accounts received of the Troops under your Command, I have Reason to believe they will halt at Trenton, and there wait further Orders. As I do not see any Advantage which can arise from your Continuance there, and the Honble. Continental Congress have committed the Disposition of them to me, until the flying Camp is formed, you will on Receipt of this proceed to Amboy in New Jersey, where General Mercer is appointed to command, and there putting yourself under his Direction, receive and obey such Orders, as he may give. I am, etc.

## To COLONEL RUDOLPHUS RITZEMA

Head Quarters, July 14, 1776.

Sir: At a Period so critical as the present, when our unnatural Enemies are in full View, and hourly expected to strike a Blow, which may be supposed in a great Measure to decide the Fate of

America, I must confess, I am not a little surprised to find an Officer of your Rank in the Army solliciting Leave to resign his Commission, more especially considering the Predicament you are now in. I should rather hope, that as you are so conscious of your Innocence, you would urge an Inquiry into your Conduct, to convince the World, that the Complaints exhibited against you are totally groundless; and that the Malice of your worst Enemies cannot do the least Injury to your Reputation, which to a Soldier ought ever to be dearer than Life.

I don't know how far I can with Propriety countermand the Order for the Court of Inquiry, as it is already given out in General Orders: however I will think of it, and give you my Answer To-Morrow. I am.

## To THE PRESIDENT OF CONGRESS

New York, July 15, 1776.

Sir: This will be handed you by Mr. Griffin[38] who has also taken upon him the charge and delivery of two Packets containing sundry Letters which were sent to Amboy Yesterday by a Flag and forwarded to me today by General Mercer. The Letter addressed to Governor Franklin came open to my hands.[39]

I was this morning honoured with yours of the 13th. instant, with its important and necessary Inclosures, and in Obedience to the Commands of Congress have transmitted General Howe, the Resolves intended for him. Those for General Burgoyne I Inclosed and sent to General Schuyler with directions immediately to forward to him. The Inhuman Treatment to the whole, and Murder of part of our People after their Surrender

---

[38] Col. Samuel Griffin. He had been elected deputy adjutant general of the Flying Camp on July 19.

[39] These papers contained Lord Howe's declaration of the appointment of himself and his brother as commissioners from the King for granting free and general pardons, and a letter to Governor Franklin requesting him to give publicity to the said declaration in New Jersey.—*Sparks.*

and Capitulation, was certainly a flagrant violation of that Faith which ought to be held sacred by all civilized nations, and founded in the most Savage barbarity. It highly deserved the severest reprobation, and I trust the Spirited Measures Congress have adopted upon the Occasion, will prevent the like in future: But if they should not, and the claims of humanity are disregarded, Justice and Policy will require recourse to be had to the Law of retaliation, however abhorrent and disagreeable to our natures in cases of Torture and Capital Punishments.[40] I have &ca.[41]

## To LUND WASHINGTON

New York, July 15, 1776.
(Forged Letter)[42]

## To SIR WILLIAM HOWE

New York, July 15, 1776.

Sir: I have it in charge from Congress to transmit the inclosed Resolutions to you;[48] And have the honor to be, etc.

## To MAJOR GENERAL PHILIP SCHUYLER

New York, July 15, 1776.

Dear Sir: Inclosed you will receive a Letter from Congress which came to Hand this Morning, with a Copy of some Resolves, to which you will pay your Attention, as their Execution will be under your Direction.

---

[40] The Americans captured at The Cedars were plundered by the Indians and several were murdered. Capt. George Forster, of the Eighth Foot, seems to have made no effort to protect the prisoners. The particulars are spread on the *Journals of the Continental Congress*, July 10, 1776.

[41] In the writing of Robert Hanson Harrison.

[42] See note to letter to Lund Washington, June 12, 1776, *ante*.

[48] The same letter was sent to Gen. John Burgoyne. The resolves referred to were those of July 10, 1776, announcing retaliatory measures for treatment received by Americans taken prisoner at The Cedars.

I have also inclosed a Letter for General Burgoyne, which I request you to seal and forward to him, as soon as you have perused the important, and necessary Resolves it contains. The spirited Measures Congress have entered into, I am hopeful, will make the British Troops more regardful of that Faith, which ought to be preserved inviolate between Nations, and that the Rights of Humanity, may not be infracted, in future.

Admiral Howe arrived on Friday last, and we hourly expect his Fleet. The same Day, just before he came in, two Ships of War, one of forty, and the other of twenty Guns, and three Tenders passed our Batteries, without any certain Damage that I could perceive, tho' an incessant Fire was kept up. They availed themselves of a brisk and favourable Wind and Tide.

Our last Intelligence is, that they are at Tappan Bay. You may readily conjecture a Variety of bad Purposes intended by this Manœuvre. I am, etc.

P. S.—I wrote to Fort Constitution and directed that Intelligence should be forwarded respecting the Ships passing by us, to Albany that, Precautions might be used to prevent Vessels falling into their Hands.—You will give further Directions in this Matter.

## To MAJOR GENERAL PHILIP SCHUYLER

Head Quarters, New York, July 15, 1776.

Dear Sir: The inclosed Resolve[44] and Extract of a Letter, you will see is of some Standing. Upon considering the Matter, I do not see how it is possible, for me to carry the Resolve into Execution with tolerable Precision or Certainty. The Persons, the

---

[44] The resolve of June 24, 1776: "That General Washington be directed to order an enquiry to be made into the conduct of the officers heretofore employed in the Canada department; that the said enquiry be made at such times and places as, in his judgment, shall be most likely to do justice, as well to the public as to the individuals; and that the result of the said enquiry, together with the testimonies upon the subject, be transmitted to Congress: that, moreover, all officers accused of cowardice, plundering, embezzlement of public monies, and other misdemeanors, be immediately brought to trial."

Witnesses and all other Circumstances are so totally unknown, that any Inquiry made by me, must prove delusive and unsatisfactory. I am, therefore, under the Necessity of passing it wholly by, or putting it under your Direction, that, as Time and Circumstances will admit, you will have it executed, in the best Manner you can, to answer the Wishes and Expectations of Congress.

Colo. Nicholson[45] (Commandant of a Regiment raised in this Province) requests that his Conduct may be inquired into; I suppose he would be included in the above general Inquiry, but as that may be long delayed and perhaps never fully had, I could wish his Case might be distinguished from the general Mass. I expected to receive from the Commissioners of Congress, who went to Canada some Vouchers and Proofs respecting him, as his Conduct did not appear to them, in the most favourable View; but none have yet come to Hand. Lieut. Colo. Visher,[46] I understand, is a material Witness against Colo. Nicholson, and will direct to such others, as are expected to support the Charge against him.

I am very sensible the General Inquiry requested by Congress must be a Work of Difficulty and Delicacy; but as they seem to desire it very earnestly, I hope it is not impracticable. I should hope, upon a Conference with Generals Gates and Arnold, some Plan may be devised to comply with it. I am persuaded you will leave nothing unattempted on your Part for this Purpose. I am, etc.

## To GOVERNOR JONATHAN TRUMBULL

Head Quarters, New York, July 15, 1776.

Sir: Since my last, two of the Enemy's Ships, one of Forty the other Twenty Guns, taking advantage of a Strong Wind and

---

[45] Col. John Nicholson, of the Fourth New York Regiment.
[46] Lieut. Col. John Vischer, of the New York Militia.

tide, passed us, notwithstanding a Warm fire from all our Batteries. they now lie in Tappan Sea, between twenty and thirty
Miles up Hudson's River, where no Batteries from the shore
can molest them. their Views, no doubt are to cut off all Communication between this and Albany by Water, which they
Effectually will do. If the Gundolas, Row Gallies &c. from
Connecticut and Providence were here, I should think of making their Station uncomfortable if Possible; I must request they
may be sent on as soon as Conveniently can be. I have wrote
Governor Cooke requesting the same of him, 'Tis but reasonable to suppose, these Ships have a Number of Small Arms on
Board, which are intended to put into the hands of the Disaffected on the North River, and in the back Parts of this Province,
when a favorable opportunity may offer, for their making use
of them against us. I am sorry to say their Number, by the best
information I can get is great. Inclosed is a Letter I wrote the
11th. Inst. which thro' mistake, was neglected by the Thursday
Post. We have one large Row Galley nearly compleated and
another which may be ready by the time they arrive from your
Honor and Governor Cooke; the whole when collected will be
sufficient to attack the two Ships up the River, as the Channel
they now occupy is narrow which will prevent working their
Guns to Advantage. I am, etc.[47]

## To THE SECRET COMMITTEE
## OF THE NEW YORK LEGISLATURE

Head Quarters, July 15, 1776.

Gentn: In answer to your favor of yesterday, I beg leave to
acquaint you, that I have consulted with such of the General
Officers as could be easily convened, with respect to the prisoners confined in the Goal of this City. We are all of opinion

---

[47] The same letter was sent to Governor Cooke.

that to enlarge them, or permit their continuance here is equally dangerous; no other Course therefore remains, than to send them to some place where they can be safely kept, can have no Influence, and consequently do us no Injury. If such a Place could be conveniently found in the Province, it would be most proper, but if not, we are of opinion they should be sent to some other and that without any delay. To obviate any difficulty which may arise, from the Authority of one Province sending its Prisoners to another, I will most chearfully Co-operate with you, so as to give the Measure the weight it may derive from my General Command. The Place which in this case, has been proposed is Farmington in Connecticut.

The Multiplicity of other Engagements obliges me to Solicit your Attention and Care to these Matters, which are rather of Civil than Military concern, and I would particularly request you, to Consult and determine upon some method to remove Persons out of Town, whose Conduct, Connections and Office afford the Strongest presumption of their remaining here, with dangerous and unfriendly Views to the American Cause. An indiscriminate order, to remove all who do not belong to the Army or Connected with it, or have not taken up Arms to defend the City, would probably involve many innocent and inoffensive Persons in Difficulty. On the other hand, to leave the City open to Spies and Emissaries from the Enemy, and facilitate their Intelligence is totally inconsistent with common prudence; I must therefore, beg your Advice and Assistance in this delicate and difficult circumstance.

## GENERAL ORDERS

Head Quarters, New York, July 15, 1776.
Parole Chatham.   Countersign Darby.
The Pay Abstracts for the month of June, are immediately to be made up carefully, examined by the Colonels or officer

commanding the Regiment, and then certified by the Brigadiers; after which to be lodged with the Pay Master General.

A working party of one hundred and fifty men, with a Field Officer, three Captains, six Subn., twelve Serjts. twelve Corporals, and three Drums and Fifes, to parade to morrow on the Grand Parade, Six O'Clock, and go up to Kingsbridge to relieve the party sent up the 7th Instant, to take their arms and two days provision, to apply to General Putnam for boats, for transportation, and when at Kingsbridge, apply to Genl. Mifflin for orders.

It is intended that all detached parties to Kingsbridge, shall be relieved once a week in future.

Genl. Scott's brigade to do duty hereafter in their own encampment.

### To LUND WASHINGTON

New York, July 16, 1776.
(Forged Letter)[48]


### GENERAL ORDERS

Head Quarters, New York, July 16, 1776.
Parole Essex.    Countersign Fairfax.

The Hon. Continental Congress have been pleased to increase the pay of the regimental Surgeons, to Thirty-three Dollars and one third, pr month, to take place from the 5th of June last; and that the pay of the troops in the middle department shall be Six Dollars and two thirds pr month, from the 10th of June last. The pay Abstracts are to be made out accordingly, and care taken to prevent confusion or delay.

The hurry of business often preventing particular invitation being given to officers to dine with the General; He presents his compliments to the Brigadiers and Field Officers of the day, and

---

[48] See note to letter to Lund Washington, June 12, 1776, *ante*.

requests while the Camp continues settled in this City, they will favor him with their company, to dinner, without any further or special invitation.

The officers under whose care and direction the Cartridges are made up, having neglected to make daily Returns to Head Quarters; they may depend upon it, that after this day, any officer omitting to send a daily Return of the number of Cartridges made, will be put under an Arrest for disobedience of orders.

### AFTER ORDERS

Col Read President of the present setting General Court Martial, being unable to attend—Col Webb is to succeed him as president; said Court Martial to assemble to morrow morning nine OClock, at the brick house near Col McDougall's encampment.

### To COLONEL THOMAS SEYMOUR AND OTHER FIELD OFFICERS OF THE CONNECTICUT LIGHT HORSE

New York, July 16, 1776.

Gentn.: In Answer to yours of this Date, I can only repeat to you what I said last Night, and that is, that if your Men think themselves exempt from the common Duties of a Soldier, will not mount Guard, do Garrison Duty, or the Service seperate from their Horse, they can be no longer of Use here, where Horse cannot be brought to Action, and I do not care how soon they are dismissed. I am, etc.

### GENERAL ORDERS

Head Quarters, New York, July 17, 1776.

Parole Georgia.    Countersign Hartford.

A working party of fifty Men properly officered to parade to morrow morning, Six OClock, with their arms, near the

Laboratory; there Capt Anderson will attend, from whom they are to receive directions; Quarter Master General to supply such Tools as they may want.

John Berrian, Henry Wilmot and John Ray Jun. a Committee of the town are appointed to give passes to Citizens going over the ferries—officers and soldiers who want passes over the ferries are to apply to their own Brigadier General; And the General desires that they will give no passes to officers or soldiers of another brigade; The officers at the Ferry Guards to attend to this order particularly and make it known to the sentries.

The two Companies of Col Van Cortlandt's Regt. at Long Island, to join their Regiment at New York—Capt. Kelsey's Company, and the Company under the command of Lieut. Borden, of Col Newcomb's Regt., to replace them to morrow morn'g 9 o'Clock.

The Court of enquiry upon Col. Ritzema's Conduct having reported, that no other of the Charges made against him was supported, except that of useing disrespectful expressions of Brigadier Genl. Lord Stirling, and his Lordship generously overlooking the personal affront offered him: The General orders that all further proceedings cease, and Col. Ritzema to be discharged from his arrest.

Yesterday the detachment of our hundred and fifty men, ordered for Kingsbridge, to march from the parade at six o'Clock, did not leave it 'till nine, by which they lost the tide, and then much short of the proportion of officers, an evil which is every day increasing: The Brigade Majors will hereafter be deemed answerable for such neglects, unless they report to the Adjutant General, the same day, what Adjutant fails in bringing on his Quota of men, on the parade in time, or put such Adjutant immediately under Arrest, and report it at Head Quarters.

The Adjutants, and Colonels of the New troops, arriving, are to take notice that Weekly Returns of their Regiments, are to be sent in at orderly time, every Saturday—Blank Returns will be given out at the Adjutant Generals Office, to those who apply for them, and an Orderly Book for each company.

A working party of one hundred and fifty Men, properly officered, to parade to morrow morning at Six OClock, with their Arms, near the Laboratory, to take one days provision with them, to relieve the party which went up the 10th. Instant; this party to stay one week, and then to be relieved.

## To BRIGADIER GENERAL GEORGE CLINTON

Head Quarters, New York, July 17, 1776.

Sir: I am favored with yours of the 15th. Instt. The Measures you have taken and directed in Consequence of the 2 Men of War passing up the North River appear to me extremely prudent and proper. The Spirit of the Militia too upon this Occasion and at so critical a Period desires the highest Commendation. As it is impossible for me to judge with Certainty what the Intentions of the Enemy are or even to know but at some Distance of Time, when they are, the dismissing the Militia must depend upon your own Judgment on a View of all Circumstances. I discharged all those from hence upon finding from all Intelligence that no immediate Attack was meditated. Your case at present is something different, not only as having the Enemy in a Manner among you but the Danger of intestine Enemies: If you can with Safety dismiss a Part I should think it very proper, but you must be governed by your own Situation and Circumstances.

With Respect to the Sloops ordered down to Fort Constitution if in the Way of Fire Ships or in any other Mode they can be used for the Annoyance of the Enemy or the Accomodation of our own Troops I am fully of Opinion with you the Expence ought not to be regarded.

The Enemy have made no Movement since my last of any Consequence, nor is there yet any Appearance of the expected Reinforcement. I am Sir, etc.[49]                    [H.S.P.]

## To MAJOR GENERAL PHILIP SCHUYLER

New York, July 17, 1776.

Dear Sir: Yesterday Evening I was favored with yours of the 12th. Inst. with its several Inclosures.

As to the Propriety or Impropriety of giving up Crown Point, and vacating that Post, it is impossible for me to determine. My Ignorance of the Country, my Unacquaintance with it's Situation, and a Variety of Circumstances, will not permit me to pronounce any certain Opinion upon the Subject, or to declare, whether it might or could not be maintained against the Enemy. I doubt not, the Measure was duly weighed by the General Officers in Council, and seem'd to them best calculated to secure the Colonies and prevent the Enemy from penetrating into them. However, I cannot but observe, tho' I do not mean to encourage, in the smallest Degree, or to give the least sanction to inferior Officers, to set up their Opinions against the Proceedings and Councils of their Superiors, knowing the dangerous Tendency of such a Practice, that the Reasons assigned by the Officers in their Remonstrance appear to me forcible and of great Weight. They coincide with my own Ideas. I have ever understood Crown Point to be an important Post, and from its Situation, of the utmost Consequence to us, especially if we mean to keep the Superiority and Mastery of the Lake. If it is abandoned by us, it is natural to suppose, the Enemy will possess it. If they do, and my Judgement does not mislead me, any Vessels or Gallies we employ upon the Lake, will certainly be

---

[49] In the writing of Joseph Reed.

in their Rear, and it will not be in our Power to bring them down to Ticonderoga or the Post opposite to it; or from thence to have the least Communication with them, or the Means of granting them Succours or Supplies of any Kind. Perhaps it is intended to employ the Gallies only on the Communication between the two Posts, that of Crown Point and the one now to be established. How far they would there answer our Views, I cannot tell. As I said before, I have not a sufficient Knowledge of the several Posts on the neighbouring Country, to form an accurate Judgement upon the Matter, and of Consequence do not design any Thing I have said, by Way of Direction, trusting, that whatever is best to advance the Interest of the important Struggle we are engaged in, will be done.[50]

I am extremely sorry to have such unfavorable Accounts of the Condition of the Army.[51] Sickness of itself is sufficiently bad; but when Discord and Disorder are added, greater Misfortunes cannot befall it, except that of a Defeat. While they prevail, there is but little Hopes of Things succeeding well. I must intreat your Attention to these Matters, and your Exertions to introduce more Discipline, and to do away the unhappy pernicious Distinctions, and Jealousies between the Troops of different Governments. Enjoin this upon the Officers, and let them inculcate, and press home to the Soldiery, the Necessity of Order and Harmony among them, who are embark'd in one common Cause, and

---

[50] In a council of officers, consisting of Generals Schuyler, Gates, Sullivan, Arnold, and Baron de Woedtke, at Crown Point (July 7), it was resolved that the post was not tenable and that the army should retire to the strong ground opposite Ticonderoga, afterwards called Mount Independence. A remonstrance against this decision was drawn up and signed by 21 of the inferior officers, at the head of whom were Cols. John Stark, Enoch Poor, and William Maxwell. Contemporary copies of the proceedings of the council and of the remonstrance are in the *Washington Papers*.

The Baron Friedrich Wilhelm de Woedtke had been a major in the Prussian Army. He came to Philadelphia with strong letters of recommendation to Doctor Franklin and was appointed a brigadier general (March 16) and ordered to Canada by Congress. He died at Lake George about three weeks after this council of war and was buried with military honors.

[51] Gates had written (July 16) that since the beginning of May the loss sustained in the northern army from the enemy, and by death and desertion, amounted to more than 5,000 men, and that 3,000 were then sick.

mutually contending for all that Freeman hold dear. I am persuaded, if the Officers will but exert themselves, these Animosities, this Disorder, will in a great Measure subside, and nothing being more essential to the Service than that it should, I am hopeful nothing on their Parts will be wanting to effect it.[52]

The Scarcity of Provision which you mention, surprises me much. I had hoped, that an ample and competent Supply, for a considerable Time, was now in Store; nor can I but believe, the most lavish and extravagant Waste has been made of it. Not longer than three or four Days ago, and just after the two Men of War and Tenders passed by, as mentioned in my last, the Situation of the northern Army in Respect to this Article, occurred to my Mind, and induced an Inquiry after the Commissary about it, being certain the Water Communication with Albany would be intirely cut off, and was happy to find from him, that the Supplies he had forwarded, with such a Proportion of fresh Meat as could be procured, would be fully sufficient for 10,000 Men for four Months. This I informed Congress of, as a most fortunate Event. To be told now, that there is none, or next to none, is so contrary to what I expected, that I am filled with Wonder and Astonishment. I have informed the Commissary of it, who is equally surprised, and must request, as our Navigation is so circumstanced, that you will direct those whose Business it is, to use every possible Means, to provide such Supplies as may be necessary, and that proper Attention be paid to the Expenditure, or it will be impossible ever to subsist that Army.

As to intrenching Tools, I have from Time to Time forwarded all that can possibly be spared.

---

[52] Schuyler had written (July 12): "The most descriptive pen cannot describe the Condition of our army. Sickness, Disorder, and Discord reign triumphant; the latter occasioned by an illiberal and destructive Jealousy, which unhappily subsists between the Troops raised in different Colonies. . . . The waste that has been made of provisions is incredible. Flour we have in plenty, but of pork not more than six hundred Barrels and fresh Beef extremely difficult to be procured." Schuyler's letter is in the *Washington Papers*.

I have directed the Quarter Master, to send such Things contained in your List, as can be had and may be transported by Land. The greatest Part it would be difficult to procure, and if they could be had, it would be attended with immense Trouble and Expence to forward them. I must, therefore, entreat your utmost Diligence and Inquiry to get them, and not only them but every Necessary you want wherever they may be had. The Water Intercourse being now at an End, but few Supplies can be expected from hence, and I make not the least Doubt, if active proper Persons are employed, in many Instances you will be able to obtain such Articles as you stand in Need of. I am under the Necessity of doing so here, and by much Pains and Industry, have procured many Necessaries.

As for the Articles wanted for the Gondolas, I should suppose many of them may be purchased of the Proprietors of Crafts about Albany, and of Persons who have Vessels there, by allowing them a good Price. The Communication by Water being now stop'd, they cannot employ them, and I presume may be prevailed on to part with most of their Tackle, for a good Consideration.

I transmitted Congress a Copy of your Letter and of its several Inclosures, and recommended to their particular Attention the Resolution No. 6, for raising six Companies to guard the Frontiers, and the high Price of Goods furnished the Soldiery, and that some Measures might be taken thereon.

There is a Resolve of Congress against Officers holding double Commissions, and of long standing, none are allowed it except Adjutants and Quarter Masters. They generally are, also first or second Lieutenants; In this Army there is no Instance of double Offices, but in the Cases I mention.

The Carpenters from Philadelphia, unfortunately had not Time to get their Tools &c. on Board a Craft here before the Men of War got up. They set out by Land next Day, and I suppose will be at Albany in the Course of this Week, as also two Companies from Connecticut.

I have inquired of Mr. Hughes, and find that the six Anchors and Cables were on Board Captn. Peter Post's Vessel belonging to Esopus; who, upon the first Appearance of the Fleet coming above the Narrows, went off without taking the Necessaries brought by Captain Douw.[53] Mr. Hughes says, Captain Douw who brought you the Lead, had Orders to get them.

I have inclosed you a List of the naval Articles the Qr. Master expects to obtain and send from hence, which will evince the Necessity of your Exertions to get the Rest elsewhere. Many of the Articles, I should suppose may be made at Albany and within the Neighbourhood of it.

I am in Hopes, in Consequence of your Application, the different Governments will take some Steps for apprehending Deserters. It is a growing Evil, and I wish it may be remedied. From the northern Army, they have been extremely numerous from Report, and should most certainly be returned, if they should be found. How far, the Mode suggested by you, may answer, the Event will shew; but I am doubtful whether many will return of themselves. I fancy a Part of your Letter was omitted to be sent. When you come to speak of Deserters, what I have on the Subject begun a new Sheet, and seems to suppose something preceding about them. After requesting Mr. Hughes to be spoke to about the Anchors &c. the next Page begins "unanimously agreed that I should write &c."

You will perceive by the inclosed Resolve, Congress mean to raise the Garrison for Presque Isle &ca. . . . in the Counties of Westmoreland and Bedford in Pennsylvania. I am, etc.

P. S. July 18th.—10 O'Clock ante Meridiem. I have this Minute spoke to Mr. Trumbull again about Provisions and

---

[53] Volckert Pieterse Douw, commissioner of Indian affairs of the Northern Department.

pressed his most vigorous Exertions; I believe he is determined to leave nothing undone on his Part and has already sent off some Persons upon the Business, of which, I suppose he will inform you or Mr. Livingston.

### To COLONEL JAMES CLINTON

Head Quarters, New York, July 17, 1776.

Sir: Your Favour of the 13th. Inst. was duly received. The Steps you have taken appear to me extremely proper; and that there may be no Discouragement in the Purchase of Arms, of which we stand in great Need, I have by the Bearer sent you the £300 you request. You will please to keep a particular Account of the Disbursement, in Order that it may be brought into it's proper Place of Settlement, at a future Day.

Before this reaches you, two Officers of the Artillery, whom I dispatched last Sunday, will have arrived to supply the Place of those so unhappily disabled. I trust these Accidents will form a Lesson of Prudence and Calmness at such Times, and particularly excite Care and Caution. It is a melancholy Consideration that in these Cases we suffer more from our own Artillery than the Enemy.

As the Enemy weighed Anchor Yesterday, with a seeming Intention to pass up the River, I trust every Thing is in the best Readiness and Preparation to receive them.

The Rafts, if properly constructed and executed with Spirit and Intrepidity, are most dangerous and alarming Enemies to Shipping. Unacquainted with the River, the Situation of the Ships, and many other Circumstances necessary to form a Judgement of the Probability of success, I can only say, that I agree in opinion with your Brother, that Expenses ought not to be regarded, if the Prospect of Success is any Way encouraging. You must, with them on whose Opinion you can depend, form the best Judgement and act accordingly. I am, etc.

## To THE PRESIDENT OF CONGRESS

New York, July 17, 1776.

Sir: I was this Morning Honoured with yours of the 15th instant with Sundry Resolves. I perceive the Measures Congress have taken to expedite the raising of the Flying Camp and providing it with Articles of the greatest use. You will see by a postscript to my Letter of the 14, I had wrote to the commanding Officer of the Pennsylvania Militia, ordering them to be marched from Trenton to Amboy, as their remaining there, could not Answer the least public Good. For having consulted with sundry Gentlemen I was informed, if the Enemy mean to direct their views towards Pennsylvania, or penetrate the Jerseys, their Route will be from near Amboy and either by way of Brunswick or Bound Brook. The lower road from South Amboy being thro.' a Woody and Sandy country; besides they will be then able to throw in succour here and to receive it from hence in cases of Emergency.

The Connecticut Light Horse mentioned in my Letter of the 11th., notwithstanding their then promise to continue here for the defence of this place, are now discharged and about to return Home; having peremptorily refused all kind of fatigue duty, or even to mount Guard, claiming an exemption, as Troopers.

Tho' their Assistance is much needed and might be of Essential service in case of an Attack, yet I judged it advisable, on their application and claim of such Indulgences, to discharge them; as granting them, would set an Example to others and might produce many ill consequences. The Number of men included in the last return by this is lessened about 500.

I last Night received a Letter from Genl. Schuyler with several Inclosures, Copies of which I have herewith transmitted. They will give Congress every Information I have respecting our Northern Army and the Situation of our Affairs in that

Quarter and to which I beg leave to refer their attention. I cannot but express my surprize at the scarcity of Provisions which General Schuyler mentions, after what the Commissary assured me and which formed a part of my Letter of the 14th. He still assures me of the same. This is a distressing circumstance, as every Article of Provision and every thing else necessary for that department, can have no other now, than a Land conveyance, the Water communication from hence to Albany being entirely cut off.

Congress will please to consider the Inclosure No. 6 about raising six Companies out of the Inhabitants about the Lakes, to prevent the Incursions of the Indians. The General Officers in their Minutes of Council have determined it a matter of much Importance, and their attention to the price of Goods furnished the Soldiery may be extremely necessary. They have complained much upon this head.

The Retreat from Crown Point seems to be considered in opposite views by the General and Field Officers. The former I am satisfied have weighed the matter well, and yet the reasons assigned by the Latter against it appear Strong and forcible; I hope what ever is done will be for the best. I was apprehensive the Appointment of General Gates over General Sullivan would give the latter disgust. His Letter I transmitted Congress seemed to Warrant the Suspicion.—he is not arrived yet, when he does, I shall try to settle the Affair and prevail on him to continue, as I think his resignation will take from the service a useful and Good Officer.[54]

---

[54] This was the age-old dispute between the line and the staff. On June 17, 1775, Gates was appointed Adjutant General of the Continental Army with the rank of brigadier general. Sullivan was appointed a brigadier general in the line of the Army June 22, 1775. Gates was promoted to major general May 16, 1776, and Sullivan was not raised to that rank until Aug. 9, 1776. Sparks quotes his letter of July 6 to General Schuyler: "I ever was desirious, that some officer superior in rank should relieve me from this disagreeable command, and should with pleasure have remained in the army and served under him; but, Congress having thought proper to supersede me by appointing General Gates, who had not, by the rank they were pleased formerly to confer upon us, the same pretension as myself, I can construe this in no other light,

By a Letter from the Committee of Orange County, received this Morning, the Men of War and Tenders were Yesterday at Haverstraw Bay, about 40 miles above this. A number of Men in four Barges from the Tenders attempted to land; with a view they suppose of taking some Sheep and Cattle that had been previously removed. A small number of Militia that was collected, obliged them to retreat without their doing any damage with their Cannon. They were sounding the Water up towards the Highlands, by which it is probable they will attempt to pass with part of the Fleet if possible.

Yesterday Evening a Flagg came from General Howe with a Letter addressed *"To George Washington Esquire &ca. &ca. &ca."* It was not received on the same principle, that the one from Lord Howe was refused.[55] I have &ca.[56]

### To THE PRESIDENT OF CONGRESS
New York, July 17, 1776.

Sir: Colonel Hand[57] having informed me that he means to purchase Regimentals for his Battalion in Philadelphia; I must

---

than to suppose Congress were apprehensive that I was not equal to the trust they were pleased to repose in me. If this be the case, I am bound in justice to my country to relinquish a command to which I am not equal. If this was not the foundation, and they had not such an opinion of me, surely my honor calls upon me to leave the service, after a person is put over me without any impeachment of my conduct." Sullivan went to Philadelphia and tendered his resignation; but after the reasons for promoting General Gates were explained to him by the President of Congress he asked leave to withdraw his application to resign, which was granted.

[55] General Howe gave the following account of this matter in a letter to Lord George Germaine (August 6): "The Commander-in-chief of the rebel forces sent me the enclosed letter and narrative of some past transactions in Canada, which I thought proper to answer in general terms, directing to 'George Washington, Esq., &c., &c., &c.' as the most unexceptionable mode of address. The officer sent to receive the flag would not receive my letter, as it did not express his General's titles. In consequence of which I sent Lieutenant-Colonel Paterson, adjutant-general, a few days afterwards to remonstrate upon this, and other circumstances relative to the usage of General Prescott, and several officers in the enemy's possession, and to mention an exchange of prisoners. This interview was more polite than interesting. However, it induced me to change my superscription for the attainment of an end so desirable; and in this view I flatter myself it will not be disapproved."—*Sparks.*

[56] In the writing of Robert Hanson Harrison.

[57] Col. Edward Hand, of the First Continental Infantry. He was colonel of the First Pennsylvania Regiment; brigadier general; Adjutant General of the Continental Army from Jan. 8, 1781, to Nov. 3, 1783; brevet major general Sept. 30, 1781.

take the Liberty to request you, will have the Nine Thousand dollars resolved by Congress on the 12th. Ulto, to be paid him here for that purpose, to be advanced to him or his order there. The State of our Chest is extremely low and many pressing demands against it, besides as the Clothes are to be paid for there, It seems unnecessary to send Money from hence. An Account of the advance, may be transmitted, in order to a Stoppage from the Mens pay. I have &ca.

## To THE NEW YORK LEGISLATURE

Head Quarters, New York, July 17, 1776.

Gentn.: Your Letter of the 15th Inst. covering the resolution of the same date [58] was duly received; which I beg leave to say was Noble and does honor to your respectable Body; It likewise adds further proof of your determination, to afford me all possible Assistance, in discharging the Important Duties of my Office. It is impossible to say *what may be* Necessary, but I shall conduct as the exigencies of the case may require, and doubt not your cheerful Aid and Assistance whenever called for. It has been out of my power, to procure more Whale Boats than are absolutely Necessary for the Night Guards, I doubt not you will be able to procure the Number you want from the Western Shore of the Sound, which may be easily transported by land or by the Way of Kingsbridge to the North River. I have the Honor etc. [59]

---

[58] Sparks quotes the resolve, which was to the effect that if the Commander in Chief thought it necessary to evacuate the city of New York the legislature would cheerfully cooperate with him in every necessary measure.

[59] On July 18 instructions were issued by Washington, through Lord Stirling, for governing the ferries in the East and North (or Hudson) Rivers. Malcom McEwen and Daniel Green were to superintend the East River Ferry to Long Island and the one at Peck's Slip. McEwen was a lieutenant in Col. John Lasher's New York Militia, and he was to receive a dollar a day for this ferry duty "after deducting his pay"; Green, having no military employment, received a dollar a day. Capt. John Johnson, of the First New York Regiment, and Lieut. Abraham Mesier, of Lasher's regiment, were to superintend the North River Ferry between Powles Hook and Hooghbook. They were to receive half a dollar in addition to their regimental pay.

## GENERAL ORDERS

Head Quarters, New York, July 18, 1776.

Parole Italy.   Countersign Kent.

Altho' the General is very sensible that the great fatigue duty of this Army (which he is highly pleased to see the officers and men go through, with so much cheerfulness and zeal) does not allow much time for manœuvring and exercising the troops; yet it is a matter of so much consequence to have them as well practiced, as time and circumstances will admit; that he earnestly recommends it to the Brigadiers, Colonels or commanding Officers of Regiments, to take time for that purpose, and particularly to have the men instructed and practice the Evolution, Manœuvring, and as much of the Manual Exercise, as respects loading and firing, not only with quickness, but calmness.

John Priest of Capt. Maxwell's[60] Company, Col. Prescott's Regiment; Duncan Grant of Capt. McFarland's[61] Company Col. Nixon's Regiment; Jason Kemp of Capt. Bolsters Company late Col Learned's Regt.; William Baker of Capt. Waterhouses[62] Company Col. Pearson's Regt.; all tried by a General Court Martial whereof Col Webb was President, for "Desertion," and found guilty, were sentenced to receive Thirty-nine Lashes each—Baker to receive his punishment at three different times, Thirteen Lashes each time.

The General approves the above sentences, and orders them to be executed at the usual time and place.

Two Guns fired from Cobble-hill, on Long Island, are to be the Signal that the enemy have landed on that Island.

Complaints having frequently been made, that the Sentries especially those along the river fire wantonly at boats and

---

[60] Capt. Hugh Maxwell, of the Seventh Continental Infantry.
[61] Capt. Moses McFarland, of the Fourth Continental Infantry.
[62] Capt. Abraham Waterhouse, of the Tenth Continental Infantry.

persons passing: Officers of Guards are to be careful upon this head and acquaint the Sentries that they are not to fire upon boats coming to the town—and that they are not to molest or interrupt, the Ferry Boats.

The present number of fatigue to be augmented with one hundred men properly officered, the whole to parade precisely at Six oClock, in the morning, to continue so 'till further orders.

Col. Malcom of Genl. Scott's Brigade, to have the superintendance of the work laid out near that encampment, and to be excused from other duty.

The General invites the Brigade Major of the day, to dine with him in course, with the other officers of the day.

## GENERAL ORDERS

Head Quarters, New York, July 19, 1776.

Parole Lewis.   Countersign Maryland.

A Detachment of three hundred men, properly officered, to parade to morrow morning, Six O'Clock, on the Grand parade, with two days provisions to go in boats, by way of East River to Kingsbridge, to execute such work as shall be laid out for them by the Engineer.

Lieut. Champion[63] of Col Wylly's Regiment, to oversee said works; Major Reed to furnish this party with such tools, as Col. Putnam shall direct.

A working party of fifty men, properly officered to parade to morrow morning at Six o'Clock on the Grand Parade, without their Arms, to receive their orders from Capt. Anderson and tools from the Laboratory.

William Herenden of Capt. Warrens[64] Company Col Reads Regiment, David Ludlow of Capt. Ledyards[65] Company Col

---

[63] Lieut. Henry Champion, of the Twenty-second Continental Infantry.
[64] Capt. Samuel Warren, of the Thirteenth Continental Infantry.
[65] Capt. Benjamin Ledyard, of the First New York Regiment.

McDougall's Regiment both tried by a General Court Martial whereof Col Webb was President for Desertion and found guilty were sentenced to receive, the former Thirty-nine Lashes, the latter Twenty.

The General approves the sentences, and orders them to be executed, at the usual time and place.

The Field Officers of the picquet are directed to attend, on the Grand Parade punctually, at a quarter after eight oClock in the morning, and to continue there 'till the Guard are marched off, for their has been great remissness lately of that kind.

### To MAJOR GENERAL ARTEMAS WARD

Head Quarters, New York, July 19, 1776.

Dear Sir: In my Letter of the 7th. Inst. I mentioned the Propriety of forwarding a Quantity of Powder and lodging it between this and Boston. I am now more fully convinced of the Necessity of such a Measure, and would wish you to forward with all convenient Speed, five hundred Barrels, to be stored at Norwich in Connecticut, till further Orders.

In a Postscript to my Letter of the 9th. Inst. I was of Opinion, it would be much easier for the Troops bound from Boston to the Northward, to proceed this Way for the Benefit of Water Carriage. This being intirely cut off by the Ships up Hudson's River, you will speed their March by the nighest and most convenient Rout.

The several Articlces wrote for in my Letter of Yesterday,[66] you will please to forward to Norwich, with Orders for them to be sent on by Water, provided the Enemy's Ships should not

---

[66] The letter of July 18 was written and signed by Samuel Blatchley Webb. "His Excellency General Washington having occasion to ride out early this morning, has dictated and Ordered me to acknowledge and answer your two Letters of the 11th Inst." The Continental agents for prizes had disposed of the cargoes of prizes without Ward's orders. The list of articles wanted are entered, with Webb's letter, in the Washington "Letter Books," and calls for all the muskets, bayonets, canteens, clothing, etc., taken in the ships *George, Anne,* and *Lord Howe,* and the brig *Annabella.*

stop the Communication, in which Case Land-Carriage must be procured. I am, etc.

P. S. In speaking of the Troops marching to the Northward, I have Reference to the three Regiments bound to Ticonderoga; The other two, I hope, will be on their Way to this Place before this reaches you.

P. S. Since writing the above, your Letter of the 15th. Inst. came to Hand. If the three Regiments you mention have marched they may proceed to this City. If not, one of them to march for Ticonderoga; the two remaining (sick) to follow to the last mention'd Place by Divisions, as fast as a Field Officer's Proportion is well enough; as they will be much the properest (having had the small Pox) for that Department. Yours &c.

## *To MAJOR GENERAL HORATIO GATES

New York, July 19, 1776.

Dear Sir: I expected 'ere this to have heard from you; as I have not I will open the corrispondance by expressing my exceeding great concern on acct. of the determination of your board of General Officers, to retreat from Crown Point to Ticonderago; assigning (contrary to the opinion of all your Field Officers) for reason, that the former place is not tenable with your present force, or the Force expected.

My concern arises from information, and a firm belief, that your relinquishing Crown point is, in its consequences, a relinquishment of the Lakes, and all the advantages to be derived therefrom; for it does not admit of a doubt, but that the Enemy will possess themselves, if possible of that pass (wch. is a key to all these Colonies) the moment you leave it, and thereby confine your Vessels to the narrow part of the Lake in front of that Post, or, by having them in the Rear of it cut off all kind of Supplies from, and intercourse between your Camp and them; securing by this means a free and uninterrupted passage into the three New England Governments for Invasion thereof. Nothing but a belief that you have actually removed the Army from the point to Ticonderoga, and demolishd the Works at the former; and the fear of creating dissensions, and encouraging a Spirit of remonstrating against the conduct of Superior Officers by inferiors, have prevented me, by Advice of the Genl. officers here, from directing the Post at Crown point to be held till Congress should decide upon the propriety of its Evacuation. As the case stands, I can give no Order in the matter, least between two opinions; and places, neither are put into such a posture of defence, as to resist an advancing Enemy. I must however express my sorrow at the Resolution of your Council, and wish, that it had never happend, as every body who speaks of it also does; and that the measure could yet be changed with Propriety.[67]

We have the Enemy full in view of us, but their operations are to be suspended 'till the Reinforcement hourly expected,

---

[67] In his reply to this letter (July 29) Gates, after stating the reasons for evacuating Crown Point, added: "It would be to the last degree improper to order those Troops to Crown Point, or even hither, untill obliged by the most pressing emergency; as that would only be heaping one hospital upon another. Those troops, when they arrive, are all ordered to halt at Skeensborough. Every thing about this army is infected with the pestilence; the cloathes, the blankets, the air, and the ground they walk upon. To put this evil from us, a general hospital is established at Fort George, where there are now between two and three thousand sick, and where every infected person is immediately sent. But this care and caution have not effectually destroyed the disease here; it is notwithstanding continually breaking out." In the same letter Gates took rather high-handed umbrage at the expression of opinion of the general officers in Washington's army. "I must now take the Liberty," he wrote, "to Animadvert a little upon the unprecedented behaviour of the Members of Your Council to their Compeers in this Department. They, Sir, having every Ample Supply at Hand, make no allowance for the Misfortunes, and wants, of this Army, nor for the Delay and Difficulty that Attends the procuring every thing Necessary here. Had we a Healthy Army, Four Times the Number of the Enemy; Our Magazines full, Our Artillery Compleat, Stores of every kind in profuse Abundance, with Vast and populous Towns and Country close at Hand, to Supply Our Wants, Your Excellency would hear no Complaints from this Army; And the Members of your Council, our Brethren and Compeers, would have as little reason then, as they have now, to Censure the Conduct of those, who are in Nothing inferior to themselves." Gates's letter is in the *Washington Papers*.

arrives, when I suppose there will soon be pretty warm Work. Lord Howe is arrived. He and the Genl. his Brother[68] are appointed Commissioners to dispense pardons to Repenting Sinners. My Compliments to the Gentlemen with you of my Acquaintance. I am, &c.    [N.Y.H.S.]

## To THE PRESIDENT OF CONGRESS

New York, July 19, 1776.

Sir: I have been duly honoured with your favours of the 16th. and 17th. with the several Resolves they contained, to the Execution of which, so far as shall be in my power, I will pay proper attention.

In my Letter of the 17th. inst. I transmitted you a Copy of one from General Schuyler and of its several Inclosures. I confess the determination of the Council of General Officers on the 7th. to retreat from Crown point, surprized me much, and the more I considered it, the more striking does the Impropriety appear. The reasons assigned against it by the Field Officers in their remonstrance, coincide greatly with my own Ideas, and those of the other General Officers I have had an Opportunity of consulting with, and seems to be of considerable Weight, I may add conclusive.

I am not so fully acquainted with the Geography of that Country, and the Situation of the different Posts, as to pronounce a peremptory Judgment upon the Matter; but if my Ideas are right, the possessing of Crown Point, is essential to giving us the Superiority and Mastery upon the Lake. That the Enemy will possess it, as soon as abandoned by us, there can be no doubt; and if they do, what ever Gallies or force we keep on the Lake, will be unquestionably in their rear. How they

---

[68] Richard, Earl Howe, and William, Viscount Howe.

are to be supported there, or what succour can be drawn from them then, is beyond my comprehension. Perhaps it is only meant, that they shall be employed, on the communication between that and Ticonderaga; It this is the case, I fear the views of Congress will not be Answered, nor the salutory effects be derived from them that were intended. I have mentioned my surprize to General Schuyler, and would by the Advice of the Generals here have directed, that that post should be maintained, had it not been for two causes. An apprehension that the Works have been destroyed, and that if the Army should be ordered from Ticonderoga or the post opposite to it, where I presume they are, to repossess it, they would have neither one place or another secure and in a defensible State. The other, lest it might increase the Jealousy and diversity in Opinions which seems already too prevalent in that Army, and establish a precedent, for the Inferior Officers to set up their Judgments when ever they would, in opposition to those of their Superiors. A matter of great delicacy, and that might lead to fatal consequences If countenanced; tho' in the present Instance I could wish their reasoning had prevailed. If the Army has not removed, what I have said to General Schuyler may perhaps bring on a reconsideration of the matter, and it may not be too late to take measures for maintaining that Post, but of this I have no hope.

In consequence of the Resolve of Congress for three of the Eastern Regiments to reinforce the Northern Army, I wrote General Ward, and by advice of my Genl. Officers, directed them to March to Norwich and there to embark for Albany conceiving that two valuable purposes might result therefrom. First, that they would sooner join the Army by pursuing this route and be saved from the distress and fatigue that must attend every long March, thro' the Country at this hot and uncomfortable season; and secondly, that they might give succour here in case the Enemy should make an Attack about the time of their passing: But the Enemy having now with their Ships of War and Tenders cut of the Water Communication from hence to Albany, I have wrote this day and directed them to proceed by Land across the Country. If Congress disapprove the route or wish to give any orders about them, you will please to certify me thereof, that I may take measures accordingly.[69]

Inclosed I have the honor to transmit you, Copies of a Letter and sundry Resolutions which I received Yesterday from the Convention of this State.[70] By them you will perceive they have been acting upon matters of great importance, and are exerting themselves in the most vigorous manner, to defeat the wicked designs of the Enemy and such disaffected Persons as may incline to Assist and facilitate their views. In compliance with their request and on Account of the scarcity of Money for carrying their Salutary views into execution, I have agreed to lend them out of the Small Stock now in hand, (not more than 60,000 Dollars) twenty thousand Dollars, in part of what they want, which they promise speedily to replace.

Had there been Money sufficient for paying the whole of our Troops and not more, I could not have done it. but as it was otherwise, and by no means proper to pay a part and not the whole, I could not foresee any Inconveniences that would attend the Loan, on the Contrary, that It might contribute in some degree to forward their Schemes. I hope my conduct in this Instance, will not be disapproved.

---

[69] "Resolved, That General Washington be informed that Congress have such an entire confidence in his judgment, that they will give him no particular directions about the disposition of the troops, but desire that he will dispose of those at New York, the flying camp, and Ticonderoga, as to him shall seem most conducive to the public good."—*Journals of the Continental Congress,* July 23, 1776.

[70] Resolutions for calling out one-fourth part of the militia of the counties of Westchester, Dutchess, Ulster, and Orange, for the defense of the State; to be engaged till the last day of December, and each man to receive a bounty of $20 and Continental pay and subsistence. They were to be stationed in the Highlands, and in the vicinity below, to guard the defiles and prevent incursions of the enemy from Hudson's River. General Washington was requested to appoint a commander of these levies. He appointed Gen. George Clinton.—*Sparks.*

I inclosed Governor Trumbull a Copy of their Letter and their several Resolves to day, by Colonel Broom and Mr. Dewer,[71] two Members of the Convention, who are going to wait on him, but did not think myself at Liberty to urge or request his Interest in forming the Camp of 6,000 Men; as the Levies directed by Congress to be furnished the 3d of June, for the defence of this place by that Government, are but a little more than one third come in. At the same time the proposition I think a good one, if it could be carried into execution. In case the Enemy should attempt to effect a landing above Kings Bridge and to cut of the communication beween this City and the Country; An Army to hang on their Rear, would distress them exceedingly. I have the Honor &ca.

P. S. After I had closed my Letter I received one from General Ward, a Copy of which is herewith transmitted.[72] I have wrote him to forward the Two Regiments now at Boston by the most direct road to Ticonderoga, as soon as they are well, with the utmost Expedition; and consider their having had the small Pox as a fortunate circumstance. when the three arrive which have marched for Norwich, I shall immediately send one of 'em on; if Congress judges it expedient, of which you will please to inform me.[73]

## To GOVERNOR JONATHAN TRUMBULL

New York, July 19, 1776.

Sir: The inclosed Extracts from the proceedings of Congress, which I have the Honor to transmit you, will discover their anxiety respecting our Army here, and their wishes to have it

---

[71] John Broome and William Duer.
[72] Gen. Artemas Ward's letter, dated July 15, 1776, is in the *Washington Papers*.
[73] In the writing of Robert Hanson Harrison, who noted that: "The Inclosed paper should have been sent before but was Omitted thro hurry," which refers to a copy of a letter of July 16 from the New York Legislature, to Washington.

reinforced. I shall only add, that the Situation of our affairs, demands the most speedy Succour, and my request that you use your good offices for Expediting the New Levies as fast as possible. I have also inclosed you a Copy of a Letter and sundry Resolutions which I received yesterday from the Convention of this State. you will perceive thereby, that they have been deliberating on Sundry important measures and are exerting themselves in the most vigorous manner, to defeat the wicked designs of our Common Enemy, and such disaffected Persons as may attempt to favor their Views. They also contain a request, that I should solicit you, to devise some mode for Keeping up a Communication and Intercourse between your State and this, and suggest the Expediency of your forming a Camp of 6000. Men about Byrom River, to co-operate with those they are Collecting, in order to hang on the rear of the Enemy, in case they land above Kingsbridge and attempt to cut off the Communication between the Country and this City. As the Quota of Men requested by Congress for the defence of this Place, is not yet arrived, I could not conceive myself at Liberty to ask of you, to furnish such an additional number, altho' I cannot but observe that the scheme seems well calculated for the purposes they have in View, and might be productive of the most salutary consequences, in case of an attempt of that sort. Colo. Broom and Mr. Duer two Members of the Convention wait on you upon the Subject and will fully point out, the object they have in view, and their Ideas of the importance and expediency of the Plan, and to them I beg leave to refer you. I am Sir, etc.

## To THE NEW YORK LEGISLATURE

Head Quarters, New York, July 19, 1776.

Gentn.: By Messrs. Broome and Duer, I was yesterday favored with your several Resolves of the 16th. Instant.

The spirit and decision in which they are formed, will I doubt not appear in their execution, and as far as I can cooperate, I shall most chearfully contribute all my Aid and Assistance. The State of this Army would make it improper for me, to send up any General Officer in the Continental Service, to take the Command of the Levies proposed to be raised; and from the nature of the Service, I should apprehend a knowledge of the Country and its Inhabitants would be very necessary. General Clinton on all Accounts appears to me the most suitable Person, and as the appointment is made dependent on me, I shall nominate him, unless some objections should be made, or Difficulty arise which I do not now know.

The Deputy Commissaries I will take advice upon, and have them appointed as soon as possible. The State of the Pay Office here did not admit a full compliance with your request of the Loan of £20,000, there not being so much in the Paymaster's hands at this time. However, that so good a work might not be delayed, I immediately gave a Warrant for 20,000 Dollars, and as fast as Circumstances will admit shall make up the remainder. I have inclosed your Resolutions to Governor Trumbull, on the Subject of forming a Camp at Byrom River, for the security of the Communication with New York, but at the same time I very much doubt his ability to carry it into execution. The Quota of Troops to be furnished by Connecticut, for the Assistance of this Army, is not half compleated, notwithstanding the most urgent and pressing Instances on the Subject, which afford a very dull prospect of fixing a New Camp, adequate to the intended design. and I very much fear, the Attempt would obstruct the raising the Levies now ordered and in the end prove ineffectual. at the same time I most heartily approve the Measure, and should rejoice to see it carried into Execution, in the compleatest manner. Since writing the above, your favor of the 18th. Inst. inclosing Colo. Cortlandt and Capt. Platt's[74] report is come to hand; the Spirit and Alacrity of the Militia in so readily turning out at this busy Season, is a very encouraging circumstance, and does them great honor. I observe Colo Fellows[75] of Massachusetts Bay, mentioned as having marched in. If his Troops compose a part of those destined for this Army, it is my intention, that all under that circumstance should come immediately down and be properly arranged; and I observe there will be the less inconvenience, as Messrs. Cortlandt and Platt observe, that they had such a surplus of Men as to enable them to discharge a Number. I am etc.

P. S. with respect to Amunition, I had flattered myself, that the Provincial Stock, would not only have been sufficient for the purposes of its immediate defence, but in case of necessity, have assisted us; I shall endeavour, under a late Direction of Congress, to procure what is to be had from the adjoining Mills.

## To THE SECRET COMMITTEE OF THE NEW YORK LEGISLATURE

Head Quarters, New York, July 19, 1776.

Gentn.: I am favored with yours of the 17th. Inst. My unacquaintedness with Hudsons River and with every other circumstance, necessary to form a judgment of the mode of defending it, will incapacitate me, from giving you the Assistance and advice you politely ask. I must entirely refer it to your own Judgment and skill, only assuring you, that it will give me great pleasure, if any thing effectual can be done, and that I will most readily give all the assistance in my power. I had some

---

[74] Capt. Richard Platt, of the First New York Regiment.
[75] Col. John Fellows. He was, later, brigadier general, Massachusetts Militia.

Intentions of throwing obstructions in the Passage at Mount Washington, but so many difficulties and obstacles have retarded it, that I much fear my being able to compleat it. however it is a Matter so purely confidential, if it can be effected, that I must desire the most profound Secresy may be observed on the Subject. I heartily wish you Success in the Measures you may adopt, and am etc.

## To THE COMMITTEE OF THE CITY OF NEW YORK

Head Quarters, New York, July 19, 1776.

Gentn.: I enclose you a Copy of a Resolution of the Provincial Convention of the State of New York, dated the 16th. Instant recommending it to all the General and Sub Committees, to apprehend and secure all such Persons, whose going at large at this Critical time, they may deem dangerous to the Safety of the State. As this City is hourly threatened with an attack from a powerful Enemy; and as there is too much reason to apprehend, from their Vicinity to this City, and from the number of Suspicious Characters still in it, that they may recieve intelligence, which may counteract all my Operations for its defence, I strongly recommend it to you to remove, for some time, all equivocal and suspicious Characters. This appears to me to be the Spirit of the Resolution of the Provincial Convention; and the propriety of it is founded on the Law of Self preservation, and confirmed by the Practice of all Nations in a State of War.

I esteem it my duty to add my recommendation, to that of the Provincial Convention, that if, through an Ill timed lenity, my attempts to secure this Province should be Baffled, the blame of it may not be imputed to my want of Vigilance.

I have inclosed a list of Persons represented as dangerous,[76] as I can only speak from Information, I must rely upon your taking proper Steps with them; unless, from your better knowledge, you determine them of different Characters than Represented. I am etc.

## *To COLONEL ADAM STEPHEN

New York, July 20, 1776.

Dear Sir: Your Letter of the 4th. Instt.[77] came duly to hand. I thank you for yr. kind congratulations on the discovery of the vile Machinations of still viler Ministerial Agents. I hope the untimely fruit of their Intentions will in the end recoil upon their own heads, all the measures heretofore projected, has done so I think; except in Canada, where an unaccountable kind of fatality seems to have attended all our Movements since the death of poor Montgomery.

We have a powerful Fleet under the Command of Lord Howe in full view of us; distant about 8 Miles from this City, the Troops (from the best Accts. amounting to about Eight or nine thousand Men) are upon Staten Island, fortifying themselves and waiting the Re-inforcement from England, which every fair Wind is expected to bring; this Reinforcement from

---

[76] Maj. Gen. Nathanael Greene handled this loyalist business. He wrote (July 27) reporting his experience with these Tories: "I have examined the prisoners, and find them to be a poor parcel of Ignorant, Cowardly fellows. Two are Taylors, named John and Isaac Dunbar, and the other two common labourers named Petit and Will Smith. They candidly confess, that they set off with an intention of going to Staten Island, but not with any intention of Joining the Enemy; but to get out of the way of fighting here. . . . There has been a draught amongst the Militia to fill the New Levies, and it was rumored that these were a part that were drawn. It was also reported, that they were to go to the Northern Army, and that almost all that went there dyed or were killed. The prospect was so shocking to them, and to their Grand-Mothers and Aunts, I believe they perswaded them to run away. Never did I see fellows more frighted, they wept like a parcel of Children, and appear exceeding sorrowful. . . . I beg your Excellency's direction how to dispose of them, they dont appear to be acquainted with one public matter. They have been Toryish; but I fancy not from principle, but from its being the prevailing Sentiment in the County." Greene's letter is in the *Washington Papers*.

[77] Stephen's letter of July 4, 1776, is not in the *Washington Papers*.

different Accts. will be from Fifteen to 20,000 Men. Our Strength greatly inferior unless the New Levies come in much faster than they have done, which I hope will be the case as harvest will soon be over and that Plea, at an end.

Two Ships on the 12th. to wit, the Phœnex of 44 Guns and Rose of 20, exhibited a proof of the incompetency of Batteries to stop a Ships passage with a brisk Wind and strong tide where there are no obstructions in the Water to impede their motion; the above Ships pass'd through an incessant Fire from our Batteries without receiving much damage; they were each hulled several times and their Rigging a little damaged but not so as to retard their way up the River to what is called the Taupon bay[78] a wide part of the River out of reach of Cannon Shot from either shore. here they now are, having cut of the Water Communication with Albany, and our Army on the Lakes, entirely.

I did not let the Anniversary of the 3d. or 9th. of this Instt. pass of with out a grateful remembrance of the escape we had at the Meadows and on the Banks of Monongahela.[79] the same Providence that protected us upon those occasions will, I hope, continue his Mercies, and make us happy Instruments in restoring Peace and liberty to this once favour'd, but now distressed Country. Give my Complimts. to the Several of yr. Corps of my acquaintances and believe me to be Dr. Sir, etc.     [N.Y.P.L.]

## GENERAL ORDERS

Head Quarters, New York, July 20, 1776.

Parole Newington.   Countersign Ormond.

Daniel Grimes of Capt. Shaw's[80] Company Colo. Marshal's Regiment tried by a General Court Martial whereof Col Webb was President was found guilty of "Desertion," but some

---

[78] Tappan Bay or, as the early Dutch settlers called it, Tappan Zee or Sea.

[79] Stephen had been with Washington at Fort Necessity and at Braddock's Defeat.

[80] Capt. John Shaw, of Col. Thomas Marshall's regiment, Massachusetts Militia.

favourable Circumstances appearing in the person's behalf, his punishment is remitted. The Provost Marshal is ordered to deliver him to Capt. Tilton,[81] in order to be put into some Regiment, to do duty here, until a good opportunity offers, to send him to his own.

### GENERAL ORDERS

Head Quarters, New York, July 21, 1776.
Parole Philadelphia.    Countersign Quebec.

William Baker of Capt. Johnsons[82] Company, in Col. McDougall's Regiment, charged with "absenting himself several days from the Camp without permission," having been tried by a General Court Martial, whereof Col Webb was President, and found guilty, was sentenced to receive Twenty Lashes. The General approves the sentence, and orders it to be executed, at the usual time and place.

Sergt. Ballard, late of General Lee's Guard, now in Custody, for having presumed to give a pass to a person to cross the East River; appearing to have done it more thro' Ignorance than Design:—The General is pleased to discharge him, but if any inferior officer shall hereafter take such a liberty, he will be severely punished: It being again declared that Passes to Citizens, or Country People, are only to be granted by John Berrian, Henry Wilmot and John Ray Junr. or one of them—Passes to officers and soldiers only by a Major General; the Brigadier General of the Brigade to which the person belongs; the Adjutant General, or General's Secretary, or Aide-de-Camps.

The General has great pleasure in communicating to the officers, and soldiers of this Army, the signal success of the American Arms under General Lee at South Carolina. The Enemy having attempted to land at the same time that a most furious

---

[81] Capt. Philip Tilton, of the Eighth Continental Infantry.
[82] Capt. John Johnson, of the First New York Regiment.

Cannonade for *twelve* hours was made upon the Fortifications near Charlestown; Both Fleet and Army have been repulsed with great loss by a small number of gallant troops just raised. The Enemy have had one hundred and seventy two men, killed and wounded, among whom were several officers; Two capital Ships much damaged; one Frigate of Twenty-eight Guns entirely lost being abandoned and blown up by the Crew and others so hurt that they will want great repair before they can be fit for service; And all with a loss on our Part of ten killed and twenty-two wounded. The Firmness, Courage and Bravery of our Troops, has crowned them with immediate Honor. The dying Heroes conjured their Brethren never to abandon the Standard of Liberty, and even those who had lost their Limbs, continued at their posts: Their Gallantry and Spirit extorted applause from their enemies, who dejected and defeated, have retired to their former station, out of the reach of our troops.

This glorious Example of our Troops, under the like Circumstances with us, The General hopes will animate every officer, and soldier, to imitate, and even out do them, when the enemy shall make the same attempt on us: With such a bright example before us, of what can be done by brave and spirited men, fighting in defence of their Country, we shall be loaded with a double share of Shame and Infamy, if we do not acquit ourselves with Courage, or a determined Resolution to conquer or die: With this hope and confidence, and that this Army will have its equal share of Honour, and Success; the General most earnestly exhorts every officer, and soldier, to pay the utmost attention to his Arms, and Health; to have the former in the best order for Action, and by Cleanliness and Care, to preserve the latter; to be exact in their discipline, obedient to their Superiors and vigilant on duty: With such preparation, and a suitable Spirit there can be no doubt, but by the blessing of Heaven, we shall repel our cruel Invaders; preserve our Country, and gain the greatest Honor.

A working party of one hundred and fifty men, properly officered, to parade to morrow morning on the Grand parade, six O'Clock, with their Arms and one days provision, to go up to Kingsbridge by water, to relieve the party which went up the 15th. Instant; to apply to General Putnam for boats.

The General is much pleased with the alacrity of the men in doing Fatigue duty; and being resolved to ease them as much as the service will admit, directs that until further Orders, the men who are to go upon Fatigue shall be excused from turning out to their Alarm posts for that day, unless in case of real alarm.

### To THE PRESIDENT OF CONGRESS

New York, July 21, 1776.

Sir: I have just time to acknowledge the receipt of your favor of the 19th. The Interesting Intelligence of the Success of our Arms in the Southern Department gives me the highest Satisfaction.[83] Permit me to join my Joy to the Congratulations of Congress upon the Event. To Morrow I will write you more fully.

2 O'Clock P. M. I this moment had report made me, that Ten Ships were seen in the Offing, coming in. I suppose part of Admiral Howe's Fleet. I have &ca.[84]

### To THE NEW JERSEY LEGISLATURE

New York, July 21, 1776.

Sir: As we have the strongest reason to believe, the period is just at hand or will soon be, when we shall have the most

---

[83] A copy of Maj. Gen. Charles Lee's letter to Congress (July 2) announcing the defeat of the British at Charleston, S. C., and also copies of the accounts of various persons of the attack on Fort Moultrie, S. C., had been inclosed in the letter of the 19th to Washington.

[84] In the writing of Robert Hanson Harrison.

pressing occasion for Troops, successfully to oppose and defeat the formidable Army we expect against us; I confess I feel myself not a little concerned for the slow manner in which the Levies come in, that were required by Congress, and which will be essential to counteract the efforts of our Enemies.

Not many more, than Twelve hundred of the Quota to be furnished by your State are yet arrived, and I am apt to conclude that it will be a long time before the whole can be made up by Voluntary Inlistments. As the succour they are meant to afford, by the delay that may attend that mode of raising them, may be too late and after an important Stroke has been given us: I submit it to your consideration, whether it may not be prudent, to devise some other way by which they may be raised, and their Aid immediately had.

Voluntary Inlistments, without doubt are preferable to any other mode, if they could be effected in time, and what I would wish for, But as there is too much reason to fear they cannot, from the small progress already made; the critical Situation of our affairs requires, that other means should be used; and in full Confidence, that nothing will be omitted on the part of your Honorable Body, to forward the Quota required of them by Congress. I am etc.

P. S. Ten Sail of Ships are just discovered in the Offing below Sandy Hook, what they are, I know not as yet.

## To THE SECRET COMMITTEE
## OF THE NEW YORK LEGISLATURE

Head Quarters, New York, July 21, 1776.

Gentn.: Yours of the 18th. Inst. I duly received and note the Contents, and am very sorry to hear the Forts in the Highlands are in so defenceless a Situation. Thro' such Variety of business, which calls my closest attention, it has been, and still is, Impossible for me personally to reconnoitre all the different

Posts under my Command: but was so sensible of the Importance of the Fortresses in the High Lands, that I ordered Lord Stirling to visit them, which he did early in the Summer, and reported to me their Situation at that time; and thro' his representations, I continued two Gentlemen in Continental pay, who were acting as Engineers, under orders from the Authority of this State; I have repeatedly pressed Col. Clinton to spare no pains to put them on the best footing Possible, and indeed, I had reason to suppose they were in tolerable order to Receive the Enemy. By the Returns there appears to be 6, 32 pounders besides some 9, 6, 4, and 3 pounders, and enclosed is a Letter for Governor Trumbull, beging him to assist you all in his power. We were so short of Matrosses, that I was necessitated to draft 600 from the different Battalions to join the Artillery in this Place. The 14. with Colo. Clinton, are of the old Regiment and experienced; to these he may add, by drafting a sufficient number of Stout Active Men from the other Corps under his Command, and put them immediately to exercising the Artillery. 'Tis not in my Power to reinforce those Garrisons with more Men; as but about 5,000 of the New Levies have yet arrived in Camp out of 15,000 Ordered; I will this day send up Mr. Machin a Lieut. of the Train, who has just returned from overseeing the Works at Boston; he is as proper a person, as any I can send, being an ingenious faithful hand, and one that has had considerable experience as an Engineer; I shall enjoin on him to attend closely to the business he is going to execute. Rest assured Gentn. that every assistance in my power shall be most chearfully granted and that I am with Esteem, Yours &c.

P. S. to the above was added the Acct. of the Battle of Sullivan's Island, Charlestown South Carolina.[85]

---

[85] See note to Washington's letter to Congress, July 19, 1776, *ante.*

## To COLONEL JAMES CLINTON

Head Quarters, New York, July 21, 1776.

Sir: The Bearer Lt. Machine I have sent to act as an Engineer in the Posts under your Command, and at such other Places as may be thought necessary. He is an ingenious Man and has given great Satisfaction as an Engineer at Boston, from which he is just returned.

I have received from the secret Committee, a Representation of your Want of Matrosses, which can be supplied in no other Way, but by drafting those that are proper, from other Corps, and exercising them to the Artillery. It is what we have been obliged to do here.

The Men thus drafted may be considered as remaining with their own Regiments, and only doing Duty with the Train on the present Occasion. I am etc.

## To LIEUTENANT THOMAS MACHIN

Head Quarters, New York, July 21, 1776.

Sir: You are without Delay to proceed for Fort Montgomery or Constitution in the High Lands on Hudson's River, and there put yourself under Command of Colonel James Clinton or commanding Officer there, to act as Engineer in compleating such Works, as are or may be laid out for the Defence of the River, and adjacent Defiles on each Side the River.

Your being steady and giving close Attention to this Business is necessary. 'Tis, therefore, expected and required of you, that you personally attend where you may be most wanted to forward the Works.

In Case of an Attack from the Enemy, or in any Engagement with them, you are to join the Train of Artillery on that Station, and act according to your Office. I am, etc.

## GENERAL ORDERS

Head Quarters, New York, July 22, 1776.
Parole Richmond.     Countersign Savoy.

The Orderly Serjeants who attend at Head Quarters, are hereafter to bring their dinners, and wait 'till they are regularly relieved.

As it is much to be feared the state of the necessary Houses in the City, may endanger the health of the troops quartered there; It is recommended to the officers, and men, to guard against it as much as possible, and if any method can be fallen on to remove or lessen the inconvenience, to apply to the Barrack Master for that purpose.

The General has noticed with pleasure the care of the Troops in the Encampments on this subject, He hopes they will continue it for the sake of their own healths and the credit of the army.

It being represented to the General, that many Regiments would at this season chuse to lessen their Rations of Meat and supply it with Vegetables, if they could be permitted: His Concern for the health of the troops, and desire to gratify them in every reasonable request, induces him to direct, that the Colonels of such Regiments, as choose to adopt this plan, signify it to the Commissary General, and in two days afterwards the Quarter Master of such Regiment, be allowed to draw one quarter part of the usual Rations in Money to be laid out in Vegetables for his Regiment.

Passes from Col Knox, for the officers and soldiers of the Artillery only, to be sufficient to pass the ferries.

## To THE PRESIDENT OF CONGRESS

New York, July 22, 1776.

Sir: Your favors of the 18th. and 19th., with which you have been pleased to honor me have been duly received with the several Resolves alluded to.

When the Letter and Declaration from Lord Howe to Mr. Franklin and the other late Governors come to be published I should suppose the warmest advocates for Dependance on the British Crown must be silent, and be convinced, beyond all possibility of doubt, that all that has been said about the Commissioners was illusory and calculated expressly to deceive and unguard, not only the Good People of our own Country, but those of the English Nation that were averse to the proceedings of the King and Ministry.[86] Hence we see the cause why a specification of their Powers were not given the Mayor and City of London on their Address requesting it, that would have been dangerous, because it would then been manifest, that the Line of Conduct they were to persue would be totally variant from that they had Industriously propagated and amused the Public with. The Uniting the Civil and Military Offices in the same Persons too, must be conclusive to every thinking one, that there is to be but little Negociation of the Civil Kind.

I have inclosed for the Satisfaction of Congress the substance of what passed between myself and Lieut. Colonel Patterson, Adjutant General, at an Interview had Yesterday in consequence of a Request, from General Howe the day before, to which I beg leave to refer them for particulars.[87]

---

[86] These letters from Richard, Lord Howe, to Govs. William Franklin, John Penn, Robert Eden, Lord Dunmore, Josiah Martin, and Sir James Wright had been sent to Amboy under a flag of truce and forwarded by Washington to Congress, which decided that the letters should "be published in the several gazettes, that the good people of these United States may be informed of what nature are the commissioners, and what the terms, with the expectation of which, the insidious court of Britain has endeavoured to amuse and disarm them, and that the few, who still remain suspended by a hope founded either in the justice or moderation of their late King, may now, at length, be convinced, that the valour alone of their country is to save its liberties." (See *Journals of the Continental Congress,* July 19, 1776.) The letters were published in the *Pennsylvania Gazette,* July 24, 1776.

[87] A memorandum of the interview between Lieut. Col. James Patterson, of the Sixty-third Foot, British Army, and General Washington was ordered published by Congress (July 26):

"The following is an exact state of what passed at the interview between his Excellency General Washington and Colonel Patterson, Adjutant General of the army under General Howe, July 20, 1776.

"After usual compliments, in which, as well as through the whole conversation, Col. Patterson addressed General Washington by the title of Excellency, Col. Patterson

Col: Knox of the Train, having often mentioned to me, the necessity of having a much more numerous body of Artillerists, than what there now is, in case the present Contest should continue longer, and knowing the deficiency in this Instance and their extreme usefullness; I desired him to commit his Ideas upon the Subject to writing, in Order that I might transmit them to Congress for their consideration, agreeable to my request

entered upon the business by saying, that General Howe much regretted the difficulties which had arisen respecting the address of the letters to General Washington; that it was deemed consistent with propriety, and founded upon precedents of the like nature by Ambassadors and Plenipotentiaries where disputes or difficulties of rank had arisen; that General Washington might recollect he had, last summer, addressed a letter to General Howe, To the Hon. William Howe, Esq., that Lord Howe and General Howe did not mean to derogate from the respective rank of General Washington; that they held his person and character in the highest esteem; that the direction, with the addition of &c. &c. &c. implied everything that ought to follow. He then produced a letter which he did not directly offer to General Washington, but observed that it was the same letter which had been sent, and laid it on the table, with a superscription to George Washington, &c. &c. &c. The General declined the letter, and said, that a letter directed to a person in a public character, should have some description or indication of it, otherwise it would appear a mere private letter; that it was true the &c. &c. &c. implied everything, and they also implied anything; that the letter to General Howe alluded to, was an answer to one received under a like address from him, which the officer on duty having taken, he did not think proper to return, but answered it in the same mode of address; that he should absolutely decline any letter directed to him as a private person, when it related to his public station. Colonel Patterson then said, that General Howe would not urge his delicacy further, and repeated his assertions, that no failure of respect was intended. He then said that he would endeavor, as well as he could, to recollect General Howe's sentiments on the letter and resolves of Congress, sent him a few days before, respecting the treatment of our prisoners in Canada. 'That the affairs of Canada were in another department, not subject to the control of General Howe, but that he and Lord Howe utterly disapproved of every infringement of the rights of humanity.' Colonel Patterson then took a paper out of his pocket; and, after looking it over, said he had expressed nearly the words. General Washington then said that he had also forwarded a copy of the resolves to General Burgoyne. To which Colonel Patterson replied, he did not doubt a proper attention would be paid to them, and that he (General Washington) was sensible that cruelty was not the characteristic of the British nation. Colonel Patterson then proceeded to say he had it in charge to mention the case of General Prescott, who, they were informed was treated with such rigor, that, under his age and infirmities, fatal consequences might be apprehended.

"General Washington replied that General Prescott's treatment had not fallen under his notice; that all persons under his particular direction, he had treated with kindness, and made their situation as easy and comfortable as possible; that he did not know where General Prescott was, but believed his treatment very different from their information. General Washington then mentioned the case of Colonel Allen, and the officers who had been confined in Boston gaol. As to the first, Colonel Patterson answered that General Howe had no knowledge of it but by information from General Washington, and that the Canada department was not under his direction or control; that as to the other prisoners at Boston, whenever the state of the army at Boston

he has done it, and the propriety of his plan is now submitted for their decision.[88] It is certain that we have not more at this Time than are sufficient for the several extensive Posts we now have, including the Drafts which he speaks of, and which, I presume, not only, from what he has Informed me, but from the Nature of the thing, can never be Qualified to render the same

admitted it, they were treated with humanity and even indulgence; that he asserted this upon his honor, and should be happy in an opportunity to prove it.

"General Washington then observed, that the conduct of several of the officers would well have warranted a different treatment from what they had received; some having refused to give any parole, and others having broke it when given, by escaping or endeavoring so to do. Colonel Patterson answered, that as to the first, they misunderstood the matter very much, and seemed to have mistook the line of propriety exceedingly; and as to the latter, General Howe utterly disapproved and condemned their conduct.

"That if a remonstrance was made, such violations of good faith would be severely punished; but that he hoped General Washington was too just to draw public inferences from the misbehavior of some private individuals; that bad men were to be found in every class and society; that such behavior was considered as a dishonor to the British army. Colonel Patterson then proceeded to say, that the goodness and benevolence of the King had induced him to appoint Lord Howe and General Howe his commissioners, to accommodate this unhappy dispute, that they had great powers, and would derive the greatest pleasure from effecting an accommodation; and that he (Colonel Patterson) wished to have this visit considered as making the first advances to this desirable object. General Washington replied, he was not vested with any powers on this subject by those from whom he derived his authority and power. But from what had appeared or transpired on this head, Lord Howe and General Howe were only to grant pardons; that those who had committed no fault wanted no pardon, that we were only defending what we deemed our indisputable right. Colonel Patterson said that would open a very wide field for argument. He then expressed his apprehensions that an adherence to forms was likely to obstruct business of the greatest moment and concern.

"He then observed that a proposal had been formerly made of exchanging Governor Skene for Mr. Lovell; that he now had authority to accede to that proposal. General Washington replied, that the proposition had been made by the direction of Congress, and having been then rejected, he could not now renew the business, or give any answer, till he had previously communicated it to them.

"Colonel Patterson behaved with the greatest attention and politeness during the whole business, expressed strong acknowledgements that the usual ceremony of blinding his eyes had been dispensed with. At the breaking up of the conference, General Washington strongly invited him to partake of a small collation provided for him, which he politely declined, alledging his late breakfast, and an impatience to return to General Howe, though he had not executed his commission so amply as he wished. Finding he did not propose staying, he was introduced to the general officers, after which he took his leave, and was safely conducted to his own boat, which waited for him about four miles distant from the city. Made public by order of Congress."

This was published in the *Pennsylvania Gazette,* July 31, 1776. A memorandum of the same, in the writing of Joseph Reed, is in the *Washington Papers.*

[88] By resolve of Congress (July 24) the plan was ordered to be put into execution as soon as possible. Knox's plan accompanies his letter, which is in the *Papers of the Continental Congress.*

service, as if they were regularly appointed and Formed into a Corps for that particular purpose.

I beg leave to remind Congress that some time ago I laid before them the proposals of some persons here for forming a Company of Light Horse, and of the President's Answer a little time after intimating that the plan seemed to be approved of, as those who wanted to make up the Troop are frequently pressing me for an Answer, I could wish to be favoured with the decision of Congress upon the Subject.

By a Letter from General Schuyler of the 14th. Instant, dated at Albany, he informs me, that the day before, some desperate designs of the Tories in that Quarter had been discovered, the particulars of which he could not divulge, being under an Oath of Secrecy. However, that such measures had been taken as to promise a prevention of the intended Mischief, and that four of the Conspirators, among them a Ringleader, were apprehended, about one O'Clock that Morning not far from the town. What the plot was, or who were concerned in it, is a Matter I am Ignorant of as yet. With my best regards to Congress. I have the Honor etc.

P. S. Congress will please to observe, what was proposed respecting the Exchange of Mr. Lovel and signify their pleasure in your next. [The last Weeks return is also Inclosed.][89]

## To THE PRESIDENT OF CONGRESS

New York, July 22, 1776.

Sir: Congress having been pleased to appoint Mr. Wilper to the command of a Company in the German Batallion now raising, I have directed him to repair to Philadelphia for their Orders.

---

[89] In the writing of Robert Hanson Harrison. The words in brackets are in Washington's writing. The return showed a strength of rank and file fit for duty, not counting officers, of 10,439. The original return is in the office of The Adjutant General, War Department, Washington, D. C.

From my acquaintance with him, I am persuaded his conduct as an Officer will meet their approbation, and thanking them for their kind attention to my recommendation of him. I have the Honor &ca.[90]

## *To JOHN AUGUSTINE WASHINGTON

New York, July 22, 1776.

Dear Brother: Whether you wrote to me or I to you last, I cannot undertake to say; but as it is sometime since a Letter has past and as I expect every hour to be engaged in two busy a Scene to allow time for writing private Letters, I will take an oppertunity by this day's post to address to you a few lines, giving a brief acct. of the Situation of Affairs in this Quarter.

To begin then, we have a powerful Fleet within full view of us, distant about 8 Miles. We have General Howes present Army, consisting, by good report of abt. Eight or Nine thousand Men upon Staten Island, covered by their Ships. We have Lord Howe just arrived (that is about 10 days ago) and we have Ships now popping In, which we suppose, but don't know, to be part of the Fleet with the expected Reinforcement. When this arrives, if the Report of Deserters, Prisoners, and Tories are to be depended upon the Enemy's number will amount at least to 25,000 Men; ours to about 15,000, more indeed are expected, but there is no certainty of their arrival, as Harvest and a thousand other excuses are urged for the Reasons of delay. What kind of opposition we shall be able to make time only can shew. I can only say that the Men appear to be in good Spirits, and if they will stand by me the place shall not be carried without some loss, notwithstanding we are not yet in such a posture of defence as I cd wish.

---

[90] In the writing of Robert Hanson Harrison.

Two Ships, to wit, the Phœnix of 44 Guns, and Rose of 20, Run by our Batteries on the 12th; exhibiting a proof of what I had long most religiously believed; and that is, that a Vessel, with a brisk Wind and strong Tide, cannot (unless by a chance Shott) be stopp'd by a Battery without you could place some obstructions in the Water to impede her Motion within reach of your Guns. We do not know that these Ships received any Capital Injury; in their Rigging they were somewhat damaged, and several Shot went through their Hulls; but few if any Lives were lost. They now, with three Tenders, which accompanied them lye up the North or Hudsons River abt. 40 Miles above this place and have totally cut off all Communication (by Water) between this City and Albany; and this Army and that of ours upon the Lakes; they may have had other motives inducing them to run up the River, such as supplying the Tories with Arms, &ca., &ca., but such a vigilant watch has hitherto been kept upon them that I fancy they have succeeded but indifferently in those respects, notwithstanding this Country abounds in disaffected Persons of the most diabolical dispositions and Intentions, as you may have perceived by the several publications in the Gazette, relative to their designs of destroying this Army by treachery and Bribery, which was provadentially discover'd.

It is the general Report of Deserters and Prisoners, and a prevailing opinion here, that no attempt will be made by Genl. How till his reinforcement arrives, which as I said before is hourly expected. Our Situation at present, both with respect to Men, and other matters is such, as not to make it advisable to attempt any thing against them, surrounded as they are by Water and covered with Ships, least a miscarriage should be productive of unhappy and fatal consequences. It is provoking nevertheless to have them so near, without being able in their weakest [part to give] them any disturbance. [The ships] that past us are also saf[ely moored] in a broad part of the River, out [of reach] of shott from either shore.[91]

Mrs. Washington is now at Philadelphia and has thoughts of returning to Virginia as there is little or no prospect of her being with me any part of this Summer. I beg of you to present my Love to my Sister and the Children; and Compliments to any enquiring friends and do me the justice to believe that I am, etc.

### To LUND WASHINGTON

New York, July 22, 1776.
(Forged Letter)[92]

### GENERAL ORDERS

Head Quarters, New York, July 23, 1776.

Parole Trenton.    Countersign Upton.

Lieut. Fuller of Capt. Keyes[93] Company, 20th. Regimt. tried by a General Court Martial of which Lieut. Col Hobby was President, for "Inoculating, and disobedience of orders"—is honorably acquitted, and discharged from his arrest.

It is with great astonishment and surprise, the General hears that Soldiers inlist from one Corps to another, and frequently receive a bounty; and that some officers have knowingly received such men; so glaring a fraud upon the public, and injury to the service, will be punished in the most exemplary manner: And the General most earnestly requests, and expects, of every good officer, who loves his Country, not only to oppose such practices, but to make the offenders known, that they may be brought to justice.

---

[91] Original mutilated; the words in brackets are probable readings.
[92] See note to letter to Lund Washington, June 12, 1776, *ante.*
[93] Lieut. Josiah Fuller, of Capt. John Keyes's company, Twentieth Continental Infantry.

## To BARON DE CALBIAC

New York, July 23, 1776.

Sir: I received your favour of Yesterday, and in answer thereto, I am to inform you, at the same time that I commend the good Intentions which you profess induced your Countrymen[94] to leave their Families and Homes, that I have done the only thing in my power to favour their views.

On their first arrival and introduction to me, I gave them a letter to the Continental Congress, to whom it was necessary to make known their wishes and from whom any Appointments they expect, must come. This, I am persuaded, you are sensible of, and would wish you to communicate to them. Their pretensions will be duly considered, and if supported by proper Credentials, I make no doubt but suitable Regard will be had to their Merits.

Your and their good Sense will readily suggest the Propriety and Expediency of their furnishing some testimonial and recommendation previous to any appointment: These would have been proper at any time, but the late instance of treachery and ingratitude in Monsieur    [95]    in deserting and taking the Command of a party of the Enemy in Canada, after he had been promoted to Office in the service of the United Colonies, makes them indispensably necessary. Though I do not entertain the least suspicion of the Honour and Integrity of the Gentlemen of whom you write, or mean to insinuate that a conduct like Monsieur        would frequently happen.

I might further add, that the unacquaintance of our Soldiers with any Language but their own, makes them rather unwilling

---

[94] Baron de Calbiac came from Guadeloupe.
[95] The name is left blank in the "Letter Book."

and impatient under the Command of Foreigners, unless they are Men of high reputation. Nor will they consent thereto but on that account and where they profess great Military knowledge. It therefore follows that any Appointments these Gentlemen may obtain, will not be attended with any good purposes or satisfaction to themselves, unless they are to [be in a] Corps of their own people, or those who understand their Language. I am, Sir, etc.

## To THE PRESIDENT OF CONGRESS

New York, July 23, 1776.

Sir: I was honoured with your favor of the 20th., by Yesterday's Post; since which and my Letter, nothing of moment has occurred.

The Ships mentioned in my Letter of the 21st. to have been in the Offing, got in that day, and are supposed to be part of the Scotch Fleet, having landed some Highlanders Yesterday.

Inclosed I have the honor to Transmit you, Copies of a Letter and Sundry Resolutions which I received last Night from the Convention of this State. They will inform you of the computed Number of Inhabitants and Stock upon Nassau Island,[96] and their Sentiments on the Impracticability of removing the Latter, and also of the means they think necessary and likely to secure them.

I have also inclosed a Letter from Mr. Faesh[97] to Lord Stirling, upon the Subject of a Cannon Furnace for the use of the States. Congress will see his plan and proposals and determine upon them as they shall Judge proper. I am &ca.[98]

---

[96] The old name of Long Island.
[97] John Jacob Faesh, owner of blast furnaces at Mount Hope, N. J.
[98] In the writing of Robert Hanson Harrison.

## To THE PRESIDENT OF CONGRESS

New York, July 23, 1776.

Sir: Since I had the pleasure of writing you by this mornings post, I was favoured with a Letter from Governor Trumbull, a Copy of which is inclosed and to which I beg leave to refer you.

In regard to the Stock he mentions, I wrote to him, requesting that they might be removed from the Islands on which they were, as I conceived it of great Importance to distress the Enemy, as much as possible, in the article of fresh provision. I wish the other Governments may follow his Example and have it removed from the Islands belonging to them respectively.

When the Ships of War and Tenders went up the River, It was thought expedient that application should be made for the Connecticut Row Gallies and those belonging to Rhode Island, in order to attempt some thing for their destruction. As soon as they arrive we shall try to employ them in some useful way; but in what, or how successfully I cannot at present determine.

Congress will please to observe what Mr. Trumbull says respecting the Continental Regiment raising under Colonel Ward. If they incline to give any Orders about their destination you will please to communicate them by the earliest Opportunity, as their March will be suspended 'till they are known.

The Orders Mr. Trumbull has given to the Officers of their Cruizers to stop Provision Vessels seem to be necessary; we have too much reason to believe, that some have gone voluntarily to the Enemy and that there are many persons who would contrive to furnish them with large supplies, and however upright the Intentions of others may be, It will be a matter of the utmost difficulty, if not an impossibility, for any to escape falling into their hands now, as every part of the Coast, it is probable, will swarm with their Ships of War and Tenders. I had proposed writing to the Convention of this State upon the Subject, before I received his Letter, and am now more persuaded of the necessity of their taking some steps to prevent further exportations down the Sound. In my next I shall inform them of the Intelligence received from Mr. Trumbull and recommend the Matter to their attention. I have the Honor to be &ca.

P. S. It appears absolutely necessary, that the Exportation of Provision should be stopped. Our Army is large and otherwise may want. Nor can Individuals be injured, as they have a ready money market for every thing they have to dispose of in that way.[99]

## To JOHN PARKE CUSTIS

New York, July 24, 1776.

Dear Sir: I wrote to you two or three posts ago, since which your letter of the tenth instant is come to hand. With respect to the proposed exchange of lands with Colonel Thomas Moore, I have not a competent knowledge of either tract to give an opinion with any degree of precision; but from the situation of Moore's land, and its contiguity to a large part of your estate, and where you will probably make your residence, I should, were I in your place, be very fond of the exchange; especially, as the land you hold in Hanover is but a small tract, and totally detached from the rest of your estate. What local advantages it may have I know not. These ought to be inquired into, because a valuable mill seat often gives great value to a poor piece of land (as I understand that of yours in Hanover is). I have no doubt myself, but that middling land under a man's own eye, is more profitable than rich land at a distance, for which reason I should, were I in your place, be for drawing as many of my slaves to the lands in King William and King and Queen as

---

[99] In the writing of Robert Hanson Harrison.

could work on them to advantage, and I should also be for adding to those tracts if it could be done upon reasonable terms.

I am very sorry to hear by your account that General Lewis stands so unfavorably with his officers. I always had a good opinion of him, and should have hoped that he had been possessed of too much good sence to maltreat his officers, and thereby render himself obnoxious to them.

We have a powerful fleet in full view of us,—at the watering-place of Staten Island. General Howe and his army are landed thereon, and it is thought will make no attempt upon this city till his re-enforcements, which are hourly expected, arrive. When this happens it is to be presumed that there will be some pretty warm work. Give my love to Nelly, and compliments to Mr. Calvert and family, and to others who may inquire after, dear Sir, your affectionate.[1]

## To GOVERNOR JONATHAN TRUMBULL

New York, July 24, 1776.

Sir: I was honoured yesterday with your favor of the 17th Inst. and return you my thanks for your kind attention to and compliance with my request for the Row Gallies. They are not yet arrived as I know of.

I wrote Congress by the return Express that brought yours, respecting Colo Ward's Regiment, and as the Post comes in every day, It is probable I shall soon have their Answer. The result, I will transmit you by the first opportunity, and would recommend, that the Regiment be put under Marching orders, that they may proceed without loss of time whatever way Congress shall direct.

The orders you have given to your Armed Cruizers, for stopping provision Vessels, appear to me extremely necessary. I

[1] The text is from George Washington Parke Custis's *Recollections of Washington*.

have mentioned the Matter to Congress, and shall warmly recommend it to the consideration of the Convention of this State. If it should be attended with Inconvenience to individuals; Yet necessity and Public utility, ought to be first considered and outweigh every thing else. But it Cannot, there is nothing but what they can readily dispose of, for the use of the Army and for ready Cash, so that every ground of Objection, must be nugatory. I am &c.

## To THE NEW YORK LEGISLATURE

New York, July 24, 1776.

Sir: I have been honored with your favor of the 20th Inst. with it several inclosures. I observe the Sentiments of your Honorable Body, on the impracticability of removing the Stock from Nassau Island, and the Measures they have adopted for securing them there and protecting the Inhabitants, and sincerely wish they may prove adequate.

I have long since and frequently requested the Commissary, to purchase all the fatted Cattle and Sheep from the Island, that he possibly could in preference to any other; he informs me that he has had many from thence, and that he now has persons employed in different parts for that purpose. The expediency of the measure strikes me so forcibly, that you may depend every means in my power, will be directed to its execution.

Agreeable to your request, I shall Continue Col. Livingston[2] at his present Post, for the protection of the Inhabitants against the Insults of the Enemy's Cruizers, unless something should happen to make his removal necessary.

When the several Regiments are raised and I am certified thereof, and of the Places of Rendesvous, I will direct the Muster Master General to attend and Compleat the Musters.

[2] Col. Henry Beekman Livingston, of the Fourth New York Regiment.

Governor Trumbull having Informed me by Letter Yesterday, that since the arrival of the Fleet at the Hook, many of the Enemy's Frigates and Ships have been stationed between Montauk Point and Block Island, to intercept the Trade from the Sound, and in which they had been but too successful in taking several provision Vessels, and of the impossibility, that any should escape falling into their hands; he had ordered the Armed Vessels in the Service of Connecticut, to stop and detain all Vessels going down the Sound with Provisions, till the Continental Congress or the Convention of the States to which they belong, could be apprized of the hazards attending their proceeding in their Voyages and give orders thereon. I beg leave to recommend the Matter to the Consideration of your Honble. Body, and submit it to them, whether it may not be expedient to lay a General Embargo, or prohibition upon all exports of this kind from your State, except such as the Congress or yourselves may order. The propriety of keeping the Enemy from supplies of this Sort, and providing a Sufficiency for our own Army is so evident, that words are unnecessary upon the Subject. However I cannot but observe as my opinion, that the former will be impossible to effect, unless some General restraining regulation is come into. No care, nor Industry, nor honesty, on the part of Exporters, will be able to elude the Vigilance and Activity of their almost Innumerable Cruizers. But when it is considered, that as long as a free export of any Articles of this Nature is tollerated, disaffected Persons may easily fall into their hands with impunity, nor any means be left us to asscertain their Guilt. When there is strong reason to believe, that some have designedly done so, and almost incontestible proof, from Sundry depositions of deserters and others, that a Ship that went from hence, sailed with no other View and joined the Enemy at the Hook; I incline to think the measure not only advisable but Necessary; Especially, as the large

Consumption of Provision by our Army, affords and will afford a ready Cash Market, for all that Individuals may have to dispose of, and take away every objection of injury on that head; were it otherwise, private advantages and Emoluments must always give place to the public good when they are incompatible.

The last deserters from the Enemy Inform us, since they have heard of our forming a Camp at Amboy, they have talked much of turning their Views to long Island and regaling themselves with large Supplies of Provisions they intend to get from thence. This is an additional circumstance, to induce the Commissary to purchase the Cattle, there before any other. I have the honor etc.

P. S. When the Ships of War &c run up the River, I wrote Governors Trumbull and Cooke for some of their Row Gallies; supposing they might be of Service, in attempting something against the Ships. I expect three or four every hour, besides the one I have. If the secret Committee are forming any plan against the Ships, in which they think they may be usefully employed, If they will let me know, I shall be glad to Co-operate with them and furnish every Assistance the Gallies can give, if not otherwise materially engaged.

I am just now informed, that the Ship mentioned above to have gone to the Enemy was fitted out by the Congress, under the Command of a Captain Hilton[3] who has acted this base part.

## GENERAL ORDERS

Head Quarters, New York, July 24, 1776.
Parole Virginia.    Countersign Wales.
Each Brigadier, with the Colonel and commanding officer of the several Regiments in his Brigade, are to meet and estimate the

---

[3] Captain Hilton's ship was captured by the Connecticut armed sloop *Spy*. Governor Trumbull wrote to the New York Legislature respecting the capture and, in reply, was favored with a resolve (July 23) forbidding the exportation of provisions from New York City under penalty of being held an enemy to the United States.

quantity of paper, absolutely necessary to serve a Regiment for Returns, and other public Uses for a Month, and make report thereof to the General at Orderly time on Friday next, that the Quarter Master General may be directed to provide & deliver the same Monthly to the Colonels, for the use of their respective regiments.[4]

The General being sensible of the dificulty, and expence of providing Cloaths, of almost any kind, for the Troops, feels an unwillingness to recommend, much more to order, any kind of Uniform, but as it is absolutely necessary that men should have Cloaths and appear decent and tight, he earnestly encourages the use of Hunting Shirts, with long Breeches, made of the same Cloth, Gaiter fashion about the Legs, to all those yet unprovided. No Dress can be had cheaper, nor more convenient, as the Wearer may be cool in warm weather, and warm in cool weather by putting on under Cloaths which will not change the outward dress, Winter or Summer—Besides which it is a dress justly supposed to carry no small terror to the enemy, who think every such person a complete Marksman.

### GENERAL ORDERS

Head Quarters, New York, July 25, 1776.

Parole Abington.    Countersign Bedford.

Care to be taken in future, that the Provost Marshal's Guard be properly officered, there having been a Complaint made on that head.

Henry Davis tried for "Desertion" is sentenced to receive Twenty Lashes; Patrick Lyons for "Drunkenness and sleeping on his post," Thirty Lashes.

---

[4] A ream per month to each regiment was thought sufficient. The estimate, dated July 25, 1776, submitted jointly by Nathanael Greene, James Mitchell Varnum, Daniel Hitchcock, Moses Little, and Edward Hand, is in the *Washington Papers*.

Philadelphia July 29. 1776

Sir,

Since I sent off my letter of this morning
the Congress has met, before whom I
laid your Letter, and I have the
pleasure to inform you the Congress
readily agreed to your having another
aid de camp

I have the honour to be
Sr.
your humble Servt
John Hancock Presit

General Washington

LETTER FROM THE PRESIDENT OF CONGRESS
JULY 29, 1776

It is with inexpressible concern, the General sees Soldiers fighting in the Cause of Liberty, and their Country, committing Crimes most destructive to the army, and which in all other Armies are punished with Death—What a shame and reproach will it be if Soldiers fighting to enslave us, for two pence, or three pence a day, should be more regular, watchful and sober, than Men who are contending for every thing that is dear and valuable in life.

The Hon. Continental Congress, in consideration of the Serjeant Majors, Quarter Master Serjeant's, Drum and Fife Majors, not having pay adequate to their Service, and hoping it will excite them to Vigilance and Industry, have been pleased to increase the pay of them, officers having no other appointment One Dollar pr Month, to commence the 16th. Inst. Those Soldiers who have entered on board the Row Galley, commanded by        Cook,[5] are to repair immediately on board, and the officers of the Regiment to which they respectively belong, are to forward them as much as possible, as the service is of the most important kind.

Peter Gusden Esqr. is appointed Major of Brigade to Brigadier General Heard, and is to be obeyed and respected as such.

## *To THE PRESIDENT OF CONGRESS

New York, July 25, 1776.

Sir: Disagreeable as it is to me, and unpleasing as it may be to Congress to multiply Officers, I find myself under the unavoidable necessity of asking an Increase of my Aid de Camps. The augmentation of my Command, the Increase of my Corrispondance, the Orders to give; the Instructions to draw, cut out more business than I am able to execute in time, with

---

[5]Probably Capt. Robert Cook, commander of an armed galley known as *Lady Washington.*

propriety. The business of so many different departments centering with me, and by me to be handed on to Congress for their information, added to the Intercourse I am Obliged to keep up with the adjacent States and incidental Occurrences, all of which requiring confidential (and not hack) writers to execute, renders it impossible in the present State of things for my family to discharge the several duties expected of me with that precision and dispatch that I could wish. What will it be then when we come into a more active Scene, and I am called upon from twenty different places perhaps at the same Instant?

Congress will do me the Justice to believe, I hope, that it is not my Inclination or wish, to run the Continent to any unnecessary expence; and those who better know me, will not suspect that shew, and parade can have any Influence on my Mind in this Instance. A Conviction of the necessity of it, for the regular discharge of the trust reposed in me is the Governing motive for the Application, and as such is Submitted to Congress by. Sir &ca: [6]

### To THE MASSACHUSETTS LEGISLATURE

New York, July 25, 1776.

Gentn.: Congress having impowred me to appoint suitable places of Rendezvous for the Battalions raising in your

---

[6] This letter was read in Congress July 29, and Washington was immediately authorized to employ another aide-de-camp.

General Greene, in a letter to Washington (July 25), described the waste of energy demanded of the higher officers in routine matters: "I am so confined, writing passes, &c., that it is impossible for me to attend to the duties of the day, which in many instances prejudices the service. Such a confined situation leaves one no opportunity of viewing things for themselves. It is recommended, by one of the greatest Generals of the Age, not only to issue Orders, but to see to the execution; for the Army being composed of men of Indolence, If the Commander is not attentive to every Individual in the different departments, the Machine becomes dislocated, and the progress of business retarded. The science or Art of War requires a freedom of thought, and leisure to reflect upon the Various incidents that daily Occur, which cannot be had where the whole of one's time is engrossed in Clerical employments. The time devoted to this employment it not the only injury that I feel; but it confines my thoughts as well as engrosses my time. It is like a merchandise of small wares." Greene's letter is in the *Washington Papers*.

Government for the Northern Army and to communicate the same to you, Also to advance them one Month's pay &c., as you will perceive by the inclosed Copy of their Resolution, which I have the honor to transmit; I must request the favor of you, to direct them to March by Companies as they are raised, to Skenesborough, and there receive orders and instructions for their conduct, from the Officer Commanding the Northern Army; and also to advance the Month's pay and take every Necessary Measure, for forwarding their March and complying with the purport of the said Resolve, assuring you that whatever money may be advanced necessarily in carrying the same into execution shall be repaid to your Order.

Before I conclude, I cannot but Confess, that I do not clearly understand what Battalions Congress allude to, and therefore beg leave to refer you to the requisition, I presume they made you upon the subject. I am etc.[7]

## GENERAL ORDERS

Head Quarters, New York, July 26, 1776.
Parole Cambridge. Countersign Darby.

The General Court Martial to sit to morrow for the tryal of Ensign Bryant now under arrest for "sending some Soldiers to take away old Iron, and other Materials, from the Ships now fitting for public use"—

A Guard at Harrison's Brewery to be mounted consisting of one Sub., one Serjt., one Corporal, and twenty-four Privates, every evening, and Sentries to be posted at proper distances from the Air Furnace along the Shore, 'till they come opposite to Col Baldwins quarters.

---

[7] The same letter was sent to the New Hampshire Legislature and to Governor Trumbull.

General Greene being particularly engaged at present, passes signed by Lieut. Blodget,[8] are to be allowed sufficient to enable persons to cross the ferries.

Complaints have been made that some of the Soldiers ill treat the Country People, who come to Market; The General most possitively forbids such behaviour, and hopes the officers will exert themselves to prevent it: Good Policy as well as Justice, demands that they should have all possible encouragement as the health of the Soldiers much depends upon supplies of Vegetables; Those who have been guilty of such practices, will do well to consider what will be our Situation, at this season, if we drive off the Country people, and break up the Market—The healthy will soon be sick, and the sick must perish for want of Necessaries: No favour will be shewn to any offenders hereafter.

## To BRIGADIER GENERAL GEORGE CLINTON

Head Quarters, New York, July 26, 1776.

Dear Sir: Yours of the 23rd. Inst. is duly received, and am pleased with the timely Notice of your Situation, Strength, Movements &c. &c. and think Time is not to be lost, or Expence regarded, in getting yourselves in the best Posture of Defence, not knowing how soon the Enemy may attempt to pass you.

The Fire Rafts you mention, are not of the best Construction; but probably are the best that can be procured with the necessary Dispatch.

Cables and Anchors, I should suppose, might easily be procured from the Vessels which used to be plying up and down the River, and are now lying idle; Salt Petre from the Manufacturers in the Country, as neither are to be had in this Place.

---

[8] Lieut. William Blodget, of the Eleventh Continental Infantry. He was, later, aide to Brig. Gen. Nathanael Greene.

The Necessity of the Case, will fully justify your taking the former wherever to be found, and the Safety of the People, I should imagine, would induce them to assist you to the latter, all in their Power.

I have sent up Lieutt. Machine,[9] to lay out and oversee, such Works as shall be thought necessary by the Officers there, and from your Representation of the Hill which overlooks the Fort, I think it ought to be taken Possession of immediately. You, who are on the Spot, must be a better Judge than I possibly can. I must leave it with you to erect such Works as you with Colonel Clinton, and the Engineer, may think necessary.

A proper Abstract or Pay Roll should be made out, of the Wages due the Artificers, examined and certified by you or your Brother, when it may be sent here and the Money drawn.

Your Method of fixing Fires with advanc'd Guard, if they are vigilant, must answer the Purpose you intend.

Your dismissing all the New England Men to 300, is a Step I approve of.

I hope you may continue to prevent the Enemy from obtaining any Supplies or Intelligence, and committing any Ravage on the distress'd Peasantry, on and about the Shores. While you are able to keep them in this Situation below the Forts, they can do little Damage.

By every Conveyance I shall like to hear of your Situation, and the Enemy's Manœuvres. I am, etc.

P S. Since the above, the Qr. Mr. General informs me, you may be supplied with Turpentine here; and thinks he can get Salt Petre enough for the present Emergency.

---

[9] Simms's *History of Schoharie County* (N. Y.) gives some additional biographical information as to Thomas Machin: That he was an English engineer who had been employed by Brindley in constructing the canal of the Duke of Bridgewater, and had come to America in 1772 to examine a copper mine in New Jersey. He joined the Colonists; was wounded at Bunker Hill; and, later, commissioned in Knox's regiment of artillery; laid out the fortifications around Boston after the British evacuation; and served with Sullivan on his Indian expedition. He was also present at the Siege of Yorktown.

## To LORD STIRLING

Head Quarters, July 27, 1776.

My Lord: Upon your representation of Capt. Butler's[10] state of health, I think it will be best to give him a discharge, tho the loss of an officer whose character for diligence and fidelity stands fair, is at all times to be regretted and never more than at the present.

With respect to Col. Parke[11] if the circumstances of his affairs render it absolutely necessary that he should have leave of absence for ten days I must consent, at the same time I can but say that I do it very reluctantly, at this critical period. I am, etc.

## To THE PRESIDENT OF CONGRESS

New York, July 27, 1776.

Sir: I was yesterday morning honored with your favor of the 24th. instant, with its several Inclosures, to which I shall pay the strictest attention. The confidence Congress are pleased to repose in my Judgment demands my warmest acknowledgements, and they may rest assured, It shall be invariably employed as far as it shall be in my power, to promote their views and the Public weal.

I have Inclosed a Letter received from Major French two days ago; Also one from him to his Lady. Congress will perceive thereby, what he says and thinks about his parole, and will be pleased to transmit me by the earliest Opportunity the result of their Opinion, and such Orders as they may think necessary to be taken upon it. The Letter for Mrs. French they will please to return me, it was only sent to shew his views more explicitly than what, that for me does.

---

[10] Capt. Joseph Butler, of the Fourth Continental Infantry.
[11] Lieut. Col. John Parke, later of Patton's Additional Continental Regiment.

Since my last nothing material has occurred. Yesterday Evening report was made that eight Ships were seen in the Offing standing towards the Hook. The Men of War and Tenders are still up the River. They have never attempted to pass the Highland Fortifications and a day or two ago quitted their Station and fell down the River Eight or Ten Miles. The Vigilance and Activity of the Militia where they were, have prevented their landing and doing much Injury: one poor Peasents Cot they plundered and then burnt.

I would wish to know whether the Allowance given to Officers the 17th. of January, of one and ⅓ Dollar for every man they inlist, Congress mean to extend to the Officers who Inlist for the New Army for three years: At first sight It may appear wrong or rather exhorbitant, supposing that many will be recruited out of the Regiments now in service and under them. but the allowance will be of great use, as it will Interest the Officers and call forth their exertions which otherwise would be feint and languid.[12] Indeed I am fearful, from the Inquiries I have made, that their utmost exertions will be attended with but little success. It is objected that the bounty of ten Dollars is too low, and Argued that if the States furnishing Men for five or Six Months allow considerably more, why should that be accepted, and when the Term of Inlistment is to be for three Years? I heartly wish a bounty in Land had been or could be given, as was proposed some time ago. I think it could be attended with salutary consequences.

In consequence of my Application to Governor Trumbull he has sent me two Row Gallies and I expect another from him. None from Governor Cooke are yet come, nor have I heard from him on the Subject. One is complete here; The fire Ships

---

[12] "Resolved, That the resolution of the 17th of January last, allowing to officers 1 dollar and 1/3d of a dollar for every man they inlist, be extended to officers who inlist for the new army for three years."—*Journals of the Continental Congress,* July 30, 1776.

are going on under Mr. Anderson's direction, but rather slowly and I am preparing some Obstructions to the Channel, nearly opposite the Works at the upper end of this Island. When all things are ready, I intend to try if it shall seem practicable, to destroy the Ships and Tenders above and to employ the Gallies, if they can be of Advantage.[13]

The Militia for the Flying Camp come in but slowly. By a return from General Mercer Yesterday, they are but a little more than 3000.

If they were in, or can be there shortly, and the Situation of the Enemy remains the same, I would make some Efforts to annoy them, keeping our posts here well guarded and not puting too much to the hazard or in any manner to to the risk. I have &c.[14]

## GENERAL ORDERS

Head Quarters, New York, July 27, 1776.

Parole Effingham.　Countersign ———.

Complaints are made, that officers who are to attend the men upon Fatigue, and other duty, grow remiss; The General hopes they will consider what the effects of so bad an example might be to the men, and as he believes it proceeds rather from inattention, than design, flatters himself there will be no occasion to remind them of their duty hereafter.

---

[13] Several plans were suggested for attacking the enemy on Staten Island. A council of war decided that a general attack was inexpedient, but that an attempt might be made by a party from the Jersey shore nearest to the island. The intrepid Major Knowlton, who was stationed at Bergen, was directed to confer with General Mercer on the subject. They determined to make the experiment on the night of July 18, and everything was got in readiness. Major Knowlton was to head a party of Continental troops and be supported by others from the Flying Camp under General Mercer, who was to take a part in the enterprise. They marched early in the evening to the point of embarkation, but the weather became so tempestuous and the waves so high that it was impossible to cross the river in time to effect the object. Another scheme was projected for an attack from the same quarter, with a body of 3,900 men, but boats could not be collected sufficient to transport half that number across the water.—*Sparks.*

[14] In the writing of Robert Hanson Harrison.

## GENERAL ORDERS

Head Quarters, New York, July 28, 1776.

Parole Gravisent.   Countersign Hungary.

William Peek Esqr. who has for some time past done the duty of Brigade Major, to General Spencer, is appointed to that office and to be obeyed and respected accordingly.

Some of the Adjutants have of late been very remiss, in making up their Returns, by eleven O'Clock on Saturday; not sending their detachments properly officered, or relieving their Orderly Serjeants, at Head Quarters; these Gentlemen will in future be pointed out in the General Orders; and after that put under Arrest if they are not more attentive. The General finding the number of sick to increase, and being desirous to have them as well accomodated as possible, directs that the Barrack Master, under the direction of the Colonel, or commanding Officer of each Regiment, fix on some house convenient to the Regiment to be improved as a Hospital for the reception of Patients just taken down, or whose disorder does not require any special assistance beyond that of their own Regimental Surgeons. One of the Surgeons of the Hospital will occasionally visit these Hospitals and determine where the nature of the case requires the Patient to be removed to the General Hospital which will hereafter be kept in different Houses contigious to each brigade. The Regimental Surgeons are to receive directions from, and be responsible to, the Director General, so far as respects the furnishing their Regimental Hospitals with conveniences for their sick. The Regimental Surgeons are also to keep a Register of their sick, and make a weekly Return to the Director and Commissary General severally of the Sick in their respective regiments.

As the Rations issued for Men in health, are very improper for those who are sick, the following Resolutions are to take place—Whenever a person is taken sick he is not to be borne on the Provision Return; but the Value of his Rations be obtained in suitable Supplies from the General Hospital to be drawn by the Surgeons of the regiment who is to conform to the rules of diet established in the General Hospitals and to account with the Director General.

The Quarter Masters of each Regiment, to apply for necessaries, at the Quarter-Master-General's, for the sick. Guards to be on the parade every morning before eight OClock.

## To THE PRESIDENT OF CONGRESS

New York, July 29, 1776.

Sir: Your favor of the 24th. I received on Saturday Evening, and agreeable to your request, shall expunge the Preamble to the resolution subjecting the property of Subjects to the British Crown, to forfeiture and confiscation.[15]

Our Stock of Musquet Powder is entirely made up in Cartridges, I therefore request that Congress will order four or five Tons more of that sort to be immediately forwarded, It being not only necessary that we should have more for that purpose, but also some Stock to remain in Barrels.

Yesterday Evening Hutchinson's and Serjeants Regiments from Boston arrived, also two Row Gallies from Rhode Island. I am fearful the Troops have not got entirely clear of the Small pox.

I shall use every possible precaution to prevent the Infection spreading, and for that purpose have ordered them to an Encampment seperate and detached from the rest.

---

[15]The expunged preamble recited: "Whereas these United States have by a long series of oppressions, been driven into a war with Great Britain and at last to the necessity of declaring themselves free and independent States; and as it is impossible to distinguish among the subjects of the same sovereign, between those who are friends and such as are enemies to the rights of America and Mankind, it is become necessary to consider as enemies all the subjects of the King of Great Britain and all others, who aid, abet, adhere to or in any way assist him in his unjust and cruel designs against these states." (See *Journals of the Continental Congress,* July 24, 1776.)

By Saturday's report from Long Island Camp, five Ships a Brig and five Schooners had got into the Hook. By Yesterday's two Ships more and a Sloop were standing in; what they are I have not been able to learn.

I have transmitted a General Return herewith, by which Congress will perceive the whole of our Force at the Time it was made.

I have inclosed you an Account of sundry prizes which was transmitted to several Gentlemen here by Saturday's Post. The two last prizes I did not see mentioned in the Letter shewn me, and I fear the report of the 2d. Provision Vessell is premature. I was also this minute informed that Captain Biddle had taken a Ship with Sugars for Britain and in bringing her in, unfortunately lost her on Fisher's Island. I have &ca.[16]

## To THE BOARD OF WAR AND ORDNANCE

New York, July 29, 1776.

Gentlemen: At length I have been able to comply with the first part of a Resolution of Congress of the 27th Ulto., relative to a return of the vacancies in the several Regiments, composing that part of the Army under my immediate command.

I thought to have made this return much sooner, but the dispersed situation of our Troops, the constant duty they are upon, the difficulty of getting returns when this is the case, especially when those returns are more than probable to undergo several corrections and the variety of Important occurrences which have intervened of late to withdraw the attention from this matter, will I hope be admitted as an excuse, and the delay not ascribed to any disinclination in me, to comply with the order, as I shall while I have the honor to remain in the service of the United States, obey to the utmost of my power and

---

[16] In the writing of Robert Hanson Harrison.

to the best of my Abilities, all orders of Congress with a scrupulous exactness.

With respect to the latter part of the aforementioned Resolution of the 27th. of June, I have to observe that I have handed in the names of such persons as the Field Officers of the several Regiments and their Brigadiers have pointed out as proper persons to fill these vacancies. I have neither added to, or diminished ought from their choice, unless the following special Information, which I conceived my indispensible duty to give, should occasion any alterations.

For the 20th. Regiment then late Arnold's there are two Competitors, towit Col: Durkee the present Lieut. Colonel who has had charge of the Regiment ever since the first establishment of it, and Lieut. Colonel Tyler of Parsons's Regiment. The pretentions of both, and a State of the case, I have subjoined to the list of vacancies given in by General Spencer, as I have also done in the case of Col: Learned, to another list exhibited by General Heath. If Learned returns to the Regiment the vacancies stand right; If he should not, I presume the Regiment will be given to the Lieut: Colonel William Shepherd who stands next to Tyler in Rank and not second to him in reputation. This change would in its consequences occasion several moves. There is a third matter in which I must be more particular, as it is unnoticed elsewhere, and that is, the Lieut: Colonel of Wyllys's Regiment, Rufus Putnam Acts here as a Chief Engineer, by which means the Regiment is totally deprived of his services, and to remove him from that department, the Public would sustain a Capital injury, for altho' he is not a man of Scientific knowledge, he is indefatigable in business and possesses more practicable Knowledge in the Art of Engineering than any other we have in this Camp or Army. I would humbly submit it therefore to Congress, whether it might not be best to give him (Putnam) the Appointment of Engineer with the pay of Sixty Dollars per month; less than which I do not suppose he would accept; as I have been obliged in order to encourage him to push the business forward in this our extreme hurry, to give him reasons to believe that his Lieutenant Colonel's pay would be made equal to this sum.

If this appointment should take place then, it makes a vacancy in Wyllys's Regiment which I understand he is desirous of having filled by Major Henly[17] an Active and Spirited Officer, now a Brigade Major to General Heath.

I am sorry to take up so much of your time as the recital of these particular cases and some others require, but there is no avoiding it, unless Congress would be pleased to appoint one or more persons in whom they can confide, to visit this part of this Army once a Month; Inspect into it, and fill up the Vacancies as shall appear proper to them upon the Spot. This cannot be attended with any great trouble, nor much expence, as it is only in the part of the Army under my immediate direction, that such a regulation would be necessary; the Officers commanding in other Departments having I believe this power already given them.[18]

---

[17] David Henly. He became deputy adjutant general to Gen. Joseph Spencer Sept. 6, 1776; lieutenant colonel of the Fifth Massachusetts Regiment Nov. 1, 1776; colonel of one of the 16 Additional Continental regiments Jan. 1, 1777; retired Apr. 23, 1779.

[18] To this paragraph the President of Congress replied (August 2): "I am particularly instructed by Congress to answer that part of your letter of 29th Ulto. directed to the Board of War, which relates to the filling up Vacancies in the Army. The Congress are Concern'd to find, that an opinion is Entertain'd, that greater Confidence has been plac'd in, and larger powers given to, other Commanders in that respect, than to yourself. They have in no instance, except in the late Appointment of General Gates to the Command in Canada, parted with the power of filling up Vacancies. The great Confusion and many Disorders prevalent in that Army, and its Distance, induc'd Congress to lodge such a power in that General for the limited space of three months, and only during his Continuance in Canada. Should Congress ever empower its Generals to fill up Vacancies in the Army, they know of no one in whom they would so soon Repose a Trust of such Importance as in yourself; but future Generals may make a bad use of it. The Danger of the Precedent, not any suspicion of their present Commander in chief, prompts them to Retain a Power, that, by you, Sir, might be exercised with the greatest public Advantage." It should be noted that Congress took no steps to improve the condition. On August 10 it approved the list submitted by the Board of War to fill the vacancies. The President's letter is in the *Washington Papers*.

I have the honor to inclose a List of the Officers of the Regiments at this place, and long ago directed the like return to be made from the Northern and Eastern Troops which I hope is complied with. I also make return of the Artillery according to Col: Knox's report and of the Ordinance Stores &ca. agreeable to the Commissary's Return.

I come now to acknowledge the receipt of your favor of the 20th. Instant, with several Inclosures, relative to a proposal of Mr. Goddard[19] and beg leave to give it as my Opinion, that the Introduction of that Gentleman into the Army as Lieut: Colonel would be attended with endless confusion. I have spoke to Colo: Parsons who is a very worthy man, upon this Subject. I have done more. I have shewn him the Memorial: in answer to which he says, that in the conversation had between him and Mr. Goddard the latter was told, that unless Lieut Colonel Tyler was provided for, The Major, Prentice[20] advanced to a Lieut: Colonelcy in some other Regiment, and his eldest Captain (Chapman)[21] not deprived of his expectation of the Majority; his coming in there would give uneasiness, but nevertheless if it was the pleasure of Congress to make the appointment, he would do every thing in his power to make it palatible. If all these Contingencies were to take place before Mr. Goddard could get into a Regiment he had been paving the way to, What prospect can there be of his getting into any other without spreading Jealousy as he goes?

With respect to the Regiment of Artificers, I have only to observe that the forming them into one Corps at the time I did, when immediate Action was expected, was only intended as a

---

[19] William Goddard.

[20] Samuel Prentiss. He was promoted to this lieutenant colonelcy Aug. 12, 1776; became lieutenant colonel of the First Connecticut Regiment Jan. 1, 1777; resigned May 27, 1778.

[21] Capt. James Chapman, of the Tenth Continental Infantry. He attained his majority Aug. 15, 1776, and was killed a month later in the fighting retreat from New York.

Temporary expedient to draw that useful body of near 600 Men into the field, under one head and without confusion. The appointment of Officers therefore in this Instance, was merely nominal and unattended, with expence.

The mode of promotion whether in a Continental, Colonial or Regimental Line, being a matter of some consideration and delicacy to determine, I thought It expedient to know the Sentiments of the General Officers upon the consequences of each, before I offered my own to your board, and have the honor to inform you that it is their unanimous Opinion, as it is also mine, from Observations on the Temper and local Attachments of each Corps to the Members thereof, that Regimental promotions would be much the most pleasing; but this it is thought had better appear in practice than come announced as a Resolution, and that there ought to be Exceptions in favor of extraordinary Merit, on the one hand and demerit on the other. The first to be rewarded out of the common course of promotion whilst the other might stand and sustain no Injury.

It is a very difficult matter to step out of the Regimental line now, without giving much Inquietude to the Corps in which it happens: Was it then to be declared, as the Resolution of Congress, that all promotions should go in this way without some strong qualifying clauses, It would be almost impossible to do it without creating a Mutiny; This is the sense of my Officers. As also that the promotions by succession, are not meant to extend to Non-Commissioned Officers further than circumstances of good behavior &ca. may direct.

As the Lists of Vacancies are returned in consequence of an Order of Congress and would I doubt not be referred to your Board, I have sent no Duplicate; nor have I wrote to Congress on the Subject, but that I may appear inattentive to their commands, I must request the favor of having this Letter or the substance of it laid before them. I have the Honor to be, etc.

## To MAJOR GENERAL ARTEMAS WARD

Head Quarters, New York, July 29, 1776.

Dear Sir: Yours of the 22nd. Inst. I received per Post and note the Contents. The Company of Artificers you mention, are much wanted, and I would have you order them on with all convenient Dispatch.

It was necessary, the Troops on their March for Ticonderoga, should be furnished with Powder and Ball.

I have wrote several Times, about the remaining Part of the Arms, which you have not noticed in your Letters. There is yet a Deficiency in the Carbines, which are not all arrived. These with the other Arms taken in different Vessels, I wish you to send on.

I am exceedingly anxious to know if you have forwarded the Powder I mentioned, what Quantity and where stored. I must beg your Answer to these Particulars in your next.

The Pork taken, from Ireland, the Commissary General requests may all be secured for the Use of the Army, and desires you will order the Dept. Commissary, Mr. Miller[22] to secure it in Store, 'till he receives his Orders respecting it.

Colonels Hutchinson's and Sergeant's Regiments have arrived, with one Man who has the small Pox; but hope to be able to prevent the spreading of that fatal Disorder.

The Enemy's Fleet are daily arriving; It appears they must have been scattered on their Passage, as they come in sometimes single; at others, three four and so on. I hope our Cruisers may pick up some of them. I am, etc.

P. S. We are in distressing Want of Artillery Men. If you can make any tolerable Shift, I must urge your sending on Captn. Burbeck with his Company as soon as possible.

---

[22] Charles Miller.

## GENERAL ORDERS

Head Quarters, New York, July 29, 1776.
Parole Jersey.   Countersign Kingwood.

The Quarter Master General is directed to furnish twelve Quires of paper, to each regiment pr month—Vizt—One Quire to the commanding officer of the Regiment; One to each Company, and one to the Adjutant; the remaining two Quires to be kept by the Colonel, as a reserve for special occasions, exclusive of orderly books and blank returns.

## GENERAL ORDERS

Head Quarters, New York, July 30, 1776.
Parole Lancaster.   Countersign Medford.

The Quarter Master General is to provide Canteens, as soon as possible, and to have the Water in the several works, in casks, examined, that there may be a fresh supply if necessary.

It is represented to the General, that the pump Water in the City, is very unhealthy; The Troops are therefore cautioned against the use of it; and the Quarter Master and Commissary Generals, are to consult together, and fix upon some mode of supply of fresh water, for the troops in the City.

## To THE PRESIDENT OF CONGRESS

New York, July 30, 1776.

Sir: I was this Morning honored with your two favors of yesterday's date and agreeable to your request have given Mr. Palfrey liberty to negociate your claim with Mr. Brimer and wish it may be satisfied, agreeably to you.[23]

---

[23] There is no mention of this Brimer claim in the *Journals of the Continental Congress.*

I last Night received a Letter from General Schuyler a Copy of which I do myself the honor to Transmit you; You will thereby perceive his reasons for leaving Crown Point and for prefering the Post, the Council of Officers determined to take, opposite Ticonderoga. I am totally unacquainted with these several posts and the Country about them. and therefore cannot determine on the validity of his observations, or think myself at Liberty to give any directions in the matter. Congress will be pleased to observe what he says of their distress for Money, from hence he can have no Relief: there being only three or four thousand Dollars in the pay Master's hands according to his Return this Morning, and all but two Months pay due the Army, besides many other demands.

I could wish that proper supplies of Money could be always kept; the want may occasion consequences of an Alarming nature. By a Letter from him of a prior date to the Copy inclosed, he tells me, that a Mr. Ryckman who has just returned through the Country of the Six Nations reports, that the Indians who were at Philadelphia have gone home with very favorable Ideas of our strength and resources, This he heard in many of their Villages. A lucky circumstance if it will gain either their Friendship or secure their Neutrality. In my letter of the 27th. I informed Congress of my views and wishes to attempt something against the Troops on Staten Island, I am now to acquaint them that by the advice of General Mercer and the other Officers at Amboy, it will be impracticable to do any thing upon a large Scale for want of Craft; and as the Enemy have the entire Command of the Water all round the Island; I have desired Genl. Mercer to have nine or ten flatt Bottom Boats built at Newark bay and Elizabeth Town, with a design principally to keep up the Communication across Hackensack and Passaic Rivers, which, I deem a matter of great importance and extremely necessary to be attended to.

Since I wrote you Yesterday, Eleven Ships more, four Brigs and two Sloops have come into the Hook. I have not yet received Intelligence what any of the late Arrivals are, but I suppose we shall not long remain in a State of Incertainty.

Having reason to believe that Lord Howe will readily come into an exchange of such Prisoners, as may be more immediately under his Command, and that some thing will be offered on this Subject within a day or two, or rather come in answer to the propositions I have made General Howe; I shall be glad to have Congress's Interpretation of the Resolve of the 22d. instant empowering the Commanders to exchange &ca. "Whether by the word Sailor they mean Sailors generally, as well those taken in the Vessels of private Adventures by the Enemy, as those belonging to the Continental Cruizers or Vessels in the Continental employ, or whether they only design to extend the Exchange to the latter, and those in their particular employ." I would also observe that heretofore Sailors belonging to Merchant Ships, that have fallen into our hands and such as have been employed merely as Transports, have not generally been considered as Prisoners. I submit it to Congress whether it may not be now necessary to pass a Resolve declaring their Sentiments on this Subject, and in General who are to be treated as Prisoners of War that are taken in Vessels belonging to the Subjects of the British Crown &ca. The result of their Opinion upon the first Question proposed, you will be pleased to transmit me by the earliest Opportunity.

I have inclosed for the Consideration of Congress a memorial and Petition by Captain Holdrige,[24] praying to be relieved against the Loss of Money stolen from him, not conceiving myself Authorized to grant his request. The Certificate which

---

[24] Capt. Hezekiah Holdridge, of the Twenty-second Continental Infantry. He was promoted to major Sept. 3. 1776; transferred to the Second Connecticut Regiment; made lieutenant colonel of the Seventh Connecticut Regiment Jan. 1, 1777; retired Jan. 1, 1781.

attends it proves him a Man of Character, and his case is hard on his State of it. Whether making the Loss good may not open a door to others and give rise to applications not so just as his may be, I cannot determine. That seems to me the only objection to relieving him.

I am informed by General Putnam, that there are some of the Stockbridge Indians here, I have not seen them myself, who express great uneasyness at their not being employed by us and have come to enquire into the cause. I am sensible Congress had them not in Contemplation, when they resolved that Indians might be engaged in our Service.

However as they seem so anxious, as they were led to expect it, from what General Schuyler and the other Commissioners did. As we are under difficulties in getting men, and there may be danger of their or some of them taking an unfavourable part, I beg Leave to submit to Congress as my Opinion under all these circumstances that they had better be employed. I have the Honor &ca.[25]

### To SIR WILLIAM HOWE

Head Quarters, New York, July 30, 1776.

Sir: Lieutenant Col. Pattison, Adjt. General of the Army under your command, at the Interview between us, having proposed an Exchange of Mr. Lovell for Govr. Skeene, I am authorized to inform you, that the Congress have not only approved of this proposition, but judging that a General Exchange of Prisoners, will be attended with mutual convenience and pleasure to both parties, have empowered their Commanders in each Department to negotiate one in the following manner, "Continental Officers for those of equal rank, either in the Land or Sea Service, Soldier for Soldier, Sailor for Sailor and Citizen for Citizen."

---

[25] In the writing of Robert Hanson Harrison.

They have also particularly mentioned the Exchange of Col. Ethan Allen for any Officer of the same or inferior rank.

You will be pleased to signify the time and place for that of Mr. Lovell and Governor Skeene, that I may give direction for the latter to be ready, who is now at Hartford about 120 miles from hence; also to favor me with your Sentiments, as well on the proposition respecting Col: Allen, as on the Subject of a Genl. Exchange. I am, etc.[26]

### To THE PRESIDENT OF CONGRESS

New York, July 31, 1776.

Sir: This will be handed you by Captain Marquisie[27] with whom I have no other acquaintance than what is derived from the inclosed Letter from General Schuyler. He says he has lost his Baggage in our service and all he had and is now going to wait on Congress to whom I suppose he means to make his pretensions known. I am &ca.[28]

### To MAJOR GENERAL PHILIP SCHUYLER

New York, July 31, 1776.

Dear Sir: Your Favors of the 14th. 17th. 20th. and 24th. have been duly received, and I am extremely happy to find, that you have discovered and apprehended some of the Ringleaders of a dangerous Plot you say was forming in the Neighbourhood of Albany; nor do I hear with little Pleasure, of the Harmony and good Agreement between you and General Gates, knowing how essential they are to the Service.

Agreeable to your Request, I communicated to Mr. Trumbull that Part of your Letter respecting Mr. Livingston's and

---

[26] In the writing of Robert Hanson Harrison.
[27] Capt. Bernard Moissac de la Marquise.
[28] In the writing of Robert Hanson Harrison.

your Apprehensions of his resigning, in Case any Person should be appointed to act independently of him, in the Business he usually managed. Upon this Occasion I must observe, that as Mr. Trumbull has the supreme Direction given him by Congress, of supplying the Northern Army, and is the Person that is to be accountable if it is not done in a proper Manner; his Appointments should, and must be regarded, or Things in this Instance will never proceed in a regular Channel and fatal Consequences will otherwise ensue. Mr. Trumbull, I believe, has wrote Mr. Livingston on the Subject, and I imagine has mentioned in what Manner he would have him to act and also given necessary Instructions to his Deputies.

It gives me great Satisfaction to hear, that taking Post at Fort Stanwix, has not given Umbrage to the Indians; and also that those that were at Philadelphia, and this Place, have returned to their several Nations. From this Circumstance, I am hopeful, you will be able to engage them in our Interest, and with the Assistance of the Reward allowed by Congress, to excite their Efforts to make Prisoners of our Enemies. I would have you press the Matter strongly in both Instances, and though you should not succeed, I flatter myself, you will secure their Neutrality. That will be an important Point to gain.

I conceive it will not be only proper, but absolutely necessary, to request General Howe to deliver the Officers, who, regardless of their Paroles, have escaped from Pensylvania; and all others that have acted in the same Manner; pointing out the Impropriety of such Conduct, and the Difficulty it lays us under, as to the Line of Treatment to be observed to others. In a Conversation with the Adjutant General of the King's Army, I touched upon this Subject, and he assured me all Complaints of this Nature would be strictly attended to by Generl. Howe, and those who gave Rise to them be handled with Severity. Lord Howe too, I am confidently informed, has express'd his great Disapprobation of such Behaviour, and said, that those that were guilty of it, should be severely noticed if they came into his Hands. Every thinking and sensible Person must see the Impropriety of it, and the Consequences that must attend it. I shoud suppose the Requisition will claim General Burgoyne's Attention and be readily complied with.

The Swivels you mention, cannot be had; but if the Experiments of a Person, who has undertaken to cast some three Pounders, should succeed; perhaps after some Time you may be furnished in Part with a Quantity of these. Colo. Knox seems to think they will be far superior to Swivels. The Man supposes, after he begins, he will be able to compleat twenty every Week.

Neither are there any Hand Granadoes. We have a large Number of 4½ Inch Shells, which might be a good Substitute; But I do not know how Things of this Sort can be forwarded to you, as the Water Communication with Albany, is entirely cut off. The Difficulty will be great, if not almost insuperable.

I observe your Reasons for quitting Crown Point, preferring Ticonderoga. My Knowledge of the Importance of the former, was not properly my own; It arose from the Information I had from Gentlemen and Persons who were, or said they were, well acquainted with it, and the Situation of the Country about it. Being founded on that, I cannot say any Thing myself upon the Subject. Your Representation of it, most certainly lessens it's Consequence in a capital Degree. However, I am fearful, the Observation of the Field Officers, "that the New-England Governments &c. will be thereby exposed to the Incursions of our cruel and savage Enemies" will be but too well verified. If that Post could not be maintained, this Evil with others greater must have happened.

In Respect to the Privilege you have given the Officers who held double Commissions, to retain which they choose, I can not object. If the Authority giving them was the same, and such as was exercised usually, and approved, I see no Cause for it, and suppose the Officers have that Right.

As to Lieutt. Colo. Buell's Case,[29] I cannot give any Direction about it, not having Authority to appoint Officers generally.

It is not in my Power to spare you any Money from hence. Our Chest is all but empty. Congress would be informed by your Letters of your Situation, doubtless. I mentioned it in mine and have suggested, as I often have, the Expediency, nay the Necessity of keeping regular Supplies.

Nothing of Moment has occurred here lately. The Enemy are growing stronger. For some Days past, Ships &c. have been coming in to them more or less.

All the Eastward Accounts say, three or four Captures have been made lately, among them a Provision Vessel from Ireland which of herself came into Boston Harbour.

In the Southern Department, we have been still more lucky. Sir Peter Parker and his Fleet got a severe Drubbing in an Attack made against our Works on Sullivan's Island, just by Charles-Town, South Carolina. A Part of their Troops, at the same Time attempting to land, were repulsed. The Papers, I presume, have reached you, announcing this fortunate Event, where you will see the Particulars, as transmitted by General Lee to Congress. I am, etc.

## GENERAL ORDERS

Head Quarters, New York, July 31, 1776.

Parole Norwalk.   Countersign Oxford.

Ensign Briant charged with "embezzling public property," having been tried by a General Court Martial whereof Col Webb is President, is acquitted of any fraudulent Intention;

---

[29] Lieut. Col. Nathaniel Buell, of Col. Charles Burrall's Connecticut State Regiment. Later he served as a colonel of Connecticut Militia.

but censured by the Court for indiscretion, in permitting some of the Soldiers taking away old Iron from the Shiping—The General approves of the sentence and orders him to be discharg'd from arrest—

It is with astonishment and concern, the General finds that precaution used to prevent the Countersign being made known to any not intitled to it, are defeated by the ignorance or misconduct of those to whom it is intrusted: In Order that none may plead ignorance hereafter, the officers and soldiers are to know, that the following Rule is established—

The Adjutant General at Six OClock P. M. will deliver the Parole and Countersign, to the Majors of Brigade, and Adjutant of Artillery, they at Retreat Beating, and not before, are to deliver them to the Adjutants of their respective Brigades; The Adjutants are to deliver them to the Field Officers of their respective Brigades if required, then to the officer of the advanced Guards, then to the officer of every other guard, in and about the City or Camp; and the General flatters himself, that when the importance and necessity of secrecy upon this head 'tis considered every officer and soldier will pride himself in his fidelity, prudence and discipline.

## GENERAL ORDERS

Head Quarters, New York, August 1, 1776.
Parole Paris.  Countersign Reading.

It is with great concern, the General understands, that Jealousies &c. are arisen among the troops from the different Provinces, of reflections frequently thrown out, which can only tend to irritate each other, and injure the noble cause in which we are engaged, and which we ought to support with one hand and one heart. The General most earnestly entreats the officers, and soldiers, to consider the consequences; that they can no way assist our cruel enemies more effectually, than making division among ourselves; That the Honor and Success of the army, and the safety of our bleeding Country, depends upon harmony and good agreement with each other; That the Provinces are all United to oppose the common enemy, and all distinctions sunk in the name of an American; to make this honorable, and preserve the Liberty of our Country, ought to be our only emulation, and he will be the best Soldier, and the best Patriot, who contributes most to this glorious work, whatever his Station, or from whatever part of the Continent, he may come: Let all distinctions of Nations, Countries, and Provinces, therefore be lost in the generous contest, who shall behave with the most Courage against the enemy, and the most kindness and good humour to each other—If there are any officers, or soldiers, so lost to virtue and a love of their Country as to continue in such practices after this order; The General assures them, and is directed by Congress to declare, to the whole Army, that such persons shall be severely punished and dismissed the service with disgrace.

## To COLONEL SAMUEL ELMORE

New York, August 1, 1776.

Sir: Having just received from Congress a Return of your Regiment[30] now in the State of Connecticut, with directions that it shall Join this Army, I request the favor of you to march immediately to this place. They have appointed John Brown Esqr. Lieutenant Colonel of it, and Robert Cochran Esqr.

---

[30] Elmore's regiment was one of the Connecticut State regiments. The American Army was made up of the Continental line regiments, which came from the different States; State regiments, like this of Elmore's, which were not considered militia; the 16 Additional Continental regiments, raised later, by order of Congress and recruited from the States at large; partisan corps, like Lee's Legion; two Canadian regiments, composed of Canadian refugees; militia; minutemen; etc. The artillery and cavalry were usually Continental line organizations.

Major. Commissions for such Officers as appear with their respective Companies, I am to fill up.[31] I am &c.

## To GOVERNOR JONATHAN TRUMBULL

New York, August 1, 1776.

Sir: Congress having been pleased to impower me, to order Colo. Ward's Regiment wherever I might think it necessary; I take the liberty of requesting you to direct him to March it immediately to this Place, where I am of opinion, the Service requires it and their Aid may be extremely material, especially as the Levies come in very slowly.

Since my last nothing of Importance has occurred or that is worthy of Notice; Except an Augmentation of about Twenty Nine Ships and Brigs, with Seven or Eight smaller Vessels to the Enemy's Fleet. I have not learned certainly what they bring; however some Troops were seen landing yesterday, which the Gentlemen who observed them, took to be Artillery Men. It is not Improbable that they were some of the Guards, whose dress is pretty much like that of the Artillery. I have the Honor etc.

P. S. The three Gallies, which you were kind enough to order, are safely arrived, as are two from Rhode Island, with these and one that we have finished here, we propose attempting something against the Ships above and are preparing for it.

## To THE PRESIDENT OF CONGRESS

New York, August 2, 1776.

Sir: Your favor of the 30th. Ulto. with its several Inclosures, I was honored with, by Wednesday's Post.

---

[31] Washington also wrote to Governor Trumbull, this date, asking him to order Elmore forward. He added: "half past 12 O'Clock. I this moment received Intelligence that Thirty Ships more were coming into the [Sandy] Hook."

Congress having been pleased to leave with me the directions of Colonel Ward's Regiment, I have wrote Governor Trumbull and requested him to order their March to this place, being fully satisfied that the Enemy mean to make their Grand push in this Quarter, and that the good of the service requires every aid here that can be obtained. I have also wrote Col: Elmore and directed him to repair hither with his Regiment; when it comes, I shall fill up Commissions for such Officers as appear with their respective Companies.

Colonel Holman[32] with a Regiment from the Massachusetts State is arrived: Col: Carey[33] from thence is also here waiting the Arrival of his Regiment which he hourly expects; he adds, when he left New London, he heard that the third Regiment from the Massachusetts was almost ready and would soon be in motion.

The Enemy's force is daily augmentg and becoming stronger by New Arrivals. Yesterday General Greene reports that about Forty sail (including Tenders) came into the Hook. What they are, or what those have brought, that have lately got in, I remain uninformed. However I think it probable they are part of Admiral Howe's fleet with the Hessian Troops. It is time to look for them.[34] I have the Honor &ca.

P.S. I am extremely sorry to inform Congress that our Troops are very sickly.[35]

[32] Capt. John Holman, of the Massachusetts Militia.
[33] Col. Simeon Carey, of the Massachusetts Militia.
[34] These vessels were those composing the fleet of Sir Henry Clinton and Lord Cornwallis from Carolina. They had attempted to capture Charleston and been repulsed by the fort on Sullivans Island, later called Fort Moultrie, in honor of its gallant defender, Col. William Moultrie. The action was fought on June 28. Sparks quotes Lord George Germain's letter to Sir Henry Clinton (August 24): "I had reason to flatter myself, that, the season being far advanced, you would not make any attempt at the southward, whereby there could be a possibility of your being prevented from proceeding with your army in due time to the northward to join General Howe, who has long impatiently expected your arrival. I was therefore extremely disappointed and mortified to learn by your letter of July 8th, that you were still in the south, and that the fleet had received a severe check at Sullivan's Island."
[35] In the writing of Robert Hanson Harrison.

## To THE MASSACHUSETTS LEGISLATURE

Head Quarters, August 2, 1776.

Sir: Your Letter of the 16th Ulto., in behalf of the Council of Massachusetts Bay, is duly Received; the Contents have been attended to; and I have the pleasure to inform you, there is a prospect of an early exchange of the Prisoners taken in the Yankee Hero Privateer. As Mr. Tracy negociated this Matter, and had an Inteview with Lord Howe on board the Eagle, Man of War, I must refer you to him for particulars.

Congress authorised Me to comply with General Howe's request of giving Governor Skene for Mr. Lovell, I have wrote informing Genl. Howe thereof, and expect soon to have Mr. Lovell sent to some part of the Continent.

Assure the Members of your Honorable Body, it gives me particular pleasure, that I had it in my power to relieve one of their Citizens from a long and tedious Imprisonment, and shall esteem myself happy in complying with any request they may make consistent with the Important Duties of my Office. I have the Honor to be etc.

Augst. 5th, P.S. on the 11th. Ulto. I wrote your Honble. Body, respecting the St. Johns, Nova Scotia and Penobscot Indians, since which I have heard nothing from them. It is a Matter of the greatest consequence, must therefore beg an Answer, acquainting me what steps they have taken, by the first post.

Since the above I have a Letter from General Howe, acquainting me he has sent for Mr. Lovell for the proposed exchange.

## GENERAL ORDERS

Head Quarters, New York, August 2, 1776.

Parole Salem.    Countersign Taunton.

The Colonels of the several Regiments, are to be particularly careful that the damaged Cartridges are preserved and sent in to Commissary Cheever at the Laboratory, as it will be a great public saving.

The Court Martials are often detained by non-attendance of Witnesses, all officers and soldiers notified to attend as Witnesses on any Court Martial are to be punctual and in future any neglect of this kind will be punished as disobedience of orders.

Notwithstanding the great abuses of Regimental Hospitals last Year, the General has out of Indulgence and kindness to the Troops, who seem to like them, permitted them to be again opened, with a full persuasion that the Regimental Surgeons will fully conform, to the Rules and Orders which have been made, and particularly that they act with the strictest Honor, and Candor, in their draughts upon the several Stores, and accounting with the Director General of the Hospital, when required— making him regular Reports of the sick, and applying what they receive to the patients only—The Colonels and Field Officers of the several Regiments, would do well, to visit their Regimental Hospitals frequently, and see these regulations observed, and in all cases, except slight, or putrid disorders, have the sick removed to the General Hospital, near the Brigade; or the General must, in justice to the public, break them up again.

Richd. Lawrence of Capt. Gilbert's[36] Company and Col. Prescott's Regiment having been tried by a General Court Martial whereof Col Webb was president and convicted of *Desertion* was sentenced to receive Thirty-nine Lashes.

The General approves the Sentence, and orders it to be executed at the usual time and place. The new Troops coming in are upon their arrival to apply to Capt. Tilton at the Quarter Master-General's Store in the Broad-Way who will give them all necessary directions.

---

[36] Capt. Samuel Gilbert, of the Seventh Continental Infantry. He was taken prisoner at Fort Washington, N. Y., Nov. 16, 1776.

## GENERAL ORDERS

Head Quarters, New York, August 3, 1776.
Parole Uxbridge.    Countersign Virginia.

That the Troops may have an opportunity of attending public worship, as well as take some rest after the great fatigue they have gone through; The General in future excuses them from fatigue duty on Sundays (except at the Ship Yards, or special occasions) until further orders. The General is sorry to be informed that the foolish, and wicked practice, of profane cursing and swearing (a Vice heretofore little known in an American Army) is growing into fashion; he hopes the officers will, by example, as well as influence, endeavour to check it, and that both they, and the men will reflect, that we can have little hopes of the blessing of Heaven on our Arms, if we insult it by our impiety, and folly; added to this, it is a vice so mean and low, without any temptation, that every man of sense, and character, detests and despises it.

Clarkson and Chase under confinement for Desertion, and reinlistment into the Artillery, from another Corps, to return to Capt. Bauman's[37] Company until Col Ellmores Regiment, wh. claims them, comes into camp.

## GENERAL ORDERS

Head Quarters, New York, August 4, 1776.
Parole Weston.    Countersign Yarmouth.

Passes signed by the Quarter Master-General, or his Assistant Mr. Hughes[38] for persons in that department to cross the Ferries to be admitted as sufficient.

---

[37] Capt. Sebastian Bauman, of the New York Artillery.
[38] Hugh Hughes.

Thomas Herbert of Capt Wyllys's Company, Col Sergents Regiment, tried by a regimental Court Martial and convicted of "Theft," was sentenced to receive Thirty-nine Lashes; but having appealed to a General Court Martial whereof Col Webb was president the sentence of the Regimental Court was revised and the prisoner acquited—The General approves the acquital, and orders him to be discharged.

Daniel McGuire of Capt. Scotts Company, Colo. Sergeants Regiment—Samuel Weaver of Capt. Farringtons[39] Company, same Regiment; both tried by the same Court Martial and convicted McGuire, of Desertion and inlisting into another Company taking a second bounty, sentenced to receive Thirty-nine Lashes: Weaver of Desertion only, sentenced to receive Thirty Lashes.

William McIlvaine of Capt Wyllys's[40] Company, and the above Regiment tried by the same Court Martial, and convicted of Desertion and sentenced to receive Thirty Lashes.

Williams Diggs of Capt Woods[41] Company, Col Baldwins Regiment, tried by the same Court Martial, and convicted of Desertion; sentenced to receive Twenty Lashes.

The General approves each of the above Sentences, and orders them to be put in execution, at the usual time and place.

The Court Martial to sit to morrow, for the tryal of Lieut: Hobby[42] of Col McDougall's Regiment, now under Arrest for "Misconduct in leaving the Vessels under his care, on the East River on Friday Evening—Witnesses to attend.

All persons are strictly forbid medling with the flat bottomed Boats, without leave from General Putnam, or unless sent on

---

[39] Capt. William Scott and Capt. Thomas Farrington, of the Sixteenth Continental Infantry.
[40] Capt. John Wiley, of the Sixteenth Continental Infantry.
[41] Capt. John Wood, of the Twenty-sixth Continental Infantry.
[42] Lieut. Caleb Hobby, of the First New York Regiment.

some special service; and those parties who have any of them are to be careful in returning them safely—The Guards at the wharves to attend to this order.

## GENERAL ORDERS

Head Quarters, New York, August 5, 1776.
Parole Amboy.   Countersign Bradford.

The General has nothing more at heart, than the Health of the Troops; and as the change of encampment has been found very salutary by such Regiments, as have shifted their ground, it is recommended to the several Brigadier Generals to have it more generally adopted; And the General once more calls upon the officers, and men, who are quartered in Houses, to have them kept clean and wholesome.

Brigadier General Scott[43] having informed the General, that some dissatisfaction had arisen in his Brigade, on account of the 1st: Battalion who had received some assurances from the Committee of the Convention, of this State, that they should not be removed out of Town, unless the Army moved generally: The General at the same time being of opinion that from their knowledge of the City, they can be more serviceable than any other equal number of men who are strangers, orders that on Wednesday General Scott's Brigade move into the City, and General Fellows with his Brigade, take their places: He also directs that no officers, or soldiers of General Fellows Brigade, take up their quarters, in the dwelling Houses, in or near their encampment except they are placed there by the Quarter Master General.

The General cannot dismiss this matter, without assuring the 1st. Battalion of General Scotts Brigade, that he will have the

---

[43] Brig. Gen. John Morin Scott, of the New York Militia. He was wounded at White Plains, N. Y., Oct. 28, 1776, and served to March, 1777.

grounds of their claim, particularly inquired into, of the Provincial Congress of the State of New York; as well because they may rest assured that at the same time public faith is preserved with them, he expects, and will require, that they observe their engagement to the public.

The arrival of new troops requiring some Change in the arrangement, and particularly with respect to the Alarm Posts— Major General Putnam, with the several Brigadiers, are desired to meet to morrow at ten O'Clock, at the City Hall, to consider thereof and make report to the General. The Adjutant General will attend at the same time.

## To THE PRESIDENT OF THE CONGRESS

New York, August 5, 1776.

Sir: I was honored with your favor of the 31st. Ulto. on Friday with its several Inclosures, and return you my thanks for the agreeable Intelligence you were pleased to communicate of the arrival of one of the Ships, with such valuable Articles, as Arms and Ammunition; also of the Capture made by a Privateer.

The mode for the Exchange of Prisoners, resolved on by Congress is acceded to by General Howe, so far as it comes within his command, a Copy of my Letter and his answer upon the Subject, I have the Honor to inclose you and to which I beg leave to refer Congress.[44]

The inclosed copy of a Letter from Col: Tupper,[45] who had the General Command of the Gallies here, will inform Congress of the Engagement between them and the Ships of War up the North river on Saturday Evening and of the Damage

---

[44] See Washington's letter to Sir William Howe, July 30, 1776, *ante*.

[45] A copy of Col. Benjamin Tupper's letter of Aug. 3, 1776, is filed with Washington's letter of Aug. 5, 1776, in the *Papers of the Continental Congress*.

we sustained; what injury was done to the Ships I cannot ascertain. It is said they were hulled several times by our Shot. All accounts agree, that our Officers and Men, during the whole of the Affair, behaved with great Spirit and bravery; the damage done the Gallies shews beyond question, that they had a warm time of it, the Ships still remain up the river and before anything further can be attempted against them, should it be thought advisable, the Gallies must be repaired.

I have also transmitted Congress, a Copy of a Letter I received by Saturday's post, from Governor Cooke, to which I refer them for the Intelligence[46] It contains. The Seizure of our Vessels by the Portuguese, is I fear, an event too true, their dependance upon the British Crown for aid against the Spaniards, must force them to comply with every thing required of them. I wish the Morris may get in safe with her Cargo. As to the Ships Captain Bucklin saw, on the 25th. Ulto., they are probably arrived; For Yesterday twenty five Sail came into the Hook.

By a Letter from General Ward of the 29th. Ulto,[47] he informs me, that two of our armed Vessels the day before had brought into Marblehead, a Ship bound from Halifax to Staten Island, she had in about 1509 £ Cost of British Goods, besides a good many belonging to Tories. A Hallifax paper found on board her, I have inclosed, as also an Account sent me by Mr. Hazard transmitted him by some of his Friends, as given by the Tories taken in her; their Intelligence I dare say is true, respecting the arrival of part of the Hessian Troops. General Ward, in his Letter mentions the day this prize was taken, Capt. Burke[48] in another of our Armed Vessels had an engagement with a Ship and a Schooner which he thought were

---

[46] A copy of Gov. Nicholas Cooke's letter, dated July 29, 1776, is filed with Washington's in the *Papers of the Continental Congress.*

[47] Ward's letter is in the *Washington Papers.*

[48] Capt. William Burke, then commanding the *Lee.*

Transports and would have taken them, had it not been for an unlucky accident in having his Quarter Deck blown up. Two of his men were killed and several more were wounded.

The Hulks and Cheveaux de frieze that have been preparing to obstruct the Channel, have got up to the place they are intended for, and will be sunk as soon as possible.

I have transmitted Congress, a Genl. Return of the Army in and about this place, on the third instant, by which they will perceive the amount of our force.[49]

Before I conclude I would beg leave to remind Congress of the necessity there is of having some Major Generals appointed for this Army: the duties of which are great, extensive and impossible to be discharged, as they ought and the good of the service requires, without a Competent number of Officers of this rank. I mean to write more fully upon this Subject, and as things are drawing fast to an Issue and it is necessary to make every proper disposition and arrangement that we possibly can; I pray that this matter may be taken into consideration and claim their early attention. I well know What has prevented appointments of this sort for some time past, but the situation of our Affairs will not Justify longer delays in this Instance; by the first Opportunity I shall take the Liberty of giving you my sentiments more at large upon the propriety and necessity of the measure. I have the Honor etc.[50]

### To GOVERNOR NICHOLAS COOKE

New York, August 5, 1776.

Sir: I have been duly honored with your two favors of the 20th. and 29th. Ulto. and wish your acceptance of my thanks for your Kind and ready Compliance, with my requisition for the Gallies, and the Matters of Intelligence transmitted in the

---

[49] The figures of this general return are given in Washington's letter to Trumbull, Aug. 7, 1776, *q. v.*
[50] In the writing of Robert Hanson Harrison.

last. The Account given Capt. Bucklin, on whose success I congratulate you, by Capt. Bell of the Portuguese seizing our Vessels, I fear is too true. Their dependance on the British Crown for protection and Aid, against their Spanish Neighbours, obliges them to comply with every thing required of them. Capt. Bucklin's information of the Fleet he saw, I dare say is not to be doubled. It is probable they arrived yesterday; for twenty five Ships then came into the Hook. These make from 90 to 100. that have come in since Thursday Sen-night.

Our Gallies, on Saturday Evening, had a Smart engagement with the Ships up the River. The Inclosed Copy of a Letter from Colo. Tupper, under whose Genl Command they were, will give you the particulars. Tho' they did not take the Ships, nor is it certain what Damage they Sustained; I have the pleasure to inform you, Our officers and Men behaved with the greatest spirit and resolution; the injury their little Fleet sustained Testifies their Courage. It is said, the Ships were several times hulled by our Shot, they still remain up the River, The Gallies must be a little repaired before anything further can be attempted, provided it should be thought advisable.

By a Letter from Colo. Hancock of the 31st. Ulto., I am Authorised to say, that a Continental Ship had arrived at Chester, not far below Philadelphia, with 366 pigs Lead, 54 Boxes of Musquet Ball, 1000 Stand of Arms with Bayonets, 1 Barrel Flints and 193 whole Barrels of Gun Powder. He also adds, that a Privateer had sent in a West India Man, having on Board, besides produce, 1100 Johans. and 700 Guineas. I wish the Ship Capt Bucklin saw may get in safe. I have the Honor to be &c.

## To JOHN BRADFORD

Head Quarters, New York, August 5, 1776.

Sir: Yours of the 29th. Ulto. is duly Received; for the future I must desire all Warlike Stores and Necessaries for an Army, taken by the Armed Vessels in public Service, may be safely Stored, under care of the Different Agents, 'till they receive Orders from proper Authority. you will please to enjoin it upon the different Commanders of the Continental Cruisers, to be particularly careful, no Embezelment is made by their Crew or others. I am &c.

## To NATHANIEL SHAW, JUNIOR

Head Quarters, New York, August 5, 1776.

Sir: This will be accompanied by four french Gentn. from the Island of Guadaloupe, who arrived from thence at Newburry pt., with a view of engaging in the Continental Service;— they came to this place about 6 Weeks since, and delivered me a letter from Genl. Ward at Boston, which I inclosed to the President of the Congress, intending to forward it by them, that it might serve as some sort of introduction: but it seems that for want of proper Credentials, added to the unsuccessfulness of some of their Countrymen, on that same Account, they declined applying to Congress,—and as it appears they are quite destitute of Money, I am Obliged to pay their Expences here, and to send them to New London, to enable them to procure a passage Home.—I have therefore addressed them to your care, requesting you will assist in providing them a passage as soon as possible. I suppose, it will not be long before an Oppertunity Offers, as I understand there are Vessels with you bound to the West Indies.

You will please to furnish them with convenient and cheap Lodgings, when they get to N. London, and I will reimburse you what you may be in advance therefor.

You are to observe tho', that I do not mean to be at the expence of supporting them in your place, more than eight or ten days at farthest. neither do I mean to be at the expence of their passages Home; they must make the best terms for themselves they can, with the Master of the Vessel, as I dont determine to burthen the Continent any more, on their Account or any of their Countrymen. I am etc.

## To THOMAS McKEAN

New York, August 6, 1776.

Sir: The French Gentleman whom you may recollect was at Philadelphia when I was there, in the character of the Baron de Calbiact, who was waiting on Congress for some promotion in the Military line, is now here, and Complains of the hardship he labours under in being refused an appointment and also in having his papers and Credentials kept from him. he informs me they are in your hands, and as he seems sollicitous about them and desirous of having them again, I request the favor of you to transmit them to and by the earliest Opportunity, that I may deliver them to him and thereby remove every protest of affected uneasiness upon this head. I am, etc.      [H.S.P.]

## GENERAL ORDERS

Head Quarters, New York, August 6, 1776.

Parole Canterbury.   Countersign Durham.

One hundred and fifty Men, with a Field Officer, three Captains, six Subs. six Serjeants, six Corporals and six Drums and Fifes, to proceed to Burdett's Ferry, opposite Mount Washington, to relieve the party now there; for this purpose to parade to morrow with Arms, on the Grand-parade, at seven o'Clock, apply to General Putnam for Boats, and attend to the tide.

Every commanding Officer of a Regiment or Corps in future is to account on the back, or at the bottom, of his return for all the officers and men returned to be on Command, expressing the place and service in which they are engaged.

Notwithstanding the orders issued, and the interest the troops have in it; Complaints are made of the bad behaviour of the troops to people at market; taking and destroying their things. The General declares for the last time, that he will punish such offenders most severely; and in order that they may be detected, an officer from each of the guards, nearest to those Markets where the Country People is, to attend from sunrise till twelve O'Clock, and he is strictly enjoined to prevent any abuses of this kind; to seize any offender and send him immediately to the Guard house, reporting him also at Head Quarters—The officers of guards in future will be answerable if there are any more Complaints unless they apprehend the offender—A Copy of this order to be put up in every Guard House in the City.

James McCormick of Capt Farrington's[51] Company, Col Sergeants Regiment; Thomas Williams of Capt. Burns's[52] Company, and the same regiment; Peter Burke of Capt Ledyards[53] Company; John Green of Capt. Johnson's[54] Company, both of Col McDougall's Regiment; all tried by a General Court Martial of which Col Webb was President, and convicted of "*Desertion*"; were sentenced to receive Thirty-nine Lashes each—The General approves the sentences and orders them to be put in execution at the usual times and places.

Hugh Lacey of Capt. Stewarts[55] Company of Highlanders, tried by the same Court Martial, and found guilty of "Impudence and Disobedience to the orders of his Captain," was sentenced to receive Twenty Lashes.

[51] Capt. Thomas Farrington, of the Sixteenth Continental Infantry.
[52] Capt. Asa Barnes, of the Sixteenth Continental Infantry.
[53] Capt. Benjamin Ledyard, of the First New York Regiment.
[54] Capt. John Johnson, of the First New York Regiment.
[55] Capt. James Stewart had been authorized by the New York Legislature (July 25) to raise a company of Scotch Highlanders. His company was attached to Malcom's regiment.

The General is pleased to pardon him on Condition that he makes a suitable acknowledgment of his fault to his Captain.

Hendrick Lent, Jacob Lent, Elias Lent, Peter Brewer, Jeremiah Hewson, Oronimus Ackerman; all of Capt Hyatts Company and Col McDougall's Regiment, having been confined for some time for "Desertion"; and no evidence appearing against them, they are ordered to be discharged for want of prosecution.

## GENERAL ORDERS

Head Quarters, New York, August 7, 1776.
Parole Essex.    Countersign Fairfield.

The Order of the 28th of July, respecting the removal of the sick from the Regimental to the General Hospital having been misunderstood by some; the General directs that it be taken with the following explanation. The Regimental Surgeons are to send at any time, with the usual Ticket, any patient to the General Hospital whose case requires it (putrid, and infectious disorders always excepted). Whenever the Director General, or any Surgeon of the Hospital by his direction, visits the regimental Hospitals, they are to direct what patients are proper to be removed, but it is expected that when any Surgeon visits the Regimental Surgeon, and if they should differ in opinion, they will refer it to the Director General, who has by the Resolutions of Congress, a superintendency over the whole. The General most earnestly recommends to the Gentlemen in both departments, to cultivate harmony and good agreement with each other, as conducive to their own Honor, and the good of the service.

A Sub: and twenty Men to be placed at Hoebuck Ferry, for examination of passengers. The officer to receive his Orders from the Adjutant General at Head Quarters.

The Pay Master having received a supply of Cash; The Colonels or commanding Officers of Regiments, are to apply for their June Pay; and make up Pay-Rolls for July, and deliver them to their respective Brigadiers for examination.

As many Soldiers discharge their Pieces, under pretence of Ignorance, of General Orders, and others having leave to do so from their officers, because they cannot draw the Charge: The General directs, that the Colonel of the Regiment, or commanding officer cause a daily inspection to be made of the state of the Arms; and when any are found loaded which cannot be drawn, they are to cause such men to assemble on the Regimental parade, or some other convenient place, but at the same time, viz:—Retreat Beating, and then discharge those peices. No alarm will then be given and the officers will see there is no unnecessary firing. It is the duty of the Colonel, and the reputation of his regiment so much depends upon the good order of the arms, that the General hopes he, as well as every other officer, and the men, will pay a special attention to it.

John Palsgrave Wyllys Esqr. is appointed Brigade Major to General Wadsworth—Mark Hopkins Esqr. to Genl. Fellows; they are to be obeyed and respected accordingly.

### To MAJOR CHRISTOPHER FRENCH

Head Quarters, New York, August 7, 1776.

Sir: I am to acknowledge the receipt of your favor of the      July, intimating your expectations of release on the 12th. of this month.

I have considered your Parole, advised with those whose Knowledge and experience gives weight to their Opinion, and otherwise endeavoured to inform myself how far your Construction of it is founded upon Justice, Reason or Usage; I do not find it warranted by either, My Duty therefore Obliges me to over rule your Claim as a matter of Right. As a matter of favor, Indulgence is not in my Power, even if your General Line of Conduct as a Prisoner had been unexceptionable.

I have therefore wrote to the Committee of Hartford, sent them a Copy of this Letter and hope you will, without Difficulty, conform to the Regulations already made with respect to Prisoners, by the General Congress.

It is probable a general Exchange of Prisoners will soon take place, it will then be a pleasing part of my Duty, to facilitate your return to your Friends and connections, as I assure you it is now a painful one to disappoint you, in an Expectation which you seem to have formed, in a full Persuasion of being right and in which on mature Deliberation, I am so unhappy as totally to differ from you. I am Sir etc.

## To THE PRESIDENT OF CONGRESS

New York, August 7, 1776.

Sir: In my Letter of the 5th., which I had the honor of addressing you, I begged leave to recall the attention of Congress to the absolute necessity there is for appointing more General Officers, promising at the same time by the first opportunity to give my sentiments more at large upon the Subject.

Confident I am that the postponing this measure, has not proceeded from Motives of frugality, otherwise I would take the Liberty of attempting to prove that we put too much to the hazard by such a saving. I am but too well apprized of the difficulties that occur in the choice. They are I acknowledge, great, but at the same time It must be allowed, they are of such a Nature as to present themselves whenever the Subject is thought of. Time on the one hand does not remove them, on the other, delay may be productive of fatal consequences. This Army tho' far short as yet, of the Numbers intended by Congress, is by much too unweildy for the command of anyone Man, without several Major Generals to assist. For it is to be observed, that a Brigadier General at the head of his Brigade is no more than a Colonel at the Head of a Regiment, except that he Acts upon a larger scale.

Officers of more General command, are at all times wanted for the good order and Government of an Army, especially when that Army is composed chiefly of raw Troops, but in an action they are indispensibly necessary. At present there is but one Major General for this whole department and the flying Camp, where as at this place alone, less than three cannot discharge the duties with that regularity they ought to be: If these Major General are appointed, as undoubtedly they will, out of the present Brigadiers, you will want for this place three Brigadiers at least. The Northern department will require one, if not two, as General Thompson is a Prisoner and the Baron De Woedtke reported to be dead or in a state not much better, there being at present only one Brigadier (Arnold) in all that department. For the Eastern Governments there ought to be one, or a Major General to superinted the Regiments there and prevent Impositions that might Otherwise be practised. These make the number wanted to be Six or Seven, and who are to be appointed, Congress can best Judge. To make Brigadiers of the oldest Colonels would be the least exceptionable way, but it is much to be questioned, Whether by that mode, the ablest men would be appointed to Office; and I would observe, tho' the Rank of the Colonels of the Eastern Governments were settled at Cambridge last year, It only respected themselves and is still open as to Officers of other Governments. To pick a Colonel here and a Colonel there through the Army according to the Opinion entertained of their abilities, would no doubt be the means of making a better choice and nominating the fittest persons; But then the Senior Officers would be disgusted and more than probable with their Connexions quit the service. That might prove fatal at this time. To appoint Gentlemen as Brigadiers, that had not served in the Army, (in this part of it at least) would not wound any one in particular, but hurt the whole equally and must be considered in a very discouraging light by every Officer of Merit.

View the matter therefore in any point of light you will, there are Inconveniences on the one hand and difficulties on the other which ought to be avoided.

Would they be remedied by appointing the oldest Colonels from each State?

If this mode should be thought expedient, the Inclosed List gives the names of the Colonels from New Hampshire to Pennsylvania inclusive, specifying those who rank first as I am told in the several Colony Lists.[56]

I have transmitted a Copy of a Letter from Mr. Jona. Glover, setting forth the nature and Grounds of a dispute between him and a Mr. Bradford respecting their Agency. Not conceiving myself Authorized, nor having the smallest inclination to interfere in any degree in the matter; It is referred to Congress, who will determine and give direction upon it in such manner as they shall Judge best. I will only observe, that Mr. Glover was recommended to me as a proper person for an Agent when we first fitted out Armed Vessels and was accordingly appointed one, and so far as I know, discharged his Office with fidelity and Industry.

---

[56] This letter was read in Congress August 8, and on the 9th that body appointed Brig. Gens. William Heath, Joseph Spencer, John Sullivan, and Nathanael Greene major generals; and Cols. James Reed, John Nixon, Arthur St. Clair, Alexander McDougall, Samuel Holden Parsons, and James Clinton brigadier generals. The list of colonels was not inclosed with the letter.

I received Yesterday Evening a Letter from General Schuyler, containing Lieutenant McMichels[57] report, who had been sent a Scout to Oswego. A Copy of the Report I have inclosed for the Information of Congress, least General Schuyler should have omitted It in his Letter, which accompanies this. he was at the German Flatts when he wrote which was the 2d Instt. and the Treaty with the Indians not begun, nor had the whole expected, then arrived, but of these things he will have advised you more fully I make no doubt. The Pay Master Informs me he received a supply of Money Yesterday. It came very seasonably, for the Applications and clamours of the Troops had become incessant and distressing beyond measure. There is now two month's pay due them. I have &ca.[58]

## To THE PRESIDENT OF CONGRESS

Head Quarters, 1. O'Clock P. M., August 7, 1776.

Sir: Since closing the Letter which I had the honor to write you this Morning, two Deserters have come in, who left the Solebay Man of War last Evening.—one of them is a Native of New York. Their Account is that they were in the Engagement with Col. Moultrie at Sullivan's Island on the 9th. July; the particulars they give nearly correspond with the narrative sent by General Lee; that they left Carolina 3 Weeks ago as a Convoy to 45 transports, having on board General Clinton, Lord Cornwallis and the whole Southern Army, consisting of about 3000 Men, all of whom were landed last week on Staten Island, in tolerable Health.

That on Sunday 13 Transports part of Lord Howe's fleet and having on board Hessians and Highlanders, came to Staten

---

[57] Lieut. Edward McMichael, of the Third New Jersey Regiment. Copies of his report are in both the *Washington Papers* and in the *Papers of the Continental Congress.*

[58] In the writing of Robert Hanson Harrison.

Island: that the remainder of the Fleet which was reported to have in the whole 12000 Men; had parted with these Troops off the Banks of Newfoundland and were expected to come in every Moment; that they were getting their heavy Carriages and Cannon on board; had launched 8 Gondolas with flatt Bottoms, and 2 Rafts on Stages to carry Cannon. These men understand that the attack will soon be made, if the other Troops arrive; That they give out they will lay the Jerseys waste with Fire and Sword. The computed Strength of their Army will be 30,000 Men. They further add, that when they left Carolina one Transport got on Shore, so that they were not able to give her relief, upon which she surrendered with 5 Companies of Highlanders to General Lee, who after taking every thing valuable out of her burnt her

That the Admiral turned General Clinton out of his Ship after the Engagement, with a great deal of abuse; great differences between the Principal Naval and Military Gentlemen; that the Ships left in Carolina, are now in such a Weakly distressed condition they would fall on easy Prey. I am, etc.

P. S: The Ships are changing their position, and the Men of War forming into a Line, but I still think they will wait the arrival of the remaining Hessians before any general attack will be made. Monday's return will shew our strength here.[59]

## To MAJOR GENERAL PHILIP SCHUYLER

New York, August 7, 1776.

Dear Sir: Before this, I presume you have received a letter from Congress, Inclosing Sundry Resolutions of the 22, 23, and 24 Ulto., among which was one, impowering their Commanders in Chief in every Department, to Negociate an Exchange of

---

[59] In the writing of Joseph Reed; the P. S. is in that of Washington.

prisoners, upon the plan therein pointed out, There were two others, mentioning the case of Colo. Allen and the persons taken with him. That the views of Congress might be carried into Execution in those Instances, as far as they could in this Department, and for the Enlargement of Mr. Lovell, whose case they have since mentioned, I wrote to Genl. Howe who has acceded to the several propositions I made him, as far as they came within the Extent of his Command. A copy of my letter and his Answer, I have Inclosed. By the Letter, you will perceive, Prisoners made in Canada are Subject to Genl. Carleton's Determination and pleasure. It is probable, you have already wrote him upon the Subject of an Exchange; but If you have not, I think you should propose It immediately, both to him and Genl. Burgoyne, and try to obtain Genl. Thompson for Genl. Prescott, and also one for the other Officers and Men, who are Prisoners in their Hands. Justice and a Regard to the merits and Bravery of the Officers, and Privates, who were taken when Genl. Montgomery unfortunately fell, Require that our Exertions should be directed, to Relieve their Sufferings, and procure their Enlargement among the first. It may not be improper, to Inform these two Gentlemen, of what has passed between Genl. Howe and Myself.—Perhaps the Copies of our Letters, will Contribute in some measure to facilitate the Worke.

I was Yesterday evening favoured with your Letters of the 1st. and 2nd., also with One from Mr. Varrick.[60] It is impossible to spare any Gunners or Mates from hence, Our posts being so extensive that we are obliged to draft upwards of Six hundred Men from different Regiments to Assist the Artillery.

---

[60] Richard Varick. He was captain in the First New York Regiment; aide to Schuyler; deputy commissary general of musters, Northern Army; lieutenant colonel and aide to Arnold; recording secretary to Washington. After the war he was recorder and mayor of New York City and attorney general of the State.

Colo. Knox Informs me you have four Comps. of Gunners and Matrosses at the Lakes, as good as any here, which is a much greater proportion than we have. You must draw what are necessary for them and other parts of the Army. As to Seamen they are extremely difficult to procure, and I wish they may be got; as it is almost certain, they would not engage in the Service you want 'em for, upon the terms usually allowed here, there seems to have been a Necessity for employing them on the best that can be had.

From Lt. McMichels report, Our Enemies seem determined to push us on all Quarters, It is nothing but what we may expect, your utmost activity and exertions must be employed, to counteract their designs and prevent their Penetrating the Country. I hope Fort Stanwix 'ere long will be compleat and defensible, against any attack they can make, If they have any such views. The Garrison should by all means have a proper supply of provision, in case It should be Invested.

In respect to the Articles, in the list Marked B. in Mr. Varrick's Letter, All that can be procured here, and those set down in the list subscribed by the Qr. Mr. General. As to the Cordage, lest a supply may not be got in Connecticut, Mr. Ivers[61] has undertaken, and will immediately set out for Poughkeepsie, in Order to Manufacture Six or Eight Tons of Hemp, he has there an Assortment of it, which will be forwarded to Albany with all possible dispatch from thence. I hope the other Necessaries will be got by the person sent to Connecticut, and the Anchors &c. at the Forges Mr. Varrick mentions. Captn. Bacon[62] sent in pursuit of Seamen &c. by Genl. Arnold, is gone to Connecticut to see what he can procure. I advanced him Five Hundred Pounds Lawful, all the Money that was in the paymasters Hands.

---

[61] Ivers was of Stratford, Conn. In 1778 he is mentioned as furnishing cordage for one of the armed vessels.

[62] Capt. Asa(?) Bacon, of Chester's Connecticut State regiment.

Having represented to Congress, the expediency of imploying the Stockbridge Indians, as they are desirous of it, they
have Authorized me to do it, as you will see by the inclosed
Copy of their Resolution, passed the 2nd. Instant. If Mr. Edwards[63] is at the Treaty you are now holding, shew him the
Resolve, and please to inform him, that it is my request, he
should adopt the most expeditiousmodeofraising them, giving
such of them that chuse it, Liberty to Join the Northern Army,
and those that prefer coming here, leave to do it, in case they
incline to divide. If they do not the whole may go to which
of the Armies they please, least Mr. Edwards should not be at
the Treaty, I will try to write him by another opportunity to the
same effect.

. Congress I see, too, have ordered Five hundred Thousand
Dollars to be sent Mr. Trumbull for the Northern Army, I am
hopeful they will be attentive to the Necessary Supplies of
Money in future.

By two deserters, we are informed Genl. Clinton with his
whole Army from the Southward, except three Companies has
arrived; they also add, that about One thousand of the Hessians
have got in, the remainder of the foreign Troops they expect
(about Eleven Thousand) will be in every day, those that have
arrived having parted with them in a Gale of Wind of the
Banks of New found Land.

Congress having Resolved, that Colo. Elmore's Regiment
should reinforce this Army; On the first Instant I wrote him,
supposing him in Connecticut, with his Regiment to repair
here, with all possible expedition; but being informed that he
is at Albany with it, or a great part of it, are now, and fully
convinced that he cannot be here in time to afford any succour,

---

[63] Timothy Edwards, Indian commissioner for the Northern Department.

I request that you will detain him and direct his Regiment to such Service as you may think Necessary, I wrote him by this Opportunity countermanding my former Orders.[64] I am etc.

## To COLONEL JONATHAN FITCH

New York Head Quarters, August 7, 1776.

Sir, The Spirit and Zeal, which the Colony of Connecticut have ever shewn in the cause of America, makes it only necessary to acquaint you with our Situation, in order to ensure your assistance.[65] General Clinton has brought his whole Body of Troops from South Carolina, the Foreign Troops are every day arriving, and we have the most Authentic account that in a little time our Enemys Army will amount to 30,000 Men; with these, a decissive Attack will be made upon the Army, which in its present Situation, from Sickness, the Deficiency of Regiments, and other Causes, is far short of its intended Compliment; under these Circumstances, I am persuaded I need only remind you, of the power given by the Laws of the Colony to the Colonels of Regiments, upon an Alarm, Invasion or Appearance of an Enemy, by Sea or Land, to call out their respective Regiments into Service. Since the Settlement of these Colonies their has never been such just Occasion of Alarm, or such an Appearance of an Enemy, both by Sea and Land; I am therefore to request you to call forth your Regiment without delay, and have them equipp'd with Blankets, Arms and Ammunition, if possible, and march them immediately to this place, agreeable to the Power given by your Constitution, as explained by His Honor Governor Trumbull, in his Letter to the Honourable Continental Congress, dated the 6th. July last. I can

[64] Washington's letter to Elmore is dated August 7 and is, in effect, what he here states to Schuyler.
[65] Colonel Fitch was at New Haven, Conn.

only add, that the greater the expedition used the more essential and honourable the Service will probably be. I am &c.[66]

## To THE NEW JERSEY LEGISLATURE

New York, August 7, 1776.

Sir: I have received repeated information, that a number of Persons known to be inimical to the cause of the American States, or of a Suspicious Character, have lately removed from this and other places into the County of Monmouth in New Jersey, with intent no doubt from its situation; of Communicating with and Aiding our Enemies. All those of Similar Characters on Long Island and the other Counties adjacent to this place, will be secured by to morrow Morning, and I must urge the necessity of your Congress adopting the same Measure, in all those Parts of your Province, which are most contigious to the Enemy. There are some also, of very dangerous Characters, who I am informed are lurking in the Neighbourhood of Hackinsack and what they call the English Neighbourhood, particularly Benjamin Hugget and Frederick Rhinelander; this Measure is now become the more necessary, as from the Intelligence I have this day Received, there is the greatest reason to believe, that the Enemy intend to begin their Operations in a very few days, and that with a very powerful force; for not only a Considerable part of the Foreign Troops, the British Guards and an additional Number of Scotch Troops are lately arrived at Staten Island; but the Army from the Southward under Genl. Clinton also joined them last Thursday; and the remainder of the foreign Troops have been spoke with on the Coast and are momently expected; this must also urge the absolute necessity, of your Congress Instantly adopting some

---

[66] The same letter was sent to Col. Ichabod Sears at Stratford, to Col. John Mead at Greenwich, to Col. Edward Hinman at Woodbury, and to Col. Joseph Platt Cooke at Danbury.

effectual measures for compleating the Troops Voted, and for affording every other reinforcement to this Place, that is in their Power; by detaching a Considerable Body of the Militia, or in such other manner, as will be more effectual. Of the 3300. voted by your State, we have but 1450, and in the same proportion from the other Colonies, so that you will easily conceive, what an Alarming Situation we are in. As the Harvest is now over and the Militia engaged most chearfully to return if Necessary, I persuade myself they will readily turn out, upon a Representation being made to them of the Necessity; what from a Deficiency of the old Regiments, Sickness, and the failure of New Levies, we are in danger of being outnumbered by the Enemy, at least doubly, if not more. The Consequences may be fatal, unless prevented by the Spirit of the Country. I have dispatched Expresses to Connecticut to call in their Militia immediately, with their Arms, Blankets and what Ammunition they have; as the Supply here, to suit their Guns is attended with much difficulty and delay. I must beg your attention to the same Circumstance, as far as the Situation of things will admit, but so as not hinder from Marching, those who cannot come so provided. I am &c.

## To GOVERNOR JONATHAN TRUMBULL

Head Quarters, August 7, 1776.

Sir: By two deserters this day, we have the following Intelligence, Vizt., that General Clinton and Lord Cornwallis with the whole Southern Army, have arrived and landed on Staten Island from South Carolina, in number about 3. or 4,000; that the Fleet which came in a few days since, are the Hessians and Scotch Highlanders, part of 12,000 who were left off Newfound Land; in the whole making about 30,000 Men; and that, it is said by Officers of the Navy and Army, they are to attack N. York, Long Island, &c. in the course of a Week. The uncommon movements of the Fleet this day, together with the above intelligence, convince us, that in all human probability, there can but a very few days pass, before a general Engagement takes place. When I consider the Weakness of our Army by Sickness, the great extent of Ground we have to defend, and the amazing slowness with which the Levies come forward, I think it absolutely necessary, the Neighbouring Militia should be immediately sent in to our assistance; and, agreeable to your Letter of the 6th July, I have ordered the Colonels, with their Regiments, to March, with all Convenient Speed, to this Place. The disgrace of the British Arms to the Southward, and the Season being far advanced, will make them exert every nerve against us in this Quarter. To trust altogether in the justice of our cause, without our own utmost exertions, would be tempting Providence; and, that you may judge of our Situation, I give you the present state of our Army:

Copy from the General Return of the Army of the United States of America, now on New York, Governor's, and Long Islands, and at Powles Hook, Augst. 3d., 1776 Vizt.

Present, fit for duty, 10,514; Sick, present, 3,039; Sick, absent, 629, on Command 2,946, on furlow 97: Total 17,225. By this, you will see, we are to oppose an Army of 30,000 experienced Veterans, with about one third the Number of Raw Troops, and these scattered, some 15 Miles apart. This will be handed you by Mr. Root, to him, I must refer you for further particulars; and have the pleasure to be etc.

### To THE COMMITTEE OF SAFETY OF HARTFORD, CONNECTICUT

Head Quarters, New York, August 7, 1776.

Gentn.: I am to acquaint you, that I lately recived a Letter from Major French, who is a prisoner in your Place, signifying that his parole would be out the 12th Inst., and that he had no intentions of renewing it. This conduct I must Confess, appears very extraordinary, as he cannot be ignorant, that he has been hitherto considered as a prisoner of War, and that accepting his parole at first was an indulgence granted, solely to make his situation more easy and Comfortable; and to prevent his experiencing the disagreeable Effects of a close confinement. I have expressed my sentiments to him freely on the Subject in my Answer, which I inclose unsealed for your perusal. I doubt not, you will pursue such measures, as are most proper on this occasion. You will please to seal and deliver the Letter inclosed, without delay, to avoid any trouble that may arise on Account of not delivering it, previous to the date beforementioned. I am, etc.

### To JESSE ROOT

Head Quarters, New York, August 7, 1776.

Sir: I have the most Authentic intelligence, that General Clinton with his whole Southern Army, 1000 Hessians and a number of Highlanders, have within these few days, joined General Howe. that 11,000 more, foreign Troops, are hourly expected having been left on the banks of Newfound Land a few days ago. An attack is now therefore to be expected, which will probably decide the Fate of America. The Levies from New Jersey, New York, and Connecticut are not compleated within one half of their Establishment and my whole Army much Short of its Compliment.

Under these Circumstances Sir, I must desire you to apply to the Several Committees or other Authority of Connecticut, to hasten down, as fast as possible, the Militia, and I cannot doubt but a sence of Public duty and the imminent Dangers, to which every thing that is dear to us is exposed, will induce every true friend and Lover of his Country, to exert his utmost Powers for its Salvation and Defence. I am etc.

## To TIMOTHY EDWARDS

New York, August 7, 1776.

Sir: The inclosed Copy of a Resolution of Congress, entered into the 2d Inst., will discover to you their Sentiments, on the Subject of employing the Stockbridge Indians in the Service of the United States.

It is certain they differed some time ago, from the Commissioners of Indian affairs and put a Stop to their proceedings in this Instance; But finding that our Enemy's are prosecuting the War, with unexampled Severity and Industry, and that these Indians are anxious to take a part in our favor; they have instructed me to employ in the Service of the American States, as many of them as I may think proper; I therefore take the Liberty to request your friendly exertions on this Occasion and that you will engage in the Service, as great a Number of them as you possibly can. I would wish you to give the Whole of them or any part that may choose it, the liberty of Joining either this Army, or that in the Northern Department under Genl. Schuyler. I do not think it will be proper, as they are desirous of becoming apart of the Army, to Oblige them to join, where they have not an Inclination to go; and therefore recommend that they should be indulged, in whatever way their fancy may lead, as to Joining either the one or the other Army, partially or wholly.

The Situation of our affairs, will readily suggest to you, the Necessity of dispatch; at the same time, that it will point out the expediency of engaging as many of them as you can. The business may be attended with a degree of trouble, which I could wish not to happen, but yet I am persuaded will be undertaken with alacrity. I am &c.

## TO COLONEL SAMUEL MILES

New York Head Quarters, August 8, 1776.

Sir: Since your Departure from hence we have received Intelligence of the utmost Importance that Gen. Clinton has arrived at Staten Island with the whole Southern Army; that the foreign Troops are arriving, the whole making a most formidable and alarming Force. By the Preparations making we have Reason to expect an early and very vigorous Attack for which we would wish to have more equal Numbers: Upon looking round I do not see any Quarter from which I may so confidently look for Assistance as the Pennsylvania Troops who have shown so much Spirit and Zeal and particularly those of the three Battalions under your Command of whom I hear a most excellent Character. I do not scrutinize with the Terms of the Inlistment of Troops at such a Time as this, nor would I avail myself of any Authority derived from that Source. Brave Men who love their Country and are resolved to defend it, will go where the Service requires at so critical and dangerous a Period as this and Men of a different Character, such I hope we have not among us, can be useful no where. I flatter myself therefore when the brave Officers and Soldiers under your special Command reflect that the Time is fast approaching which is to determine our Fate and that of our Posterity they will most chearfully persevere and comply with such Requests respecting their March and Destination as the State of Things requires. Under this Perswasion I have wrote to General Mercer to desire one of the Riffle Battalions may be forwarded over as we have not one Corps of this Kind in or near New York, and the Ground in many Places will admit them to act with great Advantage. I doubt not your utmost Influence to facilitate so important an Object. I have left it to Gen. Mercer who will doubtless consult with you on the Subject, to determine which Battalion should come, or if they could be spared, I should be glad to see a greater Number. From what I can learn I do not believe New Jersey to be included in the present Plan of Attack; if so, the Service rendered here would be of the most important Kind. If you think it will be of any Use, I have no Objection to your Communicating this Letter to your Officers and Men, and then such steps may be taken as will [     [67]] the great Cause in which we are all engaged. I am, etc.[68]

### To MAJOR CHRISTOPHER FRENCH

Head Quarters, New York, August 8, 1776.

Sir: I was unwilling to determine hastily, upon your claim of a Release founded upon your Parole, and therefore delayed the acknowledgment of your favor of the 22d July, until I should fully inform myself. I had accordingly wrote you Yesterday, that I was so unhappy as to differ from you in the construction you had put upon it, but as there was reason to believe, a General Exchange of Prisoners might soon take place, I should chearfully facilitate your return to your Friends.

Last Night I received your favour of the 5th. August waving your Claim of a Release, which makes any farther Discussion of that matter unnecessary. Your other proposal, of being exchanged for Major Meigs[69] or Col: Allen, will meet with no Objection from me; should you write to General Howe on the Subject the Letter shall be chearfully forwarded and his Answer returned.

[67] Mutilated.
[68] This letter is owned by the Mount Vernon Ladies' Association of the Union, to whose courtesy the editor is indebted for the text.
[69] Maj. Return Jonathan Meigs, of the Second Connecticut Regiment.

Should any Difficulty arise in the Exchange, I am doubtful, how far I should be authorized, without consulting the Congress, to grant you an Indulgence similar to that of Major Meigs, which I have been informed was allowed in consequence of his saving the Life of a British Officer, either nearly connected with, or much esteemed by General Carlton.

However, you may assure yourself Sir, that both Duty and Inclination lead me to relieve the unfortunate and that I agree with you, that your long and early Captivity gives you a very just Claim to special Notice, and I shall be happy in furthering your Wishes, as far as my Station will admit. I am Sir, etc.

## To BRIGADIER GENERAL HUGH MERCER

Head Quarters, New York, August 8, 1776.

Sir: The Account given you by a deserter, as brought me by Mr. Tilghman is confirmed by two Sailors who came off the Night before last from the Enemy; That Genl. Clinton is arrived with his Army from South Carolina, and that Preparations are makeing for an early and Vigorous Attack. They further add, that last Sunday 1000 Hessians landed, part of 12,000, the Remainder being left off the Banks of Newfound Land, that may be expected every Hour. under these Circumstances, and considering how much deficient this Army is, from the not filling up the new Levies, and Sickness, I must desire you to send over one of the Rifle Regiments, as we have not one Corps of that kind on this Island. I leave it to you, to fix upon that which you think will come with the most Chearfulness, and are best appointed, but would not have any time lost. The Quarter Master may set out immediately to prepare for them; from all accounts the grand Attack will be made here, and at Long Island. I cannot find any thing meditated against New Jersey at present. I have wrote to the Convention of Jersey, and to Connecticut, to send in the Militia, with all expedition. I am, etc.

## To BRIGADIER GENERAL WILLIAM LIVINGSTON

[Head Quarters, August 8, 1776.]

Sir: Before this reaches you, you will undoubtedly have heard of the unexpected arrival of the Carolina Army on Staten Island, which added to the Hessians and foreign Troops under Lord Howe, exhibit a force Justly Alarming. When I compare it with that which we have to oppose them, I cannot help feeling every anxious Apprehension. The New Levies are so incomplete, the Old Regiments deficient in their Compliment, and so much Sickness, that we must have an immediate Supply of Men. I have therefore wrote to Connecticut, and to the Convention of your Province, to call the Militia immediately. but as it may take some time, and the Necessity admit of no delay, I have thought it proper to Apply to you also, under the Resolution of Congress of last June, Copy of which was sent you when Lord Howe's Fleet first arrived, to beg you would use your utmost exertions to forward this most Necessary Measure. The Consequences to the American Interest of any Failure here, are so obvious, that I need not enlarge upon them, your own good Judgement will suggest every thing proper.

It would be a great saving of Time and expence, if the Militia, when they come, would always equip themselves with Arms, Ammunition, Blankets, Canteens and Kettles, as far as they can, and in any Order given on the present Occasion, I would wish you to notice it specially. I am, etc.

## To BRIGADIER GENERAL GEORGE CLINTON

Head Quarters, New York, August 8, 1776.

Dear Sir: Yours of the 2nd. Instant is duly received. Inclosed you have a Resolution of the Provincial Conventoin, which came to hand last evening, by which you will please to regulate your Conduct. I must beg you to inform me, as soon as possible, what Number your Brigade now consists of, and what Number it will contain, when a fourth part of the Militia are drafted, agreable to Order of Provincial Congress.

By Intelligence received and movements observed of the Enemy, we have the greatest reason to believe, a General Attack will be made in the course of a few days, our Numbers are much short of the Enemy. I hope no time will be lost, in Marching the Reinforcements expected to our Assistance from Different Quarters, with all possible dispatch. I am etc.

## To THE OFFICERS AND SOLDIERS OF THE PENNSYLVANIA ASSOCIATORS[70]

Head Quarters, August 8, 1776.

Gentlemen: I had fully resolved to have paid you a Visit in New Jersey if the movements of the Enemy, and some intelligence indicating an early attack, had not induced me to suspend it.

Allow me therefore, to address you in this Mode, as fellow Citizens and fellow Soldiers engaged in the same Glorious Cause; to represent to you, that the Fate of our Country depends in all human probability, on the Exertion of a few Weeks; That it is of the utmost importance, to keep up a respectable Force for that time, and there can be no doubt that success will Crown our Efforts, if we firmly and resolutely determine, to conquer or to die.

I have placed so much confidence, in the Spirit and Zeal of the Associated Troops of Pennsylvania, that I cannot persuade myself an impatience to return Home, or a less honourable Motive will defeat my well grounded expectation, that they

---

[70] The Pennsylvania Associators, as they were called, were the same as militia and were stationed at this date near Elizabethtown, N. J.

will do their Country essential Service, at this critical time, when the Powers of Despotism are all combined against it, and ready to strike their most decisive Stroke. If I could allow myself to doubt your Spirit and Perseverance, I should represent the ruinous Consequences of your leaving the Service, by setting before you, the discouragement it would give the Army, the confusion and shame of our Friends, and the still more galling triumph of our Enemies. But as I have no such doubts, I shall only thank you for the Spirit and Ardor you have shewn, in so readily marching to meet the Enemy, and am most confident you will crown it by a Glorious Perseverance. The Honor and safety of our bleeding Country, and every other motive that can influence the brave and heroic Patriot, call loudly upon us, to acquit ourselves with Spirit. In short, we must now determine to be enslaved or free. If we make Freedom our choice, we must obtain it, by the Blessing of Heaven on our United and Vigorous Efforts.

I salute you Gentlemen most Affectionately, and beg leave to remind you, that Liberty, Honor, and Safety are all at stake, and I trust Providence will smile upon our Efforts, and establish us once more, the Inhabitants of a free and happy Country. I am, etc.

## To THE NEW YORK LEGISLATURE

New York, August 8, 1776.

Sir: I have been favored with your Letter of the 6th. Inst. and am happy, to find the Nomination I made of Genl. Clinton,[71] in consequence of your Request to appoint an Officer to the Command of the Levies on both sides Hudson's River, has met the approbation of your Honble. Body. His acquaintance with the Country, abilities and zeal for the Cause are the Motives

---

[71] Brig. Gen. George Clinton. (See Washington's letter to the Secret Committee of the New York Legislature, July 19, 1776, *ante.*)

that induced me to make choice of him. However, I am led to conclude, from that part of your Letter which desires me to transmit him his appointment, with the Resolution Subjecting the Levies on both sides of the River at his command, that your Honorable Body entertain Ideas of the Matter, somewhat different from what I do, or ever did.

When I was honored with your Letter of the 16th Ulto, with the Resolves of Convention upon this Subject, the State of the Army under my Command would not allow me to send a General Officer in the Continental Service, to Command the Levies you then proposed to raise; supposing I had been authorised to do it; but considering myself without power in this Instance.

The Levies altogether of a Provincial Nature—to be raised by you and Subject to your direction, I esteemed the nomination of a General Officer over them, entrusted to my choice, a matter of favor and of Compliment, and as such I gratefully fill it.

I am persuaded, I expressed myself in this Manner to the Gentn. who were pleased to attend me upon the occasion and that they had the same Ideas. Under the Influence of this Opinion, all I expected was, that an Appointment would be made in conformity to my Nomination, If there was no Objection to the Gentleman I proposed, conceiving then as I do now, if he was approved by Convention, he was their Officer and deriving his appointment and Authority from them. In this light I presume Genl. Clinton must be viewed and his powers over the Levies you allude to, flow from you. Least accident may have mislaid the Letter I wrote you on the Subject, I have inclosed an Extract of it, so far as it had relation to it.

It is not in my Power to send an Experienced Officer at this time to the post you mention; I trust that Colo. Clinton[72] will

---

[72] Col. James Clinton, of the Second New York Regiment. He was made a brigadier general in the Continental Army Aug. 9, 1776; wounded at Fort Montgomery, N. Y., in Sir Henry Clinton's raid up the Hudson in 1777; served to the close of the war.

be equall to the Command of both the Highland Fortifications, they are under his direction at present.

In respect to the two Commissaries, I thought the Matter had been fixed; but as it is not, I have requested Mr. Trumbull, who has the Charge of this, to wait upon and agree with the Convention, on proper persons to conduct the business and in such a way that their purchases and his may not clash; to him therefore, I beg leave to refer you upon this Subject.

I am extremely obliged by the order for the Telescope. I have obtained it, and will try to employ it for the Valuable purposes you designed it.

I shall pay proper attention to your Members and persons employed in their Service, and give it in General Orders that they be permitted to pass our Guards without Interruption.

Before I conclude, I cannot but express my fears, lest the Enemy's Army so largely augmented, should possess themselves of the whole Stock on long Island; When the further reinforcement arrives, which they hourly expect, they may do it without a possibility on our part of preventing them.

I wish the Convention may not see Cause to regret, that they were not removed. I have the Honor to be &c.

## To THE NEW YORK LEGISLATURE

New York, August 8, 1776.

Sir: By this, I mean to Communicate to your Honble. Body, the Substance of the Intelligence I received yesterday from two deserters, that came the Evening before from the Solebay Man of War. They inform, that they were in the Engagement at Sullivan's Island and give nearly the same Account as that transmitted by Genl. Lee, which you would see published by Congress. They add, that they left South Carolina about three Weeks ago, with Genl. Clinton and his whole Army, who are now arrived and landed on Staten Island; they also say, that part of Lord Howe's fleet, with Hessian and Highland Troops on board, have got in, and that the remainder, with a considerable body, is hourly expected, which, those that have come in parted from, in a Gale of Wind of the Banks of New found land.

As the Accounts given by these Men, are direct and circumstantial, and their Authenticity corroborated by many other things that have occurred; It is not to be doubted but the number of the Enemy's Army will greatly exceed ours.

Their force which was generally expected would be considerable of itself; the unexpected augmentation of Genl Clinton's Army makes it more so. On the other hand, ours does not come up to the Intended establishment.

Under these Circumstances and as we may expect the period just at hand, when they will make their Vigorous push, I submit it to the Consideration of your Honble. Body, whether it may not be Necessary, for your Exertions to be employed in calling in, in the most expeditious manner, such reinforcements as you can Obtain, to the Aid of this Army. I have &c.

## GENERAL ORDERS

Head Quarters, New York, August 8, 1776.

Parole Greenwich.   Countersign Kennington.

Passes signed by the President of the Convention, of New York, are to be deemed authentic, and noticed as such by officers attending at the ferries.

As the Movements of the enemy, and intelligence by Deserters, give the utmost reason to believe, that the great struggle, in which we are contending for every thing dear to us, and our posterity, is near at hand—The General most earnestly recommends the closest attention to the state of the mens arms, ammunition and flints; that if we should be suddenly called to action, nothing of this kind may be to provide; and he does most anxiously exhort, both officers, and soldiers, not to be out of their quarters, or encampments, especially early in the morning, or upon the tide of flood.

A Flag in the day time, or a light at Night, in the Fort on Bayard's hill, with three Guns from the same place fired quick, but distinct, is to be considered as a signal for the troops to repair to their Alarm posts, and prepare for action, and that the Alarm may be more effectually given, the Drums are immediately to beat to Arms upon the signal being given from Bayards-hill—This order is not to be considered as countermanding the firing two Guns at Fort George as formerly ordered; that is also to be done upon an Alarm, but the Flag will not be hoisted at the old Head Quarters in the Broad way.

Col Parsons, Col Read, Col Huntington, Col Webb, Col Wyllys, Col Bailey, Col Baldwin, Col McDougall, Col: Ritzema and Lieut. Col Sheppard, to attend at Head Quarters this evening, at six o'clock.

## To THE PRESIDENT OF CONGRESS

New York, August 8, 1776.

Sir: By yesterday's post, I was honoured with your favor of the 2d. instant, with Sundry Resolutions of Congress, to which I shall pay strict Attention. As the proposition for employing the Stockbridge Indians has been approved, I have wrote Mr. Edwards, one of the Commissioners and who lives among them; requesting him to engage them or such as are willing to enter the Service. I have directed him to Indulge them with liberty to join this or the Northern Army or both, as their inclination may lead.

I wish the salutary Consequences may result from the regulation, respecting Seamen taken, that Congress have in view.

From the nature of this kind of People, and the priviledges granted on their entering into our service, I should suppose many of them would do It. We want them much.

I yesterday transmitted the Intelligence I received from the Deserters from the Solebay Man of War. The inclosed copy of a Letter by last night's post from the Honr. Mr. Bowdoin,[73] with the information of a Captain Kennedy lately taken, corroborate their accounts respecting the Hessian Troops. Indeed his report makes the fleet and Armament to be employed against us, greater than what we have heard they would be; However there remains no doubt of their being both large and formidable, and such as will require our most vigorous exertions to oppose them. persuaded of this, and knowing how much Inferior our Numbers are and will be to theirs, when the whole of their Troops arrive; of the important consequences that may, and will flow from the Appeal that will soon be made, I have wrote to Connecticut and New Jersey for all the succour they can afford, and also to the Convention of this State. What I may receive, and in what time, the event must determine. But I would feign hope, the Situation, the exigency of our Affairs, will call forth the strenuous efforts and early Assistance of those, who are friends to the Cause. I confess there is but too much occasion for their exertions. I confidently trust, they will not be witheld.

I have inclosed a Copy of a Letter from Mr. Bowdoin[74] respecting the Eastern Indians. Congress will thereby perceive, they profess themselves to be well attached to our Interest, and the Summary of the measures taken to engage them in our Service. I have the Treaty at large between the Honorable

---

[73] James Bowdoin. A copy of his letter of July 29, 1776, with Washington's letter, is in the *Papers of the Continental Congress.*

[74] A copy of this letter, dated July 30, 1776, with Washington's letter, is in the *Papers of the Continental Congress.*

Council of the Massachusetts on behalf of the United States, with the Delegates of the St. Johns and Mickmac Tribes. The probability of a copy's being sent already, and its great length, prevents one coming herewith.—If Congress have not had it forwarded to them, I will send a Copy by the first opportunity after notice that it has not been received.

August 9.

By a report received from General Greene last night, at Sun set and a little after, about one hundred Boats were seen bringing Troops from Staten Island to the Ships. Three of which had fallen down towards the narrows having taken in Soldiers from thirty of the Boats; he adds that by the best observations of several Officers, there appeared to be a General Embarkation.

I have wrote to General Mercer for Two Thousand Men from the Flying Camp: Colonel Smallwood's Battalion, as part of them, I expect this forenoon, But where the rest are to come from I know not, as by the General's last return, not more than three or four hundred of the New Levies had got in. In my Letter of the 5th. I inclosed a General return of the Army under my immediate Command, but I immagine the following state will give Congress a more perfect Idea, tho' not a more agreeable one, of our Situation. For the several posts on New York, Long and Governor's Islands and Paulus Hook we have fit for duty 10,514. Sick present 3039. sick absent 629. On Command 2946. On Furlo 97. Total 17225 in addition to these we are only certain of Colo: Smallwood's Battalion, in case of an immediate Attack.

Our posts too are much divided having Waters between many of them and some distant from others 15 Miles.

These circumstances sufficiently distressing of themselves, are much aggravated by the sickness that prevails thro the Army; every day more or less are taken down, so that the proportion of Men that may come in, cannot be considered as a real and serviceable Augmentation in the whole. These things are melancholy, but they are nevertheless true. I hope for better. Under every disadvantage my utmost exertions shall be employed to bring about the great end we have in view, and so far as I can Judge from the professions and apparent disposition of my Troops, I shall have their Support. The Superiority of the Enemy and the expected Attack, do not seem to have depressed their Spirits. These considerations lead me to think that tho' the appeal may not terminate so happily in our favor as I could wish that yet they will not succeed in their views without considerable loss. Any advantage they may get I trust will cost them dear.

8 o'Clock A. M.

By the Reverend Mr. Maddison[75] and a Mr. Johnson two Gentlemen of Virginia who came from Staten Island Yesterday and where they arrived the day before in the Packet with Colonel Guy Johnson, I am informed that nothing material had taken place in England when they left it. That there had been a change in the French Ministry which many people thought foreboded a War.[76] That it seemed to be believed by many, that Congress would attempt to buy off the Foreign Troops and that it might be effected without great difficulty. Their Accounts from Staten Island nearly correspond with what we had before. They say every preparation is making for an attack; That the force now upon the Island is about 15,000. That they appear very Impatient for the Arrival of the foreign Troops, but a very small part having got in; whether they

---

[75] Rev. James Madison, who had gone to England in 1775 to be ordained. He was instructor in mathematics and natural philosophy in William and Mary College and after the Revolution became Protestant Episcopal bishop of Virginia.

[76] This, probably, was the news of Turgot's dismissal from the Ministry of Finance, which had occurred in May, 1776. He was strongly opposed to a war between France and Great Britain.

would attempt any thing before they came, they are uncertain, but they are sure they will as soon as they arrive, if not before.

They say from what they could collect from the conversation of Officers &ca. they mean to Hem us in by getting above us and cutting off all communication with the Country. That this is their plan, seems to be corroborated and confirmed by the circumstances of some Ships of War going out at different times within a few days past and other Vessels.

It is probable that part are to go round and come up the Sound. Mr. Maddison says Lord Howe's powers were not known when he left England. That General Conway[77] moved before his departure, that they might be laid before the Commons and had his motion rejected by large Majority. I have the Honor &c.

## GENERAL ORDERS

Head Quarters, New York, August 9, 1776.

Parole Lexington.    Countersign Maryland.

Capt. Lieut. Sergeant[78] of the Artillery, with two Field Pieces, to attach himself to General Heath's Brigade, with the Ammunition Carts, as ordered by Col Knox; while time will permit, he must manœuvre with the Regiments of the Brigade, and practise as much as possible. The Horses not to be taken away from the Carts, but kept with the driver in some convenient place contigious to the Brigade so as to be ready at a moments warning.

Capt. Lieut. Carpenter[79] to do the same with Lord Stirling's Brigade.

Capt. Lieut. Johnson[80] to do the same with General Spencer's Brigade.

---

[77] Gen. Henry Seymour Conway.
[78] Capt.-Lieut. Winthrop Sargent.
[79] Capt.-Lieut. Benajah Carpenter, of Knox's artillery.
[80] Capt.-Lieut. William Johnson, of Steven's New York artillery.

Capt. Lieut. Crane[81] to do the same with General Fellows Brigade.

An Ammunition Cart is provided for each Regiment with spare Cartridges; these Carts are immediately to join the several regiments to which they belong and keep with them in some safe place near the regiment.

The Quarter Master General to have the Water Casks replenished.

The Commissary General to deliver to the Colonel of each regiment, Rum in the proportion of half a pint to a man; the Colonel to make a return of the number of his men for this purpose, and see that it is properly dealt out, by putting it under the care of a very discreet officer.

As there are some regiments yet deficient in Arms, The General directs, that the Colonels, or commanders of regiments, see what good Arms there are, belonging to the sick, and put them into the hands of those who are well; if there should still be a deficiency, they are then to apply to the Adjutant General.

The General Officers to be at Head Quarters, this evening at Six o'clock precisely.

The General exhorts every man, both officer and soldier, to be prepared for action, to have his arms in the best order, not to wander from his encampment or quarters; to remember what their Country expects of them, what a few brave men have lately done in South Carolina, against a powerful Fleet and Army; to acquit themselves like men and with the blessing of heaven on so just a Cause we cannot doubt of success.

Nicholas Fish Esqr. is appointed Brigade Major to General Scott; he is to be obeyed and respected accordingly.

Col Glover and Col Smallwoods Regiments are to be under the immediate direction of Brigadier General Sullivan 'till some further arrangement is made of the brigades.

---

[81] Capt.-Lieut. Joseph Crane, of Knox's artillery.

## To COLONEL LEWIS DUBOIS

Head Quarters, New York, August 9, 1776.

Sir: Your Letter of the 5th. by your Brother is received; by him I forward you 800 Dollars, would have you order your Regiment to March for this place,[82] as fast as any Officer's party are enlisted. you will make a return to me immediately, if the Number of men already embodied, and Continue to make your returns, by which you may call for money as wanted. I conceive that taking Men from the 4 or 5 Month's Militia, will not answer our present Necessity, as it will not add to the Number in Service; but of the Militia, which is only ordered in for a few days or Weeks, you have an undoubted right, to take such as have a mind to inlist with you. Previous to your men arriving in this City, you will order a field Officer here, to take Charge of them, as they come in. I am, etc.

## To COLONEL ANN HAWKES HAY[83]

Head Quarters, New York, August 10, 1776.

Sir: Your favours of the 2nd. and 7th. Instt. are duly received; the Commissary General, to whom I had refered the matter of your Appointment, was to have wrote and desired you to undertake the Business; since which it is determined those Troops under General Clinton, are to march to Kingsbridge, and of Consequence will receive their supplies from the General Store there. It cannot be long, before matters may take a Capital turn this way; the Issue will determine whether a Post from your part of the Country is necessary or otherways. Any movements of the Enemy which you think may be of Consequence, I shall be obliged if you will transmit me. I am etc.

---

[82] Dubois's Fifth New York Regiment was then at Poughkeepsie.
[83] Hay, then at Haverstraw, was a colonel of New York Militia. Later he was appointed a deputy commissary general in the Continental Army.

## To CAPTAIN RICHARD VARICK

Head Quarters, New York, August 10, 1776.

Sir: Your Letter of the 5th. Instant, with its several enclosures is come safe to hand, and I now enclose you a list from the Colo. of Artillery and Quarter Master General, of what is and will be forwarded from this place, which is all that can be procured. there was some Duck arrived at Providence, out of which I have requested Governor Cooke to supply the Northern Army, provided it's not otherways disposed of. The Water Communication being yet stoped makes it exceeding difficult to transport these Articles to Albany. I am &c.

## To TIMOTHY EDWARDS

Head Quarters, New York, August 10, 1776.

Sir: This will be delivered you by Saml. and John two of our friends of the Stockbridge Indians, who have been here and expressed the desire of their People, to become part of the Army of the United States. Having wrote you fully on the 7th. Inst. and transmitted a Copy of the Resolution of Congress upon this Subject, which I presume will have reached you before this comes to hand, I have referred them to you for Information, in the Instance of their Application, and have only to request the favor of your early attention to what I then recommended to your care and direction. I am &c.

## GENERAL ORDERS

Head Quarters, New York, August 10, 1776.

Parole New-Castle.   Countersign Onslow.

Great Complaints are made of the soldiers taking away the flat bottom'd Boats, which may now be wanted for the most important purposes; The General absolutely forbids any person medling with them, at the place where they are stationed but by order of General Putnam, in writing, or by one of his Aids-de-Camp; and the officer of the main guard is to detach a Sub-altern, and thirty men, who are to mount Guard over them, taking farther Orders from General Putnam. The General will be much obliged to every officer, or soldier, who seeing them out of their places, will bring them to their station.

## GENERAL ORDERS

Head Quarters, New York, August 11, 1776.
Parole Portsmouth.   Countersign Roxbury.

No Furlough, or Discharges, are after this day to be granted to officers or soldiers without the knowledge and consent of the Commander in Chief—When an Action is hourly expected, a case must be very extraordinary which can warrant an application of this kind; but if such should happen, the Colonels are to satisfy their Brigadiers in it first; the Brigadiers if they concur in it, are then to apply to Head Quarters from whence only Furloughs are to be issued 'till further orders.

The Hon. The Continental Congress having been pleased to allow a Pay Master, to each of the established Regiments, and directed the General to appoint them; he desires the Field Officers of each Regiment, to recommend to him suitable persons; they are to be persons of Integrity and Fidelity; good Accomptants and fair Writers—The Pay is Twenty-six dollars and two thirds pr Kalander Month.

When a prisoner is put under guard, the officer sending him, is not only to put down the crime he stands charged with, but the regiment and company to which he belongs; and he should also note the Witnesses names to prove the charge.

The Court Martial to sit to morrow, as a Court of enquiry, upon Lieut. Mesier,[84] of Col Lashers Regiment, for misbehaviour to his superior officer.

Joseph Martin of Capt. Hurds[85] Company, Col Silliman's Regt., tried by a General Court Martial of which Col. Wyllys was president for "abusing and robbing a woman in the market"—acquitted for want of evidence.

Hugh Cahaggan (a transient person) and Richard Keif, belonging to Col Nicholsons[86] Regiment, convicted by the same Court Martial of "stealing a Coat and several Firelocks from Capt. Dickson's[87] Company" were sentenced to receive Thirty-nine Stripes each—The General approves the above sentences—orders Martin to be discharged, and the sentences upon Cahaggan and Keif to be executed to morrow morning at Guard mounting. A Drummer from each Regiment in General Wadworths Brigade, to attend the executing the sentence upon Cahaggan, and then he is to be turned out of the camp, and taken up if ever found in it again.

The practice of Sentries setting down while on their post is so unsoldierly that the General is ashamed to see it prevail so much in the army—At Night especially, it is of the most dangerous consequence, as it occasions a Sentinel's sleeping on his post, when otherwise he would be watchful—The General requests the officers, especially those of Guards and visiting Rounds, to caution the soldiers against it, and have all conveniences for that purpose removed. Officers and Soldiers be very careful in case of damp weather, to have their Arms kept dry, and fit for action.

---

[84] Lieut. Abraham Mesier.
[85] Capt. Nathan Hurd.
[86] Col. John Nicholson's New York regiment.
[87] Capt. David Dickson, of Lasher's New York regiment.

## *To RUFUS PUTNUM

New York, August 11, 1776.

Sir: I have the pleasure to inform you that Congress have appointed you an Engineer with the Rank of Colonel, and pay of Sixty Dollars pr. Month.

I beg of you to hasten the Sinking of Vessels and other obstructions in the River at Fort Washington as fast as it is possible; advise Genl. Putnam constantly of the kind of Vessels you want and other things that no delays that can possibly be avoided may happen. I am, etc.

P. S. Congress have just sent two French Gentn. here as Engineers will either of them be of use at Fort Washington or Kings Bridge.[88]

## To GOVERNOR JONATHAN TRUMBULL

New York, August 11, 1776.

Sir: Necessity obliges me to trouble your honor with some more suspected persons, whose Characters are such, as to make it unsafe for them to remain at their usual places of abode on Long Island; and there is no retreat in this Province, where they may not do some Mischief, or be less secure than our safety requires. As they are apprehended merely on Suspicion, arising from a General line of Conduct, unfriendly to the American Cause, I have given them reason to suspect from you, every Indulgence which your good judgment will admit you to allow them, consistent with the public Safety; there are few of them who will not defray their own Expences; and those few, their Companions of better Circumstances will assist, if Convenience will admit their being together in the same Place, which will

---

[88] The original letter is in the library of Marietta College, Marietta, Ohio.

be a Saving to the Public. If there are any quite destitute, I presume they must be put on the footing with other Prisoners in like Circumstances; They express a very Earnest desire to be permitted to choose their own Lodgings and accomodations, to which I see no objection. but as I have referred them intirely to you, I do not choose to enter into any Engagement on this or any other point; only adding, generally, that I could wish they might have every accomodation and Indulgence, having a Respect to their rank and Education, which may be deemed Consistent with Safety; And they are given to understand, that your humanity and Politeness will most effectually prevent their being liable to any unnecessary Hardships. I am etc.

P. S. I am just informed that Judge Jones[89] has obtained some Letters of Recommendation to Connecticut, from which he expects to be permitted to stay at New Haven, unless very particular Circumstances should require it. I cannot but think you will agree with me, that these Prisoners should be removed from Sea Port and Post Towns, as the intention of removal from hence is not fully answered, while they have opportunities of carrying on Correspondence.

## To THE NEW YORK LEGISLATURE

New York, August 11, 1776.

Gentn.: In Answer to your favor of the 9th., with which I have been honored; I beg leave to inform you, that I neither wish or expect any thing more, than that the Levies raised by you, will be in Continental Pay, from the time they were called into

---

[89] Judge Thomas Jones, of the New York Supreme Court. He had been arrested in June, 1776, and paroled; again arrested in August, he was sent to Connecticut and again released on parole. He was arrested again in 1779. His case was one of unnecessary aggravation and was more of a persecution than a patriotic necessity. Judge Jones married Anne de Lancey and owned valuable real estate in New York City. He finally went to England. His history of New York during the Revolution is a work of merit.

Service. That Troops employed in a General Cause, should be supported at the General Expense, is so evidently just, that I cannot see any objection to it.

It is true, when the proceedings of your Honble. Body for raising these Levies, were first Communicated to me, and it was mentioned by the Committee who brought them, that it was expected they would be paid by the States; I did not think myself Authorised to take into Service so large a Number of Men, and therefore could not say the States would pay them. But the Situation of our affairs being much changed and requiring their Service, I cannot but consider them as much Intitled to Continental Pay as any Troops in this Army. In this light I am persuaded Congress will View them, It is so obvious and so equitable, that no application from me can be necessary. The Bounty I imagine, as you yourselves do, will be the expence of the State, for which Indemnification will not be made by the Public. My Letter of the 8th was not meant to Comprehend this Subject; It was particularly design'd to explain my Ideas of the authority from whence Genl. Clinton's powers were derived.

I have requested Mr. Trumbull, to take the directions of the Commissaries and to see that the Levies are properly supplied with Provisions. I am extremely Concerned that the Quotas of Men to be furnished by the Neighbouring States, have proved so deficient. The busy Season and Harvest, to which it has been ascribed, being now over in a great degree; I flatter myself from the zeal they have heretofore Manifested, they will afford every possible Assistance, they are well apprized of the Importance of this State, in the present Contest and the Necessity of maintaining it against the attempts of the Enemy.

In respect to the Militia of Albany County, as you are pleased in your proceedings of the 10th. Inst., to submit the propriety of Calling them out, to my determination; I wou'd advise, that they should not, unless the Necessity for bringing them here should be extremely great; They otherwise should remain in their County, to afford succour to the Frontier Parts of the Government, If it should be Necessary. I have Inclosed a Copy of Lt. McMichael's report transmitted me by Genl Schuyler, from whence it will appear, If the Intelligence contained in it be true, that their aid may be required there.

I have desired Genl. Greene, on the Application of the Committee sent to Kings County, to afford them every Assistance he conveniently can, for executing the business they are upon.[90]

Before I conclude, I would observe, the Letter of the 9th. which I have acknowledged to have received, is without any Signature; I presume it has been omitted thro' the hurry of Business. I have the Honor to be with great respect.

## To THE COMMITTEE OF QUEENS COUNTY, NEW YORK

Head Quarters, New York, August 11, 1776.

Gentn.: The public exigencies, having required my apprehending a number of suspected Persons in your County and sending them into another Colony, for a short time; they have expressed some apprehensions that in their Absence their property may be exposed to Injury, and their Family's deprived of the Support they would otherwise derive from it. I therefore beg leave to acquaint you, that a Temporary Restraint of their persons, is all that is intended by the present Measure; and that it would give me much pain, if it should be construed to extend to any depredation of property; that Matter resting intirely within the Jurisdiction of the Civil Authority of the Province.

---

[90] A committee of the New York Legislature was ordered to investigate conditions in Kings County, to seize all arms from the disaffected, arrest them, remove or destroy their grain, and, if necessary, lay waste to the whole country. Greene was to furnish the needed military assistance.

Until therefore some Orders are received from them to that Effect, I shall be happy in believing, you will exert your whole Power and Influence, to prevent the Mischief which these Gentlemen seem to apprehend. I am, etc.

### To MAJOR GENERAL ARTEMAS WARD

Head Quarters, New York, August 12, 1776.

Dear Sir: Your letter of the 4th. Instant, is safe to hand. an answer to the several particulars it contains, will be given soon, time will but allow me, to request your forwarding with all possible dispatch, two 13 Inch Sea Mortars, of the best in Boston, to this place, with their Beds and every thing compleat. I am &c.

### To THE PRESIDENT OF CONGRESS

New York, August 12, 1776.

Sir: I have been duly honored with your favours of the 8th and 10th Instant, with their several inclosures. I shall pay attention to the Resolution respecting Lieut. Josiah[91] and attempt to relieve him from his rigorous Usage. Your Letters to such of the Gentlemen as were here have been delivered, the rest will be sent by the first Opportunity.

Since my last of the 8 and 9th. the Enemy have made no movements of consequence:—They remain nearly in the same state nor have we any further Intelligence of their designs, they have not yet been joined by the remainder of the Fleet with the Hessian Troops.

Col: Smallwood and his Battalion got in on Friday and Col: Miles is also here with two Battalions more of Pennsylvania Riflemen. The Convention of this State have been exerting themselves to call forth a portion of their Militia to an

---

[94] Lieut. James Josiah, of the Continental Navy. By resolve of Congress (August 7) Washington was directed to propose the exchange of Josiah and to remonstrate to Lord Howe on the cruelty of his treatment.

Encampment forming above Kings Bridge, to remain in service for the space of one Month after their arrival there, and also half of those in King's and Queen's Counties to reinforce the Troops on Long Island, till the 1st. of September, unless sooner discharged. General Morris too is to take post with his Brigade on the Sound and Hudsons River for ten days, to annoy the Enemy in case they attempt to land, and others of their Militia are directed to be in readiness in case their aid should be required.[92] Upon the whole from the information I have from the Convention, the Militia ordered, are now in motion or will be in a little time and will amount to about three thousand or more.

From Connecticut I am not certain what succours are coming: By one or two Gentlemen who have come from thence I am told some of the Militia were assembling and from the Intelligence they had would march this Week.

By a Letter from Governor Trumbull of the 5th., I am advised that the Troops from that State, destined for the Northern Army, had marched for Skeenesborough. General Ward too, by a letter of the 4th. informs me, that the two Regiments would march from Boston last Week having been cleansed and generally recovered from the small Pox. I have also countermanded my orders to Col: Elmore and directed him to join the Northern Army having heard after my Orders to Connecticut for his marching hither, that he and most of his Regiment were at Albany or within its Vicinity. General Ward mentions that the Council of Massachusetts State will have in, from two to three Thousand of their Militia to defend their Lines and different

---

[92] Each militiaman in default of arms was to bring a shovel, spade, pickax, etc. One-fifth of the militia from Albany County were ordered to march immediately to the encampment north of Kings Bridge; and whenever the whole of the militia of any county should march, they were ordered, by the New York Legislature, to bring with them all the disarmed and disaffected male inhabitants, from 16 to 55 years of age, who should serve as fatiguemen to the respective regiments.

posts in lieu of the Regiments ordered from thence, agreeable to the Resolution of Congress.

The inclosed Copy of a Resolve of the Convention, of the State passed the 10th. instant, will discover the apprehension they are under of the defection of the Inhabitants of Kings County from the Common Cause, and of the Measures they have taken there upon. I have directed General Greene to give the Committee such Assistance, as he can and they may require, in the Execution of their Commission. tho' at the same time I wish the Information the Convention have received upon the Subject may prove groundless.

I would beg leave to mention to Congress, that in a Letter I received from General Lee, he mentions the valuable consequences that would result from a Number of Cavalry being employed in the Southern Department; without them, to use his own expressions, he can answer for nothing; with one thousand he would ensure the safety of those States. I should have done myself the honor of submiting this matter to Congress before at his particular request, had it not escaped my mind. From his acquaintance with that Country, and the Nature of the Grounds, I doubt not he has weighed the matter well, and presume he has fully represented the advantages that would arise from the Establishment of such a Corps. All I mean is, in compliance with his requisition, to mention the matter, that such considerations may be had upon it, If not already determined,[93] that it may be deserving of.

I have transmitted a General Return, whereby Congress will perceive the whole of our Strength, except the two Battalions under Col: Miles, which coming since it was made out are not included.

---

[93] Congress had already ordered (August 8) that General Lee be called from the South. Hancock's letter to Washington notifying him of Lee's recall, dated August 8, 1776, is in the *Washington Papers*.

I have inclosed a Letter just come to hand from Martinique. Congress will please to consider of the purport, favouring me with their Answer and a Return of the Letter.

This Moment (10. O Clock) report is made by General Greene, that a Man of War came in Yesterday, and that Sixty Sail of Ships are now standing in; no doubt they are a further part of the Hessian Troops. I have the Honor to be etc.[94]

## To THE PRESIDENT OF CONGRESS

New York, August 12, 1776.

Sir: This will be handed you by Colo. Campbell[95] from the Northern Army, whom the Inclosed Letter and proceedings of a Genl. Court Martial will shew to have been in arrest and tried for Sundry matters charged against him. As the Court Martial was by Order of the Commander in that department; the Facts committed there, the Trial there, I am much at a loss to know why the proceedings were referred to me to approve or disapprove. As my Interfering in the matter would carry much Impropriety with It, and shew a want of regard to the Rules and practice in such Instances, and as Colo. Campbell is going to Philadelphia, I have submitted the whole of the proceedings to the consideration of Congress for their decision upon his case, perfectly convinced that such determination will be had therein as will be right and Just. I have the honor to be, etc.[96]

## To THE NEW YORK LEGISLATURE

Head Quarters, New York, August 12, 1776.

Gentn.: As the time is certainly near at hand, and may be hourly expected, which is to decide the fate of this City and the Issue of this Campaign; I thought it highly improper, that

---

[94] In the writing of Robert Hanson Harrison.
[95] Col. Donald Campbell was deputy quartermaster general of the Northern Department.
[96] In the writing of Robert Hanson Harrison.

persons of suspected Characters should remain in places, where
their opportunities of doing Mischief were much greater, than
in the Enemies Camp. I therefore have Caused a number of
them to be apprehended and removed to some distance; there
to remain until this Crisis is passed. Having formerly mentioned this Subject to your Honble. Body, I would not again
trouble them in a business, which former Connections, Obli-
gations, and Interests must make very unpleasant, and which,
I apprehend, must have been in danger of failing in the
execution, unless done with all possible Secrecy and dispatch.
I postponed this most disagreeable duty till the last moment;
but the Claims of the Army upon me, an application from a
number of well affected Inhabitants, concurring with my own
Opinion, obliged me to enter upon it while time and Circumstances would admit. I have ordered a very strict attention to
be paid to the Necessities of the Gentlemen apprehended and
to their comfortable accomodations in every respect, both here
and at the Places of their Destination. I have also wrote to
the Committee of Queens County, that this step is not to be
construed as making their property liable to any Injury or ap-
propriation, unless they should receive directions from your
Honble. Body, to whom I have referred them on this Subject;
being resolved in all cases, where the most absolute necessity
does not require it, to confine myself wholly to that Line, which
shall exclude every Idea of interfering with the Authority of
the State.

Some of these Gentlemen have expressed doubts and raised
difficulties, from Engagements they lay under to your Honorable Body, or some Committees; they do not appear to me to
deserve much attention, as they cannot, with any propriety, be
charged with a breach of any Parole under their present Circumstances; but I beg leave to Submit to your Consideration
the propriety of removing the pretence. I am, etc.

## GENERAL ORDERS

Head Quarters, New York, August 12, 1776.
Parole Stowe.   Countersign Temple.

The business of granting passes proving burthensome to Messrs. Berrien, Ray and Wilmot; three others are added to them, viz: William Goforth, John Campbell and Samuel Cowperthwaite, any passes signed by either of them are to be allowed.

The Hon. The Continental Congress have been pleased to appoint the following Gentlemen, Majors General of the Army of the United States. viz:

William Heath Esqr.
Joseph Spencer Esqr.
John Sullivan Esqr.
Nathaniel Greene Esqr.

And the following Gentlemen Brigadier Generals.

James Reed Esqr.
Col John Nixon.
Col Arthur St. Clair.
Col Alexander McDougall.
Col Samuel Holden Parsons.
Col James Clinton.

They are to be obeyed and respected accordingly.

Jacob Jones in Capt. Stenrods[97] Company, late Col McDougall's Regiment; tried by a Court Martial whereof Col Wyllys was President, and convicted of "sleeping on his post"; sentenced to receive Thirty Stripes—The General approves the Sentence and orders it to be executed at the usual time and place.

A quantity of spears being arrived, the General Officers commanding posts, where they may be wanted, are to make Report, and draw for them through the Adjutant General.

---

[97] Capt. Cornelius Stenrod, of the First New York Regiment.

AFTER ORDERS

That as little shifting of regiments, and change of Alarm posts may take place, as possible at a time when an attack may be hourly expected, The General orders and directs that the following arrangement of the Army in consequence of the late promotions shall take place 'till some new disposition can be made. Viz:

Glover's, Smallwood's, Mile's and Atley's[98] Regiments; to compose one Brigade, and be under the Command of Brigadier Lord Stirling.

Late Nixon's, Prescott's, Varnum's, Little's and Hand's Regiments; to form another Brigade, and be commanded by Brigd. Genl. Nixon.

Late McDougall's, Ritzema's and Webb's Regts. and the Artificers; to be another Brigade, under the command of General McDougall.

Late Parsons's, Huntington's, Ward's, Wyllys's and Durkee's, Regiments; to compose another Brigade, under the command of General Parsons.

Late Clinton's, Reads, Baileys, Baldwins, and Learned's Regiments; to be another Brigade, commanded by Brigadier General James Clinton.

Sergeant's, Hutchinson's, and Hitchcock's Regiments; to be added to General Mifflin's Brigade: General Heards whole Brigade is to move over to Long Island. Col Gays[99] Regiment is to join his Brigade in the City of New York. Col Hitchcocks Regiment is to relieve the detachment at Burdetts Ferry, where it is to remain, and receive orders from Brigadier Mifflin. Lord Stirling, and the Colonels of the Regiments in his Brigade, are to fix upon a Brigade parade, convenient to the several

[98] Col. Samuel John Atlee, of the Pennsylvania Musket Battalion.
[99] Col. Fisher Gay, of a Connecticut State regiment. He died Sept. 27, 1776.

encampments thereof—General McDougall is to do the same with his Colonels; All the other Brigades, Parades, and Alarm Posts are to be as last settled.

The Brigadier Generals, James Clinton, Scott and Fellows, are to be under the immediate Command of Major General Putnam. The Brigadiers Mifflin and George Clinton's Brigades, to be commanded by Major General Heath. Brigadiers, Parsons and Wadworth's Brigades to be under the Command of Major General Spencer. Brigadiers Nixon and Heards Brigade to be commanded by Major General Greene 'till General James Clinton can join his Brigade at this place. Col Read is to command it. Under this disposition, formed as well as times will allow, the united efforts of the officers, of every Rank, and the Soldiers, with the smiles of providence, The General hopes to render a favourable account to his Country, and Posterity of the enemy, whenever they chuse to make the appeal to the great Arbiter of the universe.

Lieut Col Tylor[1] is appointed Colonel of the Regiment late Parsons, and Major Prentice[2] Lieut. Colonel thereof.

Lieut. Col Durkee is also appointed Colonel of the regiment late Arnolds, and Major Knowlton Lieut. Col of said regiment.

The Congress have likewise been pleased to appoint Rufus Putnam Esqr. an Engineer and have given him the Rank of Colonel in the army.

Major Henly[3] (for the present) is to do duty as Brigade Major in General James Clinton's Brigade. Major Box[4] in General Nixon's; Major Livingston[5] in Lord Stirling's, and

---

[1] Col. John Tyler, of the Tenth Continental Infantry.
[2] Lieut. Col. Samuel Prentiss, of the Tenth Connecticut Infantry.
[3] Maj. David Henley, then with General Heath.
[4] Brigade Major Daniel Box, of the Rhode Island Militia. He was badly injured by a fall from his horse in December, 1776.
[5] Maj. William Smith Livingston.

Major Peck[6] in General Parsons's; and Richard Platt Esqr. is: to do the duty of Brigade Major in General McDougall's—All of which are to be considered and obeyed as such.

## GENERAL ORDERS

Head Quarters, New York, August 13, 1776.
Parole Weymouth.   Countersign York.

Thomas Henly and Israel Keith Esqrs. are appointed Aid-de-Camps to Major General Heath; they are to be respected and obeyed accordingly.

The Court Martial to sit to morrow, for the tryal of Lieut. Holcomb of Capt. Anderson's Company, Col Johnson's Regiment, under Arrest for "assuming the Rank of a Captain and mounting Guard as such."

The Colonels of the several Regiments, or commanding officers, are to send their Quarter Masters to the Laboratory for the Ammunition Cart to be attached to each Regiment with spare Ammunition; to have it posted in some safe and proper place near the Regiment so as to be ready at a moments warning— The Horse and Driver, to be also kept near the regiment. It is the Quarter Master's duty to attend to this and in case of action to see the Cartridges delivered as they are wanted.

The Enemy's whole reinforcement is now arrived, so that an Attack must, and will soon be made; The General therefore again repeats his earnest request, that every officer, and soldier, will have his Arms and Ammunition in good Order, keep within their quarters and encampment, as much as possible; be ready for action at a moments call; and when called to it, remember that Liberty, Property, Life and Honor, are all at stake; that upon their Courage and Conduct, rest the hopes

---

[6] Brigade Major William Peck, then with General Spencer.

of their bleeding and insulted Country; that their Wives, Children and Parents, expect Safety from them only, and that we have every reason to expect Heaven will crown with Success, so just a cause. The enemy will endeavour to intimidate by shew and appearance, but remember how they have been repulsed, on various occasions, by a few brave Americans; Their Cause is bad; their men are conscious of it, and if opposed with firmness, and coolness, at their first onsett, with our advantage of Works, and Knowledge of the Ground; Victory is most assuredly ours. Every good Soldier will be silent and attentive, wait for Orders and reserve his fire, 'till he is sure of doing execution. The Officers to be particularly careful of this. The Colonels, or commanding Officers of Regiments, are to see their supernumerary officers so posted, as to keep the men to their duty; and it may not be amiss for the troops to know, that if any infamous Rascal, in time of action, shall attempt to skulk, hide himself or retreat from the enemy without orders of his commanding Officer; he will instantly be shot down as an example of Cowardice: On the other hand, the General solemnly promises, that he will reward those who shall distinguish themselves, by brave and noble actions; and he desires every officer to be attentive to this particular, that such men may be afterwards suitably noticed.

General Greene to send for ten of the flat bottomed Boats which are to be kept under Guard at Long Island: No Person to meddle with them, but by his special order.

Thirty seven Men (Sailors) are wanted for the Gallies.

Eighty men properly officered and used to the Sea, are wanted to go up to Kingsbridge, with the ships and rafts. They are to be furnished immediately and parade with Blankets and Provision, but without Arms, at General Putnam's at two o'Clock, and take orders from him.

John Gardner of Capt. Trowbridges[7] Company, Col Huntington's Regiment, tried by a General Court Martial, whereof Col Wyllys was President and convicted of "Desertion", ordered to receive Thirty-nine lashes.

John Morgan of Capt Johnson's[8] Company, Col. McDougall's Regiment, tried by the same Court Martial and convicted of "sleeping on his post,"—sentenced to receive Thirty lashes.

Francis Claudge of Capt. Speakmans[9] Company, Col. Glovers Regiment, tried by the same Court Martial and convicted of Desertion and re-inlistment—sentenced to receive Thirty-nine lashes; thirteen each day successively.

The General approves each of the above Sentences and orders them to be executed at the usual times and places.

The Court of inquiry having reported that Lieut. Mesier had behaved unbecoming an officer to one of superior Rank; the Court directed a Court Martial, unless he ask pardon of the officer he affronted: But that officer having represented to the General, that he is willing to pass it over. The General, at his request, orders Lieut. Mesier to be discharged.

AFTER ORDERS

Col Miles and Col Brodhead's Regiments of Riflemen, to discharge and clean their rifles, to morrow at Troop beating, under the inspection of their officers.

Col Smallwoods and Col Atlee's Battalions, of Musquetry, to fire at the same time, with loose powder and ball.

## To THE PRESIDENT OF CONGRESS

New York, August 13, 1776.

Sir: As there is reason to believe, that but little Time will elapse before the Enemy make their Attack, I have thought it

---

[7] Capt. Caleb Trowbridge, of the Seventeenth Continental Infantry.
[8] Capt. John Johnson, of the First New York Regiment.
[9] Capt. Gilbert Warner Speakman, of the Fourteenth Continental Infantry.

advisable to remove all the papers in my hands respecting the Affairs of the States, from this place. I hope the Event will shew the precaution was unnecessary, but yet prudence required that It should be done, lest by any Accident they might fall into their Hands.

They are all contained in a large Box nailed up and committed to the care of Lieutenant Colonel Reed,[10] Brother of the Adjutant General, to be delivered to Congress, in whose Custody I would beg leave to deposit them, until our Affairs shall be so circumstanced as to admit of their return.

The Enemy since my Letter of Yesterday have received a further Augmentation of thirty Six Ships to their fleet, making the whole that have arrived since Yesterday Morning ninety Six. I have the Honor &ca.

P. S. I would observe that I have sent off the Box privately that It might raise no disagreable Ideas and have enjoined Colo. Reed to Secrecy.[11]

### *To COLONEL THOMAS McKEAN[12]

Head Quarters, New York, August 13, 1776.

Sir: In answer to that part of your Letter of the 10th. Instt. whether, "when a Brigade is drawn up, and the oldest Colonel takes the Right, his Battalion is to be on the right with him; that is, whether the Colonel gives rank to the Battalion" I shall inform you, that to the best of my Military knowledge a Regiment never looses its Rank, consequently can derive none from its Colonel, nor loose any by having the youngest Colonel in the Army appointed to the Comd. of it. The oldest Regiment

[10] Lieut. Col. James(?) Reed, of the Pennsylvania Militia.
[11] In the writing of Robert Hanson Harrison.
[12] Of the Pennsylvania Militia. He was a Signer of the Declaration of Independence; a Delegate to Congress from Delaware and president of that body in 1781; President of Delaware, 1777; chief justice of Pennsylvania, 1777–1799; Governor of Pennsylvania, 1799–1808. He died in Philadelphia in 1817.

therefore although Commanded by the youngest Colo. is placed on the Right and the Colonel with it.

I am exceedingly sorry to hear that a Spirit of Desertion prevails among the Pensylvania Association at a time when the Cause of liberty has such a claim upon their Services, and every appearance of danger to it, invites their aid.

I thank you my good Sir for your kind and Affectionate Wishes; the day of Tryal, which will, in some measure decide the Fate of America is near at hand, and I am happy in informing of you, that a noble spirit (as far as I can judge of it) seems to prevade this Army. If we should be beaten (our numbers among friends being unequal to those of the Enemy) it will not be, I flatter myself, till after some hard knocks; which will not be very soon recovered of by the Enemy. But that superintending Providence, which needs not the aid of numbers, will lead us I hope to a more fortunate Event. With respect and esteem I am etc.

P. S. Perhaps I may not have fully understood the tendency of the question propounded to me, and consequently have given an indecisive answer; the Idea I meant to convey is this, that the Regiment takes Rank from the time it is raised, and can not be depriv'd of that Rank by the change of its Colonel; if therefore three Regiments should be formed into a Brigade the eldest of those Regiments will take the Right, although it is Commanded by the Youngest Colo., but if there shd. be no Genl. Officer to Comd. these three Regiments the Senior Colonel of course does it, not the Colonel of the Senior Regiment. In short, the Rank of a Colonel, and the Rank of a Regiment are distinct things; the first takes Rank from the date of his Commission (when in Service with those of the same denomination) the later from the time of raising. If three Regiments therefore should be Incamp'd together and no superior Officer to that of Colonel the oldest of the Colonels will Comd. those three Regiments.                                        [H.S.P.]

## To MAJOR GENERAL PHILIP SCHUYLER

New York, August 13, 1776.

Dear Sir: Your Letter of the 6 Instant I received this Morning by Bennet. The reports made by the emissaries, who have been among the Indian Nations, appear not so promising, as I could wish. However I trust, as so many have come to the Treaty, their views are Friendly, and tho' they may not consent to take an Active part, that they will not arm against us. The Difficulties attending the Vessels fitting for the Lakes, I am well apprised of, my late Letters will inform you, that I have taken every measure in my power to facilitate the work. Before this comes to hand, the Pay master I expect will have received a supply of money. The Extract of Mr. Varicks Letter shews it was much wanted, I have not failed in any Instance, to communicate your wants of this Article to Congress, when they have been mentioned to me; Urging at the same time, not only the Expediency but the Necessity of keeping the Military Chests constantly furnished. It will be well for you, always to give them early notice of what you may have Occasion for, that their Remittances may be adequate; In future I presume they will have the fullest Information upon that Subject, having by some late Resolves, enjoined their Commanders in every Department, to transmit them monthly a List of the Warrants they grant. The paymasters to return a Weekly state of their Military Chests, and the Commissaries and Quarter Masters of what they receive. I have not these Regulations by me, but if my Memory serves, they were passed the 2nd. Instant, and have been forwarded to you. I have always laid before Congress Copies of your letters and their Inclosures, when they were of a public nature or contained Intelligence any ways material, except when advised that you had done it yourself. I shall here take Occasion to request, that whenever you write to them and me of the same things, you certify me thereof, to prevent me transmitting useless Information.

In Respect to Colo. Nicholson's Regiment[13] and the places where it should be Stationed, you certainly can determine better than I, having more in your power, Intelligence of the Enemy's Movements and Designs. I would observe in answer to that part of your letter, which mentions that a Council of Officers or a Court Martial had been convened and held here to decide upon the Council of those who had sat at Crown point, that your Information is wrong. No Council, no Court of Enquiry, nor Court Martial upon that Subject Sir, was ever convened by my Order or their own accord. when Intelligence was first received here that Crown point was abandoned, It was the cause of a general Alarm and filled the minds of most who heard it with no small degree of anxiety; some Judging from the Common accepted Opinion and others from their Knowledge and Acquaintance with it and the Country round about it, that it was of the last Importance to us to possess it, to give us, in Conjunction with the Vessels we were about to build, the Superiority of the Lake, and to prevent the Enemy from penetrating into this and the Eastern States. Among others, some of the General Officers, from their own Knowledge and the rest from the Ideas they had formed, as the Matter was Occasionally mentioned, delivered their Sentiments to this Effect,

---

[13] Col. John Nicholson's Continental Infantry appears to have been a New York militia regiment taken into the Continental service for a few months in 1776.

as did every person I heard speake of it, at the time the Account first came. From the universal Chagrin that took place, the Regret that every person expressed upon the Occasion; The Remonstrance of the Officers which you transmitted, and which appeared to contain many weighty Reasons, I felt myself much concerned as every body else did, and wished according to my Information and Opinion at that time, the post had been mentioned. I do not wish to dwell longer upon the Subject, and therefore shall only add that your Letter of the 24th. Ulto. (or at least a Copy of it) was transmitted to Congress, as soon as it was received, nor shall I have any Objection to sending a Copy of the one before me now, when I have an Opportunity to make it out, if it shall be your Inclination and request. I have no news of any Importance to Communicate, unless that the Enemy are daily becoming stronger. On Monday they received an Augmentation of Ninety eight Ships to their Fleet, with a further part of the foreign Troops it is probable. They seem to be making great preparations and we have reason to expect, they are upon the point of making at Attack. The Letters which accompany this you will be pleased to deliver to Generals Gates, Reed and St. Clair, they came to hand on Sunday, and wishing you and the Army under your Command, Health and the smiles of a kind providence on all your Efforts. I am, etc.

### To THE PRESIDENT OF CONGRESS

New York, August 14, 1776.

Sir: Since I had the honor of addressing you on Monday, nothing of Importance has occurred here, except that the Enemy have received an Augmentation to their Fleet of Ninety Six Ships; some Reports make them more.

In a Letter I wrote you Yesterday by Lieutenant Colonel Reed, I advised you of this, but presuming It may not reach you so soon as this will, I have thought proper to mention the Intelligence again.

Inclosed I have the Honor to transmit, a Copy of the Examination of a Deserter, sent me this Morning by General Mercer, to which I beg leave to refer Congress for the latest Accounts I have from the Enemy. Whether the Intelligence he has given is literally true I cannot determine, but as to the Attack we daily expect it.

Your favor of the 10th. with the Inclosures was duly received, and I have instructed the several Officers who were promoted, to Act in their Stations as you requested, tho their Commissions were not sent.

As we are in extreme want of Tents and Covering for this Army; A great part of them at outposts having nothing to shelter them; nor Houses to go in, I submit it to Congress, whether it may not be prudent to remand those that were sent to Boston lately where there are no Troops at present, and if there were, the necessity for them would not be great as the Town and Barracks at several of the posts would be sufficient to receive them.

The inclosed Letter from Lieutenant Colonel Henshaw[14] will discover to Congress his views and wishes, of which they will consider and determine on, in whatever way they think right and conducive to the Public good; meaning only to lay his Letter before them.

I take the Liberty of mentioning that Col. Varnum of Rhode Island has been with me this Morning, to resign his Commission, conceiving himself greatly injured in not having been noticed in the late Arrangement and promotion of General Officers. I remonstrated against the Impropriety of the measure at this Time, and he has consented to stay 'till affairs wear a different aspect than what they do at present.

---

[14] Lieut. Col. William Henshaw, of the Twelfth Continental Infantry.

11. O'Clock. By a report just come to hand from General Greene, Twenty Ships more are coming in. I am &ca.[15]

## To MAJOR GENERAL HORATIO GATES

New York, August 14, 1776.

Dear Sir: I yesterday Morning received your Letter of the 29th. Ulto., by Bennet the Express, and am extremely sorry to find, that the Army is still in a Sickly and melancholy State. The precaution taken to halt the Reinforcement at Skenesborough, which are destined for your Succour, is certainly prudent. They should not be exposed or made liable to the Calamities already too prevailing, unless in Cases of extreme Necessity. Doctor Stringer has been here with Doctor Morgan and is now at Philadelphia, I trust he will obtain some necessary Supplies of Medicines, which will enable him under the Smiles of Providence, to relieve your Distresses in some degree. By a Letter from General Ward, two Regiments (Whitcombs and Phinneys) were to march to your Aid Last Week, They have happily had the small Pox and will not be subject to the fatal Consequences attending that disorder.

I am glad to hear the Vessels for the Lakes are going on with such Industry. Maintaining the Superiority over the Water is certainly of infinite Importance. I trust neither Courage nor Activity will be wanting in those to whom the Business is committed.

If assigned to General Arnold none will doubt of his Exertions. In answer to those parts of your Letter, which so highly resent the Conduct of the General Officers here, I would observe, Sir, that you are under a Mistake, when you suppose a Council of Officers had sat upon those who composed the Board

---

[15] In the writing of Robert Hanson Harrison.

at Crown Point. When Intelligence was first brought, that, that post was evacuated, it spread a general Alarm and occasioned much anxiety to all who heard it, it being almost universally believed, that it was a post of the last Importance, and the only one, to give us, in Conjunction with our Naval Force, a Superiority over the Lake, and for preventing the Enemy's penetrating into this and the Eastern Governments. As this matter was occasionally mentioned, The General Officers, some from their own Knowledge, and others from the Opinion they had formed, expressed themselves to that Effect, as did all I heard speak upon the Subject. Added to this, the Remonstrance of the Officers, transmitted by General Schuyler at the same time the Account was brought, did not contribute a little to Authorize the Opinion which was Generally entertained. They surely seemed to have some reason for their support, tho' it was not meant to give the least Encouragement or Sanction to preceedings of such a Nature. Upon the whole, no event that I have been informed of for a long time, produced a more General Chagrin and Consternation. But yet there was no Council called upon the Occasion, nor Court of Enquiry, nor Court Martial, as has been Suggested by some. I will not take up more time upon the Subject, or make it a Matter of further Discussion, not doubting but those who determined that the post ought to be abandoned, conceived it would promote the Interest of the great Cause we are engaged in, the others have differed from them. By the by, I wish your Description perfectly corresponded with the real Circumstances of this Army. You will have heard, before this comes to hand most probably, of the arrival of Clinton and his Army from the Southward. They are now at Staten Island as are the whole, or the greatest part of the Hessian and foreign Troops. Since Monday, Ninety Six Ships came in, which we are informed is the last Division of Lord Howe's Fleet which touched at Hallifax, and by a Deserter, are not to land their Troops. We are in daily Expectation, that they will make their Attack, all their Movements and the advices we have, indicating that they are on the point of it. I am etc.

## To THE PRESIDENT OF CONGRESS

New York, August 14, 1776.

Sir: This will be delivered you by Captain Moeballe, a Dutch Gentleman from Surinam, who has come to the Continent with a view of entering into the Service of the States, as you will perceive by the inclosed Letters from Mr. Brown of Providence and General Greene.

What other Letters and Credentials he has, I know not, but at his request have given this Line to Congress, to whom he wishes to be introduced, and where he will make his pretensions known.

I have ordered the Quarter Master Immediately to write to Mr. Brown for the Russia Duck he mentions with directions to have it made instantly into Tents, being in great distress for want of a sufficient number to cover our Troops. I have &ca.[16]

## To BRIGADIER GENERAL JAMES CLINTON

Head Quarters, August 14, 1776.

Sir: I have the pleasure of forwarding you by this Opportunity, a Letter from Congress inclosing your Commission for a Brigadier in the Continental Army, on which appointment please to accept my hearty Congratulations.

As the post you are now at, is an Object of great Importance, and I am unacquainted with the Officers under you, must

---

[16] In the writing of Robert Hanson Harrison.

request you will remain there, till you hear further from me.[17]
I am &c.

## GENERAL ORDERS

Head Quarters, New York, August 14, 1776.
Parole America.   Countersign Liberty.

Alexander Scammell and Lewis Morris Esquires, are appointed Aids-de-Camp to Major General Sullivan; they are to be obeyed and respected accordingly.

The Divisions of the Army, under Major Generals Putnam and Sullivan, having undertaken some special works are to be omitted out of the general detail of Guards and Fatigue for the present.

The General orders three days provision to be cooked immediately, that the Soldiers have their Canteens filled, and be ready to meet the enemy on a short notice.

Such Colonels of Regiments as have not sent for their Ammunition Carts, or drawn for Rum, for the refreshment of their men, in time of action, as pr Order of the 9th. Instant, are to do it immediately, and the Quarter Master must take care that it be used properly; the allowance is half a pint pr man.

The Brigadier Generals will please to recollect, that there are a number of spears, at the Laboratory, which will be of great use at the posts, and are waiting to be distributed.

In case of Alarm, the men are immediately to repair to their usual parade, where the Roll is to be called, and then march, join in Battalion, and march to their respective alarm posts—Absentees will be considered as Cowards, and treated as such.

The General flatters himself, that every man's mind and arms are now prepared for the glorious Contest, upon which so much depends.  The time is too precious, nor does the General think

---

[17] Clinton was in command at Fort Montgomery, N. Y., on the Hudson River below West Point.

it necessary to spend it in exhorting his brave Countrymen and fellow Soldiers to behave like men, fighting for every thing that can be dear to Freemen—We must resolve to conquer, or die; with this resolution and the blessing of Heaven, Victory and Success certainly will attend us. There will then be a glorious Issue to this Campaign, and the General will reward, his brave Fellow Soldiers! with every Indulgence in his power.

The whole Line to turn out to morrow morning and march to their several Alarm posts, in all points ready for action and continue 'till nine o'clock, or further orders.

William Peck and Charles Whiting Esquires, appointed Aids-de-Camp, to Major General Spencer, they are to be respected and obeyed accordingly.

## GENERAL ORDERS

Head Quarters, New York, August 15, 1776.
Parole Charlestown.   Countersign Boston.

William S. Smith Esqr.[18] appointed to act as Aide-de-Camp to General Sullivan, during the absence of Major Scammell, and to be obeyed and respected accordingly.

Henry Williams of Capt. Parks Company, Colonel Shepard's Regiment convicted by a General Court-Martial whereof Col Wyllys was President of "Desertion"—sentenced to receive thirty-nine Lashes.

The General approves it, and orders it to be executed at the usual time and place.

Lieut. Holcomb of Capt. Anderson's Company, and Col Johnson's Regiment, tried by the same Court Martial for "assuming the rank of a Captain, wearing a yellow Cockade, and mounting Guard in that capacity"—it appearing to be done

---

[18] William Stephens Smith. He, later, became a lieutenant colonel and aide to Washington.

thro' misinformation and want of experience, the Court are of opinion, he should be cautioned by his Colonel, to make himself acquainted with his duty, and that he be released from his arrest.

The General approves thereof and orders that he be discharged.

Mr. William Caldwell is appointed Pay Master to Colo. Baldwins Regiment.

Mr. John Laurence [19] to the regiment late McDougalls.

The General directs and requests that every officer will see the mens Arms and Ammunition put in order as soon as it clears up; and for that purpose have them paraded and carefully inspected. An enemy often presumes upon neglect at such time, to make an attack.

Mr. Robert Prevost Junr. appointed Pay Master to Col. Ritzema's regiment.

Col Glover's Regiment to move to morrow to Greenwich, and join General Fellow's Brigade.

General Putnam's Division, to be put into the General detail of duty as before.

Capt. James Chapman to do duty of Major to Col Tyler's Regiment (late General Parsons's) 'till further orders.

Capt. James Mellen to do the same in Colonel Ward's regiment.

Capt. Thomas Dyer to do the duty of Brigade Major to Genl. Parsons's brigade, 'till further orders.


## To THE PRESIDENT OF CONGRESS

New York, August 15, 1776.

Sir: As the Situation of the Two Armies must Engage the attention of Congress and lead them to expect, that each returning

---

[19] John Lawrence. He, later, became Judge Advocate General of the Continental Army.

day will produce some Important Events, This is meant to Inform them that nothing of Moment has yet cast up. In the Evening of Yesterday there were great movements among their Boats and from the Number that appeared to be passing and repassing about the Narrows, we were induced to believe they intended to land a part of their Forces upon Long Island, but having no report from thence from General Greene, I presume they have not done it. I have the Honor &ca.

P. S. Your favor of the 13th. was received by Yesterday's Post. I wrote on Monday by the Return Express, as you supposed.[20]

## To GOVERNOR JONATHAN TRUMBULL

Head Quarters, New York, August 16, 1776.

Sir: I have been obliged to trouble you with some more disaffected persons, whose Residence here was dangerous to the American Interest; I trust I have now done with them, at least for the present, and hope you will excuse the disagreeable Necessity I have been under, of Soliciting your care and attention to provide for them and dispose of them. As the Case of these differs in no respect from that of those before sent, I presume they will be put under the same Regulations. I am etc.

## To THE PRESIDENT OF CONGRESS

New York, August 16, 1776.

Sir: I beg leave to inform you, that since I had the pleasure of addressing you Yesterday, nothing interesting between the two Armies had happened. Things remain nearly in the situation they then were.

It is with peculiar regret and concern, that I have the Opportunity of mentioning to Congress the Sickly condition of our

---

[20] In the writing of Robert Hanson Harrison.

Troops. In some Regiments there are not any of the Field Officers capable of doing duty. In Others the duty extremely difficult for want of a sufficient number. I have been Obliged to Nominate some, 'till Congress transmit the Appointments of those they wish to succeed to the several Vacancies occasioned by the late Promotions. This being a matter of some consequence, I presume will have their early attention, and that they will fill up the several Vacancies, also mentioned in the List I had the Honor of transmitting some few days ago to the Board of War. I am Sir &ca.[21]

### To THE NEW JERSEY LEGISLATURE

Head Quarters, August 16, 1776.

Gentn.: I am informed, that in Consequence of my Letter acquainting you that a number of Persons deemed unfriendly to the Interests of America, were suspected of holding a Correspondence with the Enemy from Shrewsbury and its Neighbourhood; Mr. Isaac Low late of this City has been apprehended, and is now detained under some kind of Confinement.

Since that time, I have received Satisfaction with respect to this Gentleman, who I find has also entered into a Contract with the Congress for the Supply of a great quantity of European Goods; I should therefore be glad that any restraint laid upon him, merely upon my Representation, might be removed, and he restored to his former Liberty on such Terms and Conditions, as you may think proper, if any are necessary. I am etc.

### To FREDERICK JAY

Head Quarters, New York, August 16, 1776.

Sir: In Consequence of my Orders, the undermentioned Persons have been apprehended and are now under a guard at

---

[21] In the writing of Robert Hanson Harrison.

New-Rochelle or its Neighbourhood. As the sending a Guard, thro' to Govr. Trumbull with them, would be attended with much Inconvenience to the Public and cannot be agreeable to the Gentlemen, Upon their giving you their Word and Honor to proceed to Lebanon to Governor Trumbull, I am Satisfied to permit them to go without any other Escort, than that of the Officer who will deliver you this. I must beg the favor of you to take the Management of this Business and as soon as it is put upon a proper footing, dismiss the Guard now there. I am etc.

Col. Philips.[22]

James Jauncey and his two Sons.

Joseph Bull.

Isaac Corsa.

John Rodgers.

Ware Branson.

## GENERAL ORDERS

Head Quarters, New York, August 16, 1776.

Parole Enfield.   Countersign Danvers.

In recommending Pay Masters it is to be observed that no officer can be appointed unless he resigns his former Commission, which he is to do in person at Head Quarters.

Major Livingston,[23] and William Blodget, are appointed Aids-du-Camp to Major General Greene—they are to be obeyed and respected accordingly.

David Astin of Col Sillimans Regiment and Captain Meads[24] Company, convicted by a General Court-Martial, whereof Col Wyllys was President of "breaking open a store and stealing Rum, Molasses and Fish, sentenced to receive thirty-nine lashes.

---

[22] Frederick (?) Philipse.

[23] Maj. William Smith Livingston, of Lasher's New York regiment. Later he became lieutenant colonel in Webb's Additional Continental regiment; resigned in October, 1778.

[24] Capt. Abraham Mead, of Silliman's Connecticut State regiment.

John McAlpine and John Hopper of Capt. Smith's[25] Company, Col Malcom's Regiment convicted by the same Court Martial of "being drunk on their posts"—sentenced to receive thirty lashes each—The General approves the above sentences, and orders them to be put in execution at the usual times and places.

The Orders of the 6th. Instant respecting Soldiers abusing people at market, and taking their things, not being known to the troops who have come in since; it is now repeated that the General will punish such offenders severely: And He requires of the officers, who visit the Guards, to see whether the former Order is put up in each guard house, and whether an officer attends at the market agreeable to former orders, and report thereon to their Brigadiers.

Capt. Andrew Billinjo's[26] to do duty as Major to Col Ritzema's Regiment, 'till further orders.

Unless orders are attended to, and executed, they are of no consequence, and the greatest disorders will insue, the General therefore requests, that the officers would be very careful, not only that the orders be made known to the men, but that they see themselves that they are executed—If every one in his own department, would exert himself for this purpose, it would have the most happy effect.

The badness of the weather has undoubtedly prevented an attack, as the enemies troops have been embarked some time; The General therefore directs, that two days Victuals be kept ready dressed, by the troops, and their Canteens filled with water; so that the men may be prepared; otherwise in case of an attack, they will suffer very much.

---

[25] Capt. Robert Smith, of Malcom's New York State regiment. He was wounded at White Plains, N. Y., and Monmouth, N. J.
[26] Capt. Andrew Billings, of the Third New York Regiment.

All Tents to be struck immediately, on the Alarm being given—viz: Two Guns at Fort George; Three from Bayard's, or Bunker-hill, with a Flag in the day, and a Light at night.

The Divisions of the Army, or Brigades doing seperate duty proving very inconvenient, the whole are to be brought into the General Detail to morrow: The Brigade Majors are to be at Head Quarters, at six o'clock, to settle the detail; and the Major and Brigadier Generals are requested to send, at the same time, a note of the number of men each may want for fatigue, or direct the Engineer having the care of their Works respectively, so to do.

## GENERAL ORDERS

Head Quarters, New York, August 17, 1776.

Parole Falmouth.    Countersign Essex.

Benjamin Durant of Capt. Wadsworth's[27] Company and Col Bailey's Regiment, convicted by a General Court Martial whereof Col Wyllys was President, of "getting drunk on Guard," sentenced to receive Thirty Lashes.

Patrick Lion of Capt. Curtis's[28] Company, Regiment late Learnad's, convicted by the same Court, of "sleeping on his post" sentenced to receive Twenty-five lashes.

Benjamin Wallace of Capt. Stewart's,[29] independent Company of New-York Forces convicted by the same Court of "Desertion, and inlisting into another Company," sentenced to receive Thirty-nine lashes.

The General approves the above sentences, and orders them to be executed at the usual time and place.

---

[27] Capt. Peleg Wadsworth, of the Twenty-third Continental Infantry.
[28] Capt. Samuel Curtiss, of the Third Continental Infantry.
[29] Capt. William Stewart, of the Independent New York Company.

The General recommends to all commanding officers of divisions, brigades and regiments, in issuing their several orders, to be careful they do not interfere with General Orders, which have been, or may be issued; and those Gentlemen who have not had an opportunity from their late arrival in Camp, to know what have been issued; will do well to inform themselves, and more especially before any special order is issued, which may have a general effect.

The Guard ordered to mount at Lispenard's Brewery, in the evening, to mount in the day also, and march off the parade with the other guards.

## To THE NEW YORK LEGISLATURE

Head Quarters, New York, August 17, 1776.

Gentn.: When I consider that the City of New York, will in all human probability very soon be the Scene of a bloody Conflict; I cannot but view the great Numbers of Women, Children and infirm Persons remaining in it, with the most melancholy concern. When the Men of War passed up, the River, the Shrieks and Cries of these poor Creatures, running every way with their Children, was truly distressing and I fear will have an unhappy effect, on the Ears and Minds of our young and inexperienced Soldiery. Can no Method be devised for their removal? Many doubtless are of Ability to move themselves; but there are others in a different Situation. Some Provision for them afterwards, would also be a Necessary consideration. It would relieve me from great anxiety, if your Honble. Body would Immediately deliberate upon it and form and execute some plan for their removal and relief; In which I will co-operate and assist to the utmost of my Power. In the mean time I have thought it proper, to recommend to persons under the above description, to convey themselves without delay to some Place of Safety, with their most Valuable effects.[30] I have the Honor &c.

## PROCLAMATION[31]

Head Quarters, August 17, 1776.

Whereas a bombardment and attack upon the city of New York, by our cruel and inveterate enemy, may be hourly expected; and as there are great numbers of women, children, and infirm persons, yet remaining in the city, whose continuance will rather be prejudicial than advantageous to the army, and their persons exposed to great danger and hazard; I Do, therefore recommend it to all such persons, as they value their own safety and preservation, to remove with all expedition out of the said town, at this critical period,—trusting that, with the blessing of Heaven upon the American arms, they may soon return to it in perfect security. And I do enjoin and require all the officers and soldiers in the army under my command to forward and assist such persons in their compliance with this recommendation. Given under my hand, etc.

## To THE PRESIDENT OF CONGRESS

New York, August 17, 1776.

Sir: The circumstances of the two Armies having undergone no material Alteration since I had the honor of writing you last, I have nothing particular or Important to communicate respecting them.

---

[30] Conformably to this suggestion a committee was appointed by the New York Legislature to remove such persons as it should think proper and to afford the necessary assistance and support to the poorer citizens. The committee of safety of the State was requested to lend its aid.

[31] Printed in the *New York Journal* or *General Advertiser* of Aug. 22, 1776. A broadside copy, printed by John Holt, Water Street, New York City, is in the archives of the New York Historical Society.

In my Letter of Yesterday I forgot to mention the Arrival of Lord Dunmore here.[32] By the Examination of a Captain Hunter,[33] who escaped from the Enemy and came to Amboy on the 14th. transmitted me by General Roberdeau,[34] I am certainly informed his Lordship arrived on the 13th., The Examination does not say any thing about the Ships he brought with him. It only extends to his force which it mentions to be weak.

I before now expected the Enemy would have made their Attack; nor can I account for their defering it, unless the Intelligence given by Captain Hunter and another person who escaped from them about the same time is the cause; towit, that they are waiting the Arrival of another division of Hessian Troops which they say is still out. Whether that is the reason of the delay I cannot undertake to determine, but I should suppose things will not remain long in their present State. I have inclosed a Copy of General Roberdeau's Letter and of the Examination of these two persons which will shew Congress all the Information they have given upon these Subject.

I am just now advised by Mr. Ayres, who came from Philadelphia to build the Row Gallies; that two of our Fire Vessels attempted last night to burn the Enemy's Ships and Tenders up the River. He says they burnt one Tender, and one of them boarded the Phœnix and was grapled with her for near ten Minutes, but she cleared herself.

We lost both of the Vessels. This Account is not so particular as I could wish, however, I am certain the Attempt has not succeeded to our Wishes.

In a little time it is probable the matter will be more minutely reported. I have the Honor &ca.[35]

---

[32] John Murray, Earl Dunmore.
[33] Alexander Hunter. His examination, in the writing of Tench Tilghman, dated Aug. 4, 1776, is in the *Washington Papers.*
[34] Brig. Gen. Daniel Roberdeau, of the New Jersey Militia.
[35] In the writing of Robert Hanson Harrison.

## To SIR WILLIAM HOWE

Head Quarters, New York, August 17, 1776.

General Washington begs Leave to acquaint General Howe that he has not the least Objection to Mr. Temple's[36] Landing, and proceeding to his Family in the State of the Massachusetts Bay: On the other Hand he will meet with every Assistance and Conveniences for that Purpose.[37]

## To RICHARD, LORD HOWE

Head Quarters, New York, August 17, 1776.

My Lord: Being authorized by Congress, as their Commanders in every Department are, to Negotiate an Exchange of Prisoners; and presuming, as well from the Nature of your Lordship's command, as the Information General Howe has been pleased to Honor me with, that the Exchange in the Naval Line will be subject to your Lordship's Directions, I beg leave to propose the following mode of Exchange for your Lordship's consideration, Vizt. "Officers for those of equal Rank and Sailors for Sailors."

If the above proposal should be agreeable to your Lordship, I am charged in a particular manner to exchange any Officer belonging to the British Navy in our hands and of equal Rank, for Lieut Josiah, who was lately made prisoner in a Ship retaken by the Cerberus Frigate.

The Reason my Lord, of my being charged to propose the exchange of Lieut Josiah, in preference to that of any other Officer, is, that authentic Intelligence has been received, that regardless of his Rank, as an Officer, he has not only been subjected to the duties of a common Seaman, but has experienced many other marks of Indignity.

---

[36] Robert Temple. His claim against Congress for damages was not settled until 1779.
[37] In the writing of Joseph Reed.

As a different Line of Conduct, My Lord, has been ever observed towards the Officers of your Navy, who have fallen into our Hands, It becomes not only a matter of Right, but of Duty, to mention this to your Lordship,[38] to the end that an Inquiry may be made into the case above refered to.

From your Lordship's Character for Humanity, I am led to presume, the Hardships imposed on Lt. Josiah, are without either your Knowledge or concurrence, and therefore most readily hope that upon this representation, your Lordship will enjoin all Officers under your command, to pay such regard to the Treatment of those that may fall into their Hands, as their different ranks and Situations require, and such as your Lordship would wish to see continued by us, to those who are already in our power, or who may hereafter, by the chance of War, be subjected to it. I have the Honor etc.

## To SIR WILLIAM HOWE

Head Quarters, New York, August 17, 1776.

Sir: I do myself the Honor to transmit the inclosed Letter from Major French, and at the same time to inform you, that his Exchange for Major Meigs, whose Parole I am advised you have, will meet my Approbation. I would take the Liberty also to propose an Exchange of any Captain you may chuse, for Captain Dearborn,[39] whose Parole I have heard was delivered you with Major Meigs's.

---

[38] In Washington's "Letter Book," in the writing of Robert Hanson Harrison, there are a few verbal changes from the copy of the letter as sent, the most radical of which is the phrase noted which reads "it becomes not only a matter of duty but of right in me to mention this," etc. Howe's reply (August 19) acceded to the suggested exchange, but answered the charge of ill treatment with a general statement that all his officers disapproved insults and indignities to prisoners of every rank. Howe's letter is in the *Washington Papers*.

[39] Capt. Henry Dearborn, of the First New Hampshire Regiment. He had been captured at Quebec and was exchanged in March, 1777, and, later, was promoted to major and lieutenant colonel of the Third New Hampshire Regiment. He was Secretary of War of the United States, 1801–1809, and a major general in the War of 1812.

Give me leave to assure you Sir, that I feel myself greatly obliged by the polite conclusion of your Letter of the 1st. instant, and have a high sense of the Honor and Satisfaction I should have received from your personal Acquaintance. The different State of the Colonies from what It was last War and which has deprived me of that Happiness, cannot be regretted by any one more than Sir Your etc.

### To JAMES, LORD DRUMMOND

New York, August 17, 1776.

Sir: I have your Lordships Favor of this Day accompanied by Papers on Subjects of the greatest Moment and deserving the most deliberate consideration.

I can allow much for your Lordships well meant Zeal on such an Occasion, but I fear it has transported you beyond that attention to your Parole, which comprehends the Character of a Man of Strict Honor. How your Lordship can reconcile your past or present Conduct with your Engagement, so as to satisfy your own Mind, I must submit to your own Feelings; but I find myself under the disagreeable Necessity of Objecting to the Mode of Negociation proposed while your Lordship's Conduct appears so exceptionable.

I shall, by Express, forward to Congress your Lordship's Letter and the Papers which accompanied it; The Result will be communicated as soon as possible.

I am sorry to have detained your Lordship so long, but the unavoidable Necessity must be my Apology. I am etc.

### To THE COMMITTEE OF SAFETY, POUGHKEEPSIE, NEW YORK

Head Quarters, New York, August 17, 1776.

Sir: I am favoured with yours of the 13th. and 14th. inst. and am pleased to find you have been succesfull in procuring

Cannon for Defence of Hudsons River; also that there is such a good prospect of effectually securing the Pass at Fort Montgomery; the mention you make of General Clinton's attention to that and other important Objects gives me great satisfaction, and confirms me in the opinion that he is fully qualified for the trust reposed in him by the Congress, in their appointing him a Brigadier. I approve much of the measure for making a number of Matrosses by putting a part of the Garrison to exercising the Artillery, the same steps have been taken here. If any material advantages can be derived from fitting out the two Sloops you speak of I shall be glad you have undertaken it, tho' I confess they are not very apparent to me at present. I cannot consent to those Vessels being manned from among the Levies, unless absolutely necessary, if the Officers can inlist them out of the Militia I have no objection thereto. I shall comply with your request in furnishing Capt. Benson[40] with a sufficient quantity of Powder for the two Armed Vessels, and am, etc.[41]

## To THE PRESIDENT OF CONGRESS

New York, August 18, 1776.

Sir: I have been honored with your favor of the 16th. with its Inclosure and am sorry it is not in my power to transmit Congress a Copy of the Treaty as they require, having sent it away with the other papers that were in my Hands.[42]

The Resolution they have entered into respecting the Foreign Troops, I am persuaded would produce Salutary Effects, If it can be properly circulated among them; I fear it will be a

---

[40] Capt. Henry Benson, a sea captain.
[41] The text is from the *Magazine of American History,* vol. 6, p. 136.
[42] By a resolve (August 13) Congress requested Washington to send a copy of the treaty between Massachusetts and the St. Johns and Micmac Indians.

matter of difficulty:—However I will take every measure that shall appear probable to facilitate the end.[43]

I have the Honor to inclose you for the perusal and consideration of Congress, sundry papers marked No. 1 to No. 7. inclusive, the whole of which, except No. 2 and 7, my Answer to Lord Drummond and General Howe, I received Yesterday Evening by a Flag, and to which I beg leave to refer Congress.[44]

I am exceedingly at a loss to know the Motives and causes inducing a proceeding of such a Nature at this Time and why Lord Howe has not attempted some plan of Negociation before, as he seems to be desirous of it. If I may be allowed to conjecture and guess at the Cause, It may be that part of the Hessians have not arrived as mentioned in the examination transmitted Yesterday, or that General Burgoyne has not made such progress, as was expected, to form a junction of their two Armies: or what I think equally probable, they mean to procrastinate their Operations for some time, trusting that the Militias, which have come to our Succour, will soon be tired and return home as is but too usual with them. Congress will make their Observations upon these several matters and favor me with the result as soon as they have done.

They will observe my Answer to Lord Drummond, who, I am pretty confident, has not attended to the Terms of his parole, but has violated it in several Instances. It is with the rest of the papers; But if my Memory serves me, he was not to hold any Correspondence directly or Indirectly with those in Arms

---

[43] On August 14 Congress adopted resolves to encourage the Hessians and other foreigners to quit the British service. These were printed in German and were used as wrapping for small quantities of tobacco smuggled into the Hessians, who would, for the tobacco, conceal the wrapping from the officers. On August 27 resolves offering land to German officers were adopted, printed, and sent into the British lines.

[44] Inclosures Nos. 6 and 7 are all that are filed with Washington's letter in the *Papers of the Continental Congress,* and these are Howe's letter to Washington *re* Robert Temple and Washington's answer. It seems probable, however, that all of the Drummond correspondence is in the *Washington Papers,* as the record appears complete.

against us, or to go into any port or Harbour in America where the Enemy were, or had a Fleet, or to go on board their Ships.[45]

The Treaty with the Indians is in the Box which Lieutenant Colonel Reed I presume has delivered before this. If Congress are desirous of seeing it, they will be pleased to have the Box opened. It contains a variety of papers and all the Affairs of the Army, from my first going to Cambridge 'till it was sent away.

This morning the Phœnix and Rose Men of War with two Tenders, availing themselves of a favourable and brisk Wind, came down the River and have joined the Fleet.—Our several Batteries fired at them in their passage, but without any good Effect, that I could perceive. I am &ca.[46]

### To THE NEW YORK LEGISLATURE

New York, August 18, 1776.

Gentn.: I have been honored with your Letter of the 17th., with the Resolution of your Honorable Body, for obstructing the Channel betwixt the grand Battery and Nutten Island. Having gone into a Considerable Expence for stopping that of the North River, and such as I am not Certain I shall be justified

---

[45] "The late Conduct of Lord Drummond is as extraordinary as his motives are dark and mysterious. To judge the most favourably of his Intentions, it would seem, that an overweening Vanity has betrayed him into a criminal Breach of Honour. But whether his Views were upright, or intended only to mislead and deceive, cannot at present be a Matter of any importance. In the mean time, I have the pleasure to acquaint you, that Congress highly approve the Manner in which you have checked the officious and intemperate Zeal of his Lordship. Whether his Designs were hostile or friendly, he equally merited the Reproof you have given him, and I hope for the future he will be convinced, that it is highly imprudent to attract the Attention of the publick to a Character, which will only pass without Censure when it passes without Notice. The Congress, having considered the Matter thoroughly, are of Opinion to decline taking any publick or farther Notice of his Lordship, or his Letters, and particularly as you have so fully expressed their Sentiments on the subject in your Letter to him."—*Hancock to Washington*, Aug. 24, 1776.

Drummond attempted to vindicate himself from the charge of having broken his parole and to explain his conduct, but without success, as the facts in the case were too obvious. The difficulty, of course, was the ingrained feeling of superiority of the Britisher toward the Colonial; a feeling that must be taken into account in every attempt to understand the causes of the Revolution.

[46] In the writing of Robert Hanson Harrison.

in, and the obstructions there being far from Compleat, it will not be in my power to engage in the Business you propose, or undertake to Advance any part of the Money, which will be necessarily expended in the Execution. At the same time, give me leave to Assure you, Gentlemen, that I shall most readily afford you such Assistance, as may be derived from the Labour of the Troops here and that can be spared from other service to facilitate the design; which will be of great Importance, if it can be executed.

I have been also honored with your favor and Resolution of the same date, and am exceedingly obliged by the ready attention you have paid to my Recommendation, for the removal of the Women and Children and Infirm Persons from the City. I have the honor etc.

## To GOVERNOR JONATHAN TRUMBULL

New York, August 18, 1776.

Sir: I have been duly honored with your favor of the 13th. Instant; and, at the same time, that I think you and your honorable Council of Safety highly deserving of the thanks of the States, for the Measures you have adopted, in order to give the most early and Speedy Succour to this Army; give me leave to return you mine in a particular Manner. When the whole of the Reinforcements do arrive, I flatter my self we shall be competent to every exigency; and, with the Smiles of Providence upon our Arms and Vigorous Exertions, we shall baffle the designs of our Inveterate Foes, formidable as they are. Our Situation was truly Alarming, a little while Since; but, by the kind Interpositions and Aid of our Friends, is much bettered.

You may rest Assured, Sir, that due Consideration shall be had to the Several Militia Regiments, that have come, and are Marching to our Assistance, and that they shall be dismissed as soon as Circumstances will admit of it, I trust, as long as there is Occasion for their Services, that the same Spirit and Commendable Zeal, which Induced them to come, will Influence their Continuance. I sincerely wish, it was in my power to ascertain the particular Period when they would be needed, that they might not be detained one unnecessary Moment from their Homes and Common pursuits; But, as this cannot be done; as the Approaching Contest and Trial between the two Armies will, most unquestionably, produce events of the utmost Importance to the States; As the Issue, if favorable, will put us on such a footing, as to bid defiance to the utmost Malice of the British Nation and those in Alliance with her; I have not a doubt, but they will most readily Consent to stay, and chearfully forego every present and Temporary Inconvenience, so long as they are Necessary. I am happy Capt. Van Buren[47] has Succeeded so well in the Business he was upon, It being of great Consequence for us to fit out and maintain our Vessels on the Lake. On the Night of the 16th., Two of our fire Vessels Attempted to burn the Ships of War up the River. One of these Boarded the Phœnix of 44 Guns, and was Grappled with her for some Minutes; but unluckily she cleared herself. The only damage the Enemy sustained, was the destruction of one Tender. It is agreed on all hands, that our People, engaged in this affair, behaved with great Resolution and Intrepidity; one of the Captains, Thomas, It is to be feared, Perished in the attempt, or in making his Escape by Swimming, as he has not been heard of; His Bravery Intitled him to a better fate. Tho' his enterprize did not succeed to our Wishes, I incline to think it alarmed the Enemy greatly. For this morning the Phœnix and Rose, with their two remaining Tenders, taking Advantage of a brisk and prosperous Gale, with a favorable tide, Quitted their Stations, and have returned and joined the rest of the Fleet.

---

[47] Capt. Abraham Van Buren, of the Albany militia.

As they Passed our Several Batteries, they were fired upon, but without any damage that I could perceive.[48] The whole of the British forces in America, except those employed in Canada are now here, Clinton's arrival being followed the last week by that of Lord Dunmore, who now forms a part of the Army we are to oppose. his coming has not added but little to their Strength. I have the Honor to be &c.

### *To BENJAMIN FRANKLIN

New York, August 18, 1776.

Sir: I have been honourd with your favour of the 16th, and the several Inclosures contained therein, which are now return'd with my thanks for the oppertunity of perusing them; I also Inclose you a Letter from Lord Howe, sent out (with others) by a Flag in the Afternoon of yesterday. With it comes a Letter for Lieutt. Barrington,[49] who if not among those who broke their Parole, and went of for Canada, is in York, Pensylvania—With very great esteem and respect etc.[50]

### GENERAL ORDERS

Head Quarters, New York, August 18, 1776.
Parole Grantham.    Countersign Fairfield.

As nothing contributes so much to the good order and government of troops, as an exactness in discipline, and a strict observance of orders; and as the Army is now arranged into different

---

[48] The British ships sustained a good deal of injury in passing the upper batteries near Fort Washington and the Harlem River. General Heath's letter (August 18) reported that the *Phœnix* was three times hulled by the shot from Mount Washington and one of the tenders once and that the *Rose* was hulled once by a shot from Burdetts Ferry on the opposite side of river. The *Phœnix* and *Rose* had been sounding the river as far up as the Highlands. The tender, burned by one of the fire ships, was beached by the British the next day. A 6-pound cannon, 3 smaller ones, and 10 swivels were recovered from her by the Americans. Heath's letter is in the *Washington Papers*.

[49] Lieut.(?) Barrington, of the Seventh Foot, British Army.

[50] From the original in the *Franklin Papers* of the American Philosophical Society. The editor is indebted to that society and its librarian, Miss Laura E. Hanson, for this exact copy of the text.

divisions; those divisions formed into brigades, and the brigades composed of regiments; The General hopes and expects, that the several duties of the Army, will go on with regularity, chearfulness and alacrity:—As one means of accomplishing this he desires, that no regiment, brigade or division, will interfere with the duties of another, but walk in their own proper line; the Colonels taking care not to contravene the orders of their Brigadiers; the Brigadiers of their Major Generals; and that the whole pay due attention to the General Orders, which can only be set aside, or be dispensed with by orders of equal dignity.

The army under such a regulation will soon become respectable in itself, and formidable to the foe—It is an incumbent duty therefore, upon every officer of every rank, to be alert and attentive in the discharge of the several duties annexed to his office; his honor, his own personal safety, and for ought he knows, the salvation of his Country, and its dearest priviliges, may depend upon his exertions. Particular Causes may, and doubtless will happen, to render it necessary (for the good of the service) that a change of officers &c. should be made, from one brigade to another; but when ever there appears cause for this, it will be notified by General, or special Orders.

The General cannot quit the subject, as this may possibly be the last opportunity, previous to an attack, without addressing the privatemen, and exhorting the troops in general, to be perfoundly silent, and strictly obedient to Orders, before they come to, and also while they are in action, as nothing can contribute more to their Success, than a cool and deliberate behaviour, nor nothing add more to the discouragement of the enemy, than to find new troops calm and determined in their manner. The General has no doubt but that every good Soldier, and all the officers, are sufficiently impressed with the necessity of examining the state and condition of their arms, but his own anxiety on this head impels him to remind them of it after every spell of wet weather, least we should at any time, be caught with arms unfit for immediate use.

The regiments of Militia from Connecticut are to be formed into a Brigade under the command of Brigadier General Wolcot,[51] who is hourly expected; and in the meantime to be under the command of Col Hinman,[52] the eldest Colonel of the militia.

Though the Fire Ships which went up the North River last Friday Evening, were not so successful as to destroy either of the Men of war, yet the General thanks the officers and men for the spirit and resolution which they shewed in grappling the Vessels before they quitted the Fire Ships; And as a reward of their merit, presents each of those who stayed last, and were somewhat burnt; Fifty Dollars, and Forty to each of the others; And had the enterprise succeeded, so as to have destroyed either of the ships of war, the General could have been generous in proportion to the service.

### *To LUND WASHINGTON

New York, August 19, 1776.

Dear Lund: Very unexpectedly to me, another revolving Monday is arrived before an Attack upon this City, or a movement of the Enemy; the reason of this is incomprehensible, to me. True it is (from some late informations) they expect another arrival of about 5000 Hessians; but then, they have been stronger than the Army under my Command; which will now, I expect, gain strength faster than theirs, as the Militia are beginning to come in fast, and have already augmented our numbers in this City and the Posts round about, to about 23,000

---

[51] Brig. Gen. Erasmus Wolcott.
[52] Col. Benjamin Hinman.

Men. The Enemy's numbers now on the Island and in the Transports which lay off it, are by the lowest Accts. 20,000 Men by the greatest 27,000 to these the expected (5000) Hessians are to be added.

There is something exceedingly misterious in the conduct of the Enemy. Lord Howe takes pains to throw out, upon every occasion, that he is the Messenger of Peace; that he wants to accomodate matters, nay, has Insinuated, that he thinks himself authorized to do it upon the terms mentioned in the last Petition to the King of G. Britain. But has the Nation got to that, that the King, or his Ministers will openly dispense with Acts of Parliament. And if they durst attempt it, how is it to be accounted for that after running the Nation to some Millions of Pounds Sterlg. to hire and Transport Foreigners, and before a blow is struck, they are willing to give the terms proposed by Congress before they, or we, had encountered the enormous expence that both are now run to. I say, how is this to be accounted for but from their having received some disagreeable advices from Europe; or, by having some Manouvre in view which is to be effected by procrastination. What this can be the Lord knows, we are now passed the Middle of August and they are in possession of an Island only, which it never was in our power, or Intention to dispute their Landing on. this is but a small step towards the Conquest of this Continent.

The two Ships which went up this River about the middle of the past Month, came down yesterday, sadly frightened I believe, the largest of them, the Phœnex (a 44. Gun Ship) having very narrowly escaped burning the Night before by two Fire Ships which I sent up; one of which was grapnal'd to her for Ten Minutes, in a light blaze, before the Phœnex could cut away so as to clear herself, the other Fire ship run on board of the Tender near the Phœnex, and soon reduced her to Ashes. We lost no lives in the Attempt unless the Captn. of the Ship which made the attempt upon the Phœnex perish'd. We have not heard of him since, but it is thought he might have made his escape by Swimming, which was the Plan he had in contemplation.

As the Collection of Mercers Bonds has not been put into the hands of Colo. Peyton,[53] I have no objection to your undertaking of it if Colo. Tayloe[54] has none; accordingly, I inclose you a Letter to him on this Subject, which you may forward, and act agreeable to his Instructions, and appointment. I do not recollect enough of the Tenor of the Bonds to decide absolutely in the case of Majr. Powell;[55] true it is the design of making the Bonds carry Interest from the date, was to enforce the punctual payment of them; or, to derive an advantage if they were not. The Circumstances attending his going to Hampton, and the time when he did, I know not. He knew that those Bonds were payable to Tayloe and me; he knew that they became due (to the best of my recollection) the first of December, and should have tendered the Money at that time in strictness; however if you have the Collection, in all matters of that kind take Colo. Tayloe's, or (which I believe will be the same thing) Mr. Jas. Mercers opinion as it will be impossible for me to determine these matters at the distance I am, and under the hurry of business I am Ingaged In.

There is no doubt but that the Honey locust if you could procure Seed enough, and that Seed would come up, will make (if sufficiently thick) a very good hedge; so will the Haw, or thorn, and if you cannot do better I wish you to try these, but Cedar or any kind of ever Green, would look better; hower., if one thing will not do, we must try another, as no time ought to be lost in rearing of Hedges, not only for Ornament but use.

---

[53] Col. Craven Peyton, of Loudoun County, Va.
[54] Col. John Tayloe, of Mount Airy, Va.
[55] Maj. Joseph Powell, at one time sheriff of Fairfax County, Va.

Adams's[56] Land you will continue to Rent to the best advantage, for I believe it will turn out, that I made bad worse, by attempting to save myself by taking that pretty youths debts upon myself. As Lord Dunmore and his Squadron have join'd the Fleet at Staten Island, you will, I should think, have a favourable oppertunity of sending of your Flour, Midlings, Ship stuff &ca. Corn will, more than probably, sell well sometime hence; especially if your Crops should be as short as you apprehend. If your Ship stuff and Middlings should have turnd Sower it will make exceeding good Bisquet notwithstanding. Your Works abt. the Home House will go on Slowly I fear as your hands are reduced, and especially if Knowles fails. remember that the New Chimneys are not to smoke. Plant Trees in the room of all dead ones in proper time this Fall. and as I mean to have groves of Trees at each end of the dwelling House, that at the South end to range in a line from the South East Corner to Colo. Fairfax's, extending as low as another line from the Stable to the dry Well, and towards the Coach House, Hen House, and Smoak House as far as it can go for a Lane to be left for Carriages to pass to, and from the Stable and Wharf. from the No. Et. Corner of the other end of the House to range so as to Shew the Barn &ca. in the Neck; from the point where the old Barn used to stand to the No. Et. Corner of the Smiths Shop, and from thence to the Servants Hall, leaving a passage between the Quarter and Shop, and so East of the Spinning and Weaving House (as they used to be called) up to a Wood pile, and so into the yard between the Servts. Hall and the House newly erected; these Trees to be Planted without any order or regularity (but pretty thick, as they can at any time be thin'd) and to consist that at the North end, of locusts altogether. and that at the South, of all the clever kind of Trees (especially flowering

---

[56] Daniel Jenifer Adams.

ones) that can be got, such as Crab apple, Poplar, Dogwood, Sasa-
fras, Laurel, Willow (especially yellow and Weeping Willow,
twigs of which may be got from Philadelphia) and many others
which I do not recollect at present; these to be interspersed here
and there with ever greens such as Holly, Pine, and Cedar, also
Ivy; to these may be added the Wild flowering Shrubs of the
larger kind, such as the fringe Tree and several other kinds that
might be mentioned. It will not do to Plant the Locust Trees
at the North end of the House till the Framing is up, cover'd in,
and the Chimney Built; otherwise it will be labour lost as they
will get broke down, defaced and spoil'd, But nothing need
prevent planting the Shrubery at the other end of the House.
Whenever these are Planted they should be Inclosd, which may
be done in any manner till I return; or rather by such kind of
fencing as used to be upon the Ditch running towards Hell
hole; beginning at the Kitchen and running towards the Stable
and rather passing the upper Corner; thence round the Dry
Well, below the necessary House, and so on to the Hollow by
the Wild Cherry tree by the old Barn; thence to the Smiths
Shop and so up to the Servants Hall as before described. If
I should ever fulfil my Intention it will be to Inclose it properly; the Fence now described is only to prevent Horses &ca.
injuring the young Trees in their growth.

As my Greys are almost done, and I have got two or three
pretty good Bays here, I do not Incline to make an absolute Sale
of the bay horse you mention. But if Mr. Custis wants him, and
you and he can fix upon a price, he may take him at such valuation; paying the Money, and using him as his own; subject
however to return him to me if I should hereafter want him
and will repay him his Money; by this means he will (if it
should not prove an absolute Sale) have the use of the Horse
and I, the use of the money.

Before I conclude I must beg of you to hasten Lanphire about the addition to the No. End of the House, otherwise you will have it open I fear in the cold and wet Weather, and the Brick work to do at an improper Season, neither of which shall I be at all desirous of. My best wishes to Milly Posey[57] and all our Neighbours and friends. With sincere regard I remain, etc.

[H.L.]

## GENERAL ORDERS

Head Quarters, New York, August 19, 1776.
Parole Georgia.    Countersign Hartford.

John Green of Capt. Johnsons Company and late Col Mc-Dougall's Regiment, convicted by a General Court Martial, whereof Col Wyllys is President, of "breaking out of his quarter guard and being absent two days"—ordered to receive Thirty-nine Lashes. The General approves the sentence, and orders it to be executed at the usual time and place; and the prisoner to be then returned to his quarter guard.[58]

The Court Martial to sit to morrow, for the tryal of Lieut. Hubbel[59] of the regiment late Col McDougall's—The Judge Advocate will be informed of the witnesses by General Putnam.

A Subaltern's Guard to go over to morrow, to relieve the Guard at Hoebuck ferry.

Col Hitchcock's Regiment to move to morrow, to Burdetts ferry, and relieve the party now there; they are to join General Mifflins Brigade, and receive Orders from Major General Heath, agreeable to General Orders of the 12th. Instant. General Putnam will order boats.

The Adjutants of such regiments as have lately come in to apply at the Adjutant General's office for Blank Returns which

---

[57] Amelia (Milly) Posey, daughter of Capt. John Posey and the girlhood friend of Martha (Patsy) Custis.
[58] Quarter guard was the small guard posted in front of each battalion camp.
[59] Lieut. Caleb Hobby, of the First New York Regiment.

they are to fill up and bring in at orderly time—viz: Eleven O'Clock every Saturday.

After this day, a Major to mount at the Main Guard, at the Grand Battery, instead of a Lieut. Colonel.

## To THE PRESIDENT OF CONGRESS

New York, August 19, 1776.

Sir: I have nothing of Moment to communicate to Congress, as things are in the Situation they were when I had last the honor of Addressing them.

By a Letter from General Ward of the 12th. I find that Whitcomb's Regiment on the 8th. and Phinney's on the 9th. marched from Boston to Ticonderoga.

Governor Trumbull also, in a Letter of the 13th., advises me that Ward's Regiment in the service of the States, was on their March to this Army, and that he and his Council of Safety had, in the whole ordered fourteen Militia Regiments to reinforce us, three of them have arrived and amount to about one thousand and twenty men. When the whole come in, we shall be on a much more respectable footing than what we have been, but I greatly fear if the Enemy defer their attack for any considerable time, they will be extremely impatient to return home, and if they should, we shall be reduced to distress again. He also adds that Captain Van Buren who had been sent for that purpose had procured a sufficient supply of Sail Cloth for the Vessels to be employed in the Lake and a part of the Cordage in that State, and had a prospect of getting the remainder.

As there will be a difficulty in all probability, to circulate the papers designed for the Foreign Troops and many Miscarriages may happen before it can be effected, it may be proper to furnish me with a larger Quantity than what I already have.

Inclosed I have the honor to transmit you a General Return of our whole Force at this Time, in which are comprehended the three Regiments of Militia above mentioned. I am Sorry it should be so much weakned by Sickness. The Return will shew you how it distresses us. I have the Honor etc.

P. S: The post just now arrived, has brought a further Supply of Papers for the Hessians[60] which makes my Requisition unnecessary.[61]

## To MAJOR GENERAL WILLIAM HEATH

Head Quarters, August 19, 1776.

Sir: I received yours of yesterday's date. The Ships of War and Tenders were fired at from the Batteries here as they passed, and I suppose received similar damages to what they met with from the Forts at Mount Washington and Burdit Ferry. I shall not be able to spare any Tents for Genl. Clinton at present owing to the very small Stock on Hand, with regard to their Quarters being so scattered I can only say, that I think it of less consequence the Case should be so circumstanced there than here, at this time. I have wrote to Colo. Knox this morning, desiring him to have the Carriages for four pounders ready and sent forward with all expedition.

When I directed you to inquire into the Cause of the inactivity of some of the Row Gallies it was upon a presumption they were near you, as they are now come down to the City I shall give further Orders respecting that Affair. I am, etc.[62]

[MS. H. S.]

---

[60] See *Journals of the Continental Congress*, Aug. 14 and 27, 1776, for resolves to encourage the Hessians to desert.

[61] In the writing of Robert Hanson Harrison.

[62] In the writing of John Fitzgerald.

## To THE PRESIDENT OF CONGRESS

New York, August 20, 1776.

Sir: I was yesterday Morning favoured with yours of the 17th., accompanied by several Resolutions of Congress and Commissions for Officers appointed to the late Vacancies in this Army.

I wrote some days ago to General Schuyler to propose to Generals Carleton and Burgoyne, an Exchange of Prisoners, in consequence of a former Resolve of Congress, authorizing their Commanders in each Department to negotiate one. That of Major Meigs for Major French and Captain Dearborn's for any Officer of equal Rank, I submitted to General Howe's consideration by Letter on the 17th. understanding their paroles had been sent him by General Carleton, but have not yet received his Answer on the Subject.

In respect to the Exchange of the Prisoners in Canada, If a my Letter to Lord Howe, as well on the Subject of a General lieve it has not, the inclosed Copy of General Carleton's Orders[63] transmitted me under Seal by Major Bigelow who was sent with a Flag to General Burgoyne from Ticonderoga, with the proceedings of Congress on the Breach of Capitulation at the Cedars and the inhuman Treatment of our people afterwards, will shew it is unnecessary, as he has determined to send them to their own Provinces, *there* to remain as prisoners, interdicting at the same time all kind of intercourse between us and his Army, except such as may be for the purpose of imploring the King's Mercy.[64] The Assassination of Brigadier General

[63] A copy of Sir Guy Carleton's orders, dated Aug. 7, 1776, given to Maj. Timothy Bigelow is in the *Washington Papers*.

[64] The events attending the capitulation at The Cedars and the agreement for the exchange of prisoners entered into by Arnold were of so extraordinary and irritating a nature in regard to the conduct of the enemy that Congress, at the same time they confirmed Arnold's stipulation, resolved: "That, previous to the delivery of the

Gordon[65] is a fact entirely new to me, and what I never heard
of. I shall not trouble Congress with my Strictures on this indecent, illiberal and Scurrilous performance, so highly unbecoming the Character of a Soldier and Gentleman, only observeing
that its design is somewhat Artful, and that each Boatman
with Major Bigelow was furnished with a Copy.

---

prisoners to be returned on our part, the British commander in Canada be required
to deliver into our hands the authors, abettors, and perpetrators of the horrid murder
committed on the prisoners, to suffer such punishment as their crime deserves; and
also, to make indemnification for the plunder at the Cedars, taken contrary to the
faith of the capitulation; and that, until such delivery and indemnification be made,
the said prisoners be not delivered." (See *Journals of the Continental Congress*, July
10, 1776.)

[65] Gen. Patrick Gordon was lieutenant colonel of the One hundred and eighth Foot,
and a brigadier general in America. An American lieutenant and four men from
Ticonderoga, while on a scout within the enemy's lines, concealed themselves near the
road leading from St. John's to Laprairie. General Gordon passed them on horseback;
the lieutenant fired at and shot him through the body. The general was able to ride
to St. John's before he expired. This killing aroused the indignation of the British
officers and, occurring but two or three days before the dispatch from Congress arrived, it may have had a principal influence in dictating the paper called General
Carleton's order.

This was in effect a refusal to confirm the treaty and was so considered by the
commanding officers in Canada. The report of the committee of Congress on this
subject, and the resolves respecting the treaty, were forwarded to General Burgoyne.
The dispatch was sent under the charge of Major Bigelow from Ticonderoga. He proceeded down the lake to Isle-aux-Noix, which was then a British outpost, where he
was detained, and the dispatch was forwarded to General Burgoyne then at St. John's.
Major Bigelow stayed 10 days at Isle-aux-Noix, where he and his party were treated
very civilly by Captain Craig, the commander of that post, and by the other officers.
At length the messenger came back from St. John's with a letter directed to "George
Washington, Esquire," which was handed to Major Bigelow, and with which he
returned immediately up the lake to Ticonderoga, being escorted on his way as far as
Gilleland's by a boat with two British officers and nine Canadians.

This letter General Gates sent off by express to General Washington. When opened
it was found to be a mere envelope inclosing a paper purporting to be a military order
issued by General Carleton at Chamblee on August 7, without signature or address,
and unaccompanied by any remarks. The contents of this paper were of so singular a
character, and comported so little with the spirit and temper of a high-minded officer, that they might well have excited a strong suspicion as to their being genuine
had not the dispatch been formally entrusted to Major Bigelow as coming from General Burgoyne, or General Carleton, who was commander in chief. The order pro-
hibits all intercourse "with rebels, traitors, rioters, disturbers of the public peace,
plunderers, robbers, assassins, or murderers," and adds, "should emissaries from
such lawless men again presume to approach the army, whether under the name of
flag-of-truce men, or ambassadors, except when they come to implore the King's
mercy, their persons shall be immediately seized and committed to close confinement
and proceeded against as the law directs." After a good deal more in the same style
of rodomontade, the order concludes by directing "all the prisoners from the rebel-
lious provinces, who choose to return home, to hold themselves in readiness to
embark at a short notice, and that the commissary should visit the transports destined

I have also transmitted a Copy of the Major's Journal, to which I beg leave to refer them for the Intelligence reported by him, on his Return from the Truce.[66]

By a Letter from General Greene Yesterday Evening, he informed me he had received an Express from Hog Island Inlet, advising, that five of the Enemy's small Vessels had appeared at the Mouth of the Creek with some Troops on Board; also that he had heard two Pettit Augers were off Oyster Bay, the whole supposed to be after live Stock; and to prevent their getting it, he had detached a party of Horse and two hundred and twenty Men, among them twenty Rifle Men. I have not received further Intelligence upon the Subject.

I am also advised by the Examination of a Captain Briton,[67] Master of a Vessel that had been taken, transmitted me by General Mercer, that the General Report, among the Enemy's Troops, was, when he came off, that they were to attack Long Island and to secure our Works there, if possible; at the same time, that another part of their Army was to land above this City. This information is corroborated by many other Accounts, and is probably true; nor will it be possible to prevent their landing on the Island, as its great extent affords a variety of places favourable for that purpose and the whole of our Works on it, are at the end opposite to the City. However we shall attempt to harrass them, as much as possible, which will be all that we can do. I have the Honor etc.[68]

---

for them, and see that wholesome provisions and necessary clothing, with all possible conveniences for their passage, be prepared; and that the prisoners were to look on their respective provinces as their prisons, there to remain till further enlarged, or summoned to appear before the commander in chief in Canada." With no other explanation than the order itself it is now impossible to decide what degree of credit ought to be ascribed to it. From the tenor of Washington's letter above, and from the circumstance of his transmitting the paper to Congress, it is obvious that he considered it genuine. General Schuyler and General Gates were of the same opinion.— *Sparks.*

[66] A copy of Maj. Timothy Bigelow's journal is filed, with Washington's letter, in the *Papers of the Continental Congress.*

[67] Britton's examination, dated Aug. 18, 1776, is in the *Washington Papers.*

[68] In the writing of Robert Hanson Harrison.

## GENERAL ORDERS

Head Quarters, New York, August 20, 1776.

Parole Hampton.   Countersign Gates.

Nathaniel Mun of Capt. Peters's[69] Company, Col Reads Regiment, convicted by a General Court Martial whereof Col Wyllys is President of "Desertion and reinlistment into another corps"

James Mumford of Capt Ledyards Company, Regiment late Col McDougall's convicted by the same Court Martial of the same crime.

Alexander Moore, Serjeant in Capt Conway's[70] Company, Col Wynd's Battalion convicted by the same Court Martial of "Desertion."

Christopher Harpur of the same Company and Battalion, convicted by the same Court Martial of the same crime. Each of the above prisoners were sentenced to receive thirty nine lashes—

The General approves the sentences, and orders them to be executed at Guard mounting, to morrow morning, at the usual place.

The troops lately arrived are informed that it is contrary to General Orders, to fire in camp; such Firelocks as are loaded, and the charges cannot be drawn, are to be discharged at Retreat beating in a Volley under the inspection of an officer. The officers of such troops are desired and required to prevent all the firing in the camp, as it tends to great disorder.

The regiments of militia, now under the Command of Col Hinman, from Connecticut, are in case of alarm, to parade on the grand parade, and there wait for orders.

The officers who have lately come into Camp are also informed that it has been found necessary, amidst such frequent

---

[69] Capt. Andrew Peters, of the Thirteenth Continental Infantry. Later, he was lieutenant colonel of the Fifteenth Massachusetts Regiment.

[70] Capt. John Conway, of the First New Jersey Regiment. He was wounded at Germantown, Pa.; later became lieutenant colonel of the First New Jersey Regiment.

changes of Troops to introduce some distinctions by which their several ranks may be known—viz: Field Officers wear a pink or red cockade—Captains white or buff—Subalterns green—The General flatters himself every Gentlemen will conform to a regulation which he has found essentially necessary to prevent mistakes and confusion.

The trial of Lieut. Hubbel[71] is postponed 'till tomorrow.

The General Court Martial to set on Thursday, as a Court of enquiry, into the conduct of Adjutant Brice[72] of Col Smallwood's Battalion, charged with "disobedience of orders and disrespectful behaviour to his commanding officer"—

The General being informed, to his great surprize, that a report prevails and is industriously spread far and wide that Lord Howe has made propositions of peace, calculated by designing persons more probably to lull us into a fatal security; his duty obliges him to declare that no such offer has been made by Lord Howe, but on the contrary, from the best intelligence he can procure—the Army may expect an attack as soon as the wind and tide shall prove favourable. He hopes therefore, every man's mind and arms, will be prepared for action, and when called to it, shew our enemies, and the whole world, that Freemen contending on their own land, are superior to any mercenaries on earth—

The Brigadiers are to see the Spears in the different works, under their command, kept greased and clean—

General Sullivan is to take the command upon Long Island, 'till General Greene's State of health will permit him to resume it, and Brigadier Lord Stirling is to take charge of General Sullivan's division 'till he returns to it again.

Edward Tilghman Esqr is appointed as an Assistant Brigade Major to Lord Stirling; the duty of the whole division being

---

[71] Lieut. Caleb Hobby.
[72] Adjt. John Brice. He was, later, captain of the Third Maryland Regiment and was wounded at Camden, S. C., Aug. 16, 1780.

too great for one officer.—He is to be respected and obeyed accordingly.

## GENERAL ORDERS

Head Quarters, New York, August 21, 1776.

Parole Kingsbridge.   Countersign Jersey.

Adjutant Taylor[73] to do the duty of Brigade Major to General McDougall's Brigade during Major Platts illness; he is to be obeyed and respected accordingly.

Lieut. Hobby[74] of Capt. Hyatts Company, Regiment late General McDougalls, tried by a General Court Martial whereof Col Wyllys was president for misbehaviour in leaving one of the Hulks in the North River; was acquitted and the complaint reported groundless—Ordered that he be discharged from his arrest.

A Court of inquiry to sit on Friday at Mrs. Montagnies, upon Capts. McCleave, Stanton[75] and Tinker, charged with backwardness in duty, up the North River last week, and misbehaviour on Sunday last when the Men of war came down the river—Court to consist of the following persons, and meet at ten O'Clock—

General McDougall President.

Col. Malcom,[76] Lt Cols Shepard[77] and Wesson,[78] Major Brooks,[79] Capts. Peters,[80] and Van Dyck,[81] Members.

The Judge Advocate to attend and all witnesses.

---

[73] Adjt. Andrew Taylor, of the First New York Regiment.

[74] Lieut. Caleb Hobby.

[75] Stanton may have been Capt. William Stanton, of Burrall's Connecticut State regiment.

[76] Col. William Malcolm, of a New York State regiment.

[77] Lieut. Col. William Shepard, of the Third Connecticut Infantry. He was wounded at Long Island Aug. 27, 1776; promoted to colonel on October 2; transferred to the Fourth Massachusetts Regiment Jan. 1, 1777.

[78] Lieut. Col. James Wesson.

[79] Maj. John Brooks, of the Nineteenth Continental Infantry.

[80] Capt. Nathan Peters, of the Third Continental Infantry.

[81] Capt. Abraham C. Van Dyke, of Lasher's New York State regiment. He was taken prisoner at Fort Washington on Nov. 16, 1776.

Fifty men properly officered to parade every morning at Six O'Clock at General Putnam's; there to take Orders from him; Not to bring arms—These to be continued every day till further orders.

Fifty men also for fatigue to parade to morrow morning properly officered on the Grand parade without Arms—take orders from Capt. Post.[82]

Ten Men with one Subaltern, who have been used to the Sea, to parade at General Putnams this afternoon, two OClock, to proceed to Kingsbridge, up the North River—take three days provision.

The like number for the same service, to parade to morrow morning, Six o'Clock, at General Putnam's quarters—take three days provision; both parties parade without arms.

Twenty men, with a Subaltern, to parade for fatigue, to morrow morning without Arms, on the Grand parade to proceed to Bayard hill, and work upon the well—take orders from the person who has the direction of digging the well.

## To MAJOR GENERAL WILLIAM HEATH

### Head Quarters, New York, August 21, 1776.

Sir: Inclosed I transmit you Copy of a Letter which I have this Moment recd. from Genl. Livingston at Elizabeth Town. You will perceive by it that the Enemy are upon the point of striking the long expected Stroke, and as part of the Information seems to intimate that the Attack may be up the North River as well as at the lower posts, I have only to recommend to you to be as well prepared as possible for this important Event. Should any other Intelligence of Moment come to hand you may depend it shall be immediately communicated to you by Sir, etc.[83]    [MS.H.S.]

---

[82] Probably Capt. Anthony Post, who was with the Artificers of the Second Continental Artillery, Jan. 1, 1777.

[83] In the writing of Tench Tilghman.

## To MAJOR GENERAL PHILIP SCHUYLER

New York, August 21, 1776.

Dear Sir: On Monday I received your favor of the 16th Instant with its Several Inclosures. The time you were in Treaty, I can readily conceive was Irksome and disagreable, However, If the Good consequences you Intended, are produced, you will think it well spent.

General Carleton's Orders, for their Indecent, Illiberal Scurrility, are equal if not superior to any thing I have seen, and are such as I could not have expected from a person of his High rank. He holds forth a Language very different from General Howe, as you would perceive by the Copy of his Letter I transmitted you. The Assassination of General Gordon is a matter intirely new, having never heard of it before. The paper made up as a Letter and directed to me, which Major Bigelow brought with him, only contained a Copy of the Orders.

I am glad the works at Fort Stanwix are going on so well and that they have so much provision in Store. In a little time I hope they will be strong and Compleat.

By a letter from Governor Trumbull, I am Informed that a Captain Van Buren had procured a sufficient Quantity of Sail Cloth, and part of the Cordage wanted for the Gallies, in Connecticut, and that the rest would be probably Obtained there. Upon the whole, I hope Necessaries to fit them out, will be obtained one way or other.

The Inclosed Letter from Colonel Stark was transmitted and refered to me by General Gates, in Order that I might determine upon the Subject of it. I should suppose the Value of Rations, ought to be settled with the Commissary or Submitted to Congress for their decision. I do not conceive it is with me to direct in this Instance, and therefore think it right to give notice of It by this Opportunity.

Since my Last of the 13th, nothing worthy of mention has occurred in this Quarter, unless the Ships of War having left their Stations up the North River and Joined the Fleet again, is considered as such. On Sunday Morning they came down with their remaining Tenders. It is more than probable that an Attempt by two of our fire Vessels to destroy them a Night or two before, contributed to their departure. The Enterprize, tho' conducted with Spirit and resolution, did not succeed to our Wishes, only one Tender having been burnt. The Phœnix was grappled for some time, but cleared herself without Damage. I am &c.

### To THE PRESIDENT OF CONGRESS

New York, August 21, 1776.

Sir: Inclosed I have the Honor to transmit you, a Copy of my Letter to Lord Howe, as well on the Subject of a General Exchange of Prisoners in the Naval Line, as that of Lieut. Josiah in particular, and of his Lordship's Answer; which for its matter and manner is very different from General Carlton's Orders which were forwarded yesterday.[84]

The Situation of the Armies being the same as when I had the pleasure of addressing you last, I have nothing special to communicate on that Head, nor more to add than that I am etc.[85]

### *To MAJOR GENERAL WILLIAM HEATH

New York, August 22, 1776.

Dear Sir: As the Enemy must pass this place before they can attempt the Posts above, and as your Troops there, are now augmented, I would have you pick out a body of about Eight hundred or a thousand light active men, and good Marksmen (Including the light Infantry and Riffle Men) ready to move

---

[84] Washington's letter and Howe's answer, dated Aug. 19, 1776, are in the *Washington Papers*. (See Washington's letter to Sir William Howe, Aug. 17, 1776, *ante*.)
[85] In the writing of Robert Hanson Harrison.

this way upon the appearance of the Shipping coming up, or upon the commencement of the Canonade of any of our Works.

By the time these Troops get into the flat grounds of Harlem, they will be able (especially if you send a Horseman or two on before for Intelligence which will be proper) to determine whether the Ships Intend higher up than this neighbourhood and regulate themselves accordingly.

There is a road out of the Harlem flat Lands that leads up to the Hills and continues down the North River by Bloomingdale, Delancy's, &c., which road I would have them March as they will keep the River in Sight and pass a tolerable Landing place for Troops in the Neighbourhood of Bloomingdale; this Detachment should bring a couple of light field Pieces.

I think two, or even four, pieces of Cannon might be spared from Fort Washington to the Post over the Bridge. But query whether it might not do to run them from thence when occasion shall seem to require it as that Post never can be attacked without sufficient notice to do this. Colo. Knox will have four Carriages ready for that place immediately if we have not other Imployment upon hand, which General Putnam who is this Instant come In seems to think we assuredly shall this day as there is a considerable Imbarkation on board of the Enemy's Boats. I shall therefore only add that you should delay no time in forming your Detachment for our aid, or your own Defence as Circumstances may require. Yours &c, in haste.    [MS.H.S.]

## To THE PRESIDENT OF CONGRESS

New York, August 22, 1776.

Sir: I do myself the Honor to transmit Congress a Copy of a Letter I received Yesterday Evening by Express from General Livingston;[86] also Copies of three reports from Colonel Hand.

---

[86] Brig. Gen. William Livingston. His letter conveyed a spy's intelligence from Staten Island of the intended attack by the British.

Tho' the Intelligence reported by the Spy on his return to General Livingston, has not been confirmed by the Event he mentions, "Vizt. an Attack last night," there is every reason to induce a belief that one is shortly designed.

The falling down of several Ships Yesterday Evening to the narrows crowded with men. Those succeeded by several more this Morning and a great number of Boats parading around them as I was just now informed, with Troops; are all circumstances indicating an Attack, and it's not Improbable it will be made to day.—It could not have happened last night by reason of a most violent Gust.

We are making every preparation to receive them, and I trust, under the smiles of Providence, with our own exertions, that my next, if they do attack will transmit an Account which will be pleasing to every Friend of America and to the rights of Humanity. I have, etc.[87]

### To MAJOR GENERAL WILLIAM HEATH

Head Quarters, New York, August 23, 1776.

Sir: Yesterday Morning the Enemy landed at Gravesend Bay upon Long Island, from the best Information I can obtain, to the Number of about Eight Thousand. Colonel Hand[88] retreated before them, burning as he came along several parcels of Wheat and such other matters, as he Judged would fall into the Enemy's Hands. Our first accounts were, that they intended, by a forced march, to surprize General Sullivan's (who commands during the illness of General Greene) Line's, whereupon I immediately reinforced that post with Six Regiments; But they halted last Night at Flat Bush. If they should attack General Sullivan this day, and should shew no disposition to

---

[87] In the writing of Robert Hanson Harrison.

[88] Col. Edward Hand. He was colonel of the First Continental Infantry, First Pennsylvania Regiment, and, later, brigadier general and Adjutant General of the Continental Army.

attack me likewise, at the making of the next Flood, I shall send such further Reinforcements to Long Island as I may Judge expedient, not chusing to weaken this post too much, before I am certain, that the Enemy are not making a Feint upon Long Island to draw our Force to that Quarter, when their real design may perhaps be upon this. I am &c.

P. S. The Flood Tide will begin to make about Eleven o'Clock, at which time, if the Detachment Ordered Yesterday, were to move to the high, and open Grounds about Mr. O. Delancey's and Bloomingdale, they would be ready to come forward, or return back, as occasion should require, it will give them a little Exercise, and shew them wherein they are wanting in any matter.[89]

### To THE PRESIDENT OF CONGRESS

New York, August 23, 1776.

Sir: I beg leave to inform Congress that Yesterday Morning and in the course of the preceeding night, a considerable body of the Enemy, amounting by report to eight or nine thousand, and these all British, Landed from the Transport Ships mentioned in my last, at Gravesend Bay on Long Island, and have approached within three miles of our Lines, having marched across the Low, cleared Grounds, near the Woods at Flat Bush where they are halted, from my last Intelligence.

I have detached from hence, Six Battalions, as a reinforcement to our Troops there, which are all that I can spare at this Time, not knowing but the fleet may move up with the remainder of their Army and make an Attack here on the next flood Tide. If they do not, I shall send a further reinforcement should it be necessary, and have ordered five Battalions more to be in readiness for that purpose. I have no doubt but a little Time will produce some Important events. I hope they will be

---

[89] In the writing of Tench Tilghman; the P. S. is in that of Washington.

happy. The Reinforcement detached Yesterday went off in high Spirits and I have the pleasure to inform you that the whole of the Army that are effective and capable of duty, discover the same, and great chearfulness.

I have been Obliged to appoint Major General Sullivan to the Command on the Island, owing to General Greene's Indisposition, he has been extremely ill for several days and still Continues bad.

By Wednesday Evening's Post I received a Letter from General Ward, inclosing a Copy of the Invoice of Ordinance Stores taken by Captain Manly with the Appraisement of the same, made in pursuance of my direction founded on the Order of Congress, which I do myself the honor of transmitting.

You will also receive the Treaty between the Commissioners and Indians of the six Nations and others at the German Flats, which General Schuyler requested me to forward, by his Letter of the 18th. Instant. I have &ca.[90]

## To THE NEW YORK LEGISLATURE

Head Quarters, New York, August 23, 1776.

Gentn.: I am favored with yours of the 22d, acquainting me with a report now Circulating, "that if the American Army should be obliged to retreat from this City, any Individual may set it on fire."[91]

---

[90] In the writing of Robert Hanson Harrison.

[91] "The Convention of this State have received Information from one of the Deputies of the City and County of New York of a Report prevailing amongst the Army that if the fortune of War should oblige our Troops to abandon that City, it should be immediately burnt by the retreating Soldiery, and that Any Man is authorized to set it on fire.

"The Convention will chearfully submit to the fatal necessity of destroying that Valuable City whenever your Excellency shall deem it essential to the Safety of this State or the general Interest of America. Yet the Duty which they owe to their Constituents obliges them to take every possible Precaution that Twenty thousand Inhabitants may not be reduced to Misery by the wanton Act of an Individual.

"They therefore entreat the favor of your Excellency to take such Measures in preventing the evil Tendency of such a Report as you shall deem most Expedient."—*New York Legislature to Washington*, Aug. 22, 1776. This letter is in the *Washington Papers*.

I can Assure you Gentlemen, this Report is not founded upon the least Authority from me; on the Contrary, I am so Sensible of the Value of such a City and the Consequences of its destruction, to many worthy Citizens and their Families, that nothing but the last Necessity and that such as should justify me to the whole World, would induce me to give orders for that purpose.

The unwillingness shewn by many families to remove, notwithstanding your and my Recommendation, may perhaps have led some persons to propogate the Report, with honest and Innocent intentions; but as your Letter first informed me of it, I cannot pretend to say by whom or what purpose it has been done.

As my Views with regard to the Removal of the Women and Children, have happily coincided with your Sentiments and a Committee appointed to Carry them into execution; I submit it to your judgment, whether it would not be proper for the Committee to meet immediately in this City, and give Notice of their Attendance on this Business. There are many who anxiously wish to remove but have not the Means. I am etc.

### GENERAL ORDERS

Head Quarters, New York, August 23, 1776.

Parole Charlestown.   Countersign Lee.

The Commissary General is directed to have five days Bread baked, and ready to be delivered: If the Commissary should apply to the commanding officers of regiments, for any Bakers, they are to furnish them without waiting for a special order.

The General was sorry yesterday to find, that when some troops were ordered to march, they had no provisions, notwithstanding the Orders that have been issued. The men must march, if the service requires it, and will suffer very much if not provided: The General therefore directs, all the Troops to have two days hard Bread, and Pork, ready by them; and desires the officers will go through the encampment, and quarters, to see that it be got and kept.

The General would be obliged to any officer, to recommend to him, a careful, sober person who understands taking care of Horses and waiting occasionally. Such person being a Soldier will have his pay continued, and receive additional wages of twenty Shillings pr Month—He must be neat in his person, and to be depended on for his honesty and sobriety.

The officers of the militia are informed, that twenty-four Rounds are allowed to a man, and two Flints; that the Captains of each Company should see that the Cartridges fit the bore of the gun; they then are to be put up in small Bundles; All the Cartridges except six; writing each mans name on his bundle, and keep them safely 'till the Alarm is given, then deliver to each man his bundle; the other six to be kept for common use. In drawing for ammunition, the commanding officers should, upon the regimental parade, examine the state of their regiments, and then draw for Cartridges, and Flints, agreeable to the above regulation. Capt. Tilton will assist them in their business, and, unless in case of alarm, they are desired not to draw for every small number of men, who may be coming in.

The Enemy have now landed on Long Island, and the hour is fast approaching, on which the Honor and Success of this army, and the safety of our bleeding Country depend. Remember officers and Soldiers, that you are Freemen, fighting for the blessings of Liberty—that slavery will be your portion, and that of your posterity, if you do not acquit yourselves like men: Remember how your Courage and Spirit have been dispised, and traduced by your cruel invaders; though they have found by dear experience at Boston, Charlestown and other places, what a few brave men contending in their own land, and in the best of causes can do, against base hirelings and mercenaries—Be cool, but determined; do not fire at a distance, but wait for orders from your officers—It is the General's express orders that if any man attempt to skulk, lay down, or retreat without Orders he be instantly shot down as an example, he hopes no such Scoundrel will be found in this army; but on the contrary, every one for himself resolving to conquer, or die, and trusting to the smiles of heaven upon so just a cause, will behave with Bravery and Resolution: Those who are distinguished for their Gallantry, and good Conduct, may depend upon being honorably noticed, and suitably rewarded: And if this Army will but emulate, and imitate their brave Countrymen, in other parts of America, he has no doubt they will, by a glorious Victory, save their Country, and acquire to themselves immortal Honor.

The Brigade Majors are immediately to relieve the Guards out of the regiments order'd to Long Island, from other regiments of the brigade, and forward such Guards to the regiments.

Major Newbury's Col Hinmans, Major Smiths, Col Cook's, Col Talcots, Col Baldwin's and Major Strong's Regiments of Connecticut Militia to parade this evening precisely at five OClock on the Grand parade—Major Henly will attend and shew them their alarm posts, and direct them in manning the lines.

When any of the Field Officers for Picquet, or Main Guard, are sick, or otherwise incapable of the duty, they are immediately to signify it to their Brigade Major—but the General hopes that triffling excuses will not be made, as there is too much reason to believe has been the case.

### *To THE PRESIDENT OF CONGRESS

New York, August 24, 1776.

The irregularity of the Post prevents your receiving the early and constant Intelligence it is my Wish to communicate. This is the third Letter which you will, probably, receive from me, by the same Post. The first was of little or no consequence, but that of Yesterday gave you the best Information I had been able to obtain of the Enemy's Landing, and movements upon Long Island. Having occasion to go over thither Yesterday, I sent my Letter to the Post Office at the usual hour (being informed that the Rider was expected every Moment and wou'd go out again directly) but in the Evening, when I sent to enquire, none had come in.

I now Inclose you a report made to me by Gen. Sullivan, after I left Long Island Yesterday. I do not conceive that the Enemy's whole Force was in Motion, but a detach'd Party rather. I have sent over four more Regiments with Boats, to be ready, either to reinforce the Troops under General Sullivan, or to return to this place, if the remainder of the Fleet at the Watering place, should push up to the City, which, hitherto (I mean since the Landing upon Long Island) they have not had in their power to do, on Acct. of the Wind, which has either been ahead, or two small, when the Tide has served. I have nothing further to trouble the Congress with at present than that I am, etc.

## GENERAL ORDERS

Head Quarters, New York, August 24, 1776.
Parole Jamaica. Countersign London.

All the intrenching tools are to be collected, and delivered in to the store. Officers who have given receipts will be called upon, as they are answerable for them if there should be any deficiency.

The General has appointed William Grayson Esqr. one of his Aide-du-Camps; he is to be obeyed and respected accordingly.

In Case of action, any orders delivered by Col Moylan Quarter Master General, as from the General, to be considered as coming from him, or as delivered by an Aide-du-Camp.

The Adjutants of the Connecticut Militia, are directed to make themselves acquainted, with parapet firing; and the other officers of those Corps would do well to attend to it, and practice their men every day: their Honor and Safety will much depend upon their avoiding any confusion in manning the lines.

The Court Martial of which Col Wyllys was President is dissolved.

The Brigade Majors, in forming the new one, to be careful to have it full, and officers who can attend.

The Court Martial to proceed at their first sitting to the tryal of Adjutant Brice of Col Smallwoods Battalion, charged with "Disobedience of orders."

The changing of the regiments occasioning some difficulties in the duty—The Brigade Majors are to send, by the Orderly Serjeants, every morning, a duty Return of the officers and men in their respective brigades.

The passage of the East-River being obstructed in such a manner, with Chevaux-de-Frizes &c, as to render it dangerous for any Vessels to attempt to pass; The Sentinels along the river, contigious to where the obstructions are placed, are to hail and prevent any Vessels attempting to pass, otherways than between the Albany Pier, and a Mast in the River, which appears above water nearly opposite.

## To MAJOR GENERAL PHILIP SCHUYLER

New York, August 24, 1776.

Dear Sir: I received your favor of the 18th. with its several Inclosures on Thursday, by Mr. Allen.

My Letter of the 13th. does not, nor was it meant to contain the most distant hint of your entertaining doubts or suspicions, of my not having Communicated to Congress, such parts of your Letters as were material. It was only designed to answer yours, where you say, since my arrival here you had not written to them on Military Affairs, supposing whatever Information you might give and which was necessary for them to know, would be communicated by me. My request to be advised of the Information you might give Congress of any matters, of which you write me at the same time, was to prevent my sending them unnecessary Intelligence and the trouble of having needless Copies and Extracts made out.

I am in hopes the Articles mentioned in the Letter to Captn. Varrick will have come to hand before this. Also those contained in the Inclosed List; shippd on Board the Schooner Union, Phillip Sandford, Master, the 19th. Instt., as the Quarter Master General has reported to me.

The Treaty with the Indians, agreable to your request, I have transmitted Congress.[92]

It gives me pleasure, to find the Vessels for the Lakes are in such forwardness and going on with so much Industry. I yet hope we shall have a Navy there, equal to every exigency, and that will be superior to those the Enemy can build. Captains Hawly and Chappel[93] are now here, with permission from Governor Trumbull and myself, to Inlist, if they can, Two Hundred Seamen out of the Militia Just sent from the State of Connecticut. How they will Succeed, I can not determine.

I wish you had proceeded as your own Judgement and Inclination led in the case refered to me for my advice, respecting Colonel Dayton's[94] Officers. I am sorry that persons of their rank and of their Connections should have given into such dishonourable and disgraceful practices, and I feel myself much

---

[92] This so-called treaty was really a conference with the Six Nations at German Flats, August 8–13. The speeches are printed in full in Force's *American Archives,* Fifth Series, vol. 1, 1035–1049.

[93] Capts. David Hawley and Frederick Chappell.

[94] Col. Elias Dayton, of the Third New Jersey Regiment. He was, later, of the Second New Jersey Regiment and, finally, brigadier general in the Continental Army.

concerned for themselves and Friends. But as the matter is with me to determine; As their making concessions at the Head of the Regiment would not answer any purpose, but that of rendering them Objects of Ridicule and Contempt; As they could never after claim and support, that Authority over their Inferiors, that is necessary to good Government and discipline; As public Justice and a regard to our Military character, require that matters of such a nature should meet every possible discouragement; As my conduct might otherwise be deemed reprehensible, and to deter others from the like conduct, which is but too prevalent, I cannot but advise that the several persons concerned be subjected to the Trial of a Court Martial. If the Court should be of Opinion that they ought to be broke and dismissed the Service, Colonel Dayton, His Major and other Officers will recommend such as will be proper persons to fill the Vacancies, occasioned by their removal.[95]

On Wednesday night and Thursday Morning a Considerable body of the Enemy, said to be Eight or Nine Thousand, landed at Gravesend Bay, on Long Island; They have approached within about three Miles of our Lines, and Yesterday there was some skirmishing between a Detachment from them, and a party from our Troops. Their Detachment were obliged to give Ground, and were pursued, as far as where they had a post at a Judge Lefferts's. His House and out Houses served as Quarters for them and were burnt by our people. we sustained no loss in this Affair, that I have heard of, except having two Men slightly wounded. Our people say the Enemy met with more. They found one Dead body, in the Habit of a Soldier, with a good deal of Money in his pocket, and got three Hangers and a Fusee. They fired a shell from a Howitz, which fell on and bursted in

---

[95] Some of Dayton's officers broke open the doors of Johnson Hall and plundered the private effects therein.

a House where some of the Enemy were, but whether they were Injured by it, I have not learnt.  A Firing has been heard this Morning, but know nothing of the Event.  I am &c.

## To GOVERNOR JONATHAN TRUMBULL

New York, August 24, 1776.

Sir: On thursday last the Enemy landed a body of Troops, supposed to Amount (from the best Accounts I have been able to obtain) to Eight or Nine Thousand Men at Gravesend Bay on Long Island, Ten Miles distance from our Works, (on the Island) and immediately marched thro' the Level and open Lands to Flat Bush, where they are now incamped:—They are distant about three Miles from our Lines, and have Woods and broken Ground to pass (which we have lined), before they can get to them; some Skirmishing has happened between their Advanced parties and ours, in which we have always obtained an Advantage; what the real Designs of the Enemy are, I am not yet able to determine.  My Opinion of the Matter is, that they mean to attack our Works on the Island, and this City, at the same time, and that the Troops at Flat Bush are waiting in those Plains, till the Wind and tide (which have not yet served together) will favor the Movement of the Shipping to this place; Others think they will bend their principal Force against our Lines on the Island, which if carried will greatly facilitate their designs upon this City.  This also being very probable, I have thrown what force I can over, without leaving myself too much exposed here; for our whole Numbers, if the Intelligence we get from Deserters &c. be true, falls short of that of the Enemy, consequently the defence of our own Works, and the approaches to them, is all we can aim at.  This then in a Manner leaves the whole Island in possession of the Enemy, and of Course, of the Supplies it is capable of affording them.  Under these Circumstances, would it be practicable for your Government to throw a Body of about one thousand or more Men across the Sound, to harrass the Enemy in their rear or upon their Flanks? This would annoy them exceedingly, at the same time that a Valuable end, to wit, that of preventing their parties securing the Stocks of Cattle &c. would be answered by it. The Cattle to be removed or killed. The knowledge I have of the extraordinary Exertions of your State, upon all occasions, does not permit me to require this (not knowing how far it is practicable); I only offer it therefore, as a Matter for your Consideration and of great Public Utility, if it can be accomplished. The Enemy, if my Intelligence from Staten Island be true, are at this time rather distressed on Account of Provisions; if then we can deprive them of what this Island affords, much good will follow from it.

The foreigners are yet upon Staten Island.[96] The British Troops are upon Long Island and on Ship Board. With my great respect and Esteem, I remain etc.

## To MAJOR GENERAL ISRAEL PUTNAM

Head Quarters, August 25, 1776.

Sir: It was with no small degree of concern, I perceived Yesterday, a scattering, unmeaning and Wasteful fire, from our people at the Enemy; a kind of fire that tended to disgrace our own Men; as Soldiers, and to render our defence contemptible in the eyes of the Enemy; no one good consequence can attend such irregularities, but several bad ones, will inevitably follow from it. Had it not been for this unsoldierlike and disorderly practice, we have the greatest reason imaginable to believe, that numbers of deserters would have left the Enemy's Army, last

---

[96] This was an error, as a part of the Germans, Colonel Donop's corps of chasseurs and Hessian grenadiers, were landed on the 22d. Lieutenant General von Heister, commander in chief of the Hessian forces in America, with two brigades of Hessians, joined the army on Long Island on the 25th.—*Ford*.

year, but fear prevented them from approaching our Lines then, and must for ever continue to operate in like manner whilst every Soldier conceives himself at Liberty to fire when, and at what he pleases.

This is not the only nor the greatest evil resulting from the practice; for as we do not know the hour of the Enemy's approach to our lines, but have every reason to apprehend that it will be sudden and violent, whenever attempted; we shall have our men so scattered, and (more than probable) without Ammunition, that the consequences must prove fatal to us; besides this there will be no possibility of distinguishing between a real and false alarm.

I must therefore Sir, in earnest terms, desire you to call the Colonels and commanding Officers of Corps, (without loss of time) before you[97]; and let them afterwards do the same by their respective Officers, and charge them, in express, and positive terms, to stop these irregularities, as they Value the good of the service, their own Honor, and the safety of the Army; which under God, depends wholly upon the good order and Government that is observed in it.

At the same time, I would have you form a proper line of defence, round your Encampment and Works, on the most advantageous ground; your guards, which compose this, are to be particularly instructed in their duty, and a Brigadier of the day, to remain constantly upon the lines, that he may be upon the spot to command, and see that orders are executed; Field Officers should also be appointed to go the rounds and report the Situation of the Guards; no person to be allowed to pass beyond the Guards, without special order in writing.

By restraining the loose, disorderly and unsoldierlike firing before mentioned, I do not mean to discourage Partizan and

---

[97] Putnam had just been sent over to take the general command on Long Island. Sullivan had the immediate command of all the troops not within the lines at Brooklyn.—*Sparks.*

scouting parties; on the contrary I wish to see a Spirit of this sort prevailing, under proper regulations, and Officers either commissioned or non commissioned (as cases shall require) to be directed by Yourself or Licensed by the Brigadier of the day, upon the spot, to be sent upon this service. Such skirmishing as may be effected in this manner, will be agreable to the rules of propriety, and may be attended with salutary effects; inasmuch as it will inure the Troops to Fatigue and danger; will harrass the Enemy, may make prisoners and prevent their parties from getting the Horses and Cattle from the interior parts of the Island, which are objects of infinite importance to us, especially the two last.

All the Men not upon duty, are to be compelled to remain in, or near their respective camps, or Quarters, that they may turn out at a moments warning; nothing being more probable, than that the Enemy will allow little enough time to prepare for the attack.

The Officers also are to exert themselves, to the utmost to prevent every kind of abuse to private property, or to bring every Offender, to the punishment he deserves; shameful it is to find that these men, who have come hither in defence of the rights of mankind, should turn invaders of it, by destroying the substance of their friends.

The burning of Houses, where the apparent good of the Service is not promoted by it, and the pillaging of them, at all times, and upon all Occasions, is to be discountenanced and punished with the utmost severity. In short, it is to be hoped, that men who have property of their own, and a regard for the rights of others, will shudder at the thought of rendering any Man's Situation, to whose protection he had come, more insufferable, than his open and avowed Enemy would make it, when by duty and every rule of humanity, they ought to Aid, and not Oppress, the distressed in their habitations.

The distinction between a well regulated Army, and a Mob, is the good order and discipline of the first, and the licentious and disorderly behaviour of the latter; Men, therefore, who are not employed, as mere hirelings, but have steped forth in defence of every thing that is dear and Valuable, not only to themselves but to posterity, should take uncommon pains to conduct themselves with uncommon propriety and good Order, as their honor, reputation &c. call loudly upon them for it.

The wood next red Hook should be well attended to, put some of the most disorderly rifle men into it; The Militia are most indifferent Troops (those I mean which are least tutored and seen least service) will do for the interior Works, whilst your best Men should at all hazards prevent the Enemy's passing the Wood, and approaching your Works. The Woods should be secured by Abattis &c. where Necessary to make the Enemy's approach, as difficult as possible; Traps and ambuscades should be laid for their parties, if you find they are sent out after Cattle &c.

### GENERAL ORDERS

Head Quarters, New York, August 25, 1776.

Parole Marlborough.   Countersign Newtown.

A special Court Martial to sit this day at twelve OClock, at Mrs. Montagnies for the tryal of Lieut. Col Zedwitz,[98] charged with "carrying on a treasonable correspondence with the enemy" to be composed of a Brigadier General and twelve Field Officers—General Wadsworth[99] to preside.

---

[98] Lieut. Col. Harman Zedwitz, of the First New York Regiment. He had been called upon to translate into German the resolves of Congress (August 14) enticing the Hessians to desert. He wrote to Governor Tryon, informing him of the resolves and offering to serve as a British spy; his letter was intercepted. The court-martial proceedings are in the *Washington Papers*, and Zedwitz's letter is published in facsimile in Force's *American Archives,* Fifth Series, vol. 1.

[99] Brig. Gen. James Wadsworth, of the Connecticut Militia; major general of the same, 1777–1779.

The General Order against working on Sunday is revoked the time not admitting of any delay. The same number of fatigue men to turn out, as yesterday, this afternoon at three OClock, as well Militia as other troops.

Col Smallwood[1] to command Lord Stirling's Brigade during his absence on Long Island.

## GENERAL ORDERS

Head Quarters, New York, August 26, 1776.

Parole Newcastle.   Countersign Paris.

Six hundred men properly officered, from General Wolcot's Brigade, to parade to morrow morning, at six o'clock, on the Grand Parade, without arms for fatigue: Four hundred to take directions from General McDougall, and two hundred from Lieut. Fish;[2] and the same number to be continued 'till the works are completed; to leave work at young flood, and go on again at the ebb.

The General is very anxious for the state of the arms and ammunition, the frequent Rains giving too much reason to fear they may suffer; He therefore earnestly enjoins officers and men to be particularly attentive to it and have them in the best order.

## To THE PRESIDENT OF CONGRESS

New York, August 26, 1776.

Sir: I have been duly honored with your favors of the 20th. and 24th. and am happy to find my Answer to Lord Drummond has met the approbation of Congress. Whatever his

---

[1] Col. William Smallwood, of a Maryland regiment. He was wounded at White Plains, N. Y., and was, later, a brigadier and major general in the Continental Army. He was thanked by Congress for his conduct at Camden, S. C., in August, 1780.

[2] Lieut. Nicholas Fish, of Malcolm's New York State regiment. He was brigade major to General Scott in August, 1776, and major of the Third New York Regiment in November, 1776, serving to June, 1783.

views were, most certainly his conduct respecting his parole is highly reprehensible.

Since my Letter of the 24th., almost the whole of the Enemy's Fleet have fallen down to the Narrows and from this circumstance, the striking of their Tents at their several Incampments on Staten Island, from time to time, previous to the Departure of the Ships from thence; we are led to think, they mean to land the Main Body of their Army on Long Island, and to make their grand push there. I have ordered over considerable Reinforcements to our Troops there, and shall continue to send more as circumstances may require. There has been a little Skirmishing and irregular firing kept up between their and our advanced Guards, in which Colonel Martin[3] of the Jersey Levies has received a Wound in his Breast, which is apprehended will prove Mortal. A private has had his Leg broke by a Cannon Ball, and another has received a shot in the Groin from their Musquetry. This is all the Damage they have yet done us. What they have sustained is not known.

The Shifting and changing the Regiments have undergone of late, has prevented their making proper returns and of course put it out my Power to transmit a general one of the Army. However I believe our Strength is much the same, that it was when the last was made, with the Addition of Nine Militia Regiments more from Connecticut averaging about 350 Men each these are 9 of the 14 Regiments mentioned in my Letter of the 19th.—Our people still continue to be very sickly.

The Papers designed for the foreign Troops, have been put into several Channels, in order that they might be conveyed to them, and from the Information I had Yesterday, I have reason to believe many have fallen into their Hands.[4]

---

[3] Col Ephraim Martin, of the New Jersey Militia. He was appointed colonel of the Fourth New Jersey Regiment Nov. 23, 1776, but never joined, presumably on account of his wound. He died in 1806.

[4] See note to Washington's letter to Congress, Aug. 18, 1776, *ante.*

I have inclosed a Copy of Lord Drummond's second Letter[5] in Answer to mine, which I received since I transmitted his first and which I have thought proper to lay before Congress; that they may possess the whole of the correspondence between us, and see how far he has exculpated himself from the Charge alleged against him. The Log Book he mentions to have sent Colonel Moylan, proves nothing in his favor; That shews he had been at Bermuda and from thence to some other place, and on his passage from which to this place, the Vessel he was in was commanded by a pilot who brought her into the Hook, where he found the British Fleet which his Lordship avers he did not expect were there, having understood their destination was to the Southward. I am &ca.[6]

## To MAJOR GENERAL ARTEMAS WARD

Head Quarters, New York, August 26, 1776.

Sir: I am now to Acknowledge the Receipt of your's of the 15th. and 19th. Instant and am much obliged for your care and dispatch in forwarding the Two Sea Morters which I wish may come safe to hand. The number and strength of the Enemy and the many different posts we have to occupy together with the late Manoeuvres of General Howe render it utterly impossible for me to relieve you by sending a General Officer from this to take Command in Boston, Congress seeing the Situation pass'd the enclosed Resolve,[7] and I cannot but hope you will conclude to keep the Command till something decisive is done with our formidable Enemy in this Quarter, who have landed most of their Army on Long Island and advanced part of them as far as Flatt Bush within three Miles of our Works; between them and the Works is a Ridge of Hills covered wt. Woods in

---

[5] Drummond's letter, dated Aug. 19, 1776, is in the *Washington Papers*.
[6] In the writing of Robert Hanson Harrison.
[7] The resolve of Aug. 21, 1776, requesting Ward to continue in the service.

which I have posted a large Body of the Army, which have once repulsed an advanced party of them in an attempt to get through and I cannot but hope will prevent or at least weaken them much should they effect their purpose of passing. I am, etc.[8]

[MS. H. S.]

## To MAJOR GENERAL WILLIAM HEATH

Head Quarters, New York, August 26, 1776.

Dr. Sir: I have now before me your letters of the 23rd. and 24th. of this Inst. with respect to the detachment I directed on the 23rd., I conceive it to be highly expedient that they be kept in the most perfect readiness to act as the circumstances of affairs may render necessary; the present appearance of things seems to indicate an intention in the enemy to make their capital impression on the side of Long Island; but this may possibly be only a feint, to draw over our troops to that quarter, in order to weaken us here; As to the floating bridge you have mentioned for keeping open the communication on Harlem river, I entirely approve of the application of the fire rafts to that purpose provided they will answer the design, to which you intend to convert them; I should think that a General or Garrison Court martial at your quarters for tryal of offenders (in cases not capital) would be useful and proper; The Qur. M. Genl. informs me he has sent up a person last week for the purpose of securing the sails and rigging taken from the vessels lately sunk near Mount Washington.

I have spoke to some gentlemen on the subject of Hardenburgh's[9] death who (I make no doubt) will convey the account to his brother, I am, etc.[10]

[MS. H. S.]

---

[8] In the writing of Samuel Blatchley Webb.

[9] Heath's letter (August 24) gives the name as Hardenbrook, but Washington interpreted it as Hardenbergh. There were several officers by the name of Hardenbergh among the New York troops. Heath's letter is in the *Washington Papers*.

[10] In the writing of William Grayson.

## To THE PRESIDENT OF CONGRESS

New York, Eight O'Clock, P. M., August 27, 1776.

Sir: I this minute returned from our Lines on Long Island, where I left his Excellency the General. From him I have It in command to Inform Congress, that yesterday he went there, and continued till Evening, when, from the Enemy's having landed a considerable part of their Forces, and from many of their movements, there was reason to apprehend they would make in a little time a General Attack. As they would have a Wood to pass through before they could approach the Lines, it was thought expedient to place a number of men there on the different Roads leading from whence they were stationed, in order to harass and annoy them in their March. This being done, early this morning a Smart engagement ensued between the Enemy and our Detachments, which, being unequal to the force they had to contend with, have sustained a pretty considerable loss. At least many of our Men are missing, among those that have not returned, are General Sullivan and Lord Stirling. The Enemy's loss is not known certainly; but we are told by such of our Troops as were in the Engagement, and what have come in, that they had many killed and wounded. Our party brought off a Lieutenant, Sergeant, and Corporal, with twenty privates, prisoners.

While These Detachments were engaged, a Column of the enemy descended from the Woods, and marched towards the Centre of our Lines with a design to make an Impression, but were repulsed. This Evening they appeared very numerous about the Skirts of the Woods, where they have pitched Several Tents; and his Excellency Inclines to think they mean to attack and force us from our Lines by way of regular approaches, rather than in any other manner. To day Five Ships of the

Line came up towards the Town, where they seemed desirous of getting, as they turned a long time against an unfavorable Wind; and, on my return this Evening, I found a Deserter from the 23d Regiment, who Informed me that they design, as soon as the Wind will permit 'em to come up, to give us a Severe Cannonade, and to Silence our Batteries, If possible. I have the honor etc.                    ROBT H. HARRISON.

## To THE NEW YORK LEGISLATURE

Long Island, August 28, 1776.

Sir: I was just honoured with your favour of this date, with General Woodhull's[11] letter, and should esteem myself happy were it in my power to afford the assistance required; but the enemy having landed a considerable part of their force here, and at the same time may have reserved some to attack New York, it is the opinion not only of myself, but of all my General Officers I have had an opportunity of consulting with, that the men we have are not more than competent to the defence of these lines, and the several posts which must be defended. This reason, and this only, prevents my complying with your request.

I shall beg leave to mention, in confidence, that a few days ago, upon the enemy's first landing here, I wrote to Governour Trumbull, recommending him to throw over a body of one thousand men on the Island, to annoy the enemy in their rear, if the state of the Colony would admit of it. Whether it will be done, I cannot determine. That Colony having furnished a large proportion of men, I was, and still am doubtful whether it could be done. If it could, I am satisfied it will, from the zeal and readiness they have ever shown to give every possible

---

[11]Brig. Gen. Nathaniel Woodhull, of the New York Militia. He was captured by the British and wounded after being taken prisoner at Brooklyn, N. Y., on August 28 and died of his wounds on September 20.

succour. I am hopeful they will be in a condition to do it, and, if they are, those troops I doubt not will be ready and willing to give General Woodhull any assistance he may want. But cannot the Militia effect what he wished to do? They, I believe, must be depended on in the present instance for relief. I have the honour to be, etc.[12]

## To THE PRESIDENT OF CONGRESS

Long Island, August 29, half past four, A. M., 1776.

Sir: I was last night honoured with your favor of the 27th. accompanied by sundry Resolutions of Congress. Those respecting the officers, &c that may be wounded in the service of the States are founded much in Justice, and I should hope may be productive of many salutary consequences. As to the Encouragement to the Hessian Officers, I wish it may have the desired effect, perhaps it might have been better, had the offer been sooner made.

Before this you will probably have received a Letter from Mr. Harrison of the 27th. advising of the Engagement between a Detachment of our Men and the Enemy on that day.[13] I am sorry to inform Congress. that I have not yet heard either of General Sullivan or Lord Stirling, who were among the missing after the Engagement; nor can I ascertain our loss, I am hopefull part of our Men will yet get in, several did yesterday morning. That of the Enemy is also uncertain. The accounts

---

[12] The text is from Force's *American Archives*. He apparently took it from the *Journal of the New York Convention*.

[13] Washington remained on Long Island. Stirling's letter to Washington from the British man-of-war *Eagle* (August 29), Colonel Haslet's letter to Thomas Rodney (October 4), and General Sullivan's to the President of Congress (October 25), all of which Sparks prints, are the official sources supplementing Washington's report to Congress. (*See* Washington's letter to the President of Congress, Aug. 31, 1776, *post*. Harrison's letter from New York City, a short, 2-page account, is in the *Papers of the Continental Congress*. (See Harrison's letter to the President of Congress, Aug. 27, 1776, *ante*.) Sparks prints it in the Appendix to volume 4 of his *Writings of Washington*.

At a Council of War held at Long Island
Aug. 29. 1776

Present His Excell. G. Genl. Washington

Maj. Gen. Putnam    B. Gen.ds Parsons
              Spencer          Scott
                               Wadsworth
Brig. Generals Mifflin         Nixon
              McDougal

It was submitted to the Consideration of the Council
whether under all Circumstances it is not eligible
to leave Long Island & remove to New York. The Dependencies & remove to New York. — Unanimously agreed
on the Affirmative —    Israel Putnam
                        Jos. Spencer —
                        Thomas Mifflin
                        Alexr. McDougall
                        Sam H. Parsons
                        Jn. Morin Scott
                        James Wadsworth

COUNCIL OF WAR ON EVACUATION OF LONG ISLAND
AUGUST 29, 1776

are various, I incline to think they suffered a good deal. Some Deserters say five Hundred were killed and wounded. There was some skirmishing the greater part of yesterday, between parties from the Enemy and our People. In the Evening it was pretty smart, The Event I have not yet learned.

The weather of late has been extremely wet. Yesterday it rained severely the whole afternoon, which distressed our people much, not having a sufficiency of Tents to cover them, and what we have not got over yet, I am in hopes they will all be got to day[14] and that they will be more comfortably provided for, tho the great scarcity of these Articles distress us beyond measure, not having any thing like a sufficient number to protect our people from the Inclemency of the weather which has occasioned much sickness and the men to be almost broke down. I have the honor to be, &c.[15]


## GENERAL ORDERS

Head Quarters, New York, August 29, 1776.

Parole ———. Countersign ———.

One Orderly Serjeant from each Regiment in General Wadsworths, General Wolcot's and General Fellows's Brigades, and one from Col Knox's Command, to attend daily at Head Quarters until further orders.

The commanding officers of each company, in the several regiments in this post, are strictly required to attend, to the orders that have been given, by the Commander in Chief, from time to time, to see that their respective Rolls are looked over, and the orders of the day published to their whole company.

---

[14] Shee's, Magaw's, and Glover's regiments from Fort Washington. The order of August 29, ascribed by Johnston (*Campaign of 1776*) to Washington, is not of record in the General Orders of the Commander in Chief. It was probably issued by Putnam.

[15] In the writing of Robert Hanson Harrison.

And as it is the pleasure of the Commander in Chief of the Continental Forces, that all Soldiers that pass from Long Island here without passes, should immediately be sent back. All the Guards especially, and all others, belonging to the Army in this post, are required to take up all soldiers coming from Long Island without passes signed by a proper officer, and send them immediately back to Long Island.

The Colonels or commanding Officers of each Regiment must take care that the arms and ammunition of each soldier be in good order; that they be equipped and constantly ready for action. They must be particularly attentive to see that the Cartridges suit their peices.

All the guards, and also all others belonging to the Army, are to be vigilant in taking up, and confining, all persons guilty of disorderly firing, or firing without leave. All the guards supplied by general detail, are to be punctually on the Grand Parade by eight o'clock in the morning, and in case any Brigade Major does not punctually bring on the men, he is to furnish, the Brigadier of the day is to report him immediately, and if such Brigade Major is delayed by the negligence of an Adjutant, he is to put such Adjutant immediately under an arrest.

It is hoped that every officer and soldier, in this post, will exert himself for the good of the service, to the utmost; and as there are many intrenchments, now begun that are unfinished, that necessity requires should be immediately completed; it is justly expected that every brave man will exert himself to complete every needful fortification.

## To THE NEW YORK LEGISLATURE

New York, August 30, 1776.

Sir: Your favor of this date is just come to hand. Circumstanced as this Army was, in respect to Situation, Strength, &c,

it was the unanimous advice of a Council of General Officers,to give up Long Island; and not, by dividing our force, be unable to resist the Enemy in any one point of attack. This reason, added to some others, particularly the fear of having our Communication cut off from the Main, (of which there seemed to be no small probability), and the extreme fatigue our Troops were laid under, in guarding such extensive Lines, without proper shelter from the Weather, induced the above Resolution.

It is the most intricate thing in the World, Sir, to know in what Manner to conduct one's self with respect to the Militia; if you do not begin, many days before they are wanted to raise them, you cannot have them in time: if you do, they get tired and return; besides being under but very little order or Government whilst in Service. However, if the Enemy have a design of serving of us at this Place, as we apprehend they meant to do on Long Island: It might not be improper to have a Body in readiness, to prevent or retard a landing of them, on the East of Harlem River, if need be. In haste, and not a little fatigued, I remain, etc.

## To MAJOR GENERAL WILLIAM HEATH

Head Quarters, New York, August 30, 1776.
Sir: As Numbers of the Militia are going off without License, I desire you will stop all such at Kings bridge, as are not furnished with regular Discharges. I am, etc.[16]          [MS. H. S.]

## GENERAL ORDERS

Head Quarters, New York, August 30, 1776.
Parole Liberty.   Countersign Hancock.
All commanding Officers of regiments are to parade on their regimental parade, this evening at five o'Clock, examine the

---

[16]In the writing of Tench Tilghman.

state of their men's ammunition and arms, get them in the best Order—All damaged Cartridges are to be returned and in this case fresh ones drawn without farther order. The Returns of the regiments are to be made as soon, and as exact as possible. No Arguments can be necessary at such a time as this, to induce all officers to a strict attention to this duty.

The constant firing in the Camp, notwithstanding repeated Orders to the contrary, is very scandalous, and seldom a day passes but some persons are shot by their friends—Once more therefore the General entreats the officers to prevent it, and calls upon the Soldiers to forbear this practice—Peices that cannot be drawn are to be discharged in a Volley, at Retreat Beating, and not otherwise, and then by command of the officer.

The loss of two General Officers by the late Action having occasioned a necessary change in the brigades; the Brigade Majors are to attend ten OClock to morrow to receive a new arrangement.

As the Tents are wet, and Weather unfavorable, the troops are to remain in the City till further Orders; those not supplied with Barracks, to apply to Mr. Roorbach,[17] Barrack Master: Officers and Men are charged to see, as little damage as possible, done to houses where they are quartered.

General Wadsworth to send two Regiments from his Brigade, to reinforce Col Sergeant at Horns hook, as soon as possible.

In case of an Alarm this evening, which may be expected from the nearness of the enemy, and their expectation of taking advantage of the late Rains, and last nights fatigue; the following disposition is to take place and the regiments are to parade accordingly—General Mifflin's to parade on the Grand Parade, they are then to join the regiments lately composing Lord Stirlings Brigade, and the whole to parade on the parade lately assigned by him to them; these are to act under General Mifflin

---

[17] Garret Roorbach.

as a Reserve Corps. The Regiments of General Nixon's Brigade are to join General Spencer's division who will assign them their alarm posts—The Jersey Troops to join General McDougall's Brigade, and parade at, or near, said ground.

## GENERAL ORDERS

Head Quarters, New York, August 31, 1776.
Parole Harlem.   Countersign Flushing.

Major Livingston, charged with having ordered a Negroe to fire on a Soldier of Col. Newcomb's[18] Regiment is ordered to be confined and brought to trial: But the General is sorry to see Soldiers, defending their Country, in time of imminent danger, rioting and attempting to do themselves justice.

The Plunderers of Lord Stirling's house, are ordered to restore to the Quarter Master General, what they have taken, in failure whereof they will certainly be hanged.

It is the Generals orders that the remainder of Lutz's[19] and Kachlein's[20] Battalions be joined to Hand's Battalion; that Major Hays[21] be also under the special command of Col Hand; that then those Battalions, with Shee's, Col. Magaw's, Col. Huchinson's, Col Atlee's, Col. Miles, Col Wards Regiments be brigaded under General Mifflin, and those now here march, as soon as possible, to Kingsbridge. The Quarter-Master will supply waggons if to be spared, if not, to apply to Lieut. Achbolt[22] on the North River, Boat Station; or Ensign Allen[23] on the East; who will supply boats. A careful officer with a small

[18] Col. Silas Newcomb, of the New Jersey Militia. Later he was colonel of the First New Jersey Regiment and brigadier general of New Jersey Militia. He resigned in December, 1777.
[19] Lieut. Col. Nicholas Lutz, of the Pennsylvania battalion of the Flying Camp. He was wounded at Long Island and taken prisoner; exchanged in September, 1779, and did not reenter the service.
[20] Col. Peter Kachlein, of the Pennsylvania Militia.
[21] Lieut. Col. William Hay, of the Pennsylvania battalion of the Flying Camp.
[22] Lieut. Edward Archbald, of the Fourteenth Continental Infantry.
[23] Ensign Jonathan Allen, of Brewer's Massachusetts regiment.

guard to attend them. Major Lord will supply, from General Walcot's Brigade, an officer and six men to each boat, to bring boats back, except those that are ordered to stay.

Both officers and soldiers are informed that the Retreat from Long Island was made by the unanimous advice of all the General Officers,[24] not from any doubts of the spirit of the troops, but because they found the troops very much fatigued with hard duty and divided into many detachments, while the enemy had their Main Body on the Island, and capable of receiving assistance from the shipping: In these circumstances it was thought unsafe to transport the whole of an Army on an Island, or to engage them with a part, and therefore unequal numbers; whereas now one whole Army is collected together; without Water intervening, while the enemy can receive little assistance from their ships; their Army is, and must be divided into many bodies, and fatigued with keeping up a communication with their Ships; whereas ours is connected, and can act together: They must affect a landing under so many disadvantages, that if officers and soldiers are vigilant, and alert, to prevent surprise, and add spirit when they approach, there is no doubt of our success.

Ebenezer Gray is appointed Brigade Major to General Parsons.

The following disposition is made of the several Regiments, so as to form Brigades, under the commanding officers respectively mentioned.

[Brig.] Genl. [Samuel Holden] Parsons .  { [Jedidiah] Huntington  
[William] Prescot  
[Jonathan] Ward  
[John] Durkee  
[John] Tyler

---

[24] This council was held in Brooklyn, N. Y., on August 29. Washington, Maj. Gens. Israel Putnam and Joseph Spencer, Brig. Gens. Thomas Mifflin, Alexander McDougall, Samuel Holden Parsons, John Morin Scott, James Wadsworth, and John Fellows were present. The proceedings, in the writing of Robert Hanson Harrison and William Grayson, are in the *Washington Papers*. (See note to Washington's letter to Congress Aug. 31, 1776, *post*.)

[Brig.] Gen. [Alexander] McDougall . .
- McDougall
- [Rudolphus] Ritzema
- [William] Smallwood
- [Charles] Webb
- Artificers

[Brig.] Gen. [John Morin] Scott . . . .
- [Abraham] Lasher
- [William] Malcom
- [Samuel] Drake
- [Cornelius] Humphrey

[Brig.] Gen. [James] Wadsworth . . . .
- [Samuel] Chapman
- [Comfort] Sage
- [Samuel] Selden
- [Fisher] Gay
- [Philip Burr] Bradly

[Col.] Comdt. [Gold Selleck] Silliman .
- Silliman
- [Jabez] Thompson
- [Lt. Col. Ichabod] Lewis
- [Maj. Matthew] Mead
- [Benjamin] Hinman

[Brig.] Gen. [John] Nixon . . . . . .
- [James Mitchell] Varnum
- [Moses] Little
- [Daniel] Hitchcock
- Nixon
- [John] Bailey

[Brig.] Gen. [George] Clinton . . . .
- [John] Glover
- [James] Read
- [Loammi?] Baldwin
- [Ebenezer] Learned

[Brig.] Gen. [Nathaniel] Heard . . . .
- [Philip Van] Cortlandt
- [Philip] Johnson
- [Silas] Newcomb
- [Maj. Robert] Freeman
- [Ephraim] Martin

[Brig.] Gen. [John] Fellows . . . . .
- [John] Holman
- [Archibald?] Cary
- [Isaac?] Smith

| [Col.] Comdt. [John] Douglass . . . . . | Douglass |
|  | [Jonathan] Pettiborne |
|  | [John] Cook |
|  | [Matthew ?] Talcott |
|  | [Maj. Jabez?] Chapman |
| [Col.] Comdt. [John] Chester . . . . . . | Chester |
|  | [George] Pitkin |
|  | [Jonathan] Baldwin |
|  | [Maj. Simeon] Strong |
|  | [Maj. Roger] Newburry |
| [Col.] Comdt. [Paul Dudley] Serjeant . . | Serjeant |
|  | [Elisha] Sheldon |
|  | [Elizur ?] Talcot |

They are to chuse out capable, active and spirited persons, to act as Brigade Majors, who will be allowed for their service.

The General hopes the several officers, both superior and inferior, will now exert themselves, and gloriously determine to conquer, or die—From the justice of our cause—the situation of the harbour, and the bravery of her sons, America can only expect success—Now is the time for every man to exert himself, and make our Country glorious, or it will become contemptable.

Commanding Officers of regiments, are to take care to have hard Bread and Pork for two days kept by them constantly— The neglect of former orders, in this respect, has occasioned some of the hardships the troops have lately sustained—If there is any delay at the Commissary's, good officers will compose and quiet their men, and mention it by way of letter to the General.

## To MAJOR GENERAL WILLIAM HEATH

Head Quarters, New York, August 31, 1776.

Dr. Sir: I have receiv'd your letter of this day, and concur with you in sentiment as to the probability of the Enemy's endeavouring to land their forces at Hunts point, or some place not far distant from it; in order to prevent such an attempt from being carried into execution, I have sent up General Mifflin with the troops he brought from your quarters strengthened by a reinforcement; with this assistance, I hope you will be able to defeat their intentions; I beg you will exert yourself to the utmost of your abilities on this momentous occasion; In particular I must request of you, that the cheveaux de frise be immediately sunk; was it in my power to send you Col. Putnam, I would willingly comply with your request but we have so much business for him here, that he cannot by any means be spared; Colo. Knox has directed Capt. Bryan[25] to go up immediately; he recommends him as a good officer and equal to any that he has in the artillery; As to passes signed by Colos. of Regiments they are not to be permitted; none but those under the hand of a Brigadier general or one of superior rank are to have any reguard paid to them unless you hear something farther from me on that subject. I am, etc.[26]          [MS.H.S.]

### To MAJOR GENERAL HORATIO GATES

Head Quarters, New York, August 31, 1776.

Sir: As Congress have been pleased to give the Bearer Monsier Jean Artur De Vermonet a Commission for a Captaincy in the Continental Army, and he having expressed a Desire to act in the Northern Department on acct. of his being unacquainted with the English Language and thereby incapable of being so usefull here as he might be under you, I am therefore to request you will find some employment for him and the other Gentleman who accompanies him who means to act as a Volunteer, and has a Letter of Recommendation from Mr. Hancock approving of his intentions. I am, etc.[27]          [N.Y.H.S.]

[25] Capt.-Lieut. David Bryant, of Knox's artillery. Later he transferred to the Third Continental Artillery and was captain of same in May, 1777. He died of wounds received at Brandywine, Pa., in September, 1777.

[26] In the writing of William Grayson.

[27] In the writing of Richard Cary (?).

## To THE PRESIDENT OF CONGRESS

Head Quarters, New York, August 31, 1776.

Sir: Inclination as well as duty, would have induced me to give Congress, the earliest information of my removal of the Troops from Long Island and its dependencies to this City, the night before last; but the extreme fatigue, which myself and family have undergone (as much from the Weather as any thing else) since the incampment of the 27th. rendered me entirely unfit to take a pen in hand. Since Monday, we have scarce any of us been out of the Lines, till our passage across the East River was effected yesterday Morning, and for the 48 hours preceeding that; I had hardly been off my horse and had never closed my Eyes, so that I was quite unfit to write or dictate till this Morning.

Our Retreat was made without any loss of Men or Ammunition and in better order than I expected, from Troops in the Situation ours were; we brought off all our Cannon and Stores, except a few heavy pieces, (which in the condition the Earth was, by a long continued rain) we found upon tryal impracticable; the Wheels of the Carriages sunk up to the Hobbs, and rendered it impossible for our whole force to drag them; We left but little Provisions on the Island, except some Cattle, which had been driven within our Lines and which after many attempts to force across the Water, we found impossible to effect. I have inclosed a Copy of the Council of War held previous to the Retreat,[28] to which I beg leave to refer Congress for the reasons or many of them that led to the adoption of that measure.

---

[28] Held August 29. These proceedings, in the writing of Robert Hanson Harrison and William Grayson, are in the *Washington Papers.* They are accompanied by a minute of the unanimous decision to withdraw from Long Island to New York, in the writing of Joseph Reed, and signed by all the council except Washington and Fellows. From the appearance of the papers it seems that the advisability of obtaining a signed decision was an afterthought. (See General Orders, Aug. 31, 1776, *ante.*)

Yesterday Evening and last Night, a party of our Men were employed in removing our Stores, Cannon, Tents &ca. from Governors Island, which they nearly compleated. some of the Cannon yet remain but I expect will be got away to day.

In the Engagement on the 27th. Generals Sullivan and Stirling were made prisoners; The former has been permitted on his parole to return for a little time. From Lord Stirling I had a Letter by General Sullivan, a Copy of which I have the honor to transmit.[29] It contains his Information of the Engagement with his Brigade. It is not so full and certain as I could wish, he was hurried most probably, as his Letter was unfinished. Nor have I been yet able to obtain an exact amount of our Loss, we suppose it from 700 to a 1000 killed and taken.[30] General Sullivan says Lord Howe is extremely desirous of seeing some of the Members of Congress, for which purpose he was allowed to come out and to communicate to them what has passed between him and his Lordship. I have consented to his going to Philadelphia, as I do not mean or conceive it right to withhold or prevent him from giving such Information as he possesses, in this Instance.[31]

[29] This letter is in the *Washington Papers* and is printed by Sparks in Appendix to volume 4 of *Writings of Washington*. (See note to Washington's letter to Congress, Aug. 29, 1776, *ante*.) Howe's account of the battle is printed in Force's *American Archives*, Fifth Series, vol. 1, 1255–1256, from the *London Gazette Extraordinary*, Oct. 10, 1776. There are a number of monographs on the battle, T. W. Fields's being a satisfactory one.

[30] According to General Howe's return of the American prisoners taken on Long Island, the whole number amounted to 1,076. This list includes General Woodhull, and the militia under him, probably about 200, who were not in the action, but were taken afterwards at Jamaica. The British loss, as stated by General Howe, was 94 killed and missing and 283 wounded.—*Sparks*.

[31] Sullivan's visit and delivery of Lord Howe's message to Congress caused sharp debate in that body. John Adams referred to him as "a decoy duck whom Lord Howe has sent among us to seduce us into a renunciation of our independence," and he remarked *sotto voce* that he wished the first shot fired by the British in the Long Island engagement had gone through Sullivan's head. (See Benjamin Rush's *Memorial*.) A committee, consisting of Benjamin Franklin, John Adams, and Edward Rutledge, was finally appointed (September 6) to confer with Howe. They met on Staten Island, and the conference came to naught when it was discovered that Howe had no power to grant peace except on condition that the Declaration of Independence be rescinded.

I am much hurried and engaged in arranging and making new Dispositions of our Forces, the movements of the Enemy requiring them to be immediately had, and therefore have only time to add that I am, with my best regards to Congress, and to you. Their and your &ca.[32]

## REASONS OF COUNCIL OF WAR FOR EVACUATING LONG ISLAND

1st. Because Our advanced party had met with a defeat, & the wood was lost, where we expected to make a principal Stand.

2nd. The great loss sustained in the death or Captivity of Several valuable Officers and their Battallions, or a large part of them, has occasioned great confusion and discouragement among the Troops.

3rd. The Heavy rains which fell Two days and Nights with but Little Intermission have Injured the Arms and Spoiled a great part of the Ammunition, and the Soldiery being without Cover and obliged to lay in the Lines, were worn out, and It was to be feared would not be retained in them by any Order.

4th. From the Time the Enemy moved from Flatbush, Several large Ships had attempted to get up as Supposed into the East River to cut off our Communication by which the whole Army would have been destroyed. But the wind being N. E. could not effect It.

5th. Upon consulting with persons of knowledge of the Harbour, they were of Opinion that Small Ships might come between Long Island and Governors Island where there are no obstructions and which would cut off the communication effectually, and who were also of Opinion the Hulks sunk, between Governor's Island, and the City of New York, were no sufficient Security for obstructing that passage.

6th. Tho' our Lines were fortified with some strong Redoubts, yet a Great part of them were weak being only abbattied with Brush, and affording no strong cover, so that there was reason to apprehend they might be forced, which would have put our Troops in confusion, and having no retreat, they must have been cut to pieces, or made prisoners.

7th. The Divided state of the Troops rendered our defence very precarious, and the duty of defending long and extensive Lines, at so many

[32] In the writing of Robert Hanson Harrison.

different places, without proper conveniences and cover so very fatiguing, that the Troops have become dispirited by their Incessant duty and watching.

8th. Because the enemy had sent several ships of war into the sound, to a place called flushing bay, and from the information received, that a part of their troops, were moving across long island, that way, there was reason to apprehend, they meant to pass overland, and form an incampment above King's bridge, in order to cut off, and prevent all communication between our army and the country beyond them or to get in our rear.

# INDEX

# INDEX

*By* David M. Matteson

Crimes; Drill; Eastern department; Flying Camp; Fortifications; Funds; General orders; Guards; Health; Hudson River; Invalids; Military science; Militia; New York campaign; Officers; Prisoners of war; Quarters; Recruiting; Returns; Staff.

Washington, George, movements, 62, 67, 70, 74, 76, 76*n*, 78, 87*n*, 101, 103, 481, 494; on independence or reconciliation, 92; on framing state constitutions, 92; on obedience to Congress, 140, 347; on lack of military experience, 152; Hickey plot, 193; confidence of Congress, 306*n*, 342, 349*n*; right to fill vacancies, 349; telescope from New York Legislature, 400; sends papers from New York, 427, 452; prolonged exertion, 506. *See also* Addresses; American Revolution; Commander in chief; Estates; Mount Vernon; Proclamation; Spurious letters.

Washington, John Augustine, letters to, 91, 325.

Washington, Lund, Custis estate, 28; letters to, 29, 457; forged letters to, 126, 235, 280, 285, 327.

Washington, Martha, inoculation, 93; forged letter to, 175; movements, 327.

Water, wells, 208, 471; filling casks and canteens, 229, 230, 407, 436, 442; supply, 353.

Waterbury, *Col.* David, letter to, 41; command, 41, 42.

Waterbury's Battery, 74.

Waterhouse, *Capt.* Abraham, company, 89, 299.

Watkins, Thomas, court-martial, 32.

Watson, William, on prizes, 26; letter to, 233; prize papers, 233.

Wayne, *Col.* Anthony, for Canada, halted, 2, 15, 54, 180; lack of arms, proposed supply, 18, 19; muster, 136.

Weaver, *Corp.* John, court-martial, 5.

Weaver, Samuel, court-martial, 368.

Webb, *Col.* Charles, muster, 39, 97; details, 78, 94; fatigue parties, 81, 99, 208; returns of arms, 107; regiment, 111, 142; at courts-martial, 286, 299, 301, 313, 360, 366, 368, 376; order to headquarters, 402; regiment brigaded, 422, 503.

Webb, Samuel Blatchley, insult by soldier, 111; service, 111*n*; aide to Washington, rank, 165; letters written by, 301*n*, 493*n*.

Welch, *Corp.* William, court-martial, 74.

Wells, *Maj.* ——, at court-martial, 89.

Wells, digging at encampments, 208, 471.

Wentworth, Joshua, prize agent, letter to, 139.

Wesson, *Lieut. Col.* James, at court of inquiry, 470.

Westchester County, N. Y., militia called out, 306*n*.

Whaleboats. *See* Boats.

Wheelwrights, detail, 88, 158.